THE MANY DIMENSIONS OF AGING

Robert L. Rubinstein, PhD, is Professor in the Department of Sociology and Anthropology at the University of Maryland, Baltimore, County. He was a Senior Research Anthropologist at the Polisher Research Institute of the Philadelphia Geriatric Center from 1981–1997 and worked closely with M. Powell Lawton. Rubinstein served nearly 5 years as Director of Research at PGC. His research interests include older men, environment and aging, social relations of older people, and death and dying. He has conducted research in the United States and Vanuatu (South Pacific).

Miriam Moss, PhD, is a Senior Research Sociologist at the Polisher Research Institute of the Philadelphia Geriatric Center. Since joining PGC in 1970, she has worked closely with M. Powell Lawton in projects involving assessment, activity and morale, changing tenants' needs, caregiving and mental health, and quality of life and the valuation of life.

Morton H. Kleban, PhD, is Senior Research Psychologist and Director of Psychometrics at the Polisher Research Institute of the Philadelphia Geriatric Center. He received his doctorate in Psychology from the University of North Dakota in 1960. He joined the staff of the Philadelphia Geriatric Center in 1966 and has worked with M. Powell Lawton since that time.

THE MANY DIMENSIONS OF AGING

Robert L. Rubinstein, PhD
Miriam Moss, PhD
Morton H. Kleban, PhD
Editors

 Springer Publishing Company

Springer Publishing Company, Inc.
536 Broadway
New York, NY 10012–3955

Cover design by James Scoto-Lavino
Acquisition Editor: Bill Tucker
Production Editor: Pamela Lankas

00 01 02 03 04 05/ 5 4 3 2 1

Library of Congress Cataloging-in-Publication Data

The many dimensions of aging / Robert L. Rubinstein, Miriam Moss, and
  Morton H. Kleban, eds.
     p.   cm.
  Includes bibliographical references and index.
  ISBN 0-8261-1247-1
    1. Aged—Psychology, 2. Aged—Health and hygiene. 2. Aged—
Social conditions. 4. Quality of life. 5. Gerontology.
I. Rubinstein, Robert L. II. Moss, Miriam. III. Kleban, Morton H.
HQ1061.M337 1999
305.26—dc   99-31415
                                                     CIP

Printed in the United States of America

This volume is dedicated to M. Powell Lawton.

Contents

Contributors

Steven M. Albert, PhD
Columbia University
New York, NY

Elaine M. Brody
La Jolla, CA

Habib Chaudhury
University of Wisconsin
Milwaukee, WI

Laura N. Gitlin, PhD
Thomas Jefferson University
Philadephia, PA

Allen Glicksman, PhD
Polisher Research Institute
Philadelphia Geriatric Center
Philadelphia, PA

Carrie Griffin
University of California,
   San Francisco

Douglas Holmes, PhD
Hebrew Home for the Aged
Riverdale, NY

Ira R. Katz, MD, PhD
University of Pennsylvania
Philadelphia, PA

Barry D. Lebowitz, PhD
National Institutes of Mental
   Health
Rockville, MD

Sandra Litvin, PhD
Polisher Research Institute
Philadelphia Geriatric Center
Philadelphia, PA

George L. Maddox, PhD
Duke University
Durham, NC

Keith Diaz Moore
University of Wisconsin
Milwaukee, WI

Lucille Nahemow, PhD
University of Connecticut
Storrs, CT

Robert Newcomer, PhD
University of California
   San Francisco

Marcia Ory, PhD
National Institue of Aging
Bethesda, MD

Margaret A. Perkinson, PhD
Washington University
St. Louis, MO

Rachel A. Pruchno, PhD
Boston College
Boston, MA

Avalie Saperstein
Philadelphia Geriatric Center
Philadelphia, PA

K. Warner Schaie, PhD
Pennsylvania State University
University Park, PA

Abby Spector
Philadelphia Geriatric Center
Philadelphia, PA

Jeanne A. Teresi, PhD
Hebrew Home for the Aged
Riverdale, NY

Kimberly Van Haitsma, PhD
Polisher Research Institute
Philadelphia Geriatric Center
Philadelphia, PA

Gerald D. Weisman, PhD
University of Wisconsin
Milwaukee, WI

Sherry Willis, PhD
Pennsylvania State University
University Park, PA

Acknowledgments

Several individuals have worked with the editors to make this book possible. We are very grateful for their help and support. We would like to acknowledge them here. Bill Tucker and Ursula Springer of Springer Publishing Company have supplied support and encouragement, which has made this work a reality.

Evelyn Gechman, of the Polisher Research Institute of the Philadelphia Geriatric Center, and Pat Richardson, of the Department of Sociology and Anthropology of the University of Maryland at Baltimore County, have helped in preparation of the final manuscript. We thank them for their help.

Foreword

M. Powell Lawton arrived at the Philadelphia Geriatric Center (PGC) in August 1963. Though we did not realize the full import of that event at the time, his appearance was inextricably linked with massive changes and growth in that unique facility. Indeed, his work ultimately effected positive changes in the lives of older people everywhere, changes that continue now and will continue to have ripples beyond our ability to mark them. Although that statement may sound extravagant, this is the time for truth-telling, not for understatement.

This is not a preface to a book in the usual sense. The huge number and diversity of content areas in which Powell worked, the prodigious output of writings, lectures too numerous to count, the substantive contributions he made—all these will become apparent in the chapters to follow. Rather, this is a preface to an extraordinary man whose character, personality, and talent shaped his work and that of countless others.

I was privileged to be at the Philadelphia Geriatric Center when Powell arrived, having preceded him by half a dozen years. He was discovered by and in turn discovered a true original—an imaginative genius named Arthur Waldman, then Executive Director of the organization. It was Art's style (as he phrased it) "to bet on people"—to have a hunch about someone and then to let those people do what they liked in shaping their own work directions. In luring Powell to the PGC, Art's bet and approach not only paid off, but hit the jackpot. Art and Powell were practical visionaries whose mutual joy in new ideas and in discovery of knowledge that could "do good" had an extraordinary synergy.

I say "luring" advisedly; for Art was patient in his determined efforts to bring Powell to the PGC—3 years of patience, to be exact. In 1960, he met a colleague of Powell's at a party who introduced the two men (Powell was then at Norristown State Hospital). Art's explicit notion was to establish a research unit at the PGC, but recruiting Powell, who said he was not interested in gerontology, was not that easy. Several meetings of the two over the next few years solidified Art's resolve. And he finally succeeded.

Powell had been at Norristown State Hospital for 5 years as Director of Clinical Training of psychologists. This followed a 5-year stint as Chief Clinical Psychologist at the VA in Providence, Rhode Island. Born in Atlanta, he was educated at Haverford College and awarded his doctorate at Columbia University. He nearly took a very different career path: A gifted musician, he had been admitted to Oberlin to continue his oboe studies, but changed to Columbia at the 11th hour. Music was implicated in his marriage, since he met Fay on a blind date at a Leonard Bernstein concert.

To put Powell—the man and the researcher—in perspective, one does well to remember the context of his courageous and creative venture into research in aging; in 1963, no home for the aged included a research unit, and very few (if any) organizations of any kind had a research program focused on older people. The elderly and their families in the main were neglected, ignored, and in many ways oppressed by society. Old people in general were poor and very often dependent economically on their children. Social Security was just beginning to take hold. Medicare and Medicaid would not come into being until 1965, and Supplemental Security Income did not exist until 1972. In those early 1960s, there was virtually no specialized housing for older people, nor were there long-term-care services. Even the phrase "long-term care" did not exist, waiting until 1978 for an attempt at definition by the U.S. National Committee on Vital & Health Statistics (1978). The number and proportion of old people in the population was increasing rapidly with a concomitant rise in those suffering from chronic ailments such as cardiovascular disease, arthritis, and Alzheimer's disease.

The latter ailment—Alzheimer's disease (AD)—became the focus of one of Powell's most concentrated and strenuous research efforts. I use Powell's activities regarding AD as illustrative here, though I could have chosen any of a dozen areas of interest. In the early '60s, those who suffered from that ailment (successively called "senility," "mental impairment," "organic brain syndrome," "chronic brain syndrome," etc.) were warehoused in state mental hospitals, denied admission to homes for the aged and nursing homes, or lived with suffering families. The sanctimonious deinstitutionalization movement—"send these people back to the community"—was dumping huge numbers of individuals out of the state psychiatric hospitals, mainly into bootleg nursing homes euphemistically called "boarding homes." The PGC not only was the pioneer among voluntary homes in admitting Alzheimer's patients, but was led by Powell into an organized, systematic effort to research appropriate environments and social treatment programs for them. Concurrently, he carried out related streams of research concerning all older people in, for example, functional assessment, housing and community planning, morale, services for caregiving families, determinants of well-being, and so on. All could be placed under the rubric of what several decades ago he called "the good life," a phrase that has yielded to "quality of life" (QOL) and that has lately preoccupied him.

The concept "quality of life" is much more to Powell than an intellectual exercise in research. Always in mind was the social utility of his work along the continuum from the micro-standpoint of the individual to the macro-standpoint of broad social planning and policy.

Though acutely aware of the social and physical environments of older people, Powell appears to be totally unaware of his own work environments—most often undecorated rooms piled high on every surface and in every corner with journals and papers. Yet he can unerringly pull what he wants (or what *you* want) from the middle of a stack, and hospitably clear a chair so that his visitor can be seated. My first sight of Powell, soon after his arrival, was of him sitting in his "office," which until the preceding day had been a windowless storage room for wheelchairs and other equipment. Himself a Quaker, he was laboriously copying large letters in Yiddish onto poster-board: A Yiddish translation of the Kahn-Goldfarb mental status questionnaire in order to use it with the Yiddish-speaking older people. When we reminisced about this recently, he laughed and said that the English-to-Yiddish translation was not a great problem; the main problem was translating the Yiddish responses into English.

As a researcher, Powell is a "class act." Always his own man, his independence of thinking, soaring intelligence, pristine conceptualizations, meticulous insistence on accuracy, prodigious capacity for work, encyclopedic knowledge, astonishing output, adventurous explorations—one could go on and on without exhausting the inventory of good things that characterize his work. With all that he has always been and remains unassuming and unpretentious.

But there is still more to be said. One of his great contributions is that Powell has given us generations of researchers trained in his traditions. Starting as a one-person department, he built PGC's research institute so that at one time it numbered over 60 people. It became a virtual mini-Camelot. He deliberately attracted and employed professionals from a wide spectrum of disciplines: psychology, sociology, medicine, psychiatry, nursing, social work, and anthropology. Never restrictive, he encouraged all to follow their interests, think independently, and to grow to their own fullest capacities. Always he was there for consultation, advice, warm encouragement, back-up, steering (when asked), and honest critiques. Steadfast and loyal, he *never* let anyone down. Rather, he has an army of disciples and admirers whose values he shaped and who in turn are shaping those of the next generations of researchers. It is they, both those still at PGC and those scattered in the field to universities and other organizations, who are his professional children and grandchildren and who will perpetuate him in their activities.

Finally, a personal note. I deeply appreciate having been asked to write this Foreword. I am among those whose lives Powell changed and enhanced, whose quality of life he improved. I experienced unbelievable good luck in being the friend of this remarkable man in benefitting from his knowledge, generosity, and integrity for more than three decades.

—ELAINE M. BRODY.

References

U.S. National Committee on Vital and Health Statistics. (1978). *Long-term health care: Minimum data set* (Preliminary report of the Federal Consultant Panel on the Long-Term Health Care Data Set). Washington, DC: U.S. Government Printing Office.

Introduction

Robert L. Rubinstein, Miriam Moss, and Morton Kleban

It is with a deep sense of gratitude and love that we offer this book of essays to honor M. Powell Lawton. Powell Lawton, our mentor, colleague, and friend, has been a mainstay for us, and for the discipline of gerontology, for decades. As these essays demonstrate, he has many interests and has conducted research in many areas, attesting to the multidimensional nature of aging. His scholarly work has shaped the discipline of gerontology, influencing both the world of ideas and their practical applications. Today, he continues his productive and influential work unabated.

Although Powell Lawton himself is multidimensional, two aspects of his personality strike us as especially important. His friendly, loyal, and supportive nature has made him mentor and colleague to many. Despite working full-time at a research institution, the Polisher Research Institute of the Philadelphia Geriatric Center, he has mentored dozens, if not hundreds, of students and young scholars and researchers. He has shown and has retained an openness to new ideas and new ways of thinking that is profound. Indeed, the authors of the essays in this book range from most junior to most senior, attesting quite clearly to the far-ranging and significant sets of contacts and influences Powell has made. Second, Powell Lawton's scholarly work is a model of creativity, thoughtfulness, and scientific meticulousness that has been a model for the field. Powell's work has always been undertaken with the view that research should have some practical application. The combination of this belief and Powell's long-term tenure at the Philadelphia Geriatric Center, one of the nation's premier geriatric centers, has made sure that practice and policy matters are always significant. The influence of Powell's work in environmental design for the aged, in assessment, in identification and treatment of depression, in behavioral treatment of dementia victims, and in so many other areas, is without peer.

Powell's scholarly output has been staggering. He is author or editor of 26 books; he has published literally hundreds of articles. His ideas on person and environment relations, on assessment, on the measurement of health, on assessing emotion in dementia victims, on affect, and on quality of life have been germinal and paradigmatic, clarifying our thinking about major domains, and engendering important research agendas on the part of others.

Powell is a native Southerner, born in Atlanta, who came North to go to college. He received his Ph.D. from Columbia University in 1952. He held jobs as a psychologist at the VA Hospital in Providence, from 1952–1957; in Pottstown, PA, from 1959–63, and at Norristown State Hospital, Norristown, PA, prior to his coming to the Philadelphia Geriatric Center in 1963, where he has been situated ever since. He holds adjunct appointments at the Pennsylvania State University and Temple University School of Medicine. He has been the recipient of nearly 30 major research, intervention, or evaluation grants, largely from the National Institutes of Health. These include major studies of quality of life, health, and valuation of life (NIA); emotion in dementia (The Alzheimer's Association); use of a stimulation vs. retreat treatment program for Alzheimer's patients (part of the NIA Special Care Units initiative); caregiving and mental health (NIMH); affect, normal aging, and personal competence (funded by NIA and chosen as a MERIT award); a major Clinical Research Center on psychopathology among the aged (NIMH); a Teaching Nursing Home award (NIA); a multiservice respite program for family caregivers of patients with Alzheimer's disease and its evaluation (Glenmede Trust and the John A. Hartford Foundation); and many studies of senior housing and prosthetic impacts of architecture and design. The number, range of topics, areas of expertise, methodological sophistication, and depth of knowledge is truly staggering!

Powell's work, although in the mainstream of gerontology, has consistently stretched the envelope into new concepts and new perspectives. DeMaupassant wrote to Flaubert, words that apply to Powell: "Originality is paying enough attention to something until you see it in a way no one else has ever seen it before." Considering the breadth of this work, and his encyclopedic knowledge, it is understandable that he has been called on repeatedly as consultant to the work of his peers. Further, it is only fitting that Powell was the one to review the major Maddox and Birren encyclopedias of gerontology (Lawton, 1996, 1997).

It is important to note that this book is not a systematic summary and review of Powell's opus. Powell is still hard at work and the work is nowhere near done! Rather, this book represents a way of saying "Happy Birthday!" This book contains a selection of essays by persons who have worked with Powell or with his ideas over the last few decades. We asked the authors to take some idea or thought from something Powell had written or said, and develop it as an essay. The results are unique statements about the effects of Powell's work. They vary widely in presentation and form. Many of the authors have worked with Powell at one time or another at the Philadelphia Geriatric Center; others have worked with him on a number of special projects over the last decade. One of our major regrets in doing this book is that we could not include everyone whose professional work has been significantly influenced by Powell. We anticipate that many readers will ask why he or she was not included here. For this we apologize. A more inclusive book would no doubt include many hundreds of authors and run to several volumes.

Part One focuses on Powell Lawton's work on the environment and aging and features three chapters. Gerald D. Weisman, Habib Chaudhury and Keith Diaz Moore, of the University of Wisconsin at Milwaukee, write on "Theory and Practice of Place: Toward an Integrative Model." In this chapter, they identify the strong moral component to Powell Lawton's work in assuming that the right to a decent environment is universal and inalienable. They map Lawton's influence on their work through a series of propositions about research and values, the relation of theory to practice, the multiple levels of environmental experience, the differences among objective, consensual and subjective understandings of the environment, and various attributes of place experience. They show how the influence of Lawton's work is found in their own through the creation of the Professional Environmental Assessment Protocol (PEAP).

Lucille Nahemow, of the University of Connecticut, a co-author with Powell Lawton of a seminal paper on the ecological theory of aging (1973), describes some of the scholarly influences of that paper through a description and analysis of some publications about it or in response to it in recent years. Nahemow reviews her and Lawton's classic description of environmental press, individual competence, and adaptation level. She shows how this basic idea of the ecological theory of aging, aimed at understanding personal competence and environmental press in relationship, has been subject to a variety of empirical tests and studies and how follow-up research has generated and evaluated a number of useful hypotheses. This chapter clearly shows the ripple effect of Powell Lawton's conceptualizations over both time and intellectual space.

Lastly, Laura Gitlin, of Thomas Jefferson University in Philadelphia, explores the relationship of person–environmental fit, "aging in place," and "the good life." This latter notion was Powell Lawton's early and influential conceptualization of what is now standardly labeled "quality of life" in the gerontological, geriatric, and medical literatures. Gitlin shows how theories of "staying in place," home adaptation, home modification, environmental adjustment, prosthetic environments, and the like are informed by Powell Lawton's theoretical and empirical specifications. Lawton is well known for his work on nursing home environments and especially how such environments shape the lives of those suffering from dementing illnesses. Here, Gitlin has adapted Lawton's ideas for standard, community residential environments.

In Part Two, we present four chapters on "Health and Quality of Life." Early in his work on aging, Lawton recognized the need to develop adequate assessment tools that effectively measure the abilities of elders in a variety of domains including health, cognition, social competence, time use, environment and psychological well-being; both theoretically, and in reality, the end product for this measurement was the "good life," of maximal functioning in all domains, often made more possible through attention to personal competence and to levels of environmental press as defined broadly. Thus, research on health assessment, functioning and competence, health impacts, health quality of life, and health and affect have long been central to Powell Lawton's research program.

Steve Albert, of Columbia University, discusses the relationship of time use and health and functioning in the first chapter of this section simply titled, "Time and Function."

Time use in everyday life has been of great interest to Lawton who, with several colleagues, has conducted a number of time budget studies. Albert reviews the value of time use studies for health research from multiple perspectives and in a broad range of contexts, while recognizing their less-than-enthusiastic acceptance in mainstream gerontology. Albert argues that time use studies are not only excellent ways of understanding people's psychological and social lives and the subjective context of their experiences, but also that they have untapped potentials for understanding important aspects of health and functioning.

In a broad and synthetic chapter, Jeanne Teresi, of the Hebrew Home for the Aged and Columbia University, Douglas Holmes, of the Hebrew Home for the Aged, and Marcia Ory of the National Institute of Aging analyze the notion of quality of care, an increasingly important specification. They show how this concept has benefited from the conceptual influence of Powell Lawton's work and where Lawton's ideas might continue to add clarity to it. Their chapter, "Assessing Quality of Care Among Chronic Care Populations: Conceptual and Statistical Modeling Issues" shows how quality of care as a meaningful construct has seen and should continue to see Lawton's influence through a view of health measurement as multidimensional in nature, thus defining quality of life and of care more broadly. They acknowledge, with Lawton, that these constructs cover many conceptual domains, that they include a focus on the social and physical environment; person-environment fit; and bend to fit hard-to-assess and hard-to-reach populations—this, too, a long-time concern of Lawton's work.

Margaret Perkinson, of Washington University of Saint Louis, describes "Family and Nursing Home Staff's Perceptions of Quality of Life in Dementia." This chapter, as with so many, cross-cuts topic areas that have been at the center of Lawton's interests. Here, life in nursing homes, dementia, measurement of quality of life, and multiple perceptions of participants in social life are described, and each has been focal in Lawton's work. Perkinson focuses on Lawton's special interest in quality of life in dementia, again an example of interest in assessment in hard-to-reach persons. Perkinson uses several case studies and a number of concepts from anthropologists to illuminate family member and staff definitions of quality, and suggests ways to maximize individualized care for nursing home residents with dementia.

Last in this section, Allen Glicksman, of the Philadelphia Geriatric Center, deals with the cultural basis of well-being (also known as morale or psychological well-being) in his chapter, "Style Versus Substance: The Cross-Cultural Study of Well-Being." Measurement of morale or well-being and of positive and negative affect have been important components of Powell Lawton's larger model of "the good life" and "quality of life" and his concern with health, functioning, and assessment. Glicksman discusses a number of methodological issues and conceptual concerns in dealing with measurement of this construct, and describes some research designed to explore and unpack some cultural dimensions of response to well-being items and to culturally distinctive content in the well-being concept. Glicksman's chapter also resonates to Powell Lawton's long-standing concerns for minority aged and for ethnic differences in aging.

Part Three presents two chapters that deal with components of affect. Studies of the emotional life of elders has been one of Powell Lawton's major preoccupations since 1985, primarily through two means: an NIMH-funded Clinical Research Center on Depression and Psychopathology, for which Powell Lawton was the original Principal Investigator (now labeled the Intervention Research Center [IRC] and of which Ira Katz, of the University of Pennsylvania, is the current Principal Investigator), and Powell Lawton's 10-year MERIT research award, "Affect, Normal Aging, and Personal Competence." The former project featured some of the very first systematic and high-quality scientific studies of depression among residents of nursing homes and congregate housing sites. The latter study saw the development of general theories of emotions in later life, with an eye to positive and negative affect. In addition, funding from the Alzheimer's Association has enabled Powell Lawton to study emotional expression among victims of dementing illness, as one nonverbal way of "reading" people when they can no longer speak for themselves (see Perkinson, Chapter six).

In this section Kimberly Van Haitsma, of the Philadelphia Geriatric Center, describes "The Assessment and Integration of Preferences Into Care Practices for Persons with Dementia Residing in Nursing Homes." Here Van Haitsma discusses the assessment of Alzheimer's disease victims in terms of their preferences for pleasant events and how these might best be incorporated into a care planning regime. Her work is based on three sets of theoretical ideas pioneered by Powell Lawton. These are (1) his work on quality of life; (2) his work (with Lucille Nahemow) on the ecological model of aging; and (3) a development from this model, Lawton's work on demented nursing home resident preferences for "stimulation" or "retreat" in terms of environmental stimulation. This latter issue was explored in an NIA-funded Special Care Unit project award to Lawton and the Philadelphia Geriatric Center. Van Haitsma indicates that Lawton's model of quality of life has not at all been static, and has been modified to incorporate measurements of "positive behavior and directly observed emotional states" for persons with dementia.

In the second chaper in this section, entitled "Opportunities for Redefining Late Life Depression *ab initio*, " Ira Katz, of the University of Pennsylvania, outlines progress in understanding depression among the elderly since he and Powell Lawton began working in this area in the early 1980s. There remain, however, difficulties in the reliability of diagnosing major depression among elders who have medical illness or who may have subclinical, minor, or subdysthmic depressions. Katz notes that these remain poorly understood in later life. Katz also discusses the need for simpler tools to diagnose depressive disorders in healthy aged, and to discriminate these from other psychiatric problems. Moreover, Katz discusses remaining problems in how depression is defined or the epistemology of definition, variations in symptomatology, the potential for underestimating the rate of depression among the aged. Katz also examines both Powell Lawton's methodological and substantive contributions to understanding the phenomenology of depression in later life, particularly Lawton's key finding of variation in the daily experience of negative emotions by elders with a major depression. By way of Lawton's insights, Katz calls for the possibility of a "fundamental, unbiased reevaluation of depression in the frail elderly."

Part Four, "Human Development," consists of a single chapter by K. Warner Schaie and Sherry L. Willis of The Pennsylvania State University entitled, A Stage Theory Model of Adult Cognitive Development Revisited." Powell Lawton has been an Adjunct Professor of Human Development at Penn State since 1972 and has collaborated on various projects with Schaie. This chapter reviews Schaie's original stage theory of adult development and describes some new stages to be added to the model. The reorganization stage is focused around the need to plan for dependency and balance maximal quality of life versus frailty and the possibility of medical illness. Such a stage may include concern with living arrangements, housing, social relationships, advanced medical directives, and similar proactive planning. The legacy-leaving stage centers on the self through time and may include activities as diverse as writing an autobiography, concern for prized possessions, legacies, oral histories, and heirlooms. The chapter also discusses the "lasting effects of basic cognitive skills for functioning at all life stages." Citations of work by Powell Lawton clearly show the relevance of his work for issues of development, for differential functional capacities, and for understanding the tasks that must be faced in the aging process.

In Part Five, two chapters discuss the topic of caregiving, a matter that has been at the center of gerontological research for nearly 20 years. Lawton was Principal Investigator on an NIMH-funded program project on caregiving and mental health that began in 1985; Elaine Brody, a long-time research collaborator of Powell Lawton's and one of the central figures in caregiving research, and Rachel Pruchno, were co-Principal Investigators. A series of related projects in the early 1980s examined issues concerning caregiving, gender and living arrangements.

First in this section, Rachel Pruchno, presents an up-to-date review of caregiving research, where it has been and where it should go. Her chapter "Caregiving Research: Looking Backward, Looking Forward" inventively enlarges the field of caregiving as it is typically rendered in the aging literature by focusing on the broad family context of intergenerational linkages, examining children, parents and grandparents, as well as spouses as potential caregivers or care-receivers. Additionally, Pruchno focuses on parents of persons with developmental disabilities or mental illness. Sections on the effect of caregiving on mental health echo Lawton, Brody, and Pruchno's earlier theoretical conceptualizations of stress and coping, resources, negative emotions, and uplifts that influence or result from the difficulties and accomplishments of caregiving.

Sandra Litvin's chapter, "Appraisals of Dependence Versus Independence Among Care-Receiving Elderly Women," reports on findings from a research project in the early 1990s that grew out of Lawton's caregiving and mental health program project by focusing exclusively on the world views of the older care-receivers themselves: namely, how did they evaluate the caregiving they were receiving. Litvin reports on the self-appraisals of care-receiving women, specifically, how and whether they perceived themselves to be a "care-receiver" or rather just someone who received some help every once in a while. Litvin notes clearly the influence of Powell Lawton's work on her conceptualizing this research and on the significance of subjective self-appraisal in understanding the person.

The last set of chapters in this book, Part Six, centers on practice and policy outcomes. As noted above, the practical side of what is sometimes theoretically driven or abstract research has always been at the forefront of Powell Lawton's research program.

This section contains four chapters. First, George Maddox of Duke University echoes this theme of practice in his essay, "If You Want to Understand Something, Try to Change It." Maddox describes the seeming ease with which Powell Lawton has been able to move between the world of academic theories and that of clinical practice and pragmatic endeavor. Maddox, a long-time collaborator with Lawton on the Annual Review of Gerontology and Geriatrics, highlights some of Lawton's distinctive accomplishments. More to the point, he paints a picture of the intellectual eras of gerontology in which both he and Lawton have worked, focusing on productive and unproductive arenas of gerontological conceptualization therein.

Second, Robert Newcomer (with the assistance of Carrie Griffin, both from the University of California at San Francisco), in his essay on "Community Planning and the Elderly" also sketches out some of the historic and social context of Powell Lawton's original work on aging and the environment. This essay begins with a discussion of community planning, the large context in which numerous germinal and classic studies of older people in living environments were set. In addition, he focuses on the social movements of the post-war years, the 1950s and 1960s, and the intellectual, political and social contexts that highlighted the possibility of social planning for cities and other living environments. They review influential studies of aging, the community and environment, from which community planning for the aged emerged and grew. Such studies coalesced around complex concerns such as elders with low income; needs and situations of minorities; the plusses and minuses of city life; urban infrastructures such as transportation and housing stock; age mixing; social and instrumental amenities; neighborhood attachment and urban renewal; the increased presence of elders in urban settings; forced relocation and the destruction of vital urban communities; and city politics. Modern community planning emerged from such studies of aging and the environment and detailed consideration of these issues. Newcomer's chapter provides some context for Lawton's interest in and studies of community settings, as well as for Newcomer's own substantial work in these areas.

Third, Avalie Saperstein and Abby Spector, both of the Philadelphia Geriatric Center, address "Research as a Resource for Planning and Practice." The chapter works on two levels. First, it is a description of Powell Lawton's pragmatic research-based contributions to one geriatric setting, the Philadelphia Geriatric Center, for nearly four decades. PGC is a setting in which Powell's ideas have been actively put to the task of improving the lives of frail and sick elders. Powell's influence and work has helped PGC to develop many programmatic firsts that have been pioneered locally and exported nationally and internationally. The chapter by Saperstein and Spector reports on several of these programs and how they came about. Second, Saperstein and Spector present what can be viewed as a model for collaboration between research and the helping professions. The immediacy of PGC and its residents, the willingness of administration and staff, and the creativity and scientific rigor of Powell Lawton's work have blended to make research-based program innovation a first goal.

Last in the section is an essay by Barry Lebowitz, of the National Institute of Mental Health, on "Outcomes Research in Mental Disorders of Late Life: Alzheimer's Disease as an Example." This essay treats in part the difference between understanding treatments as they exist in clinical trials versus how they actually work in real life. Answers to this difficult and vexing question can be found in Powell Lawton's work, Lebowitz contends. He identifies a "public health model of treatment research" that incorporates many of the contributions of Powell Lawton, so that standard therapeutic modality research also incorporates some consideration of issues of function, frailty, disability, comorbidity, and quality of life so evident in the Lawton approach to research and assessment. Further, Lebowitz notes the compelling need to adapt standard treatment protocols to the characteristics of persons and their specific environments, be they a nursing home, primary care setting, assisted living setting, or some other environment.

Powell Lawton is a unique person whose combination of scientific talents, creativity, and personal integrity and warmth have placed him in a leadership position in gerontology and identify him as a colleague, mentor, and friend to so many. His steady course continues. His long-term colleagues see him as inspired and as inventive as the day they began to work with him. We hope these essays, in some small way, show the breadth of Powell Lawton's extraordinary vision, dedication, and insight into the aged, and indeed, all people. He has in many ways done so much to help older people and their families and to train and direct generations of researchers and practitioners toward this goal.

References

Lawton, M. P. (1996) All gerontology is divided into 500 articles. Review of *The Encyclopedia of Aging. Gerontologist, 36*, 555–557.

Lawton, M. P. (1997) A weighty guide for the gerontologist. Review of *Encyclopedia of Gerontology:* Age, again, and the aged. *Gerontologist, 37*, 838–840.

Lawton, M. P. & Nanemow, L.E. (1973). Ecology and the aging process. In C. Eisdorfer & M. P. Lawton (Eds.), *The psychology of adult development and aging* (pp. 619–674). Washington, DC: American Psychological Association.

I

Environment
and Aging

Theory and Practice of Place: Toward an Integrative Model

Gerald D. Weisman, Habib Chaudhury, and Keith Diaz Moore

There was no doubt in our minds, as we set about writing this chapter, that our work over the years has been profoundly influenced by M. Powell Lawton. The exact shape and character of this influence, however, was not nearly so clear at the outset. Therefore the task we set for ourselves has been two-fold: first to review that subset of Lawton's multifaceted writings most related to our own work, and in doing so to elicit what we perceive to be key themes, or as we will refer to them here, propositions; then to review and reflect on our own work so we might better understand the ways, sometimes explicit but often implicit, in which these propositions have shaped what we believe and what we have endeavored to accomplish. We have identified and have organized this chapter in terms of five such propositions, each linked to and building upon those which precede it. Collectively, these propositions are meant to provide the first outlines of a model for a theory and practice of "place." Such a model is meant to help us better understand and more effectively design those environments—homes, day care centers, congregate housing, nursing homes, special care units—in which older persons live their lives. This concept of place, unlike more familiar notions of "building," "setting," or "social institution" is meant to capture and convey the complex yet lawfully patterned nature of these environments as psychological, sociological, and organizational as well as architectural systems.

PROPOSITION 1: REGARDING RESEARCH AND VALUES

As a problem in social science, person–environment relations are only beginning to be systematically addressed. Part of the problem is the social scientist's limited view of his or her mission: the persistent search for a statistical correlation between human behavior and an aspect of "the environment." . . . Demonstration of such environmental effects affirms the occupational purpose of the environmental researcher. Typically, however, these "environmental effects" are rather small, and extended apologies for their size are often offered . . . in light of the demonstrated importance of the environment . . . the amount of research effort expended to prove that environment matters begins to seem extreme. . . . The right to a decent environment is an inalienable right and requires no empirical justification." (Lawton, 1980, p. 160)

Concern for the quality of life of chronically ill persons begins with the goal of "adding quality to years," a socio-humanitarian goal. (Lawton, Winter, Casten, & Ruckdeschel, in press)

Almost 20 years ago, at a time when many social scientists still maintained—or hoped—that research must be value-free, Lawton made clear the value system which underlies his own work, and in so doing gently challenged the rest of us to do the same. Traditionally, values have been seen as a threat to "validity," compromising the researcher's claims of objectivity. However, in the behavioral as opposed to the physical sciences, such an ostensibly value-free perspective may in fact not be possible given the values and goals inherent in efforts to understand and influence the places in which people live, work, engage in social interchange, or receive care. Indeed such "value-free" social research, once conducted, is all too often judged to be "not applicable" to the very problem(s) it was meant to address. In the context of organizational behavior, Susman and Evered (1978) argue that what is often perceived to be a crisis of applicability is in fact a crisis of epistemology, rooted in the underlying assumption of value-free research.

What appears at first to be a crisis of relevancy or usefulness . . . is, we feel, really a crisis of epistemology. This crisis has risen, in our judgment, because researchers have taken the positivist model of science which has had great heuristic value for the physical and biological sciences and some fields of the social sciences, and have adopted it as the ultimate model of what is best. (Susman & Evered, 1978, pp. 582–583)

In Lawton's work, an unabashed concern for the well-being of older persons is revealed; the dilemma simply dismissed: "The right to a decent environment is an inalienable right and requires no empirical justification." This simple statement of conviction lays the foundation upon which Lawton's subsequent work builds; it is understood that not all questions are empirical in nature and not all answers have significance levels. There are two bases upon which confidence is built—empirical and ethical—and Lawton illustrates that one can, does, and must inform the other.

It is perhaps in the discussion of the concept of Quality of Life that this value-laden nature of research—and of human interaction with the world in general—can be seen most clearly. In his Kleemeier Memorial Lecture, Lawton (1983) reviewed his own work, summarizing it as an attempt to understand what he then referred to as "the good life." This concept had four sectors—behavioral competence, psychological well-being, perceived quality of life, and the objective environment—which "together include every aspect of behavior, environment, and experience" (Lawton, 1983, p. 349). At the core of the four sectors of "the good life" is the self, which George (1990, p. 194) has defined as "a dynamic process of interaction between the individual and the environment." It is through these interactions that people give meaning to their world and, in turn, come to understand themselves. By using the term "good," Lawton conveyed the notion that each sector, as well as their amalgamation (self), is capable of being evaluated positively or negatively. It is this idea of quality or value which is central to Lawton's work, the clear assumption being that individuals would rather have positive than negative experiences in their lives.

Lawton further suggests that these evaluations are not only individual in nature but also consensual (also see discussion of Proposition Four, below): "Translating the good life into social goals, well-being in the different sectors might be looked upon as the right to health, happiness, satisfaction with daily life, and a good environment" (Lawton, 1983, p. 356). Through his attempts at operationalizing various aspects of "the good life," Lawton endeavors to advance our ability to understand the given situation in service of achieving those social goals. There is a comforting coherence of underlying purpose linking such seemingly diverse efforts as the development of the Multilevel Assessment Instrument (Lawton, Moss, Fulcomer, & Kleban, 1982), the Philadelphia Geriatric Center Affect Rating Scale (Lawton, Van Haitsma, & Klapper, 1996), and theorizing regarding objectives to be achieved in nursing home design (Lawton, 1980, developed six nursing home design objectives: safety, orientation, negotiability, aesthetics, personalization and social interaction). It is through the articulation of value-driven goals that problems, both theoretical and practical, emerge and are addressed, and it is in terms of these goals that these endeavors can be meaningfully (re)connected.

PROPOSITION 2:
THE INTEGRATION OF THEORY AND PRACTICE

A theoretical framework is more than a toy for the theoretician. An abstract concept, if properly articulated, can lead us to identify holes in our practice, to question assumptions that have hindered the improvement of our practice, and to devise new strategies for our practice. As we face the growing demands that will be placed on our national resources by an aging society, it behooves us to extend every effort to see that theory, empirical research, service delivery, and policy develop in mutually reinforcing fashion. (Lawton, 1980, p. 164)

Much as Lawton (1980) adapted the ecological equation of Kurt Lewin, it would appear Lawton has adapted much of Lewin's "action research" perspective—embracing the need for clear, strong linkages between theory and practice. Lewin argued for research that stemmed from a commitment to social change and a willingness to challenge existing practices; "Research that produces nothing but books will not suffice" (Lewin, 1946, p. 35).

This use of theory, framed by a clear goal orientation in the service of an applied problem, is clearly illustrated in the development of the Weiss Institute at the Philadelphia Geriatric Center. Designed to serve those with what at that time was characterized as senile dementia and related brain pathologies, the Weiss Institute was planned with the explicit goal of "compensating wherever possible for the disorientation, memory loss, loss of social skills and sense of self typically demonstrated by organically brain damaged older persons" (Liebowitz, Lawton & Waldman, 1979, p. 59). The process was initiated with a national conference (Lawton & Lawton, 1965) the goal of which was "the articulation of a view of person-environment relationships that stressed the holistic quality of architectural design, treatment, and the quality of life of the inhabitants of a setting." Informed by Lawton and Nahemow's (1973) competence-press model, a prosthetic environment was created to maximize competence in terms of individual orientation and socialization, based on the sociopetality concept of Osmond (1957).

The choice of this theoretical conceptualization resulted in a groundbreaking approach to nursing home design. With rooms arrayed around the perimeter of a very large (40' × 100') central space, Weiss Institute residents could survey all important activity areas from the thresholds of their rooms. It was intended that this immediately visible area both serve as a "landmark" for spatial orientation and encourage involvement in the activities which occurred there. The Weiss Institute was a significant departure from the normal double-loaded corridor layout found in most skilled care facilities, an arrangement reflective of the implicit view of residents as passive recipients of care. Once completed and occupied, the facility was the focus of an extended longitudinal evaluation study (Lawton et al., 1984). This process—defining the "problem," planning and action taking, and evaluating to specify learning—clearly follows the Lewinian model of "action research" and has informed the development of other model facilities for those with dementia, including the Corinne Dolan Center, the Helen Bader Center, and Woodside Place (Kovach, Weisman, Chaudhury, & Calkins, 1997).

As a model facility meant to inform both practice and theory, the Weiss Institute may be seen adopting an epistemology at variance with more traditional behavioral science paradigms. Viewing people, program, and setting as subsystems of an integrated whole, normal strategies of defining dependent and independent variables and the apportioning of variance became problematic:

The independent variable itself was distressingly gross, in that the change in treatment locale subsumed an immense variety of components whose effects are unquestionably related to one another in very complex ways. (Lawton et al., 1984, p. 755)

Because of this complexity, what is held to be true is not based on the establishment of cause and effect relationships, but rather the pragmatic utility of achieving a defined outcome. Such an approach seems to presage a neo-pragmatist epistemology currently emerging in the behavioral sciences. Taking such a neo-pragmatic perspective, Polkinghorne (1992) argues that, at best, practice hopes to establish fragments of understanding and patterns of relationships which appear to achieve certain goals. This concept is well exemplified in the current trend of documenting "best practices," such as those found in case studies of assisted living facilities (e.g., Regnier, 1994), activity programming (e.g., Zgola, 1987) or long-term care management techniques (Teresi, Holmes, & Benenson, 1993).

Such patterns can be both substantive and procedural in nature, and the Weiss Institute provides both. Substantively, the elimination of double-loaded corridors and the provision of direct visual access from resident rooms to social space represent patterns increasingly often found in facilities for those with dementia (cf. Cohen & Weisman, 1991). In terms of process, the model of setting goals as part of an extensive planning process, development of design guidelines informed by theory and empirical research, and systematic evaluation of the resultant facility has been replicated and proven successful in the development of several other model facilities (cf. Kovach et al., 1997; Weisman, 1997). Each such demonstration project contributes to our understanding of patterns of environment-aging relationships, informs better practices, and thereby improves resulting therapeutic milieus. Polkinghorne (1992) emphasizes the role of such patterns in practice: "The more open we are to increasing and revising our patterns, and the greater variety of organizing schemes we have at our command, the more likely we are to capture the diversity of organization that exists in the world (p. 152)." This reflects the importance of developing "better ways of describing and classifying . . . important environmental features (to) integrate more of the components of the complex . . . person–environment interaction" (Parr, 1980, p. 391).

PROPOSITION 3:
MULTIPLE LEVELS OF ENVIRONMENT

The environment has yet to be subjected to a successful classificatory effort. If we knew the most meaningful dimensions of the environment and how they were related to one another, this taxonomy would be enormously useful in the further development of the science of person/environment relations, much as the periodic table served this function in chemistry. (Lawton, 1980, p. 17)

This statement, likely no less true now than when written close to two decades ago, still represents a significant challenge to the conventional wisdom of the behavioral sciences. Traditionally, each of the behavioral sciences has approached its task in terms of one level of analysis—psychologists focus on individuals and social psychologists on smaller groups, while sociologists and anthropologists deal with increasingly larger aggregations of people. The physical environment, needless to say, had little or no role to play in any of these formulations. As an initial step toward a more ambitious taxonomic effort, Lawton (1980) presented a five-fold "ecosystems" model. While acknowledging that the distinctions between these components is not always clear, Lawton nonetheless emphasized their heuristic value. In brief, the personal environment is taken to include significant others in the life of an individual, such as parents, spouse, or co-workers. The group environment reflects the influences of an aggregation of individuals, "in some structural relationship to the subject" (1980, p. 17). The supra-personal environment is defined by the aggregate characteristics of those others in proximity to an individual (e.g., average age, income, or ethnicity). By social environment Lawton means larger socio-cultural forces such as political movements, economic cycles, or cultural values. Finally, "the physical environment is the natural or built environment, reducible to grams, centimeters, and seconds" (1980, p. 18).

Here again, as in his explicit incorporation of values and concern with practice, Lawton's goal of dealing with environment at multiple levels of aggregation presages more recent approaches to the study of environment-aging relationships (cf. Weisman, 1997) and environment-behavior studies more generally (cf. Proshansky, 1987; Stokols, 1987). Lawton's inclusion of the physical environment presages the greatly increased interest in recent years in the context within which people lead their lives and the impact of such contextual factors upon their experience of place. These areas of research endeavor to redress "the deficiencies of decontextualized research" as perceived within "every major area of the discipline of psychology" (Stokols, 1987, p. 42) and to do so in a manner respectful of the holistic nature of place experience. It is for this reason that Rowles and Ohta requested that contributors to their 1983 volume "focus on the environmental context of aging, not merely considered from a physical or architectural perspective, but rather in terms of the old person's total milieu—physical, social, cultural, clinical, phenomenological, and so on" (Rowles & Ohta, 1983, p. xiii). The challenges in execution of such multi-level models, however, remains great:

If we conceive of person–environment relationships as being arranged in hierarchical order of complexity the specificity of a relationship confirmed at one level may not be preserved on the next. Thus the units of causal relationships at lower levels are frequently transformed into more complex units that include the lower level units but require new concepts or methods. (Parmelee & Lawton, 1990, pp. 476–477)

PROPOSITION 4:
OBJECTIVE, CONSENSUAL, AND
SUBJECTIVE ENVIRONMENTS

Quality of life is the multi-dimensional evaluation, by both intrapersonal and social-normative criteria, of the person-environment system. (Lawton, 1991, p. 6)

Much as Lawton endeavored to broaden the definition of environment, and integrate levels of analysis typically as separate as the disciplines from which they emerge, Lawton's proposal to consider "both intrapersonal and social-normative criteria" represents another level of epistemological and methodological challenge for environment-aging research. A decade previously, Lawton extended Lewin's classical ecological equation—$B = f(P, E)$—to include the P x E transaction [i.e., $B = f(P, E, PxE)$ (Lawton, 1980, p. 17)]. The PxE term was meant to reflect the fact that human experience is the consequence of more than just person (P) and environment (E) defined in purely objective terms; it is also necessary to take into account

the interface between the two elements, exemplified in the internal representation of the external environment . . . this interface is similar to what the statistician calls an "interaction"; the combination of subjective experience and external environment may have an effect on behavior that is in addition to and independent of either the person or the "objective" environment. (Lawton, 1980, p. 17)

This PxE term muddies the water of empirical research, for no longer can one truly understand the situation solely through examining those aspects which lend themselves to objective measurement. As is evident from this section's opening quote, consideration of the subjective, or intrapersonal is, in Lawton's view, equally as pertinent. This particularly rings true in the area of quality-of-life research, where many conceptions of quality of life are solely subjective in nature. In recent years, disciplines or research domains such as humanistic geography, qualitative social gerontology, and nursing home ethnography have utilized a variety of qualitative approaches to meaningfully illuminate the subjective aspect of environmental experience. However, in many instances, this focus has come at the expense of more objective aspects. The challenge is how one can empirically understand person and environment as integral part of a transactional reality, yet also take into account the more objective aspects of person and environment and integrate these dimensions as part of a holistic, yet applicable knowledge base.

It is in this regard that Lawton's recognition of the consensual environment plays a critical role. The PxE component cannot be thought of as solely constituted of the individual's idiosyncratic understanding of their environment. Rather, Lawton recognizes that the schemata that one uses to understand and evaluate one's situation are developed through the processes of socialization and enculturation and hence, have a consensual aspect. Barker (1968) discusses settings as having a "program:" a set of shared expectations or rules regarding the activities which are to occur there and how such activities are likely to be evaluated by others. "These rules are followed, implicitly or explicitly, though, in order to act within (or against) the actions that are physically or socially possible in that place" (Canter, 1991: 197). It is for similar reasons that Proshansky, Babian, and Kaminoff (1995, p. 94) surmised "there is no physical environment that is not also a social environment."

With the recognition of the consensual order, Lawton brings to light the social and cultural processes which are at work in the person-environment system. All three environments—objective, subjective and consensual—are necessary to understand experience of place: the objective environment sets the context within which the drama of human experience unfolds; subjective measures tap the various viewpoints and impressions of those somehow engaged in that drama; and the consensual environment renders the constraints and resources upon which actor improvisation may draw. These three environments require the use of multiple methods and means of analysis and interpretation. The ecological equation, which stimulated the awareness of the need for evaluation of the objective, subjective and consensual, also suggests the need for measuring person and environment separately (i.e. P and E) as well as measuring the PxE holistic transaction. Taken together, these points are the driving force behind Parmelee and Lawton's challenge that, a longitudinal design with a mix of qualitative and quantitative methods that allows person and environment to be measured both separately and transactionally offers the best opportunity to move the field beyond its current languishing state (Parmelee & Lawton, 1990, p. 483).

PROPOSITION 5:
MODALITIES AND ATTRIBUTES OF PLACE EXPERIENCE

> Many . . . highly specific physical, personal, staff-related, and service-related characteristics of institutions may be thought of collectively as some of the attributes of "milieu," a higher-order abstraction whose specification has occupied many gerontologists. (Lawton, 1980, p. 114)

Environmental experience has traditionally been conceptualized in terms of psychological processes; within environment-aging studies these include action, knowledge, feeling and fantasy (Rowles, 1983), paralleling constructs such as perception, cognition, evaluation, and action (cf. Canter, 1991) in environment-behavior studies more generally. Initially viewed as both discrete and sequential, these processes have, in recent years, increasingly been recognized to be overlapping and reciprocal. While unquestionably a useful heuristic for study of the psychological processes which underlie the intake, organization, and utilization of environmental information, such conceptual-izations neglect both the ecological context of real life situations (Kirasic, 1989) and the substantive character of environments as experienced, or in Moos' (1981) felicitous phrase, their "personality."

We may think of the above processes (perceptual, cognitive, etc.) as the "modalities" of place experience. However, if we consider how to study environmental experience in the terms which are suggested by the preceding propositions—driven by values, being multi-valent in the service of both theory and practice, studied at multiple levels that are considered in complementary objective, consensual, and subjective aspects—these modalities no longer serve the greatest utility. These modalities have become institu-tionalized as arenas of study, dismantling experience from its fundamentally synthetic and integrated nature. Therapeutic intentions are difficult to articulate in terms of each modality and lead to stated desired outcomes such as "reduced aggressive behavior." However as many researchers have pointed out (e.g., Kolanowski, 1995; Rader, Doan and Schwab, 1985), it behooves practitioners to consider the intent behind the behav-ior—to gain a more holistic sense of the experience—in order to respond appropriately.

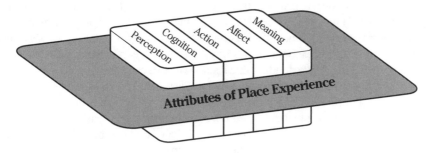

Figure 1.1 The traditional approach to modalities of place experience can be integrally expressed through the attributes of place experience.

In response to the preceding propositions, we suggest that the modalities of experi-ence need to be merged into a seamless, holistic entity—one we characterized as "place experience" (see Figure 1.1). Once thought of in this way, place experience can be dis-aggregated in terms other than modalities of perception, cognition, behavior, and affect. In particular, following Lawton's concept of "milieu," we can conceptualize place expe-rience in terms of some set of "attributes of place experience." In the following years there have been multiple efforts to conceptualize and assess such attributes of place expe-rience (cf. Calkins, 1988; Cohen & Weisman, 1991; Moos & Lemke, 1994; Norris-Baker, Weisman, Lawton, & Sloane, in press; Pynoos & Regnier, 1991). Interestingly, there is considerable consensus in attributes across these investigators. Taking the Norris-Baker and colleagues' taxonomy as an example, one finds attributes including safety & security, awareness & orientation, support of functional abilities, regulation & quality of stimulation, opportunities for personal control, provision of privacy, facilitation of social contact, and continuity of the self.

The threads of these experiential attributes run through the different modalities of place experience (i.e., cognition, perception, and behavior). Thus the experience of "privacy" or its absence in a place reflects the intake of information from our surroundings, our categorization and evaluation of that information, and action taken or not taken as a consequence. Further, these attributes bring to surface the integrated nature of place experience in a way that is meaningful for environmental design. For example, the attribute of "legibility" (those qualities of a place with support orientation and way finding) is purposefully used in the design of the Weiss Institute, particularly its central living/activity space surrounded by residents' rooms. The residents can see (perception) the activity space immediately after coming out of their rooms, hopefully remember (cognition) its location and function, carry out activities (action) in the space, form certain affect (feeling) about the space, and attach certain meaning (meaning) to it.

At a deep, phenomenological level, the attributes of place experience distill into the subjective core of place experience and form the basis of self-identification with the environmental experience. A growing body of literature (e.g., Boschetti, 1984; Howell, 1983; Rowles, 1983) has suggested that it is personal experience that gives meaning to places and contributes to self-identity. This literature also suggests that places are important symbols of the self, cues to memories of important life experiences, and a means of maintaining, reviewing, and extending one's sense of self, especially in old age. Further, the temporal aspect of place experience—which Parmelee and Lawton (1990) suggest is another crucial variable in the person-environment system—has been explored by Rowles (1983) in his conceptualization "environmental fantasy." "Fantasy" refers to the integration of our real or imagined experience of places and can be either reflective— involving past experience, projective—being imagination of geographically separated place experience, or prospective— corresponding with the temporal dimension of experience (Rowles, 1983). All of this taken together suggests that the nature of one's present experience of place is shaped by the past, and that the reflection of the past experience is likewise influenced by our present experience. Individuals, groups, organizations, and physical settings both acquire and lose features, attributes, and qualities over time. Consequently the nature of place experience changes, gains new meanings, and adds meaning.

We posit that places emerge as individuals, groups, and/or organizations come together in a physical setting for the realization of some set of goals. Places may—like Barker's "behavior settings" (Barker, 1968)—be the creation of a formal organization (e.g., a high school algebra class as brought into being by a school board), or an individual or group (e.g., a grocery store); conversely—as is the case with empty lots where people may congregate—places may come into being without any formalized organizational involvement. Recognizing the temporal dimension of place experience, the model is dynamic; the home which was once a setting for family actions and meanings cannot be experienced in the same way when one returns after a number of years. The context of the physical environment, the individuals' perceptions of spaces, and social and organizational contexts all change in a natural course over time.

INTEGRATION AND APPLICATION

For us, the five propositions presented above come together in what we characterize as a "model of place." We strongly believe in the benefits of clear conceptual models to guide the study of environments for the elderly and have previously argued that they are essential to our understanding of the environmental context of older persons (Weisman, 1997; Weisman, Calkins, & Sloane, 1994). Such models or frameworks have clear value for analysis, understanding, evaluation, and design of environments for older persons.

Building on previous developments in environmental gerontology and environment-behavior studies more generally, this model encompasses both the subsystems or "components of place" which comprise environments for older persons and the "experience of place" which these components create. "Components"—organizational, psycho/social, and architectural—emphasize the history, goals, and models of care which underlie specific place types for the elderly (e.g., assisted living versus special care units [SCUs]), as well as key features and characteristics of their physical settings. The interaction of these organizational, social, and architectural components in turn defines those "attributes of place experience" which shape the overall character or "personality" of a place (cf. Moos, 1981).

The resultant "model of place" developed in Weisman (1997) is represented in Figure 1.2. The epistemological origins of the model may be found in an "organismic" or, more appropriately, "systemic" world view which permits a simultaneous focus on both components and the whole (cf. Altman & Rogoff, 1987; Von Bertalanffy, 1976). Consistent with such a systems perspective, our conceptual model posits that all places—whether these be nursing homes, schools, prisons, or commercial facilities—are shaped by an overarching philosophy and are thus driven by some goal-orientation. Schools may be predicated on models as different as "open education" or "the three R's," prisons may be designed for punishment or for rehabilitation, retail environments may focus on "deep discounting" or the carriage trade. Similarly, our understanding of what SCUs are meant to accomplish and how such goals may be realized organizationally, socially, and architecturally is defined by such a "philosophy" or "model of care." Such philosophies both reflect and reinforce prevailing social attitudes (cf. Silverstein & Jacobson, 1985) and shape patterns of expected and encountered behavior within particular place types (cf. Canter, 1991). Finally, it is posited that relationships between the various components of place—organizational, social, architectural, experiential—are typically far from random; rather these several subsystems work together synergistically in support of overall place goals.

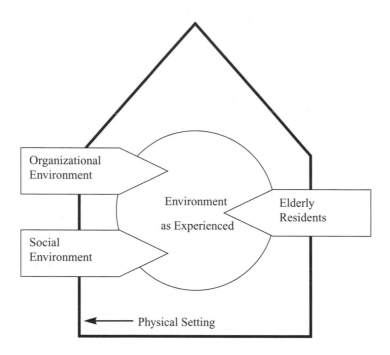

Figure 1.2 An integrative model of place that has at its core the environment as experienced where one would focus upon the attributes-of-place experience. These attributes are created through the dynamic interrelationships among the individual, social, organizational, and physical environments that constitute place.

This framework underlies a range of projects—theoretical as well as applied—currently underway in our Institute on Aging and Environment. Each in turn, as we have endeavored to demonstrate in previous sections, has its origins in the concepts and values inherent in the work of Powell Lawton.

Pulse of a Place

In an effort to both utilize and "test" the integrative model discussed above, Diaz Moore (1997) conducted an intrinsic case study evaluation, to investigate the social life of a 24-resident special care unit. This study endeavored to understand the given situation in order to make recommendations for improvement of the "social affordance" of this unit. (One of the stated goals of this unit was to provide opportunities for socialization and this was consistent with the therapeutic goals found in the literature, and provided a meaningful issue for evaluation). Using the diagnostic approach found in other professional fields, the study employed a three-step process model of presentation of the case, diagnosis, and prescription of action. Presentation of the case began with a thorough description of the special care unit in terms of the most "objective" aspects of the four subsystems—organization, social, individual, physical—of the integrative model (i.e., plans of the facility, staffing patterns, and descriptive statistics on residents such as mean age, gender distribution, and average length of stay). Once these most objective aspects were laid out, the process endeavored to spiral inward toward more consensual (i.e., behavioral observation) and subjective (i.e., self-report) data. All three types of data were seen as necessary to set the stage for diagnosis of the SCU as an integrated place.

Diagnosis endeavored to assess the "pulse of the place," in this case, defined in terms of the social affordance of the SCU. To do so required recognition that the place as a whole is comprised of an integrated hierarchies of systems as found in Proposition Three. This position reflects Parmelee and Lawton's (1990) observation that "If we perceive of person-environment relationships as being arranged in a hierarchical order of complexity the specificity of a relationship confirmed on one level may not be preserved on the next (p. 476)." Thus, in the diagnosis phase, relationships occurring within each system were analyzed first, followed by analysis of interrelationships between systems. Finally, iterative cycling back and forth between subsystems and relationships helped to clarify the SCU as a whole place. By way of example, abusive behavior is often measured in terms of frequency of occurrence, without recognition that resident behavior is often the result of staff interaction and intervention. While one could blame the staff person, often the staff member is acting in accordance with organizational policy. Similarly, it is rarely the case that potentially constraining aspects of the physical environment, which might increase the likelihood of such behaviors, are considered. The study specifically endeavored to broadly "contextualize" the patterns of relationships that emerged in order to avoid the dangers associated with simply studying the manifestations of a problem, as such an approach may not, in the final analysis, reveal what is truly occurring in the complex, systemic transactions of place.

Once patterns of relationships began to emerge within the study, it was possible to prescribe actions to be taken in order to enhance social affordance. These prescriptions again involved all four dimensions of the integrative model with clear recognition of the impact each prescriptions had upon multiple aspects of the environment. These recommendations were informed by the interpreted patterns of relationships existing in the SCU, which in turn were informed by the collected data, by theory and by values—with all three working in concert. This study is reflective of the spirit of evaluation found in Lawton et al.'s, (1984) study of the Weiss Institute where existing patterns were documented and evaluated in terms of their efficacy in achieving a stipulated goal.

Reminiscence of Place and Place-Therapy

This ongoing study tries to access "ground zero" of the phenomenological core of place experience as retained in the images of memory possessed by people with dementia of the Alzheimer's type (Chaudhury, 1996). The study takes as its departure the body of literature which suggests that places and things are important symbols of the self, cues to memories of important life experiences, and a means of maintaining, reviewing, and extending one's sense of self, especially in old age (Cooper, 1974; Csikszentmihalyi & Rochberg-Halton, 1981). Reminiscence is one of the processes by which individuals are continually structuring, maintaining, and reconstructing their self-identities. For people with cognitive impairments in long-term care settings, autobiographical recollection has been hypothesized to help counter the threat to selfhood inherent in multiple changes brought about by diminished cognitive functioning, behavioral difficulties, the loss of personal control, and the overall unfamiliarity of an institutionalized setting. There is evidence that reminiscence sessions with institutionalized people with dementia can be therapeutic with increased self-esteem (Kiernat, 1979), increased MMSE scores (Goldwasser, Auerbach and Harkins, 1987), enhanced life satisfaction (e.g., Fallot, 1980) and lowered depression (Woods & McKiernan, 1995). Given the evidence that places are important aspects of lived experience, this study proposes that having those with dementia remember past places from their current perspective may prove to a be a quite powerful means of reminiscence therapy—a kind of "place-therapy."

The potential of tapping into memories of past place as a resource for programmatic interventions for older people echoes Lawton's (1991) conceptualization of Quality of Life with self being at its core. In particular, "place-therapy" has the potential of a positive intervention in at least three dimensions. First, the process of remembering places from the personal past, as well as events and emotions associated with these places, can provide cues for remembering one's life course for older people in general, and particularly in long-term care settings. This, in turn, could help maintain a sense of continuity of past life and self-identity, which may have a positive impact on cognitive and behavioral functioning. Second, knowing an individual's environmental history can open a window of understanding for the caregiver in a long-term care setting. This would be a powerful tool for viewing and understanding the person with dementia as an uniquely interesting individual. Third, recalled environmental features could be incorporated into the physical environment of dementia care settings, which may provide appropriate environmental stimuli for the residents in recollection of meaningful environments from the past.

Professional Environmental Assessment Protocol

The Professional Environmental Assessment Protocol (PEAP) (Norris-Baker et.al., in press) was originally designed in conjunction with the multi-disciplinary National Institute on Aging Collaborative Research Project on Special Care Units (Ory, 1994). The PEAP was initially designed to use global, subjective, and evaluative measures integrated within one instrument to be utilized by a trained professional during a walk-through observation of a place. Later it was amended to include a brief open-ended interview with the care supervisor to gain greater insight into the life of the place, as will be discussed in this section.

The goal of the PEAP is the focused evaluation of specialized dementia care facilities (Special Care Units) with respect to eight dimensions of the environment as experienced (e.g., Environmental Awareness & Orientation) judged to be therapeutic with respect to the care of persons with Alzheimer's Disease or related dementias. This approach differs from other commonly employed approaches to environmental description and assessment, going beyond the simple documentation of objective properties of a setting (e.g., enumeration of all spaces comprising an SCU, calculation of square footage of each). Thus indicators included in discussion of each of the eight attributes of the PEAP are just that—indicators—and are not meant to constitute a checklist. At the same time, the PEAP is meant to be more focused than totally global evaluations (e.g., everything else being equal, is this a good or bad environment for dementia care?).

The primary focus of the PEAP is the physical setting and the extent to which it supports the needs of people with dementia. At the same time it is recognized that the physical world does not exist in isolation. The interrelated nature of the various dimensions of place, as reflected in the integrative model, makes it clear that the physical environment must be understood and evaluated within the larger context of such issues as unit philosophy of care and program, level of resident capability, constraints of budget and regulations, and the like. This served as the impetus for inclusion of an open-ended interview within what is otherwise a survey protocol. The inclusion of both scalar and open-ended questions and an open-ended interview results in various data types being produced by the instrument. Various types of data require various analytic techniques which proves challenging but in the end produces a rich profile of the physical environment and its role in the "personality of the place."

The PEAP is strongly influenced by all five propositions set forth above. The eight attributes which the PEAP addresses have all been informed by the value position that people have an inalienable right to a decent environment. These eight attributes attempt to define aspects of place experience critical to those with cognitive impairments. The protocol is designed to provide information which researchers can use to inform theory-building, but also that practitioners can use to inform their practice. The PEAP's development was greatly affected by the conceptualization of the ecological nature of the environment having multiple levels as well as by the utility of accessing objective, consensual, and subjective criteria. Finally, the PEAP has at its core place-experience, here addressed in terms of attributes of experience, which results from the dynamic transactions involving all four dimensions of place. In so doing, while the PEAP's focus is on the physical environment, as a model protocol it foreshadows potential development of similar protocols for each of the other dimensions of place.

CONCLUSIONS

Our work in the Institute on Aging and Environment is attempting to meaningfully address five propositions we have found within the work of Lawton:

1. That research into quality of life issues such as the quality of one's environment, will necessarily be evaluative in nature and hence value-laden;
2. The need for mutual reinforcement of theory and practice;
3. That the environment has multiple levels which are nested and transact in a systemic fashion;
4. The need for utilizing objective, consensual and subjective measures; and
5. That at the core of the study of person-environment systems is the concept of milieu whose attributes may be thought of as attributes of place experience.

These five propositions have helped shape the core assumptions by which we endeavor to conduct ourselves. Epistemologically, we have adopted a systemic perspective that recognizes the need for analysis as well as synthesis; allows components to be separated for the purposes of analysis, yet retains the understanding that the whole is more than the sum of the parts. Our research methodology has adopted multiple methods, multiple data types, and multiple data points in an effort to triangulate from multiple perspectives on the experience of place. As researchers, our axiology unabashedly asserts the right that people have for decent housing, particularly on behalf of those whom otherwise may have no voice in what is an oftentimes harsh society. Lastly, as practitioners in arenas of facility architectural design, development, and programming, we adhere to the need for design decisions to be made with an informed knowledge base and clearly articulated goals based on a firm value position.

These propositions have led us toward developing a theory and practice of place in which we attempt to address theoretical or practical considerations with the same underlying premises. The integrated model of place serves as a powerful heuristic which identifies areas for future research and assessment activities as well as areas or issues that may be neglected in practice. To be able to bring our practice and research efforts together in terms of the lexicon of the attributes of place experience helps one inform the other through effective dialogue. It is our belief that such a dialogue can only enhance our collective efforts at improving the quality of life—through the creation of quality places—for older persons and others with special needs.

REFERENCES

Altman, I., & Rogoff, B. (1987). World views in psychology: Trait, interactional, organismic, and transactional perspectives. In I. Altman & D. Stokols (Eds.), *Handbook of environmental psychology* (Vol. 1, pp. 7–40). New York: Wiley.

Barker, R. (1968). *Ecological psychology: Concepts and methods for studying the environment for human behavior.* Stanford, CA: Stanford University Press.

Barker, R. (1987). Prospecting in environmental psychology: Oskaloosa revisited. In I.

Altman & D. Stokols (Eds.), *Handbook of environmental psychology* (Vol. 2, pp. 1413–1432). New York: Wiley.

Boschetti, M. A. (1984). *The older person's emotional attachment to the physical environment of the residential setting.* Unpublished doctoral dissertation, University of Michigan.

Calkins, M. (1988). *Design for dementia: Planning environments for the elderly and confused.* Owings Mills, MD: National Health Publishing.

Canter, D. (1991). Understanding, assessing, and acting in places: Is an integrative framework possible? In T. Garling & G. W. Evans (Eds.), *Environment, cognition, and action* (pp. 191–209). New York: Oxford University Press.

Chaudhury, H. (1996). *Self and reminiscence of place: Exploring theories among people with dementia in long-term care settings.* Unpublished doctoral dissertation proposed, University of Wisconsin—Milwaukee.

Cohen, U. & Weisman, G. (1991). *Holding on to home.* Baltimore, MD: Johns Hopkins University Press.

Cooper, C. (1974). The house as a symbol of self. In J. Lang, C. Burnett, W. Moleski, & D. Vachon (Eds.), Designing for human behavior: Architecture and the behavioral sciences (pp. 130–146). Strodsburg, PA: Dowden, Hutchinson, & Ross.

Csikszentmihalyi, M., & Rochberg-Halton, E. (1981). *The meaning of things: Domestic symbols and the self.* Cambridge, MA: Cambridge University Press.

Fallot, R. (1980). The impact on mood of verbal reminiscing in later adulthood. *International Journal of Aging and Human Development, 10,* 385–400.

George, L. (1990). Social structure, social processes, and social-psychological states. In R. Binstock & L. George (Eds.), *Handbook of aging and the social sciences,* (3rd ed., pp. 186–204). San Diego, CA: Academic Press.

Goldwasser, A. N., & Auerbach, S. M., & Harkins, S. W. (1987). Cognitive, affective and behavioral effects of reminiscence group therapy on demented elderly. *International Journal of Aging and Human Development, 25,* 209–222.

Howell, S. C. (1983). The meaning of place in old age. In G. D. Rowles & R. J. Ohta (Eds.), *Aging and milieu: Environmental perspectives on growing old* (pp. 97–1077). New York: Academic Press.

Kiernat, J. (1979). The use of life review activity with confused nursing home residents. *Physical and Occupational Therapy in Geriatrics, 3,* 35–48.

Kirasic, K. C. (1989). Acquisition and utilization of spatial information by elderly adults: Implications for day-to-day situations. In L. W. Poon, D. C. Rubin, & B. A. Wilson, (Eds.), *Everyday cognition in adulthood and late life* (pp. 265–283). Cambridge: Cambridge University Press.

Kolanowski, A. (1995). Aggressive behavior in institutionalized elders: A theoretical framework. *American Journal of Alzheimer's Disease, 10,* 23–29.

Kovach, C., Weisman, G., Chaudhury, H., & Calkins, M. (1997). Impacts of a therapeutic environment for dementia care. *American Journal of Alzheimer's Disease, 12*(3), 99–116.

Lawton, M. P. (1980). *Environment and aging.* Belmont, CA: Brooks-Cole.

Lawton, M. P. (1983). Environment and other determinants of well-being in older people. *Gerontologist, 23*, 349–357.

Lawton, M. P. (1991). A multidimensional view of quality of life in frail elders. In J. Birren, J. Lubben, J. C. Rowe, & D. Deutchman (Eds.), *The concept and measurement of quality of life in the frail elderly* (pp. 3–27). San Diego, CA: Academic Press.

Lawton, M. P., Fulcomer, M., & Kleban, M. (1984). Architecture for the mentally impaired. *Environment and Behavior, 16*(6), 730–757.

Lawton, M. P., & Lawton, F. (Eds.). (1965). *Mental impairment in the aged.* Philadelphia, PA: Philadelphia Geriatric Center.

Lawton, M. P., Moss, M., Fulcomer, M., & Kleban, M. (1982). A research and service-oriented Multilevel Assessment Instrument. *Journal of Gerontology, 37*, 91–99.

Lawton, M. P., & Nahemow, L. (1973). Ecology and the aging process. In C. Eisdorfer & M.P. Lawton (Eds.), *Psychology of adult development and aging* (pp. 619–674). Washington, DC: American Psychological Association.

Lawton, M. P., Van Haitsma, K., & Klapper, J. (1996). Observed affect in nursing home residents with Alzheimers disease. *Journal of Gerontology, 51B*, P3–P14.

Lawton, M. P., Winter, L., Casten, R., & Ruckdeschel, K. (in press). *Valuation of life: The positive side of health-related quality of life.*

Lewin, K. (1946). Action research and minority problems. *Journal of Social Issues, 2*, 34–36.

Liebowitz, B., Lawton, M. P., & Waldeman, A. (1979). A prosthetically designed nursing home. *American Institute of Architects Journal, 68*, 59–61.

Moore, K. D. (1997). *Social life in an SCU: The pulse of the Mayer Hebrew Home.* Unpublished manuscript, University of Wisconsin-Milwaukee.

Moos, R. (1981). The practical utility of environmental evaluation of sheltered care facilities. In R. Stough & A. Wandersman (Eds.), *Optimizing environments: Research, practice and policy* (pp. 7–21). Washington, DC: Environmental Design Research Association.

Moos, R., & Lemke, S. (1994). *Group residences for older adults.* New York: Oxford University Press.

Norris-Baker, C., Weisman, G., Lawton, M. P., & Sloane, P. (in press). Assessing special care units for dementia: The Professional Environmental Assessment Protocol. In E. Steinfeld & G. Danford (Eds.), *Measuring enabling devices.* New York: Plenum.

Ory, M. (1994). Dementia special care: The development of a national research initiative. *Alzheimer's Disease and Associated Disorders, 8*(Supp.1), S389–S404.

Osmond, H. (1957). Function as the basis of psychiatric ward design. *Mental Hospitals, 8*, 23–30.

Parmelee, P., & Lawton, M. P. (1990). The design of special environments for the aged. In J. Birren & K. W. Schaie (Eds.), *Handbook of the psychology of aging* (pp. 464–488). San Diego, CA: Academic Press.

Parr, J. (1980). Environmental issues: Introduction. In L. Poon (Ed.), *Aging in the 1980s: Psychological issues* (pp. 393–406). Washington, DC: American Psychological Association.

Polkinghorne, D. (1992). Postmodern epistemology of practice. In S. Kvale (Ed.), *Psychology and post modernism* (pp. 146–165). Newbury Park, CA: Sage.

Proshansky, H. (1987). In I. Altman and D. Stokols (Eds.), *Handbook of environmental psychology* (Vol. 1, pp.). New York: Wiley.

Proshansky, H., Fabian, A., & Kaminoff, R. (1995). Place-identity: Physical world socialization of the self. In L. Groat (Ed.), *Readings in environmental psychology: Giving places meaning* (pp. 87–113). London: Academic Press.

Pynoos, J., & Regnier, V. (1991). Improving residential environments for frail elderly: Bridging the gap between theory and application. In J. Birren, J. Lubben, J. Rowe, & D. Deutchman (Eds.), *The concept and measurement of quality of life in the frail elderly* (pp. 91–119). San Diego: Academic Press.

Rader, J., Doan, J. & Schwab, M. (1985). How to decrease wandering, a form of agenda behavior. *Geriatric Nursing*, 196–199.

Regnier, V. (1994). *Assisted living housing for the elderly: Design innovations from the United States and Europe*. New York: Van Nostrand Reinhold.

Rowles, G., & Ohta, R. (1983). *Aging and milieu: Environmental perspectives on growing old*. New York: Academic Press.

Rowles, G. D. (1983). Place and personal identity in old age: Observations from Appalachia. *Journal of Environmental Psychology, 3*, 299–313.

Silverstein, M., & Jacobson, M. (1985). Restructuring the hidden program: Toward an architecture for social change. In W. Preiser (Ed.), *Programming the built environment* (pp. 7–26). New York: Van Nostrand.

Stokols, D. (1987). Conceptual strategies of environmental psychology. In I. Altman and D. Stokols (Eds.), *Handbook of environmental psychology* (Vol. 1, pp. 41–70). New York: Wiley.

Susman, G., & Evered, R. (1978). An assessment of the scientific merits of action research. *Administrative Science Quarterly, 23*, 582–602.

Teresi, J., Holmes, D., & Benenson, E. (1993). A primary care nursing model in long-term care facilities: Evaluation of impact on affect, behavior and socialization. *Gerontologist, 33*, 667–674.

Von Bertalanffy, L. (1976). Introduction. In H. Werley, A. Zuzich, M. Zajkowski, & A. D. Eagolnik (Eds.), *Health research: The systems approach* (pp. 5–13). New York: Springer.

Weisman, G. D. (1997). Environments for older persons with cognitive impairments: Toward an integration of research and practice. In G. Moore & R. Marans (Eds.), *Advances in environment, behavior, and design* (Vol. 4, pp. 3315–346). New York: Plenum.

Weisman, G. D., Calkins, M., & Sloane, P. (1994). The environmental context of special care. *Alzheimer's Disease and Associated Disorders, 8*(Supp.1), S308–S320.

Woods, B., & McKiernan, (1995). Evaluating the impact of reminiscence on older people with dementia. In B. K. Haight & J. D. Webster (Eds.), *The art and science of reminiscing: Theory, research, methods, and applications* (pp.). Washington, DC: Taylor & Francis.

Zgola, J. (1987). *Doing things: A guide to programming activities for persons with Alzheimers disease and related disorders*. Baltimore, MD: Johns Hopkins University Press.

2

The Ecological Theory of Aging: Powell Lawton's Legacy

Lucille Nahemow

Powell Lawton and I first presented the Ecological Theory of Aging (ETA) 25 years ago. At that time, the new field of environmental psychology was developing, systems theory was beginning to be applied to the social sciences and "ecology" was being used both as a field of study and as a slogan. In the original paper, we pointed out that *adaptation* was a key concept in both ecology and in the aging process. From the central concern with adaptation the theory was born. The ETA took off, and many now consider it a classic. It has been referenced more in the '80s and '90s than it was in the '70s. When Powell Lawton and I first worked on the theory privately we had hopes about how the ETA would be used. I remember being steeped in scientific principles at that time: I saw the theory primarily as a structure to be tested and modified. Powell was more realistic, hoping to offer intellectual stimulation to scholars in the new field. At this time let us consider what did happen to the theory that Powell Lawton spent much of his creative professional life furthering.

This chapter will consider the many ways in which the ETA has contributed to the work of researchers, scholars and practitioners in the intervening years. The theory has been used by many different disciplines and taken on qualities of those disciplines. In the tradition of environmental psychology (see Stokols, 1995), the ETA has been more diffused than subjected to rigorous testing. It has frequently been used as a springboard for new concepts and methodologies, and in the process the theory has sometimes been unwittingly modified. Some elements have been emphasized and others all but lost. Therefore, despite its familiarity to many, I will once again describe the Ecological Theory of Aging.

DESCRIPTION OF THE ECOLOGICAL
THEORY OF AGING

The Ecological Theory of Aging (Lawton & Nahemow, 1973) explores the interplay between individuals and their environments. It is an adaptation level theory based upon that of Harry Helson (1964) who explained that

> Adaptation is a mechanism for acquainting us with changes in the environment. If the same stimulation continues, adaptation gradually counteracts its effects to the point where it may no longer be sensed or its quality becomes neutral (Helson, 1964, p. 43).

Adaptation is the key concept in ecology. In the first issue of *Ecological Psychology* (1989), Reed said, "The function of the nervous system is to keep it in adaptive contact with its environment (p. 97)." Helson explained the adaptive mechanism in the following way:

> For every condition or complex of conditions in which a receptor system is stimulated, there is an initial rapid change in activity and sensitivity which is followed by a constant level of activity and sensitivity if the stimulation is continued at a constant intensity (p. 45).

In other words, individuals tend to adapt to external stimuli in such a way that after a period of time, the present stimuli are perceived as neither strong nor weak; in fact, they are barely perceived at all. When this occurs, adaptation level (AL) has been achieved. However, there is a limitation. Adaptation occurs only in the middle range of stimulation. While under most conditions our eyes automatically adapt to increased illumination, they never adapt to staring directly into the sun. Helson interprets these limits to human adaptability as survival features of the species.

While the adaptation level concept was formulated by Helson to explain psychophysical phenomena, the Ecological Theory of Aging extends it into other realms of experience. Adaptation level is applied to the total environment in the same way that Helson applied it to specific stimuli. The principle is the same, although the measurement is more difficult. We can expect most people to reach an AL in most environments. However, there are environments to which it is almost impossible to adapt, and there are some people who adapt with difficulty and require a benign environment to be able to reach their AL.

The Ecological Theory of Aging can be applied to individuals of any age, even though the theory was developed with older people in mind. Older people require more time to reach their AL—as they require more time to do all things. Since reduced competence often accompanies aging at the very end of life, older people sometimes have difficulty reaching an AL. This effectively narrows the mid-range of stimulation to which humans can adapt. It has been formalized as the "Environmental Docility Hypothesis" (Lawton & Simon, 1968). In the following schematic presentation of the theory, the strength of environmental press is shown on the abscissa, the degree of individual competence is shown on the ordinate, and the Adaptation Level (AL) is represented by the central diagonal line surrounded by an adaptive range.

Murray (1938) defined environmental press as forces in the environment that together with individual need evoke a response. Environmental press can be both objective (alpha press) reflecting factors like complexity, and subjective (beta press), reflecting the perceived demand character of the environment. Under most circumstances, there is a strong positive relationship between alpha and beta press. Murray states that "When there is wide divergence between alpha and beta press we speak of delusion" (p. 122). It is beta press, or the perceived environment, which influences AL. Most researchers who have used the theory, particularly sociologists and urban planners, use alpha, or objective press. According to Murray, that would be alright for large samples.

Individual competence is a global concept with many dimensions including biological, psychological, and social components. Unlike the concept of intelligence, which was once thought to measure genetic potential, the concept of competence deals with functional issues. The question usually addressed is whether individuals have the skill required to perform a particular task, not how well they can function or whether they are functioning at some ideal level.

Adaptation Level (AL) shows continuous oscillation around a central point. Because of this perpetual oscillation, AL should be conceived as a range, not as a point. Helson (1964) states: "Our ability to change the environment by moving about in it allows us to determine to a large extent the nature and degree of stimulation we receive" (p. 53). An individual will normally seek his or her own level of environmental press. Typically, highly competent individuals will be adapted to complex environments with high press, whereas individuals with low competence will be adapted to simpler environments with

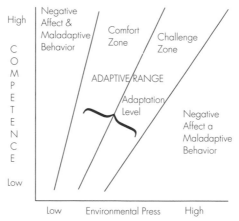

Figure 2.1 Ecological theory of aging.

low press. There is an area surrounding the AL in which the individual is comfortable and behaves appropriately. Beyond that range, behavior is maladaptive and affect is distinctly negative.

Provided one remains within the AL range, heightened environmental press will be perceived as challenge. When this occurs for a sufficient period of time, adaptation level will elevate, and in time, personal competence will increase. Conversely, lowered environmental press will be perceived as relaxing. Many people seek low press environments for vacations, and some find it difficult to get back to work. If one were to stay on vacation for a very long time, the AL would decrease. Eventually competence would decline. After such an interval it would require retraining and considerable discipline to resume work again. Thus the environment not only creates a surround conducive to certain kinds of behavior; it can actually alter the individual.

The adaptive range bordering the AL is much wider for highly competent individuals than for less competent ones. The lower the level of functioning, the more dependent the individual is upon the immediate environment and the less able he or she is to change or leave that environment. Lawton & Simon (1968) referred to this greater vulnerability of less competent individuals as the "Environmental Docility Hypothesis." For the lower functioning individual, it is more critical that the initial placement is such as to maximize person-environment fit and that changes are closely monitored over time.

Environments do not remain static. Environmental press decreases as a direct function of time spent within them. All novel environments, no matter how "simple" they may be objectively, require new learning and adjustment to their demands. We can relax and take the environment for granted only after an initial period of adaptation, enabling us to reach an AL. During the initial phase we first focus on those elements in the environment that we fear may be life-threatening; then we become sensitized to what behaviors are expected of us, and we learn meaningful environmental pathways, such as where the bathroom is located. The more competent the individual, the faster the AL will be reached.

Although the diagram represented in Figure 2.1 shows three dimensions, there is actually a very important fourth dimension, which is time. Adaptation Level is a function of time. With time spent in an environment we adapt to the relevant stimuli in that environment. Consequently a long-term care facility may provide perfect person/environment congruence at time 1, and at time 2 may be inappropriate because it provides too little press to be stimulating (Nahemow, 1989).

TESTING THE ECOLOGICAL THEORY

Rigorous tests of the ETA have produced mixed results. Three attempts are described in detail to permit the reader to understand the research procedures. Morgan et al. (1984) tested the ETA's environmental docility hypothesis. They state:

The purpose of the present study . . . was to test simultaneously the generalizability of the hypothesis (in a standardized fashion) across all three domains of potential competence: a) physical health or sensory capacity, b) access to caregiver networks, and c) personality characteristics commonly associated with successful coping . . . less competent individuals in physical, social or psychological terms have a narrower range of adaptability to increasing environmental demands and should be able to tolerate less environmental press before reaching stress thresholds. (p. 240)

A self-report index of environmental press contained four subscales with four items each: (a) *safety* of home and neighborhood, (b) *proximity* to services and ability to get around (c) *ease* with which they could communicate needs and (d) *predictability* in the environment. Competence was defined as (a) having high self-esteem, (b) an internal locus of control, (c) being assertive, and (d) accepting needed help. One hundred and two volunteers between 60–92 years of age were dichotomized as high or low competent. Correlations between environmental press and adjustment were performed separately for those who were high and low in competence. The authors conclude that "The present data provide considerable support for the generalizability of Lawton and Simon's environmental docility hypothesis across relevant dimensions of physical health, social support and personality" (Morgan et al., 1984, p. 242).

Booth (1986) tested an induced dependency hypothesis in the UK. He stated:

It is a well-attested fact that residential homes are potentially harmful places in which to live. The apathy, helplessness, withdrawal, and disorientation that research has shown to be so widespread among their residents have been linked with the way homes are run and the nature of institutional regimes. . . . The weight of informed opinion now accepts that the process of care may itself induce dependency. . . . The more institutional regimes deny residents control over their own lives . . . tend to foster their dependency.

Booth predicted that restrictive environments, which induce dependency, would reduce the individual's competence level.

Information about personal functioning of residents of 175 homes for the elderly was obtained. Some 6,947 residents were assessed in 1980, 7,024 in 1981, and 6,891 in 1982 in the same homes using the same methods. Four dependency scales were created assessing self-care, continence, social integration and alertness, and orientation. An Institutional Regime Questionnaire asked 31 questions of managers regarding "objective features of daily routine."

In this large, well-conducted study, no evidence was found that the more restrictive regimes resulted in greater dependency or mortality over time. Thus predictions based upon the ETA were not supported. The author argued that his finding does not mean that the way residents are treated is of no consequence. It does suggest that the case for more liberal regimes and ways of working, in terms of the amount of control that residents have over their own lives, should be argued on the basis of residents' rights instead of the assumption that they diminish the effects of institutionalism.

Booth and Phillips (1987) conducted a subsequent longitudinal study of group living in which residents of group homes were compared to those in traditional homes for the elderly. They argued that "Principles of group living in old people's homes are derived from the theoretical assumptions of the induced dependency hypothesis. Group living environments intend to create a more family-like setting" (p. 47). They noted that while early findings often showed group homes to be superior, this could be accounted for by a combination of methodological weaknesses and the possibility that observers may have seen what they wanted to see. In contrast, in the Booth and Phillips study, the data showed very little difference. Again, in a well-designed, controlled study, Booth failed to support a key implication of the ETA. Clearly, much more research is needed to test the theory; unfortunately prospective, well-controlled studies are expensive and rare. It has been much more common for researchers to use the ETA to generate research hypotheses.

GENERATING HYPOTHESES FROM THE ETA

Wister (1989) studied "aging in place." He used the ETA as his theoretical base because "Lawton's ecological model of aging has had the greatest impact on research and policy" (p. 268). He described the model in detail, explaining that "the principal components are individual competence and environmental press" (p. 269). He indicated the Environmental Docility Hypothesis is central to the theory. Wister missed a critical element in the ETA when he referred to its principal components as competence and environmental press. The central concept of the theory is actually adaptation level. Without considering the way in which AL mediates between competence and press, it is impossible to state whether the individual is beyond his or her range of comfort.

Wister discussed critiques of the model which required the model to take a more holistic approach by addressing the issues of needs and preferences and the individual's impact upon the environment. Lawton respond by saying that the ETA addressed those issues implicitly, for "it is people who create social structure and the individual is not a passive recipient of the environment" (p. 271).

Wister studied community-living elderly individuals residing in a tri-city region of Canada. He investigated several aspects of environmental adaptation. He found that the majority did not make any design changes to their homes, and were not considering future changes. Competence proved to be a predictor of design alterations, and selecting a dwelling for its special features resulted in a more optimistic view of future moves. He interpreted this as support for the ETA. He found that "Most elderly seem to be able to adapt without serious consequence under conditions of relatively low competence and moderate environmental press," and stated that "Older people are much more psychologically adaptive and resilient than is often assumed" (p. 289). According to the theory, when a person rises to the occasion by adapting to a difficult environment, not only does the individual demonstrate "resilience," but he or she will also show increased competence with time. Like several other researchers, designers, and planners, Wister used the ETA as an argument when recommending design decisions for building for the elderly.

Reitzes, Mutran, and Pope (1991) used a national sample of retired men 60–74 years of age "to investigate the influence of the local environment on the psychological well-being of elderly persons (p. 5195)." They studied urban, suburban and "non-metropolitan" retired men and found differences in both well-being and in the size of social networks depending upon location. They found that, in general, suburban men scored highest on well-being, but that poor health reduced the well-being of suburban men more than it did for urban men.

Reitzes and colleagues used the ETA primarily to propose and develop relationships among several social and psychological factors. They discuss ways in which theories of urbanism predict different strengths in social bonds in urban and non-metropolitan places; they imply that urban centers may serve to challenge the mental health of inhabitants. They note, "Location may also influence well-being in another way. Lawton and Nahemow's environmental docility hypothesis proposed that older people with reduced cognitive and physical competence would be affected more than other older people by their local environment" (p. 5196). They reasoned that since the local environment was expected to have a greater impact on those in poor health, they would study the interaction between location and poor health on well being.

ENVIRONMENTAL ASSESSMENT

Probably the most widespread use of the Ecological Theory of Aging has been for purposes of environmental assessment. Parmelee and Lawton (1990) reviewed the literature regarding special environments for the aged. They posited a dialectic between autonomy and security. Since both are needed, purpose-built housing for older people must offer a careful balance of the two. In considering applications of the ETA, we can see the dialectic at work. To assess environments it is necessary to consider complex methodological issues involved in measuring environmental press. Distinguishing between alpha and beta press was a concern for several authors whose work is described in this section.

With the active collaboration of the Housing Authority and the Department of Social Services, researchers and practitioners at Duke University designed an assisted living facility in order to permit residents to function maximally (Fonda , Maddox, Clipp, & Reardon, 1996). Based upon theoretical constructs of the ETA, the designers planned to avoid excess disabilities and increase competence when possible. A longitudinal research component was built in to assess the effectiveness of the design. The ETA was used as part of the explanation for designing the facility.

Stahler, Frazer, and Rappaport (1984), remodeled a psychiatric geriatric ward to "provide a more humane environment and improve adaptive behavior." They found that immediately following remodeling, patients were less effective socially. Hostility and tension increased, and self-maintenance skills decreased. However, 5 weeks later, the trend reversed. In the remodeled ward, pathological behavior was reduced, while on a comparison ward it was not. The immediate effect of environmental alterations in a ward with geriatric psychiatric patients—a population with low competence—would be to throw the patients outside their adaptive range. The expected negative affect and maladaptive behavior was evidenced. However, with time in a superior environment, these patients would be expected to establish a new AL at a slightly higher functional level, and that appears to have happened. These findings are important because they demonstrate rather dramatically the need for considering the temporal dimension when developing before—after experimental designs. With any test of the ETA, and particularly when examining the practical effects of an intervention, one must make measurements at different intervals.

Chapman and Beaudet (1983) studied a random sample of a population at high risk for institutionalization. They found that a high-quality neighborhood located at some distance from the center of town was related to both personal well-being and neighborhood satisfaction. They related this finding to the ETA in the following manner:

Living in the central city is associated with living in relatively easy-to-maintain apartments rather than detached homes, the convenience of nearby services due to more mixed residential- commercial uses, and access to similar others due to the concentration of older persons near downtown [they stated]. Viewed from the perspective of Lawton and Nahemow's ecological model, these attributes characterize a neighborhood environment that should be relatively low in environmental press and thus suited to the competence levels of this frail sample.

Recall that Reitzes and his colleagues conceptualized the probable impact of the urban environment quite differently. In fact, they felt that central cities constituted a "challenge to mental health" (p. 5195). The opposite hypotheses of the two research teams occurred because both used a limited analysis of the myriad of factors producing environmental press. Regarding Chapman and Beaudet's analysis, it is reasonable to assume that convenient amenities would reduce environmental press. However, the analysis must also take into account other factors in the individually perceived environment. When Murray originally described "press," he explained:

Everything that can supposedly harm or benefit the well-being of an organism may be considered pressive, everything else inert. The process in the subject, which recognizes what is being done to him at the moment (that says "this is good" or "this is bad," may be conveniently termed pressive perception. The process is definitely egocentric and gives rise almost invariably, to some sort of adaptive behavior. (Murray, 1938, p. 119)

Chapman and Beaudet (1984) were well aware that crime rate might affect neighborhood satisfaction. The authors included the available crime data in a regression analysis, which failed to show a statistically significant contribution to satisfaction, and they did not pursue it further. However, as is often the case, detailed crime data was not readily available. When poor or minimal data are plugged into a regression analysis, it may not register even if a strong relationship actually exists. Moreover, no information was collected regarding individual perceptions of danger. This information is difficult to gather, and the issue of crime and fear of crime was not central to Chapman and Beaudet's study. However from the standpoint of the ETA it could be a central issue. In Murray's scheme, fear of crime would definitely be considered pressive, while convenient amenities might prove to be simply inert, particularly if the individual had little need for them. Thus fear of crime could increase the press more than objective social convenience would decrease it, resulting in higher beta press than Chapman and Beaudet estimated—and possibly lower satisfaction.

La Gory, Ward, and Sherman (1985) studied sources of environmental satisfaction with the neighborhood in a large population of older people. They found that it was the subjective rather than the objective press that explained most of the variance. They found that mental portraits (perceptions) of the neighborhood were the most significant source of neighborhood satisfaction. This is a very important point, which is often overlooked by investigators who would like to simplify the model as much as possible. La Gory, Ward, and Sherman accept the complexity of the person/ environment transaction with the comment: "Older persons sharing the same neighborhoods do not necessarily occupy the same environmental worlds (p. 405)." The original definition of environmental press by Murray (1938) in which alpha was distinguished from beta press is maintained and corroborated in this exploration of the theory. The authors concluded that "Lawton and Nahemow's press theory proves useful in predicting person-environment congruence among the elderly" (p. 416).

CONTRIBUTIONS TO HEALTH PSYCHOLOGY

In his review of environmental psychology, Stokols (1995) commented that the development of environmental psychology paralleled that of the emerging field of health psychology. It is probably not surprising, then, that there has been cross-fertilization between the fields and that the ETA has proven useful in health psychology. Whereas in environmental assessment it was environmental press that was the key concept, here it is individual competence and the Environmental Docility Hypothesis.

The Environmental Docility Hypothesis has appealed to those interested in improving clinical skills. Niederhe (1997) discussed the pattern of current clinical research on the mental health of older people. He states:

> Situational factors in the problems and syndromes of older adults get relatively little attention in these papers even though, according to the influential environmental docility hypothesis, environments play an increasingly influential role in shaping

the adjustment of older adults as their intrinsic skills weaken. . . . Given the strength of behavioral assessment techniques in identifying how behavior patterns relate to situational stimuli and reinforcers, research efforts might well place a heightened emphasis on such considerations (p. 102).

Corcoran and Gitlin (1991) were concerned with an adaptation of the Environmental Docility Hypothesis. They stated that individuals with Alzheimer's Disease are likely to experience heightened sensitivity to influence from the environment, which might contribute to maladaptive behaviors. These maladaptive behaviors create difficulties for the caregiver. They list 12 intervention principles, which are derived from an extension of the model, which can be used by health care professionals to guide treatment.

Rogers (1982) applied the ETA to the work of the occupational therapist. She states that "Competence is a transactional concept that involves effectiveness in interacting with the environment" (p. 709). Basically, she argues that the purpose of occupational therapy is to increase an individual's competence. She is sensitive to the nuances of the ETA, stating:

The lower one's competence, the lower the environmental demands that can be met. For those who are severely disabled, and those who are newly disabled, the difference between an over-demanding and an under-demanding environment is slight. There is a fine line between protection from overwhelming environmental stress and exposure to environmental deprivation (p. 712).

This is accomplished in two stages. Initially, the therapist tries not to further traumatize the individual. Behavioral expectations are lowered and environmental demands are reduced. The client is excused from the normal requirements of independent living. Later, "challenge is achieved by increasing the environmental demands above the client's functional level" (p. 712). The occupational therapist gradually increases the environmental press, even risking failure in the process, to find what she calls the "just right" challenge. Rogers' sensitive analysis provides a valuable application of the ETA.

Pruchno, Burant, and Peters (1997) developed family typologies based upon the extent of agreement among families concerning the elder member. The authors argued that caregiving demands fall under the domain of environmental "press." From this vantage point they noted that "caregiving is not prejudged as stressful; rather the demands associated with caregiving have the potential to become stressful when there is incongruence between the strength of the demand and the competence of the caregiver" (p. 158). In this way, Pruchno, Burant and Peters distinguished between objective and subjective press in the caregiving role.

McConatha, McConatha, and Dermigny (1994) examined the effects of computer-based training on the rehabilitation of long-term care residents. They look upon the training as a means of enhancing personal autonomy and creating a match between person and environment. Making use of the personal computer is an innovative approach, which can lend itself readily to these goals. Using interactive computer services can provide mental stimulation and challenge in an environment which often lacks both. The article goes on to document how the training was conducted.

The application of the ETA to issues of rehabilitation has demonstrated an important strength of the theory. Sensitive therapists consider the timing of interventions with as much care as they consider the nature of the intervention. Because this has always been true, it becomes second nature to link the two elements in a treatment. The implication in the adaptation-level concept, which is so central to the ETA, is that one adapts to an environment over time. All novel environments, including simple ones, have considerable press. In long-term care facilities, residents often enter in a state of confusion and illness, which reduces their level of competence. At that time staff members should reduce stress as much as possible. However, with time in the setting the press becomes considerably reduced. If health improves as well, residents are ready for some challenge. It is at this point that computers can offer an invaluable window to the outside and to life in different places. According to the ETA, a timely increase in press can produce increased competence.

THE ETA AS A SPRINGBOARD

It is gratifying to discuss some of the very creative ways in which researchers have used the theory to advance their particular areas of interest. The following experimental studies are examples of this recent trend:

Karuza, Zevon, Gleason, Karuza, and Nash (1990) were primarily interested in the attribution of responsibility for the cause of and the solution to a problem that an individual may face. They postulate four models with different attributions for the meaning of a problem and its solution. The Moral model treats individuals as responsible for both causing and solving their problems; "The variety of self-help approaches currently in vogue typifies this model" (p. 195). "The Compensatory model treats individuals as responsible for solving problems but not causing them"; They see others who need help "as good individuals who are handicapped or constrained by environmental pressures" (p. 195). The Enlightenment model sees individuals as responsible for causing but not for solving their problems; "Alcoholics Anonymous is an example of this model" (p. 195). In the Medical model, individuals are not responsible either for causing or solving problems. Experts take over (p. 196).

In four consecutive studies, Karuza et al. (1990) found the elderly more likely to endorse the Medical model. The fourth experiment in the sequence, used the ETA to consider specific domains of perceived control. There were two different hypothetical situations: one in which the target person broke a leg, and the other a case of depression. The target person was sometimes presented as young and sometimes as old. They found that elderly people were seen as less responsible than younger people for causing their broken leg, but more responsible for their depression. They were also less responsible for solving their broken leg, but as responsible as younger people for solving their depression.

This ingenious experimental study used the ETA to develop and support the domain-specific paradigm. Karuza et al. say:

In keeping with the logic of person-environment fit models (Lawton & Nahemow, 1973), which hold that the form that adaptive behavior takes is a function of perceived personal resources and environmental pressures, we would expect that the age of the recipient will interact with the type of problem to determine the model preference of helpers. Specifically, the higher relative risk for functional losses associated with old age would be expected to enhance the preference for the medical model when helping elderly recipients who suffer a health-related problems compared with young adults. For non-health related problems (e.g., social or emotional problems), the higher relative risk for functional losses would presumably be less relevant, so no differences would be expected in helping-model choices when helping an elderly or young adult (p. 203).

Another experimental study used the ETA creatively to make a case for environmental selectivity of old people. Fredrickson and Carstensen (1990) studied how individuals of different ages respond to descriptions of hypothetical people. With whom would they choose to socialize, and what benefits would they anticipate from the socialization? Carstensen's selectivity theory postulates that throughout life people become more selective in choosing their social partners. Selectivity, she reasons, serves two functions: It allows the individuals to conserve physical energy, and it operates as a mechanism for affect regulation.

The authors found that novel partners were considered most important to teens, less important for the middle-aged and community elderly, and least important for nursing home residents. The authors interpreted this as an endorsement of Powell Lawton's proactivity hypothesis, which contends that older people actively affect their environments. If the press is rather high in one area, they will do what they can to get it in line with their individual coping ability. Toward this end, the authors argue, older people have every reason to be selective in their choices of partners.

Baltes and Wahl, in a series of studies (Baltes, Wahl & Reichert, 1991; Wahl, 1991) and a comprehensive literature review (Baltes, Wahl, 1992a, 1992b, 1996), considered the nature of daily behavioral interactions between older adults and their social partners. They concluded that the social world of older adults can be characterized as one in which their dependent behaviors are immediately attended to, while independent behaviors are widely ignored. Their research showed very little reinforcement for independent behaviors in long-term care facilities. In the community there was some reinforcement, but probably not enough to maximize functioning. Expectations of incompetence were found to be part of the helping role in institutions. According to the ETA such expectations would constitute a self-fulfilling prophecy. Still, the elders credited themselves with more competence than the staff felt they had. Staff tended to attribute incompetence to the elders, while they saw themselves as helping to assure competent self-care. This pattern should be studied further and, hopefully, corrected.

USING THE ETA TO SHOWCASE OTHER IDEAS

White (1982) used the ETA to underline the importance of the environment in long-term-care facilities. His main point is that it is highly desirable to continue sexual activity into old age. He obtained sexual histories from 250 residents in 15 nursing homes in Texas. His hypothesis was that "sexual attitudes and knowledge regarding the aged and sexual activity will be significantly related to reported sexual activity in the institutionalized aged" (pp. 16–17). The questions asked were appropriate for testing the hypothesis. However, the hypothesis is tangential to the ETA. No environmental assessments were made. Thus, for White, the ETA was used to support his assertion: "The institutionalized aged are clearly more controlled by their environment than the noninstitutionalized aged" (p. 16). While I agree with the author's point of view, the ecological model does not seem to be an essential element in the research.

Barresi, Ferraro, and Hobey (1984) also used the ETA as background to showcase their ideas. The authors used a path model to predict well-being among urban elderly from data collected by the Social Security Administration. They found different causal pathways indicated for men and women. They stated:

> This finding is consistent with the position of Lawton and Nahemow that the adaptation level, which measures the balance between individual competence and environmental press, is different for aged men and women. (p. 287)

Actually, the ETA makes no mention of gender differences. It would be a valuable extension to the theory to do so. A focus on gender issues would be timely in light of the rapid accumulation of data in the field.

THE ETA AS THEORETICAL SPRINGBOARD: NEW MODELS

Hogue (1984), a nurse who studied falls in the elderly, used the ETA as a basis for her own model. She uses a schematic representation. In it both environment and competence filter through "cognitive appraisal." Functional health is not seen as a component of competence as it is in the ETA. Instead, functional health is a primary variable, which feeds back to both competence and environment. The new theoretical focus is congruent with the concerns of a nursing professional. It is an interesting attempt to extend the theory. The problem is that concepts are broadened so that measurement of any one variable, always difficult, becomes nearly impossible. Perhaps this is why Hogue does not realize the potential for developing a cogent, different point of view. However there are several valuable elements in the model she presents.

Brown (1995) also used the ETA as a precursor of her *Urban* Ecological Model of Aging in order to examine the *suprapersonal envioronment* of impoverished urban areas. She found the ETA influential in both research and policy development. Brown's more focused model permits her to consider the suprapersonal face of the urban environment—by which she means the perception of the environment as one with a great many unemployed people, teen age mothers, female heads of household, welfare participants, and so on. She wanted to include both objective assessments and those based on media reports. she focused her attention on environmental factors often overlooked by researchers but duly noted by both inhabitants and visitors to these distinctive areas. Brown's Urban Model required further development and, one hopes, will result in necessary empirical work.

THE ETA AS A POLITICAL TOOL

Anderson, Chen, and Hula (1985) used the ETA to support the notion of a "continuum of housing environments" (p. 48). They developed one of the implications of the theory—that, all things being equal, individuals will seek and create their own level of environmental press. They stated: "Lawton and Nahemow's theory suggests the existence of optimal housing environments for older citizens." The authors reason that only by creating a diversity of environments for older people can the elderly select a set of services consistent with their needs. Housing choice is necessary to maximize life satisfaction.

The model suggests that the elder can move towards the appropriate level—either by changing the environmental press or by influencing his or her competence. Presumably, the set of alternatives will make it possible for individuals of different competencies to maximize their adaptive and affective behavior. (p. 48)

Anderson, Chen, and Hula concluded that "the model has provided justification for many seeking to optimize housing opportunities for the elderly" (p. 57). In this case, the model is used as a political tool in a good cause.

Stolper (1978) also used the theory to make a political statement. She argued that environmental design for the frail elderly is extremely important. She included an excellent discussion of Pastalan's idea of environment as language, suggesting that we "keep it plain." She discussed the effectiveness of reality orientation, a procedure developed by Jim Folsom, a physician who worked with demented patients. By providing consistent orientation cues to older demented people, in a soothing tone, he could ameliorate some effects of dementia. Thus, Stolper used the ETA in a very general way; it became a backdrop to permit her to highlight her own ideas, and to support the contention (with which I heartily agree) that the environment of long-term care facilities is important and deserves consideration.

DISCUSSION AND CONCLUSIONS

The Ecological Theory of Aging has been applied creatively to problems in many different disciplines and has been modified and adapted to changing circumstances. Sometimes the theory has been used in its entirety to generate hypotheses. More frequently, one or another element has been selected in accordance with the particular interest of the researcher. Relatively few studies have been conducted to evaluate the Ecological Theory of Aging, and those that were undertaken yielded mixed results. Morgan et al. (1984) found strong support for the Environmental Docility Hypothesis across different domains of competence. But Booth and his colleague (Booth, Booth, & Philips, 1986; 1987), in an exceptionally well-executed study conducted in the UK, did not find support for the ETA. Other researchers discussed the strengths and weaknesses of the ETA, but did not actually test it (Brown, 1995; Wister, 1989). It is true that the theory is very broadly based and not easily subject to verification, and perhaps that is one reason why there are so few tests of the theory. However, the lack of rigorous tests of an influential theory is not only true for the ETA, but is characteristic of contemporary research scholarship in general.

Several investigators were concerned with the issue of person/environment congruence. Chapman and Beaudet (1983), LaGory et al. (1985), Reitzes et al. (1991) and Wister (1989) all used large, representative samples to study the impact of neighborhood factors on individual well-being. These investigators wanted to go beyond descriptions of those elements of the environment which are good for people. All wanted to have an influence upon public policy. Anderson et al. (1985) and Stolper (1978) studied elderly housing. They, too, were interested in influencing decision making. They wanted to have an impact on design decisions affecting the elderly.

Environmental press was studied by both Pruchno et al. (1997) and LaGory et al. (1985) who defined subjective press in interesting ways. Pruchno and her colleagues discussed the press inherent in caregiving, indicating that whether it was positive or negative depended upon the interpretation of the individual caregiver. La Gory and colleagues argued that older people occupying the same neighborhood need not share the same environmental world. Thus, attention is being paid to the measurement of environmental press, with questions of the relationship between objective and subjective press being addressed if not often resolved. The suprapersonal environment received some attention from Brown in 1995, and hopefully it will receive more. The suprapersonal environment is the dominant element in urban areas, where environmental press consists largely of people occupying the space.

The Environmental Docility Hypothesis has triggered some interesting research. Both Corcoran and Gitlin (1991) and Niederhe (1997) focused upon this element in the theory. The Environmental Docility Hypothesis has always been of great interest to those who care for the old and infirm. Therapists attempt to improve functioning and several looked at the Environmental Docility Hypothesis as a way to conceptualize person/environment relationships of older or impaired people. It has been used creatively by occupational therapists (Rogers, 1982), nurses (Hogue, 1984) and even computer users (McConatha et al., 1994). Happily, planners and designers are finding ways to create suitable environments, and therapists are helping people to adapt to them.

The ETA has been used as for political purposes as well as for intellectual ones. Researchers concerned with the public good often want to affect policy. It is rare for anyone to study design without drawing conclusions about how things should be done. It is natural to want to implement the insights obtained. The need for person/environment congruence necessitates better planning and requires more thoughtful architectural innovation. Moreover, the ETA has served as a way of helping people make their case to those in a position to implement decisions.

The issue of time and timing has not been used as much as it could be. Rogers (1982) and La Gory et al. (1985) specifically dealt with this aspect of the theory with very good results. I think that this area holds the most promise for development, and for useful extensions of the theory. The core of the ETA lies in the concept of Adaptation Level, which is a direct function of time in an environment. Of course it is hard to work in four dimensions, and that is probably why the time dimension of the theory has not been sufficiently explored. It is no surprise, either, that the work in this area was done by a therapist who did not amass large samples, and by theorists who were speculating rather than measuring.

The Ecological Theory of Aging has generated both "think pieces" and hard research. It seems to me that the time may be ripe for pursuing the element of time in the theory. With the extraordinary development of applied mathematics and computer technology, the complexity of true multidisciplinary work can be accommodated. Thus, the ETA, with its four-dimensional theory, should soon be more accessible to rigorous research. This kind of analysis may be particularly useful when looking at the dialectic between autonomy and security posited by Parmelee and Lawton; the prominent need for one or the other will surface at different times.

THE FUTURE OF ETA

The ETA has been part of environmental psychology and shares its history. Stokols, in "The Paradox of Environmental Psychology" (1995), considered that history. He found that six major trends have emerged in environmental psychology. Four of them have relied to some extent upon the ETA. These are: a) development of novel constructs and methods for analyzing the links between environment and behavior; b) increased emphases on cross-paradigm research; c) transactional models of environment and behavior; and d) expanded application of environment and behavior research to the development of public policies and community problem-solving. He concluded that environmental psychology has made major contributions to knowledge. The field has been influenced by an array of societal concerns, which have constituted a dominant theme in the field and continue to do so. As the field has responded to such concerns, it has shared the methodology of other disciplines and become increasingly "transparent" to them. While research proliferated, the field became diffuse, its constructs and insights imbedded in the literature of psychology, architecture, anthropology, sociology, geography, and urban planning. That is true of the Ecological Theory of Aging as well. It has been used by practitioners of all those disciplines as well as by occupational therapy, physical therapy, sex therapy, and nursing.

It is gratifying that the ETA has found so many uses and has extended into so many disciplines. In reviewing these many varied and creative applications of the ETA, one cannot help but be struck by the fact that a theory is far more than a scientific construct. It is a showcase for the ideas of others, and a jumping-off point for new ideas. It is a political as well as a scientific tool. The theory needs more scientific testing. It is my hope that with more work directed toward clarification of the concepts used in the model, more serious testing will take place in the years to come. The Ecological Theory of Aging has generated creative thought and interesting research for the last 25 years. We anticipate, and certainly hope, that it will continue to do so.

REFERENCES

Anderson, E. A., Chen, A., & Hula, R. C. (1985). Housing strategies for the elderly: Beyond the ecological model. *Journal of Housing for the Elderly, 2*, 47–61.

Baltes, M. M., & Wahl, H-W. (1992b) Dependency-support script to institutions: generalizations to community settings. *Psychology and Aging, 7*, 409–418.

Baltes, M. M., & Wahl, H-W. (1992a). Behavior systems of dependency in the elderly: Interaction with the social environment. In *Aging, health and behavior* (pp. 83–106). Newburg Park, CA: Sage.

Baltes, M. M., & Wahl, H. W. (1996). Patterns of communication in old age: the dependence-support and independence-ignore script. *Health Communications, 8*, 217–231.

Baltes, M. M., Wahl, H-W., & Reichert, M. (1991) Successful aging in long-term care institutions. In *Annual review of gerontology and geriatrics* (Vol. 11, pp. 311–337). New York: Springer Publishing Co.

Barresi, C. M., Ferraro, K. F., & Hobey, L. L. (1984). Environmental satisfaction, sociability, and well being among urban elderly. *International Journal of Aging and Human Development, 18*, 277–293.

Booth, T. (1986). Institutional regimes and induced dependency in homes for the aged. *Gerontologist, 26*, 418–423.

Booth, T., & Phillips, D. (1987). Group living in homes for the elderly: A comparative study of the outcomes of care. *British Journal of Social Work, 17*, 1–20,

Brown, V. (1995) The effects of poverty environments on elders' subjective well being: A conceptual model. *Gerontologist, 35*, 541–548.

Chapman, N. J., & Beaudet, M. (1984). Environmental predictors of well-being for at-risk older adults in a mid-sized city. *Journal of Gerontology, 38*, 237–244.

Corcoran, M., & Gitlin, L. N. (1991). Environmental influences on behavior of the elderly with dementia: Principles for intervention in the home. *Physical and Occupational Therapy in Geriatrics, 9*, 5–22.

Fonda, S. J., Maddox, G. L., Clipp, E., & Reardon, J. (1996). Design for a longitudinal study of the impact of an enhanced environment on the functioning of frail adults. *Journal of Applied Gerontology, 15*, 397–413.

Fredrickson, B. L., & Carstensen, L. L. (l990). Choosing social partners: How old age and anticipated endings make people more selective. *Psychology and Aging, 5*, 335–347.

Guttmann, D. (1989). *Reclaimed powers*. New York: Basic Books.

Hogue, C. C. (1984). Falls and mobility in late life: An ecological model. *Journal of the American Geriatrics Society, 32*, 858–861.

Karuza, J., Zevon, M. A., Gleason, T. A., Karuza, C. M., & Nash, L. (1990). Models of helping and coping, responsibility attributions and well-being in community elderly and their helpers. *Psychology and Aging, 5*, 194–208.

La Gory, M., Ward, R., & Sherman, S. (1985). The ecology of aging: Neighborhood satisfaction in an older population. *Sociological Quarterly, 26*, 405–418.

Lawton, M. P., & Nahemow, L. (1973). Ecology and the aging process. In C. Eisdorfer & M. P. Lawton (Eds.), *The psychology of adult development and aging* (pp. 619–674). Washington, DC: American Psychological Association..

Lawton, M. P., & Simon, B. (1968). The ecology of solid relationships in housing for the elderly. *Gerontologist, 8*, 108–115.

McConatha, D., McConatha, J. T., & Dermigny, R. (1994). The use of interactive computer services to enhance the quality of life for long-term care residents. *Gerontologist, 34*, 553–556.

Morgan, T. J., Hansson, R. O., Indart, M. J., Austin, D. M., Crutcher, M. M., Hampton, P. W., Oppegard, K. M., & O'Daffer, V. E. (1984). Old age and environmental docility: The roles of health, support and personality. *Journal of Gerontology, 39*, 240–242.

Murray, M. A. (1938). *Explorations in personality*. New York: Oxford University Press.

Nahemow, L. (1989). *The ecological theory of aging as it relates to elderly persons with mental retardation*. Paper presented at the International Congress of the IASSMD, Dublin, Irland.

Niederhe, G. (1997). Future directions for clinical research in mental health and aging. *Behavior Therapy, 18*, 101–108.

Parmelee, P. A., & Lawton, M. P. (1990). The design of special environments for the aged. In J. E. Birren, & K. W. Schaie, (Eds.), *Handbook of the psychology of aging* (pp. 464–488). New York: Academic Press.

Pruchno, R. A., Burant, C. J., & Peters, N. D. (1997). Typologies of caregiving families: Family congruence and individual well-being. *Gerontologist, 37*, 157–167.

Reed, E. S. (1989). Neural regulation of adaptive behavior. *Ecological Psychology, 1*, 97–117.

Reitzes, D. C., Mutran, E., & Pope, H. (1991). Location and well-being among retired men. *Journal of Gerontology Social Sciences, 46*, (Suppl.) #4 5195–5203.

Rogers, J. C. (1982). The spirit of independence: The evolution of a philosophy. *American Journal of Occupational Therapy, 36*, 709–715.

Stahler, G. J., Frazer, D., & Rappaport, H. (1984). The evaluation of an environmental remodeling program on a psychiatric geriatric ward. *Journal of Social Psychology, 123*, 101–113.

Stokols, D. (1995). The paradox of environmental psychology. *American Psychologist, 50*, 821–837.

Stolper, J. H. (1978). Environmental design considerations for long term care facilities. *Long-Term-Care and Health Services Administration Quarterly*, 15–23.

Wahl, H-W. (1991). Dependence in the elderly from an interactional point of view: Verbal and observational data. *Psychology and Aging, 6*, 238–246.

White, C. B. (1982). Sexual interest, attitudes, knowledge, and sexual history in relation to sexual behavior in the institutionalized aged. *Archives of Sexual Behavior, 11*, 11–23.

Wister, A. V. (1989). Environmental adaptation by persons in their later life. *Research on Aging, 11*, 267–291.

3

Adjusting "Person–Environment Systems": Helping Older People Live the "Good Life" at Home

Laura N. Gitlin

INTRODUCTION

Over the past decade, long-term care practice has gravitated towards a home-based approach that enables older people to remain in their own residence for as long as possible. The home, as the natural environment of older people, has become the focal point for medical, rehabilitative and health promotion activities (K. J. Mann, 1997; Medalie, 1997). The provision of health and human services in the homes of older people actually dates back more than a century. However, this "back to the future" (Stricklin, 1997) movement is differentiated from its previous history by advancements in technological knowledge and service management systems. As part of this recent movement, new service approaches are being developed and tested. One relatively new home-based service involves the prosthetic alteration of the permanent or non-permanent features of the home environment and adjustment to a person's interaction within that context to facilitate the continuance of meaningful life tasks. This approach has been variably labeled in the literature as home modification (Pynoos, Cohen, Davis & Bernhardt, 1987), or environmental adjustment (Jackson, Longino, Zimmerman & Bradsher, 1991), terms that are used interchangeably here.

The therapeutic use of the home environment represents a potentially powerful intervention, the outcomes of which are projected to improve overall quality of life for older people who are aging with chronic health conditions and related functional needs. Surprisingly, the effectiveness of home modification for different target populations has not been rigorously tested using randomized controlled trials (Gitlin, 1999). One of the barriers to the empirical study of home modification outcomes has been the lack of adequate theoretical conceptualization of this intervention approach (Gitlin, 1998b). This approach has been viewed primarily from a medical, rehabilitative framework, with little attention given to the broader theoretical context of its potential impact on aging in place and the underlying psychosocial mechanisms associated with its use and non-use by older people. To advance this health care intervention, the use of home environmental adjustment must be anchored within a broad conceptual framework that specifies the structure of expected change and its relationship to the multiple dimensions of well-being for older adults at different levels of behavioral competencies.

The "good life" or its modern label, "quality of life," and associated principles and underlying structure represents one of Dr. Lawton's core constructs that has stimulated a profusion of research with important implications for health policy, architectural design, and clinical practice. The good life, as quality of life, has been defined recently by Dr. Lawton (1991, p. 6) as the "multidimensional evaluation, by both intrapersonal and social-normative criteria, of the person-environment system of an individual in time past, current, and anticipated." It is composed of four overlapping sectors—objective environment, perceived quality of life, behavioral competence, and psychological well-being—each with its own internal structure, set of dimensions, and relationships that have been extensively examined (Lawton, 1982; Lawton, 1983; Lawton, Brody, & Turner-Massey, 1978). This broad framework, with its conceptual tools of multidimensionality, person–environment system, and four subsectors offers an organizing framework or backdrop from which to advance health care practice involving home modification.

The purpose of this chapter is to explore ways of linking the metatheoretical constructs of quality of life to micro-level principles that can guide clinical actions involving home modification. It articulates a few of the pressing issues and questions that require further discussion and empirical examination to advance this promising area of intervention. As such, it is necessarily exploratory and formative, and perhaps raises more questions than it answers.

Two broad queries are posed, a few components of which are then explored in this essay. The first query asks: What is the relationship of environmental adjustment to specific subsectors and dimensions of the "good life" model? This query is in keeping with Dr. Lawton's (1991, p. 10) recommendation that specific dimensions of each broad category of quality of life be "custom-selected to match the purpose of the inquiry."

The second broad query concerns the dynamic structure of the physical home environment and its evaluation. Here there are several related matters. The first issue is the obligation to understand the "intrapersonal aspects" or "internal standards" (Lawton, 1991, p. 7) that individuals apply to the physical home environment and their personal needs and how these impact acceptability and usability of environmental modifications. Another issue is the need to examine the "social-normative aspects" or objective evaluative criteria from which to rate home environments and derive modification recommendations. It logically follows, then, that both objective and subjective evaluations must be integrated to derive a home modification intervention that is relevant and meaningful to the particular life context of the older person.

Case vignettes are introduced in this essay to help particularize conceptual points and connect macro considerations to real-life behaviors (Stake, 1995; Yin, 1989). The cases are drawn from two research studies; one study examined the acceptance and use of different types of home modifications for older rehabilitation patients (Gitlin, Schemm, Landsberg, & Burgh, 1996; Gitlin, Luborsky, & Schemm, 1998), while the other examined the use of environmental adjustment among families caring at home for individuals with dementia (Gitlin & Corcoran, 1993, 1996).

CONCEPTUALIZING ENVIRONMENTAL ADJUSTMENT

Environmental adjustment represents an approach to health care that differs from conventional medical or psychosocial interventions. Traditional behavioral interventions focus on changing a particular lifestyle choice or behavior. In contrast, the target of change in a home modification intervention is the physical environment and a person's interaction within that context. The fundamental objective of an environmental adjustment is to accommodate health and age-related decrements by reducing the demands of the physical environment on daily task performance. That is: an adjustment simplifies the environment to facilitate the ability to perform a basic activity, such as self-care, leisure, or other instrumental tasks. Applied environmental psychology, with its ecological model of competence-environmental press, developed initially by Lawton and Nahemow (1973), and subsequently expanded by Lawton (1981, 1982), as well as human factors research (Czaja, Weber, & Nair, 1993; Faletti, 1984; Fozard, 1981; Lawton, 1990a), provides the theoretical underpinning and empirical rationale for the clinical significance of adapting a dwelling unit as a basis for regulating person-environment transactions.

Adjustments to the home environment include an extensive array of possibilities. These range from expensive alterations of the physical home structure (widening doors, lowering cabinets, building ramps), to less costly installation of special equipment (grab bars), to no-cost changes to the material or non-permanent features of a home (removal of clutter, arrangement of furniture, or use of visual cues or memory aids). An adjustment may also include person-based changes, such as an assistive device for mobility or dressing, a behavioral strategy, such as changing footwear, or conserving energy through modification of task performance. Any one environmental adjustment may serve multiple purposes, and each type of modification may have a different outcome. For example, a grab bar in the bathroom may improve safety, accessibility, and functional level, whereas an adapted leisure game may enhance socialization, time use, and engagement.

Viewed from the vantage point of person–environment transactions, the use of a home modification is simultaneously an outcome of an adaptive, coping process as well as predictive of certain behavioral outcomes. This reciprocal process—environmental adjustment as outcome and predictor—has not been systematically considered. Furthermore, the individual as responder to the physical environment and initiator to its alteration can be conceptualized along Lawton's docility–proactivity continuum (Lawton, 1989; Lawton, 1990b). That is, using an environmental strategy which is either self-initiated or obtained through professional intervention, reflects proactive involvement in constructing a meaningful and supportive home environment to sustain continued engagement in selected life activities. There is strong evidence from national probability surveys of the presence of certain types of physical adaptations in elderly households (see Gitlin, 1998b; 1999 for overviews). This suggests an ongoing level of proactive involvement of older people in self-managing the functional consequences of chronic illness. However, the reasons why some older people are better environmental problem solvers than others are poorly understood.

The power of home modification to regulate a problematic person–environment transaction is perhaps best understood through illustration. Consider the case of a 70-year-old married man, Mr. M, who is in rehabilitation with a below-the-knee double amputation. He returns home from the hospital to confront an invariant environment that poses significant physical barriers to his ability to resume daily self-care. Two flights of stairs exterior to the home reduce Mr. M's capacity to ambulate outside, socialize, and attend doctor visits. Another flight of stairs interior to the home leading to the bedroom and bathroom prevents resumption of previous sleep, bathing, and grooming routines. Mr. M must become increasingly dependent upon his wife, and his personal choices and sense of autonomy are restricted. Additionally, the household setup places increased physical demands on his wife, who must assist in transfers and frequently ascend the stairs to obtain clothing and other needed items for Mr. M's self-care. She, in turn, has multiple health problems, including a heart condition that requires energy conservation and minimization of stair use (Gitlin, 1998a). Mr. M and his wife develop a number of immediate environmental solutions, such as transforming the first floor space into a sleeping area and organizing what Dr. Lawton (1990b) has called a control center, a central space that contains the necessary objects for self-care and other meaningful activities. Despite proactive reshaping of the home by Mr. and Mrs. M, environmental barriers prevail, with serious negative affective consequences for them both. The reduced capacity for socialization, leisure participation, and maintenance of health, combined with increased physical and emotional dependence on his wife, places Mr. M at risk for further psychological upset and physical decline.

Two immediate home-modification solutions include an exterior ramp and interior stair glide. These break down the inaccessibility of the physical environment and begin to restore a balance between the physical dimensions of the home, daily task demands, and the level of physical competency of both Mr. and Mrs. M. Thus, the importance of including an environmental perspective in medical treatment is clearly evident, the potential outcomes of which include the enhancement of multiple dimensions of quality of life.

RELATION TO QUALITY OF LIFE

What, then, are the particular gains and limitations of home environmental adjustment as a quality improvement strategy in the context of a broad quality-of-life model? Are gains and limitations specific to person–environment systems such that older people who manifest lower or higher levels of behavioral competencies and environmental needs evidence different outcomes? That is, home modifications may elevate distinct dimensions of quality of life based on the level and/or type of frailty experienced at home as well as the particular fit within the home environment. For example, whereas simplification of the environment may enhance awareness and orientation, and hence the behavioral competence of an elder with cognitive impairment, this simplification may induce boredom, and hence psychological malaise, in an elder with physical impairment.

Defining the potential gains, as well as the limitations or boundaries of home modification in light of a multidimensional conceptual framework has important implications for theory and practice. Chiefly, such a conceptual framework provides a basis from which to examine whether, for a given targeted behavioral outcome, home modification alone or in combination with other health and behavioral interventions impacts quality-of-life components. There has been insufficient theoretical and empirical consideration of the multicausal, interrelated nature of environmental change and other adaptive mechanisms and their combined affect on quality-of-life indicators.

Clearly, an environmental adjustment is just one of a number of potential strategies for regulating change in competencies as older people age in place. Mr. M needed other health modifications such as exercise and dietary changes. We do not want to overstate the benefits of an environmental adjustment, while at the same time, we want to account for all possible areas of its potential impact.

Environmental modification can be characterized in several ways using the quality-of-life model and its underlying structure. It represents an intervention that targets the physical dimension within the subsector "objective environment." As such, its immediate impact is on the objective physical environment and/or the person in the environment (e.g., two dimensions of this subsector described by Dr. Lawton). It may also alter the small-group environment (another dimension of this subsector) in that an alteration may minimize the level of involvement of others in assisting in daily care needs. We see evidence of this in the case of Mr. M, in which an interior stair glide minimized the amount of time and type of assistance his wife provided.

While the immediate impact of a home modification is on the objective environment, its purpose is to affect behavioral competence and derive a balance between these two subsectors of the quality-of-life model. As discussed earlier, the relationship between behavioral competency and environment has been richly explored. The impact on other subsectors however, awaits further empirical study. Recent discussions in the disability literature suggest that environmental adjustment may impact components of psychological well-being such as self-efficacy, as well as perceived quality of life, such as satisfaction with daily life (Schulz, Heckhausen, & O'Brien, 1994).

A typology of likely outcomes of home modification might range from factors that reflect an immediate impact on person-environment transactions in the domain of the objective environment (e.g., improved objective environmental conditions); to those that reflect proximal gains in the domains of behavioral competence (e.g., increased independence in functional health or self-care) and psychological well-being (e.g., improved mastery); to those that reflect more distal outcomes related to perceived quality of life (e.g., satisfaction with staying in place, delayed relocation to residential care).

INTRAPERSONAL CONSIDERATIONS

The symbolic meaning and importance of objects to older people may become potent factors that influence the level of environmental proactivity or willingness to alter physical elements of the home. The physical environment presents as a rich symbolic context that has been examined by only a few researchers (Albert, 1990; Rubinstein, 1989, 1990).

Consider, for example, Mrs. B, who cares for her husband with dementia. He was beginning to wander outside the home. While Mrs. B had a double bolt lock on the front door that successfully blocked Mr. B's wandering attempts, he was able to exit using a back kitchen door. In examining different strategies with an occupational therapist to control his wandering behavior, Mrs. B agreed to have a dead bolt lock installed on the back door. However, once the lock was installed, she was unable to actually use it, and expressed that she felt "locked in" and overwhelmed by its use. Shortly after the installation of the lock, a wandering episode occurred in which Mr. B exited the home by that door. Mrs. B found it necessary to place her husband in a nursing home (Gitlin, 1997).

Although the subjective meanings of the home with age has been understudied, three themes related to environmental adjustments can be gleaned from existing literature: the home as source of continuance of self, environmental adjustment as a source of biographical upset, and personal tradeoffs in using an environmental strategy.

Continuance of Self

A central theme in housing research is the importance of continuity of place and self for older adults. The ability to remain at home among familiar surroundings and carry out lifelong habituated activities has been discussed in the housing literature as providing an important source of ego-strength, personal comfort, and security among older people. The home environment may serve as an important focal point for enabling older people to adjust to life-course disruptions.

Following the onset of acute illness and disability, proactive manipulation of the environment can be viewed as a constructive process, the goal of which is to preserve or reestablish personal continuity. Thus, the home environment may become a symbolic context enabling older people to reestablish some level of sameness in daily life following a disruption caused by either an acute onset of a condition or an age-related deficit.

Removing the Throw Rug and Other Biographical Upsets

While the physical environment serves as an important source for maintaining biographical integrity or sense of personal continuity, its alteration, in turn, may be a source of personal disruption or upset. The difficulty of removing a throw rug—a common qualitative observation among health care professionals—perhaps offers some insight as to the potential biographical disruption caused by an environmental adjustment. This seemingly simple environmental action may in fact challenge ego integrity and self-definition. An environmental adjustment, especially one that is publicly visible (e.g., mobility aid, stair glide, ramp, grab bar), may heighten feelings of loss and serve as a visual reminder that things are not like before.

The drive for environmental continuity, to keep the physical home "as it always has been," is a qualitative observation we have made in our study of families caring for individuals with dementia. This is illustrated by the case of an 85-year-old spouse caring for her 90-year-old husband at the moderate-to-severe stage of dementia. The caregiver maintained the home as it had always been, and enforced a daily routine that reflected the premorbid activities and behaviors of her husband. Of central importance to this caregiver was maintaining a sense of "normalcy" and biographical integrity of her husband and how she chose to remember him. Therefore, objects for care, such as a commode, medications, mobility aid, were concealed and brought out only at the immediate time of need.

A number of home modifications were offered by an occupational therapist to offset the objective burden of care. Modifications included a stair glide for safety, adapted utensils to facilitate eating, and bathroom equipment. None, however, were acceptable to the caregiver because they fundamentally altered the notion of normalcy that guided her care practices and use of objects in the home (Gitlin, Corcoran & Leinmiller-Eckhardt, 1995). Modifications that were acceptable to this caregiver were those that were environmentally imperceptible (e.g., cutting up food into smaller portions, serving one item of food, using tactile cueing in descending stairs) and fit into the physical structure and daily routines that she had established.

Whereas small incremental environmental changes may be less costly to ego integrity, other more visible alterations, such as special equipment, may raise issues of stigma. Qualitative studies on disablement have shown the role of sociocultural notions of disability in shaping personal evaluations and acceptance and use of special equipment and home modifications (Kaufert, Kaufert, & Locker, 1987; Luborsky, 1993).

Trade-Offs

The use of an environmental adjustment poses an interesting dilemma. Its use reflects the discontinuation of previous ways of performing, or doing a valued activity, in order to achieve some level of sameness or continuity in performing that valued activity. Of significance is that home modification may have a dual outcome; it simultaneously promotes autonomy and independence while contributing to emotional, physical, and/or social disruption (Gitlin, Luborsky, & Schemm, 1998). This dilemma, between a positive (e.g., obtaining a functional gain) and a negative outcome (e.g., encountering personal and social consequences), appears to be an essential feature of the experience of using certain home modifications. Weighing the personal trade-offs may represent a contextual factor that influences successful adaptation to this type of intervention.

OBJECTIVE ENVIRONMENTAL CONDITIONS

Objective environment is defined by Dr. Lawton as all that "lies outside the individual and is capable of being counted or rated consensually by observers other than the subjects." (Lawton, 1983, p. 352). Identifying objective evaluative criteria for home modification practice may not be easy to achieve. For example, the home safety inspection conducted by a health professional represents one example of an attempt to evaluate elderly households along objective criteria. However, even within the environmental domain of safety, little consensus has been attained among health professionals and researchers as to what constitutes a hazard and its measurement. What constitutes a hazard may in large part be determined by particular objective characteristics of the person in that household as well as subjective considerations, such as personal notions of safety and preferred environmental routines that are rooted in "time past, current, and anticipated," (Lawton, 1991, p. 6) An objective environmental measure of the home that does not systematically account for the person and the level of his or her susceptibility to the environmental situation may not be ecologically valid.

Here the concern is twofold. We must be able to identify characteristics of homes that are desirable, or that maximize independence, individual choice, and autonomy. Also, we must develop a measurement approach that is reliable and ecologically valid, e.g., one that accounts for the person as a contextual factor. These represent difficult methodological tasks, given the extreme variation in the physical arrangements of homes, the differentiated relationship between persons and household characteristics, and the highly individualized needs and task preferences demonstrated by older adults.

PRINCIPLES FOR PRACTICE

The case of Mr. M illustrates the point that although older people self-initiate environmental adaptations, they may also require professional assistance to attain personal goals and desired household behaviors. Individuals may not possess the prerequisite resources (e.g., knowledge, physical materials) to set up their environment to facilitate its meaningful use. Four principles to guide research and clinical practice are suggested from this discussion.

First, examining environmental modification from a global quality-of-life perspective shifts the focus of intervention from a rehabilitative framework to a multidimensional consideration in which the environment is one part of a larger personal and social system. The shift from a medical to holistic quality-of-life perspective offers an important advantage to the practice of home modification. It suggests that assessment must be multidimensional, focusing on the person within a complex environmental system. Furthermore, the framework offers a broader understanding that older people may derive important benefits from environmental adjustments that extend beyond functional health to include higher-order level behavioral competencies such as those categorized by Dr. Lawton (1983) as time use (e.g., stimulus variation, leisure participation, engagement in meaningful activity) and social behavior (e.g., intimacy, nurturance, resumption of work and family roles). Thus, in seeking meaningful environmental quality at home, the full range of potential areas of function (physical, cognitive, and social) needs to be considered.

The second principle concerns the need to consider both the subjective view of the environment and its objective conditions. The concern with both perceived notions of the home environment and objective determinations of its defining features is congruent with Dr. Lawton's underlying structure of quality of life in which "the whole story requires . . . both" (Lawton, 1991, p. 7). Thus, professional intervention in the personal life space of older people must be guided not only by an objective determination of its dysfunctional status, but also by special attention to intrapersonal considerations of the home environment. The subjective experience of the home environment may have important implications for what types of home modifications will be accepted and used. There may not be congruence between subjective evaluations by older people of their home environment and normative assessments of its objective features by health professionals. There is empirical evidence to suggest that older people underreport home environmental problems and have difficulty discerning conditions that may place them at risk or minimize their functional capacity (W. C. Mann, Hurren, Tomita, Bengali, & Steinfeld, 1994; Steinfeld & Schea, 1993). The potential for dissonance between personal goals and the meanings of home objects and physical arrangements, and professional judgments of home safety and functionality, is great and has important implications for the approach assumed in intervention. The older person's personal goals and considerations may need to supersede objective determinations in developing appropriate home-modification interventions.

The third principle concerns the way in which environmental change is implemented in a household. It may be preferable to introduce small, incremental changes in the environment so as not to upset the balance or trade-offs that may be inherent in the use of certain types of modifications. Also, maximizing the choices offered to older people as well as providing knowledge as to how to manipulate the environment to achieve desired goals, would be important aspects of intervention to enhance their participation in the intervention process and their ability to make autonomous decisions.

Finally, the focus of a home-modification intervention is necessarily on the transactional piece: the interactive and reciprocal relation of person and environment. Thus, home modification represents a highly individualized type of intervention that addresses specific person-environment transactional needs. A solution for one person may not work for another with a similar deficit due to differences in the objective conditions of their physical environment, intrapersonal considerations, level of competency, or particular interaction of person and environment. While this point might seem obvious, it has critical implications for service delivery. It is not possible to develop a standardized delivery approach, and for certain transactional situations, highly skilled professionals may be required.

CONCLUSIONS

Although much progress has been made in environment–behavior research, less attention has been given to the empirical study of the use of the physical home environment as an agent for behavioral and functional change and support among older people. The life-enhancing potential of modifying the home environment has only recently been discussed in the gerontological literature for older people with functional decline, although occupational therapists, nurses, and other rehabilitation and home care therapists have long recognized its role and importance in geriatric care. The primary focus on relocation in previous research on housing is perhaps not surprising in that it constitutes a major life event with multiple health and psychological consequences. Still, the vast majority of older people choose to remain in their long-term residence, and would benefit from intervention to help achieve the good life, or their own personal life goals within the context of home. As such, future research needs to be directed at examining the links between a person, the physical home environment and subsequent adaptational mechanisms that are brought into play, at the conceptual and empirical levels of inquiry.

My take-off point for this essay has been several key, robust macrotheoretical constructs that Dr. Lawton has developed and advanced over the past several decades in order to broaden the theoretical discussion of home environmental modification. Environmental adjustment, as intervention, can be considered as an outgrowth of Dr. Lawton's conceptualization of the person-environment system and his ongoing theoretical and empirical efforts to "link the physical environment to the behaving older person" (Lawton, 1982, p. 33). The person–environment system, as a component of the multidimensional quality of life schema, represents a fundamental starting point for conceptualizing mean-ingful environmental based interventions to support home life for older people who are experiencing age-related deficits or functional decline. Understanding the gains and lim-itations of environmental adjustment vis-a-vis a broad multidimensional quality-of-life model offers certain advantages. It transforms home modification from a rehabilitative, restorative, medical model framework to a holistic perspective of the interrelated actions available to older people to adapt to their changing functional abilities. This broad per-spective also offers a basis for thinking comprehensively about home modification and the potential dimensions of each component of quality of life that it may impact. Four postulates for clinical practice are embedded in this perspective: The importance of exam-ining environmental change as part of a multidimensional approach to long-term care; the importance of assessing personal interpretations and meanings of home and its objects to inform intervention; the need to consider personal life style choices and internal dilem-mas posed by sociocultural notions of disability; and the importance of individualizing home modification services to address a specific person-environment transactional sys-tem. These guiding principles need further explication and require the development of assessment tools that reflect person-environment transactions and client-driven approaches to intervention.

REFERENCES

Albert, S. M. (1990). The dependent elderly, home health care, and strategies of house-hold adaptation. In J. F. Gubrium & A. Sankar, (Eds.), *The home care experience: Ethnography and Policy* (pp. 19–36). Newbury Park, CA: Sage.

Czaja, S. J., Weber, R. A., & Nair, S. N. (1993). A human factors analysis of ADL activ-ities: A capability-demand approach [Special Issue]. *Journal of Gerontology, 47,* 44–48.

Faletti, M. V. (1984). Human factors research and functional environments for the aged. In I. Aitmans, M. P. Lawton, & J. Wohlwell (Eds.), *Elderly people and the environ-ment* (pp. 191–237). New York: Plenum.

Fozard, J. L. (1981). Person-environment relationships in adulthood: Implications for human factors engineering. *Human Factors Society, Inc., 23*(1), 7–27.

Gitlin, L. N. (1997, November). *Challenges of implementing a home-based caregiver intervention involving environmental modification.* Paper presented at the 50th Annual Meeting, Gerontological Society of America, Cincinnati, OH.

Gitlin, L. N. (1998a). From hospital to home: Individual variation in the experience with assistive devices among the elderly. In D. Gray & L. Quadrano (Eds.), *Designing and using assistive technology: The human perspective.* Baltimore: Brookes Press.

Gitlin, L. N. (1998b). The role of social science research in understanding technology use among older adults. In M. Ory & G. DeFriese (Eds.), *Self-care in late life.* New York: Springer Publishing Co.

Gitlin, L. N. (1999). Testing home modification interventions: Issues of theory, measurement, design and implementation. In R. Schulz, M.P.Lawton, & G. Maddox, (Eds.), *Annual review of gerontology and geriatrics (Vol. 18). Intervention research with older adults (pp.).* New York: Springer Publishing Co.

Gitlin, L. N., & Corcoran, M. (1993). Expanding caregiver ability to use environmental solutions for problems of bathing and incontinence in the elderly with dementia. *Technology and Disability, 2,* 12–21.

Gitlin, L. N., & Corcoran, M. (1996). Managing dementia at home: The role of home environmental modifications. *Topics in Geriatric Rehabilitation, 12,* 28–39.

Gitlin, L. N., Corcoran, M., & Leinmiller-Eckhardt, S. (1995). Understanding the family perspective: An ethnographic framework for providing occupational therapy in the home. *American Journal of Occupational Therapy,* 49, 802–809.

Gitlin, L. N., Luborsky, M., & Schemm, R. L. (1998). Emerging concerns of older stroke patients about assistive device use. *Gerontologist, 38,* 169–180.

Gitlin, L. N., Schemm, R. L., Landsberg, L., & Burgh, D. Y. (1996). Factors predicting assistive device use in the home by older persons following rehabilitation. *Journal of Aging and Health, 8,* 554–575.

Jackson, D. J., Longino, C. F., Zimmerman, R. S., & Bradsher, J. E. (1991). Environmental adjustments to declining functional ability: Residential mobility and living arrangements. *Research on Aging, 13,* 289–309.

Kaufert, J. M., Kaufert, P. A., & Locker, D. (1987). After the epidemic: The long-term impact of poliomyelitis. In D. Coburn (Ed.), *Health and Canadian Society.* (pp. 345–362). Toronto: Fitzhenry.

Lawton, M. P. (1981). An ecological view of living arrangements. *Gerontologist, 21,* 59–66.

Lawton, M. P. (1982). Competence, environmental press, and the adaptation of older people. In M. P. Lawton, P. G. Windley, & T. O. Byerts (Eds.), *Aging and the environment: Theoretical approaches.* (pp. 33–59). New York: Springer Publishing Co.

Lawton, M. P. (1983). Environment and other determinants of well-being in older people. *Gerontologist, 23,* 349–357.

Lawton, M. P. (1989). Environmental proactivity in older people. In V. L. Bengtson, & W. Schaie, (Eds.), *The course of life: Research and reflections* (pp. 15–23). New York: Springer Publishing Co.

Lawton, M. P. (1990a). Aging and performance of home tasks. *Human Factors, 32,* 527–536.

Lawton, M. P. (1990b). Residential environment and self-directedness among older people. *American Psychologist, 45,* 638–640.

Lawton, M. P. (1991). A multidimensional view of quality of life in frail elders. In J. E., Birren, J. E. Lubben, J. C. Rowe & D. E. Deutchman (Eds.), *The concept and measurement of quality of life in the frail elderly* (pp. 3–27). San Diego: Academic Press.

Lawton, M. P., Brody, E. M., & Turner-Massey, P. (1978). The relationships of environmental factors to changes in well-being. *Gerontologist, 18,* 133–137.

Lawton, M. P., & Nahemow, L. E. (1973). Ecology and the aging process. In C. Eisdorfer & M. P. Lawton (Eds.), *The psychology of adult development and aging.* (pp. 619–674). Washington, DC: American Psychological Association.

Luborsky, M. R. (1993). Sociocultural factors shaping technology usage: Fulfilling the promise. *Technology and Disability, 2,* 71–8.

Mann, K. J. (1997). The home as a framework for health care. *Disability and Rehabilitation, 19,* 128–129.

Mann, W. C., Hurren, D., Tomita, M., Bengali, M., & Steinfeld, E. (1994). Environmental problems in homes of elders with disabilities. *Occupational Therapy Journal of Research, 14,* 191–211.

Medalie, J. H. (1997). The patient and family adjustment to chronic disease in the home. *Disability and Rehabilitation, 19,* 163–170.

Pynoos, J., Cohen, E., Davis, L., & Bernhardt, S. (1987). Home modifications. Improvements that extend independence. In V. Regnier & J. Pynoos (Eds.), *Housing the aged. Design directives, policy considerations* (pp. 277–304). New York: Elsevier.

Rubinstein, R. L. (1989). The home environments of older people: A description of the psychosocial processes linking person to place. *Journal of Gerontology, 44,* S45–S53.

Rubinstein, R. L. (1990). Culture and disorder in the home care experience: The home as sickroom. In J. F. Gubrium & A. Sankar (Eds.), *The home care experience: Ethnography and policy* (pp. 37–57). Newbury Park, CA: Sage.

Schulz, R., Heckhausen, J., & O'Brien, A. T. (1994). Control and the disablement process in the elderly. *Journal of Social Behavior and Personality, 9,* 139–152.

Stake, R. E. (1995) *The art of case study research.* Beverly Hills, CA: Sage.

Steinfeld, E., & Schea, S. (1993). Enabling home environments. Identifying barriers to independence. *Technology and Disability, 2,* 69–79.

Stricklin, M. L. (1997). Community-based care: back to the future! *Disability and Rehabilitation, 19,* 158–162.

Yin, R. K. (1989). *Case study research: Design and methods.* Beverly Hills, CA: Sage.

II

Health and Quality of Life

4

Time and Function

Steven M. Albert

T ime use is an indicator of psychological and social space, a measure of the ways people traffic with their environments to meet needs and accomplish goals. Insofar as good health is required for such active engagement with an environment, we can expect time use to reflect health status. That is, we think of a health condition as more or less impairing according to how much it limits us in doing what we want to do. Limitation in this sense can be measured in terms of change in time use: in the proportion of the day spent at home, in time spent alone or receiving care, or, finally, in time allocated to particular kinds of tasks (e.g., tasks that are physically strenuous or cognitively challenging, or, conversely, tasks that are relatively undemanding, energy-conserving, or perhaps "null" and hard to define as engagement of any type).

The series of time-use studies conducted by Lawton and colleagues (Lawton, 1999; Lawton, Moss, & Fulcomer 1986–87; Moss & Lawton 1982; Moss, Lawton, Kleban, & Duhamel 1991) developed these insights well, across a variety of settings. After reviewing salient findings from this research, I discuss more recent efforts, from a number of different fields, in which time allocation has been used as an indicator of health status, and, more particularly, as an indicator of functional competency.

Lawton and colleagues did not directly examine time allocation as an indicator of functional status. Their focus instead stressed time allocation as an indicator of behavioral competency and psychological well-being, with the effects of functional limitation or other health conditions subsumed within this broader model. They also recognized that time allocation, which is, after all, how one spends one's time, must have a variety of determinants, including environmental opportunity, personality, and even the particular events of any given day (since these may influence how the remainder of a day is spent). Clearly, health or functional status is likely to be only one of these determinants and perhaps hot the most important one for most people (who, after all, are healthy). Thus, Lawton and colleagues considered time allocation more an indicator of lifestyle than health status. Yet we will argue that this body of research powerfully shows the value of time use as an indicator of functional status, and that this insight has not been well exploited in gerontology and health services research.

Finally, the position of these time allocation studies in Lawton's research trajectory should be noted. They represent a logical bridge between Lawton's early research on well-being (in which environment was always an important factor) (Lawton, 1983, 1985; Lawton & Simon, 1968), and more recent research examining the relationship between events and affect in daily life (Lawton, DeVoe, & Parmelee, 1995); observed affect among patients with dementia (Lawton, Van Haitsma, & Klapper, 1996); and the role of psychological and environmental resources for the quality of life of frail elders (Lawton, 1991). We single out only one strand of a finely woven, rich intellectual tapestry.

TIME USE AND HEALTH STATUS

As indicated above, one difficulty with time use as an indicator of health and functional status is that many nonhealth factors also influence the way people spend their time. Time use indicates lifestyle, psychological proclivities, environmental options beyond the control of an individual, and daily variability with little or no apparent relation to health. For this reason, Moss and Lawton (1982) first spoke of time use as a "window on a lifestyle," with functional status as only one of many determinants of that lifestyle. Still, they were able to show significant differences in time use across lifestyles defined mainly in terms of functional status. Older adults living in independent community settings spent their time differently than older adults receiving in-home services or awaiting placement in long-term care facilities. Results from this study showed that older adults living independently "spent more time away from home, performed more obligatory activities, spent less time in personal and sick care or with social agency personnel, and spent more time in shopping, housework, cooking, and in travel" (Moss & Lawton 1982, p. 119). Functional status, then, was a major determinant of "the behavioral day" over and above variability due to individual differences in lifestyle and environment. Moreover, a fairly straightforward record of the duration and context of activities over the prior day (the "yesterday" time budget), could elicit this behavioral day with reasonable reliability, as later confirmed by an extensive set of methodological studies (Juster & Stafford, 1985).

An additional finding from this important research was the direction of change in time use according to health status. Not unexpectedly, more highly functional people spent less time in rest and relaxation and a greater proportion of the day out of the home. Less expected was the greater proportion of the day spent performing obligatory tasks, such as housework, cooking, shopping, and travel. The more highly functional older adults allocated more time to these tasks; moreover, they also reported greater pleasure in performing them. This finding shows that time use reflects not just health, but also an important feature of the psychology of health. Moss and Lawton suggested that more highly functional older adults spend more time in such obligatory tasks, in part, because they perform them with greater variation, perhaps purposefully extending the time they allocate to these tasks to make such task performance an occasion for challenge, recreation, and satisfaction. Impairment, by contrast, forces people to perform everyday tasks with less variation and less opportunity to affirm competencies. Thus, impaired function means alteration in time use but also alteration, perhaps, in the experience of time: "Impaired function means that a greater proportion of all behavior becomes routine, and the negative experience of many routine activities is emphasized because they are harder to perform" (Moss & Lawton, 1982, p. 123). Recognition of this feature led the authors to recommend the introduction of greater novelty in the home settings of impaired elders, "opportunities to perform unusual instrumental behaviors under low-threat conditions" (p. 123).

A second study examined the time budgets of caregivers to frail elders, who completed "yesterday" time budgets at baseline and again 3 months later. By design, the caregivers were all providing support to elders at high risk of nursing home placement, and about half did, in fact, enter nursing homes within the study period (Moss et al., 1991). The authors were largely interested in the change in caregiver time allocation that follows an elder's entry into a nursing home. They found that caregivers whose elders entered a nursing home showed increases in time out of the home, time with others beside the elder, and time devoted to instrumental tasks, relative to caregivers whose elders did not enter nursing homes. Not surprisingly, these caregivers also spent far less time providing help to elders than did those whose elders remained in the community.

The authors were also able to examine differences in time allocation at baseline between caregivers whose elders remained in the community 3 months later and those whose elders went on to nursing home placement by the time of the follow-up interview. This contrast is especially informative, since elders who entered nursing homes in the study period were likely to be more impaired at baseline than those who remained in the community. Thus, the baseline comparison of the two gives an indication of the effects of more severe elder functional impairment on caregiver time. Caregivers to elders who entered nursing homes were providing 60% more time in overall assistance and 40% more time in instrumental support. They also spent more time alone and at home with the elder, and had less time to themselves for household tasks, social activity, and leisure.

In fact, the effects of elder functional deficit on caregiver time allocation are likely to be even stronger. In this study, correlations between caregiver reports of elder ADL deficits and time-budget counts of ADL care were reassuringly high (.74 in the case of assistance with eating). Thus, it is likely that comparisons based on actual elder deficits would show even stronger differences in caregiver time allocation.

Finally, a third study confirmed these findings for proxy reports of elder time allocation. Caregivers to these elders at risk for nursing home placement were also asked to report on the ways these elders spent their time, again completing the 24-hour "yesterday" interview, but this time for the elder. Lawton (1999) reports that these elders, all of whom were severely impaired and at high risk for nursing home placement, showed extremely impoverished time use. Rest and passive leisure (radio/television) occupied the greatest portion of the day; elders were alone for more than half the time accounted for; and elders spent more than half of their time in bed or in bedrooms. The bland and undifferentiated quality of this way of spending time was reinforced by caregivers' inability, in more than half the cases, to identify even a single activity over the prior month that gave an elder pleasure.

All three studies converge on a common conclusion. Greater functional impairment means restriction in activity: more time at home, less time in instrumental activities, less variety in the way tasks are performed, and less satisfaction with time use. It also means alterations in time use for caregivers, who must render support to such elders. This includes increased time providing assistance to elders and a similar narrowing of the range of activities performed in a day. These results emphatically support Lawton's conclusion that social space, as seen in extra-household resources, is one of the most sensitive indicators of biological decline, and that this process of contraction in space ultimately extends to the individual's immediate living area (Lawton, 1985, 1990).

But Lawton also recognized additional complexity in attempts to use altered time use as an indicator of health limitation: "It is well worth pursuing the idea that the process that ends in constricted social space may be as proactive as the process that expands social space" (Lawton, 1990, p. 639). Individuals forced into restricted activity patterns may yet increase their control of remaining space and adopt strategies that allow them to maximally use the more limited time available for challenging activities. Lawton (1985) and Rubinstein (1989) vividly describe the ways impaired elders make constricted spaces (such as the bedrooms or living rooms to which they may be confined) maximally stimulating and maximally meaningful. The density of control increases even as the space contracts, as elders seek to secure maximum stimulation in these settings. Fredrickson & Carstensen (1990) similarly describe how impaired elders with limited time for challenging activity (such as social interaction) optimally use such time by choosing engagements that are most likely to maximize positive affect, or at least minimize the risk of negative affect. While time budgets capture constriction in activity and contraction of space, other methodologies may be required to measure the proactive use of such restrictive resources.

NEW EFFORTS IN ASSESSING TIME USE AS A METRIC FOR FUNCTIONAL COMPETENCY

Despite the success of time-budget studies in documenting variation in functional ability, the methodology has not been widely adopted in studies of adult health. In describing the hard journey of a manuscript using the time-budget approach, Lawton (1999) noted that many researchers do not value and do not see the practical point of time-budget studies. This very generous conclusion should be compared to reviewers' less than charitable comments ("About all anyone did was eat, rest, or sit/lie in front of TV"; "Do the activities of a normal population . . . have any meaning/relevance for the seriously impaired?"). The junior researcher can take some comfort from seeing that even a prominent, senior scholar must sometimes take his lumps; but the more troubling conclusion is that "everyday life," and the diagnostic significance of alterations in such behaviors, is often not taken seriously as a research focus. The thoughtless comment on the irrelevance of "normal" behaviors for the seriously impaired is particularly galling. At this point, then, it is worth marshalling some of the more recent, accumulating evidence on the value of time-budget measures in health research. While the time budget has gained a limited number of advocates in gerontological research (see the edited volume of Altergott, 1988), it remains an underutilized tool for health research in elderly populations.

Maternal Time Allocation and Caregiving

The reluctance of the gerontological community to use the time-budget approach for health research should be contrasted with the response of researchers in pediatric health, who have used the method for some time. Two recent studies from developing nations provide good examples of the effect of childhood illness on maternal time allocation.

These studies relied on a combination of spot sampling and self-reports, in which households were repeatedly visited over follow-up periods of close to 1 year. In a study from a Peruvian village, Bentley and colleagues showed that maternal caregiving time was increased during episodes of childhood illness (for some, but not all, child age groups); that such increases were greatest when children had symptoms of disease perceived to be more severe (i.e., mucus in stool in the case of diarrheal disease); and that mothers spent more time trying to get children to eat during illness (Bentley et al., 1995). Gryboski (1996), on the other hand, did not find a significant difference in maternal caregiving time for children when each child's symptom days were compared to preceding or following non-symptom days. This latter study has the virtue of a within-subject design (unlike Bentley's, which involved group contrasts), but also has the fault of comparing symptom days to prodromal or convalescent days, when the proper contrast is more appropriately "sick" versus "healthy" days; this may have obscured differences in time allocation related to illness. In any case, the two studies show that maternal care is responsive to childhood illness, but that the magnitude of such response is constrained by competing activities. In Bentley's Peruvian community and Gryboski's Indonesian village, women were also major economic producers, whose productive efforts were critical for entire households. They were constrained in the extent that they could alter activity patterns in response to childhood illness.

Recognition of the limit to which one can alter activity is also relevant to caregiving research involving impaired elders. Albert and colleagues have shown that formal care hours (that is, paid hours of care provided by home health attendants, homemakers, and housekeepers) may be more highly correlated with degree of elder impairment than care hours provided by informal caregivers (i.e., unpaid family and friends). The number of informal care hours is determined, in part, by the availability of such caregivers, i.e., whether they work, whether they live nearby, whether their own health allows them to provide care, and their investment in the role of caregiver. Formal hours, by contrast, do not face such constraints, and in the service-rich setting of New York City may be a better indicator of elder impairment (Albert et al., 1998).

Cognitive Deficit

Albert and colleagues used the time-budget approach to examine the effect of human immunodeficiency virus (HIV), and in particular, neurocognitive deficit associated with HIV, on activity patterns (Albert et al., 1994). They used the "yesterday" time budget to compare the activity patterns of HIV-positive gay men to the activity patterns of uninfected gay men and showed that the HIV-positive group spent significantly less time awake, more time at home, and more time resting. Across both infected and uninfected men, time spent in passive leisure (TV, radio, reading) was significantly correlated with neuropsychological test performance, number of neurological signs and symptoms, and self-reported deficits. Finally, increased time in medical care or self-care was associated with poorer neuropsychological performance. The correlations reported in this study were modest (.25-.35), but these results emerged from time budgets that had been completed by respondents without the supervision of researchers, supporting the robust nature of these associations. They are likely to be underestimates.

In a second study of the effect of HIV-associated neurocognitive deficit on everyday function, Albert and colleagues noted that respondents did not report deficits in instrumental tasks (e.g., taking medicine, using the telephone, handling money) even when performance tests indicated deficit in these domains. In this research, we used an observed medication performance test based on the Observed Tasks of Everyday Living (Diehl, Willis, & Schaie, 1995). Results were striking; for example, in one series of 20 patients, only one reported a need for help in taking his medicines, when, in fact, five could not follow prescription information to place a series of five medicines in a medication timer (Albert et al., 1997). Why did these patients fail to perceive and report deficits in the medication domain? We cannot be sure; cognitive deficits may have been responsible for both poor performance and lack of insight on perceived competency, or patients may have understandably overestimated their abilities in the clinical setting. It is also possible that our medication test is a poor guide to actual everyday competencies, though high correlations between medication performance test and neuropsychological performance (.40-.50 for tests of memory, motor planning, and reaction time) make this explanation less likely.

An alternative explanation, however, can be investigated with the time budget. It may be that subjects with cognitive impairment alter their activity patterns to simplify or avoid cognitively challenging tasks. In this way, respondents with cognitive impairment would be less likely to confront tasks that might force recognition of impaired competencies. To test this hypothesis, we compared the activity patterns of HIV-positive subjects who met criteria for mild dementia with those who did not meet these criteria; the sample included men and women, and both gay men and people whose infection was acquired through injection drug use. We found that the demented group spent significantly less time performing instrumental tasks (food preparation and related household activities) and significantly more time in passive leisure activity. The nondemented group spent about a quarter of their waking time in passive leisure activity, while the group meeting criteria for dementia spent over a third of their time in such minimally demanding activity. Finally, the nondemented group spent nearly four times as much time in work or volunteer activity, nearly 10% of their waking time, while subjects meeting criteria for dementia spent <3% of their waking hours performing these more demanding tasks (Albert et al., 1997).

Thus, the time budget proved useful in explaining, to some degree, respondents' tendency not to report instrumental deficits. They had already altered their behavior to minimize the impact of deficits in this domain.

Work Disability

An obvious use of the time budget is to assess the impact of health conditions on the capacity to work, measured most directly in time allocated to productive activities. In occupations where people "punch in and out" of work, such recording is straightforward, but a number of studies have examined the effect of illness or work productivity in Third World societies as well. For example, Parker (1992) showed that parasite infection in the Sudan led women to alter activities in notable ways: they worked fewer hours, but were able to maintain overall productivity by working faster in the fewer hours available to them; they also maintained this work productivity by neglecting other activities, such as self-care, to conserve energy for work activities. These women do not have the option of withdrawing from productive activities. In a similar vein, Picard and Mills (1992) have shown that reductions in work time among Nepali villagers were related to malaria infection, type of parasite species, time since treatment, and treatment course.

For an example closer to home, Cady and colleagues recently reported results from a study of effects of migraine on work productivity in the setting of a double-blind, placebo-controlled clinical trial of sumatriptan (Cady et al., 1997). Subjects in this study were all migraineurs who used a diary to record "productivity loss" following migraine attacks. Productivity loss was defined as the sum of time lost to work and time in which subjects may have worked but at reduced effectiveness. To derive the amount of work time with reduced effectiveness, subjects recorded both time worked and self-perceived effectiveness on the job for each interval of work time. Work time could thus be weighted for effectiveness. A similar approach has been developed for cognitively and socially challenging activities performed by schizophrenic patients, though here the weights for activities were developed by researchers (Olbrich, Voss, Mussgay, & Pfeiffer, 1993). In the migraine study, the primary outcomes were mean productivity loss and median time to return to normal work performance following migraine attack. Compared to the placebo group, sumatriptan injectors showed lower productivity loss and lost only half as much time to reduced productivity.

This important study demonstrates the sensitivity of the time budget to record both time in activity and variation in the quality of such activity. It is thus an important advance in time-budget methodology that, to our knowledge, has not yet been applied to gerontological health research. For example, O'Leary and colleagues used a time-budget methodology to examine behaviors of Alzheimer's patients and coded behaviors as simply "adaptive" or "ineffective" (O'Leary, Haley, & Paul, 1993). A weighting approach might allow finer coding of such behaviors, which in turn may make the time budget more useful for clinical trial research (see below).

Illness Recognition

Another series of time-budget studies has begun to explore illness recognition, that is, when people change activities in response to sickness. Sauerborn, for example, has noted that recognition of mild illness (as opposed to disease that leaves no choice but reduction of activity and adoption of the role of patient) may be related to the opportunity cost of time (Sauerborn, Nougtara, Hien, & Diesfeld, 1996). In a Third World setting, illness episodes, help-seeking, care for the ill, and alterations in activity due to illness were less frequent in the more highly productive rainy season than in the dry season. This finding is especially provocative given the increased risk of malnutrition and greater transmission of infectious disease typical of the rainy season.

Clinical Trials

Recognition that caregiver time is correlated with level of elder deficit has led to use of caregiver time allocation as an outcome in clinical trials. Clipp and Moore (1995) have shown that informal care hours were correlated with level of cognitive deficit and behavioral symptoms at baseline, and that informal caregiver time decreased in the treatment arm of this double-blind, placebo-controlled trial. For example, caregivers in the high-dose treatment arm were able to reduce total patient supervision, on average, by 3.3 hours per day. The authors conclude that incorporation of caregiver measures, such as time allocation, in clinical trials for Alzheimer's disease has an advantage over patient-centered measures. The clinical significance of small but statistically significant improvements in patients' cognitive function is hard to establish; but if such changes are also associated with increased independence or lower stress for caregivers, a case can be made for the clinical relevance of even small patient treatment effects.

Effect on Households

Finally, and more generally, it should be noted that time allocation measures move the patient off center stage to stress household responses to illness. This is implicit in a number of the studies summarized here. Assessing alteration in patient activity draws attention to household processes: who performs tasks the patient would have performed, who performs tasks required for patient care, and how a household may have to reorganize or allocate resources differently to meet the challenge of health limitation in one of its members. Broad differences in such household processes may characterize developing and more developed societies. For example, in a rural African population, Sauerborn, Adams, and Hien (1996) reported that the time costs of care for household members (i.e, time valued at current costs of replacing labor) represent about two-thirds of the total household costs of illness, and that caregivers lose about as much time providing care as the sick person loses because of illness. One would expect the time costs of illness to be lower in developed societies because of access to more efficient therapies, prosthetic technologies that allow caregivers to leave patients unattended, and related advantages.

CONCLUSIONS

Powell Lawton's research on time use represents only one of many accomplishments. One might even argue that it represents a minor theme of his oeuvre, when arrayed next to such central, enduring interests as functional assessment, quality of life, affect and lifespan development, the experience of nursing home residence, and environmental psychology. Yet this assessment is not quite right. The interest in time use and use of the time budget should be seen in the context of Lawton's overarching research strategy. One feature of Powell's research has always been a continual search for observable, measurable outcomes that can be used to assess theoretical models. Time use is one such operational criterion, an indicator of behavioral competence (Lawton, 1991). Thus, the interest in time use is a logical development from the more fundamental project of understanding components of the good life.

But even this is perhaps too limiting. For we have seen earlier that time use may also relate to psychological well-being, as when routine tasks become oppressive because health conditions reduce a person's capacity to perform tasks in different ways and thus limit the extent to which someone can control the timing and execution of tasks. In such cases, we have seen that the experience of time may also change, with people reporting more boredom, less satisfaction with life, and poorer affect.

Following Lawton's example, I have argued that time use can be seen as an indicator of functional status. It is also an index of lifestyle, and it is sometimes hard to separate the two, as Moss and Lawton (1982) recognized early on. Ways to disentangle the two, however, are available. Research designs allow us to compare groups with comparable lifestyles that differ in a health condition, as we have done with investigations of the effects of HIV on neurocognitive function (Albert et al., 1994). Methodological revisions may also help. In a current project we are restricting the time budget to capture only particular health-indicative behaviors, i.e., behaviors resistant to lifestyle differences, such as medication management. Weighting activity by measures of "challenge," "perceived effectiveness," or other indicators of quality may also help take into account differences in lifestyle and make the technique more sensitive. Here again, though, we follow Lawton, who first proposed degree of "liking" as an indicator of the quality of time use.

To conclude, the time budget remains a promising but underdeveloped research tool. It well illustrates Powell Lawton's recognition that everyday life, and the mundane activity of which it is made, is actually complex and, when carefully assessed, can be a valuable indicator of more basic competencies and an important guide to policy and care planning.

REFERENCES

Albert, S. M., Marder, K., Todak, G., Clouse, R., Polanco, C., & Stern, Y. (1997, October). *Functional status of patients with HIV-1-associated cognitive-motor disorder.* Paper presented at the 122nd annual meeting of the American Neurological Association, San Diego, CA.

Albert, S. M., Sano, M., Bell, K., Merchant, C., Small, S., & Stern, Y. (1998). Hourly care received by people with Alzheimer's disease: Results from a community-based study. *Gerontologist, 38,* 704–714.

Albert, S. M., Todak, G., Elkin, E., Marder, K., Dooneief, G., & Stern Y. (1994). Time allocation and disability in HIV infection: A correlational study. *Journal of Occupational Science: Australia, 1,* 21–30.

Altergott, K. (Ed). (1988). *Daily life in later life.* Newbury Park, CA: Sage.

Bentley, M. E., Elder, J., Fukumoto, M., Stallings, R. H., Jacoby, E., & Brown, K. (1995). Acute childhood diarrhea and maternal time allocation in the northern central sierra of Peru. *Health Policy and Planning, 10,* 60–70.

Cady, R., Ryan, R., Jhingran, P., O'Quinn, S., Pait, D. G., Watson, C., & Batenhorst, A. (1997, May). *Sumatriptan injection reduces productivity loss during a migraine attack: Results of a double-blind placebo-controlled trial.* Paper presented at the 49th annual meeting of the American Academy of Neurology, Boston, MA.

Fredrickson, B. L., & Carstensen, L. L. (1990). Choosing social partners: How old age and anticipated endings make people more selective. *Psychology and Aging, 5,* 335–47.

Clipp, E. C., & Moore, M. J. (1995). Caregiver time use: An outcome measure in clinical research on Alzheimer's disease. *Clinical Pharmacology and Therapeutics, 58,* 228–236.

Diehl, M., Willis, S. L., & Schaie, K. W. (1995). Everyday problem solving in older adults: Observational assessment and cognitive correlates. *Psychology and Aging, 10,* 478–491.

Gryboski, K. L. (1996). Maternal and non-maternal time allocation to infant care, and care during infant illness in rural Java, Indonesia. *Social Science and Medicine, 43,* 209–219.

Juster, T. F., & Stafford, F. P. (1985). *Time, goods, and well-being.* Ann Arbor: University of Michigan, Institute for Social Research.

Lawton, M. P. (1983). The dimensions of well-being. *Experimental Aging Research, 9,* 65–72.

Lawton, M. P. (1985). The elderly in context: Perspectives from environmental psychology and gerontology. *Environment and Behavior, 17*, 501–519.

Lawton, M. P. (1990). Residential environment and self-directedness among older people. *American Psychologist, 45*, 638–640.

Lawton, M. P. (1991). A multidimensional view of quality of life. In J. E. Birren, J. E. Lubben, J. C. Rowe, & D. E. Deutchman (Eds.), *The concept and measurement of quality of life* (pp. 3–27). New York: Academic Press.

Lawton, M. P. (1999). Methods and concepts for time-budget research on elders. In W. Pentland, A. Hawey, M. P. Lawton, & M. A. McCall (Eds.), *Intervention with older adults: Vol. 18. Annual review of gerontology and geriatrics*. New York: Springer Publishing Co.

Lawton, M. P., DeVoe, M. R., & Parmelee, P. (1995). Relationship of events and affect in the daily life of an elderly population. *Psychology and Aging, 10*, 469–477.

Lawton, M. P., Moss, M., & Fulcomer, M. (1986–87). Objective and subjective uses of time by older people. *International Journal of Aging and Human Development, 24*, 171–188.

Lawton, M. P., & Simon, B. (1968). The ecology of social relationships in housing for the elderly. *Gerontologist, 8*, 108–115.

Lawton, M. P., Van Haitsma, K., & Klapper, J. (1996). Observed affect in nursing home residents with Alzheimer's disease. *Journal of Gerontology: Psychological Sciences, 51B*, P3–15.

Moss, M., & Lawton, M. P. (1982). Time budgets of older people: A window on four lifestyles. *Journal of Gerontology, 37*, 115–123.

Moss, M., Lawton, M. P., Kleban, M., & Duhamel, L. (1991). Time use of caregivers of impaired elders before and after institutionalization. *Journal of Gerontology, 48*, S102–111.

Olbrich, R., Voss, E., Mussgay, L., & Pfeiffer, H. (1993). A weighted time budget approach for the assessment of cognitive and social activities. *Social Psychiatry and Psychiatric Epidemiology, 28*, 184–188.

O'Leary, P. A., Haley, W. E., & Paul, P. B. (1993). Behavioral assessment in Alzheimer's disease: Use of a 24-hour log. *Psychology and Aging, 8*, 139–143.

Parker, M. (1992). Re-assessing disability: The impact of schistosomal infection on daily activities among women in Gezira Province, Sudan. *Social Science and Medicine, 35*, 877–890.

Picard, J., & Mills, A. (1992). The effect of Malaria or work time! Analysis of data from two Nepal districts. *Journal of Tropical Medicine and Hygiene, 95*, 382–389.

Rubinstein, R. L. (1989). Themes of the meaning of caregiving. *Journal of Aging Studies, 3*, 119–1xx.

Sauerborn, R., Adams, A., & Hien, M. (1996). Household strategies to cope with the economic costs of illness. *Social Science and Medicine, 43*, 291–301.

Sauerborn, R., Nougtara, A., Hien, M., & Diesfield, H. J. (1996). Seasonal variation of household costs of illness in Burkina Faso. *Social Science and Medicine, 43*, 281–290.

5

Assessing Quality of Care Among Chronic Care Populations: Conceptual and Statistical Modeling Issues

Jeanne A. Teresi, Douglas Holmes, and Marcia Ory

It is becoming increasingly important to develop and implement methods for determining the quality of care provided to elderly persons. There are several major reasons why this is so. First, the oft-cited accelerating growth of the population of elderly persons—particularly the old-old—means that there will be increasing numbers of dependent persons relying on various components of the health care system. Second, the growing costs of caring for this population have focused attention on ensuring that health- and social-care dollars are being spent judiciously. Finally, the growth of managed care, which reflects consumer ascendancy in the health care marketplace, requires that consumers—both organizational and individual—have available some means for assessing the relative adequacies of care, as a basis for market selection decisions. For some decades, Powell Lawton has been at the forefront of those concerned with quality-of-care issues; as a result, his work has had substantial direct and indirect impact on models and techniques used in evaluating care.

The first portion of this chapter includes a review of recent conceptualizations regarding the measurement of quality of care, including specification of the domains which define the construct. The second portion presents and discusses major models relating to quality of care, and their theoretical antecedents. As will be seen in this portion of the discussion, Lawton's work has been seminal in bringing to the fore the critical distinction between process and outcomes as criteria in the measurement of quality of care. In this portion there is also discussion of risk adjustment as it relates to the assessment of quality of care. Finally, there is a brief discussion of selected advanced statistical techniques which may be involved in quality of care assessment. Throughout these sections there is repeated reference to Lawton's work; by their very breadth, his contributions reflect his comprehensive interests and expertise, and his ongoing involvement in learning of and contributing to the leading edge of conceptual progress.

Quality of care has been discussed in numerous contexts over the past 30 years. As noted, there has been recent enhanced interest in the topic, particularly as it relates to managed care and prediction of costs and outcomes (Brooten, 1997; Hogan, 1997). For example, the December, 1997 issue of *Health Services Research* is devoted to managed care, including several articles addressing quality of care issues. This focus has been true in other contexts, as well, including several conferences resulting in journal supplements devoted entirely to the topic. A conference on Measuring the Effects of Medical Treatment, sponsored by the Agency for Health Care Policy Research (AHCPR), included papers developed by the Patient Outcome Research Teams (PORTs). These papers were published in an April 1995 supplement to *Medical Care*, which contained many methodological articles dealing with the measurement of health status and of the quality of life. Another conference, Outcome Measures and Care Delivery Systems (Mitchell, Heinrich, Moritz, & Hinshaw, 1997), was sponsored in June 1996 by the American Academy of Nursing. It focused on outcomes in relation to the delivery of medical care in hospital settings, although home health care (Shaughnessy, Crisler, Schlenker, & Arnold, 1997) and other settings (Lamb, 1997) were also considered. The proceedings were presented in a special issue of *Medical Care*, published in November, 1997. Another conference held in September 1996, was sponsored by the Alzheimer Association, AHCPR, the Advisory Panel on Alzheimer's Disease to the Department of Health and Human Services, the National Institute of Aging (NIA), the National Institute of Mental Health (NIMH) and the Department of Veterans Affairs. The focus of this conference was on outcomes relevant to treatment interventions for patients with Alzheimer's disease; the proceedings were published in a December, 1997 special supplement to *Alzheimer Disease and Associated Disorders Journal*. Finally, in March, 1996, the AHCPR and the NIA jointly sponsored a conference on "Aging and Primary Care: Organizational Issues in the Delivery of Health Care Services to Older Americans," held in Washington, D.C. This meeting has resulted in a special issue of *Health Services Research (HSR)*, edited by Ory, Cooper, and Siu (1998), which examines social and behavioral theoretical approaches to understanding intra- and inter-organizational care process and outcomes for older Americans. Finally, a forthcoming publication by the Institute of Medicine (IOM) addresses the quality of long-term care in terms of advances made since the recommendations of the 1986 IOM report on quality of care in nursing homes.

The 1994 *Annual Review of Gerontology and Geriatrics* edited by Lawton and Teresi (1994) reviews measures that can be used for research outcomes across the spectrum of older adults. Two recent books, one edited by Robert L. Kane (1997) and the other by Andresen, Rothenberg, and Zimmer (1997), discuss health care outcomes, comorbidity, risk adjustment and health status measures. Other publications focusing on process and outcome measurement include two volumes (published in 1996 and 1997) of *Mental*

Health and Aging, edited by Teresi, Lawton, Holmes and Ory. These volumes contain reviews of outcome measures for use with chronic care populations; authors include investigators of the NIA collaborative studies of Special Care Units, and members of the Workgroup on Research and Evaluation of Special Care Units (WRESCU).

In the present chapter we attempt to integrate quality-of-care literature across fields because we have found a disturbing trend for different disciplines to independently "discover" or rediscover equivalent domains, using different terminology, but without referencing or evidencing awareness of similar efforts elsewhere. For example, the health services literature frequently does not reference the medical outcomes literature which, in turn, does not reference the gerontological literature on health-related quality of life. Most probably, an integrated approach would better advance both theory and empirical findings related to quality of care.

While the ensuing discussion focuses on conceptual models for the study of quality of care, rather than on specific measures, we do include a description of selected illustrative, widely used assessment measures. Consistent with our perceived need for theoretical integration, we review the current state-of-the-art across a number of disciplines.

BACKGROUND OF QUALITY OF CARE ASSESSMENT

Much of the recent work on quality of care has appeared in the literature of the 1990s and has focused on hospitals and on medical outcomes. Some of the earliest work, however, was conducted in psychiatric institutions and Veterans Administration facilities during the 1950s and 1960s. Emphasis was on organizational variables such as staffing, process variables reflecting the social environment such as ward atmosphere (Moos & Houts, 1968; Spiegel & Younger, 1972), or on social interactions such as staff and patient perceptions and involvement (Cohen & Struening, 1964). Measurement of outcomes focused not so much on quality of care as on the delivery of treatment, specifically its effectiveness and patient tenure in the community (Kellam, Goldberg, Schooler, Berman & Shmelzer, 1967). In this vein, some of Lawton's earliest contributions focused on role perceptions and personality traits of psychiatric aides in relation to performance and methods of maximizing their therapeutic potential (Lawton, 1965; Lawton & Goldman, 1965). Among psychiatric aides, Lawton (1965) found a positive relationship between their job performance ratings and lowered authoritarianism and dominance and lessened tendency to perceive wide differences between patients and non-patients.

In the 1980s the Institute of Medicine (1986) issued a report on improving quality of care in nursing homes; this was in part an outgrowth of the nursing home scandals of the 1970s and accompanying concern about quality of care in long-term care facilities. The IOM report identified areas which should be targeted for improvement. Many of the recommendations have been followed, e.g., the reduction of restraints, and the development and collection of a national database (Morris et al., 1990). But other areas, e.g., staffing, have not been fully addressed. For example, in the context of similar case mixes, staff–patient ratios are still quite variable across institutions; staff training and support are still inadequate (see Teresi, Grant, Holmes and Ory, 1998). A recent review (Binstock & Spector, 1997) calls for investigations of technological and staffing innovations which support quality in a cost-containment environment.

DOMAINS RELATING TO THE QUALITY OF CARE

In order to guide research into the determinants of the quality of care, as well as to develop proxy measures of quality of care, it is imperative that models be created which reflect each of the domains which bear on the construct. Therefore, these domains are listed below as the prelude to a discussion of the various conceptual models currently in use. In each case, titles in parentheses () reflect designations used in the major models. In discussing the following domains we have attempted to integrate the key components of several models used in the study of quality of care. The classifications for the domains follow the work of Lawton (1982) (Behavioral Competence, Objective Environment, Perceived Quality of Life, and Psychological Well-Being); Donabedian (1980) (Structure, Process and Outcome); Anderson and Newman (1973) (Predisposing, Enabling, Need and Outcomes); and Mechanic (1979, 1989), and Johnson and Wolinsky (1993) (Health Status), in addition to the classification developed here (Formal, Informal, Environment, Individual, Outcome). Actual elements come from the work of many authors, e.g., Mitchell and Shortell (1997); Teresi, Lawton, Ory, and Holmes (1994); Montgomery (1994); Lawton (1983); Lawton (1997); Lawton and Lawrence (1994); Gurland and Wilder (1984); Shaughnessy et al. (1997).

Formal Support System (Predisposing Structural)

This is comprised of such subdomains as *Organizational factors* [e.g., size, ownership, locality, proportion of residents Medicaid-reimbursed, structure of the facility and the degree of bureaucratic function, coordination of resources, technology available, and external pressures, such as funding source, family involvement, and organizational affiliation(s)]; *Unit factors* (e.g., size of units(s), staff/resident ratios); *Community factors* (e.g., available community services and facilities, and role of regulatory agents); *Staffing factors* (e.g., professional- & subprofessional-to-resident ratios, certification/training, available professions or specialties, and patterns of assignment); *Clinical factors* (e.g., numbers of residents with each of specific diagnoses, availability and use of information systems for case management and tracking, and such care structural elements as team composition and interdisciplinary care).

Informal Support System (Predisposing, Enabling, and Need Factors)

This is comprised of such subdomains as Caregiver Demographics, Extendedness, and Involvement (e.g., the number of supports, their knowledge of resources, the degree to which the supports act as a link with existing bureaucracies, the identity of the supports (kin or friends or other), and the hours' input given); and Burden experienced by Informal Supports (e.g., emotional economic, physical, and social).

Environmental Characteristics (Enabling Process)

This is comprised of such subdomains as Social Environment (e.g., atmosphere, group cohesion, nature of interactions and communication, nature of care planning behaviors, team skills, and conflict management); and Physical Environment (e.g., noise, smells, space, lighting, colors, configuration, privacy, safety, orientation, functionality, stimulation, personal control, social interaction, continuity, and change).

Characteristics of the Target Individual (Predisposing, Enabling Process, and Need)

This is comprised of such subdomains as Target Individual Demographics; Medication Compliance; Personality Attributes (e.g., aggression, adaptability, affect, psychiatric symptoms, coping style, dependence, energy level, degree of interest(s)); Knowledge; Resources; Cultural Values; Objective Health States such as Acute Comorbid Conditions (e.g., orthopedic, cranial, pulmonary, endocrine, and communicable disease); Current Treatments (e.g., wound care, IV/infusion, oxygen, enteral/parenteral, and catheter); Subjective Health Status (e.g., pain, self-rated health); Functional Status (e.g., activities of daily living (ADL), instrumental activities of daily living (IADL), Social ADL, continence, mobility, range of motion, upper and lower body strength, biomechanics); Perceptual Status (e.g., vision, auditory status); Mental/Neurological Status (e.g., affect, psychiatric, cognitive, and communication disorder); and Behavioral Characteristics (e.g., behavior disorder, and agitation).

Care Outcomes

This is comprised of such subdomains as Medical Outcomes (e.g., mortality, complications, and adverse events); Service Use Outcomes and Health Behavior (e.g., number of professional visits, disability days, hours of personal care, hospital transfers, and lengths of stay, and service use transition status); Health Status Outcomes (e.g., functional decline, and emergence of additional comorbidities); Mental Health Outcomes (e.g., psychological well-being and perceived quality of life); Consumer Satisfaction (e.g., expressions/measures of resident, staff, family, and informal caregiver satisfaction); Staff

Outcomes (e.g., tardiness, turnover, burnout, and unexplained absences); Family and Other Informal Caregiver Outcomes (e.g., maintenance of informal function, psychiatric distress, and morbidity); and Cost Outcomes.

General Observations Regarding the Domains:
Outcomes versus Process

Several observations related to the above domains are relevant to quality-of-care research. First, *not* included are measures of the actual care process, which can be considered as an intervention with elements which must be defined, e.g., specific staff acts such as turning patients every 2 hours, toileting practice, and timely restraint removal. Related to this is the considerable confusion in the literature as to whether outcome measures such as health status are measures or the results of quality of care. For example, a decubitus ulcer may result from any of many factors. In order to argue that such an indicator constitutes a quality measure, one must show that it is caused by only one latent factor, in this instance, quality of care. Using commonly applied methods, the assessor would identify outlier facilities (in terms of "excess" ulcers among their residents) and term them poor-quality facilities. Thus, use of indicators such as the presence or absence of decubitus ulcers in the assessment of quality might be misleading. Even if case-mix adjusted, this begs the issue, as quality relates not so much to this discrete and sometimes misleading outcome as it does to the process of care. If this were a perfect world to the extent that risk adjustment could account for all factors which relate (in this instance) to the formation/maintenance of decubitus ulcers, then—and only then—could ulcers be used as a proxy for the quality of ulcer-related elements of care. However, there are two restrictions in such a formulation.

First, risk adjustment can never be "perfect." That is, given all the demographic and other investigated and noninvestigated factors contributing to risk and propensity scores, this ideal control constitutes an unlikely scenario; as Shaughnessy and colleagues (Shaughnessy, Kramer, Hittle, & Steiner, 1995, p. 77) warn, "Risk adjustment is an inexact science—not because statistical methods are egregiously inadequate, but largely because we cannot typically collect data on all risk factors that should be taken into consideration."

Second, the process of caregiving relates to many aspects of "quality"—and to single out a limited set of indicators such as decubitus ulcers is essentially an instance of criterion insufficiency, in that the overall quality of care might be dreadful, with attention being given only to those facets of caregiving (e.g., turning, nutrition and direct wound care) which are known to relate to ulcers. In other words, quality indicators should be restricted to care process variables; unless process indicators are incorporated into the definition and protocol for a quality improvement intervention, there exists major potential for error or, more critical, for gaming the assessment system.

DEFINING AND CONCEPTUALIZING MODELS FOR STUDY OF QUALITY OF CARE

We turn now to a discussion of models commonly used in the study of quality of care. No single model incorporates all of the elements of all of the domains suggested above; in the aggregate, however, all domains are represented.

Defining Quality of Care

Donebedian (1980, 1988) suggests that quality of care consists of the maximization of patient welfare, after controlling for the balance of expected gains and losses associated with the process of care. In an industrial context, quality has been defined as a continuous effort to meet the needs and expectations of the customer (in health care, this becomes the stakeholder, client, patient, resident, and/or caregiver) (Laffel & Blumenthal, 1989). The Institute of Medicine (Institute of Medicine, 1986) defined quality of long-term care as: "The extent to which health services increase the probability of desired health outcomes and are consistent with current professional knowledge." Palmer and Chapman (1997) review several aspects of quality; these include accessibility (receipt of appropriate care in a timely fashion); clinical performance (e.g., selecting appropriate tests, providing treatment in the specified time interval, (for example, antibiotics within 2 hours of surgery and communicating with patients), medical satisfaction (consumer feelings about the care), effectiveness (improvement of patient outcomes), and efficiency (the balance of quality of care with cost). We would argue that the latter three components, medical satisfaction, effectiveness, and efficiency, are outcomes, rather than indicators, of quality care.

Modeling Quality

One of the most widely used models of quality of care builds on three domains: structure, process and outcomes (Donabedian, 1980; Donabedian, Wheeler, & Wyszewianski, 1982; Patrick, 1997). As viewed by Donebedian, Structure includes the resources, benefits, and organizational features which are characteristic of the health care system. Process refers to the availability, accessibility, affordability, acceptability, and actual use of services by consumers (in the languages of social exchange theory, sometimes referred to as stakeholders) (Patrick, 1997). Outcomes include consumer satisfaction, quality of life, adverse events, morbidity, mortality, and cost. To date, the most frequently studied outcome has been mortality (Aiken, Sochalski, & Lake, 1997), although a more comprehensive approach to measuring health-related and general quality-of-life outcomes is reflected in the work of Lawton (see Lawton, 1991, 1993, 1997) and Stewart and Ware (1992).

Process versus Outcomes

In a recent review, Palmer and Chapman (1997) support the view expressed above, suggesting that use of outcome measures as indicators of quality of care blurs the distinction between process and outcome variables. For example, Sainfort and colleagues (Sainfort, Ramsay, & Monato, 1995) argue that the findings related to quality of care in nursing homes suffer from inconsistencies in several areas: conceptualization, measurement, sampling, unit of analyses, and methods of analyses. They argue that

> Most quality measures do not account very well for variation in health status among residents and tend to equate poor health condition with poor quality of care. Anecdotally, it appears that the more outcome based the measure of quality, the more pronounced the bias . . . such a bias is likely due in part to inadequate organizational case-mix adjustment. (p. 71)

Davis (1991a) argues that the inconsistencies are partially due to different preferences expressed by different constituencies (e.g., administrators, regulators, residents, families). He further suggests that the widely used approach of examining interrelationships among structure, process, and outcome variables actually has been detrimental to quality-of-care research because the mere presence of certain structural or process features may represent paper compliance with regulations, which may bear little relationship to the actual delivery of quality care.

Adhering to Lawton's conceptualization of constructs such as health status and the environment as latent variables measured by indicators, quality of care can be conceived of as several latent variables measured by several indicators (preferably scales) which are caused by the latent variable. For example, causally prior (exogenous) variables might include several latent variables reflecting physical environmental quality which might be measured by scales reflecting availability of supplies, cleanliness, odors, and glare. (However, see Lawton, Weisman, Sloane, & Calkins, 1997 for a more detailed conceptualization.) Similarly, staffing quality of care might be measured by staff load (e.g., number of patients/nurse aide), staff turnover, frequency of staff rotation, and staff communication. Such latent quality variables would be distinctly different from outcomes such as decline in health status (adjusted for comorbidity). They would be causally antecedent to process or mediating latent variables which might include medical status or adverse events (measured by conditions such as decubitus ulcers, catheterization, urinary tract infection, contractures, or incontinence). Exogenous environmental and staffing quality variables may have direct effects on decline in health and indirect effects through adverse events. Core process variables such as prompted voiding programs would constitute moderator or independent variables in research, and would be measured by staff actions reflecting implementation of the programs.

Organizational Factors

A recent volume edited by Ory, Cooper, and Siu (1998) contains several review articles reflecting current issues relating to managed care and quality of care issues. Sofaer (1998) presents various models which have been or might be used in the study of quality of care. These include organizational theory, information processing theory (cognitive processing), social learning (behavioral change) theory, health care utilization, health status and determinants, and contingency theory. The last is a formulation for operationalizing the "gestalt" of an organization in terms of formalization, specialization, standardization, complexity, and centralization (Zinn & Mor, 1998). In the review, Sofaer (1998) argues for a shared conceptual framework lest we continuously reinvent the wheel, although she concedes that such a process will be difficult, given the multiplicity of disciplines involved in quality-of-care research. While numerous models link quality of care to delivery mechanisms, few studies have compared managed care to other forms of care. Those studies that do exist often do not take into account the complex influences of external factors such as patients' contributions to health (diet, exercise, self-care), or factors such as the timing of the measurement of the outcome so as to adequately capture effects (Palmer & Chapman, 1997).

Organizational theory has been used as the cornerstone of a number of analytic models. The central components of the organizational theory model are uncertainty (the difference between what is known initially and the knowledge requirements of the task) and interdependence (the degree to which a patient's condition requires cooperation among specialists and ancillary services, Wholey, Burns, & Lavizzo-Mourey, 1996). An assumption of some of the models is either the conditional minimization of costs (given some fixed level of quality) or the maximization of quality given a fixed level of cost. Structures of services can be classified in terms of degree along these dimensions.

It is posited that certain types of patients are more or less suited for particular constellations of uncertainty and interdependence. For example, Wholey et al., (1996) point out that a team approach may not be the ideal for patients who are high on longitudinal interdependence but low on lateral interdependence (requirement for a specialist). Based on organizational theory, the authors propose to enhance quality of care by greater use of primary care physicians and nurse case managers, and "vertical integration" (e.g., directly engaging the patient in the information- gathering process). For example, a California HMO (PacifiCare Health Systems) routinely surveys patients about their health (Wholey et al., 1998). Satisfaction measures are routinely used by many managed care organizations. One study by Kaiser (Frederick & Schneiders, 1995) of focus groups comprised of older consumers aged 60 to 65 found that consumers identified bedside manner, caring about patients, and listening skills as the most important qualities of physicians (see Palmer & Chapman, 1997). Based on such results, physicians have been encouraged to change their bedside manners and interaction styles in order to increase consumer satisfaction and revenues. While such efforts may be successful, as discussed later, it is unclear how well, if at all, intermediate outcomes such as satisfaction impact on long-term and ultimate outcomes. Further longitudinal research is needed in this area.

Mitchell and Shortell (1997) review the literature related to quality-of-care outcomes found in hospital and nursing home studies, and conclude that most research relating organizational variables to adverse events (a) was conducted in the 1990s; (b) was conducted in acute care, rather than in long-term care settings; (c) has produced equivocal results regarding the role of process variables such as quality of the working environment and interactions among professionals in relation to outcomes; and (d) has shown that more sophisticated risk adjustment methods have rendered the patient variables most important in outcome prediction and have reduced the variance explained by organizational factors. They conclude from their review that organizational structure variables such as size, ownership, location of the country (urban, rural), and teaching hospital status are not related to mortality in hospitals or nursing homes. However, few hospital studies in either setting have examined environmental context variables, although the environment has been studied relatively more in psychiatric facilities and nursing homes than in other settings. For example, organizational climate (lower staff cohesion, poor human relations, greater laissez-faire climate, and greater disdain for non-professional staff was related to failure on nursing home surveys (Sheridan, White, & Fairchild, 1992).

Modeling Process

Conceptual efforts have attempted to integrate organizational management and technology theory; the resulting model resembles the person-environment fit concept developed by Kahana (1975). The congruence between the organizational context and environmental demands is posited to impact on clinical interventions affecting patient outcomes. As an example, this formulation has been applied to the study of pain (Hester, Miller, Foster, & Vojir, 1997), and has resulted in the development of measures such as the Organizational Context Battery which is a compilation of several measures of eight domains: customer orientation, organizational characteristics, burnout, job satisfaction, caring, innovation, professionalism, and leadership.

A conceptual model proposed by Aiken et al. (1997) posits that different organizational forms, e.g. different hospital and unit models (such as magnet hospitals, hospices, ICUs, and SCUs) directly affect operant mechanisms such as nurse autonomy, control, and specialization which, in turn affect nurse, patient and organizational outcomes such as nurse burnout and satisfaction, patient satisfaction, complications, morbidity, and costs. However, some (Shaugnessy et al., 1997) view the staff outcomes as intermediary outcomes resulting in indirect effects on other variables.

Physical and Social Environment

Outcomes are moderated by organizational process variables which include group dynamics and environmental characteristics. Typically, the medical outcomes literature does not focus as much on the physical as on the social environment. However, the physical environment becomes more important as a process variable in models because elderly persons often are housed in institutions for long periods of time or are confined to their own homes, where the physical environment may constitute a major factor in quality of care.

Addressing issues relating to physical and social environments, Lawton (1970) proposed a five-group categorization of the environment: personal, small-group, supra-personal, social, and physical. The first four categories relate to relationships and interactions with individuals or organizations, while the last relates to things which can be counted. Recently, Lawton and colleagues (Lawton et al., 1997) reviewed the conceptual models related to the environmental sector, dating from Kleemeier (1959) to the most recent work of Moos and Lempke (1994). They present work conducted in the 1990s for use in chronic care settings, including the home (Trickey, Maltais, Gosselin, & Robitaille, 1993). They classify the environment into four dimensions relevant to assessing chronic care populations: Social vs Physical Environment (Lawton, 1982); Objective vs Subjective quality; Descriptive vs Evaluative quality (description vs evaluation in terms of liking, satisfaction, and preference); Global vs Discrete quality (large, complex environments vs. single attributes; Weisman, Calkins, & Sloane, 1994). They examine the major environmental quality of care measures in terms of common constructs. These are safety, orientation, functionality, stimulation, personal control, social interaction, continuity, and change.

Clinical Performance

Clinical performance constitutes a critical process variable in much of the quality-of-care literature. Clinical performance review methodology, including the selection of quality indicators, is currently being undertaken in several state-level efforts as well as by federal agencies such as Health Care Finance Administration (HCFA), for measuring quality of managed and fee-for-service care as well as of long-term care. In national studies, such research is being conducted by the National Committee for Quality Assurance (NCQA) using the Health Plan Employer Data Information System (HEDIS), and by the Joint Commission on Accreditation of Health Care Organizations (see Palmer & Chapman, 1997). The Agency for Health Care Policy Research (AHCPR) has sponsored several efforts to develop clinical performance measures and to create networks for dissemination of information about the psychometric properties and utility of quality measures. Information about these programs is available on the Internet and through the AHCPR (AHCPR Public Affairs). Some studies linking actual care process variables to outcomes have found positive results. For example, a meta-analysis of studies linking quality of inpatient care to hospital readmission found that process-of-care variables such as ratings of care; use of residents vs experienced staff; examination of physicians who were taught discharge care vs those who were not; and early discharge planning vs regular planning were related to lower risk of early readmission (Ashton, DelJunco, Souchek, Wray, & Mansyur, 1997).

Brooks, McGlynn, and Cleary (1996) provide five methods for assessing quality using process data; three are based on clinician review of data such as medical records to determine if the process of care was adequate, if it could have been improved, and if the process and outcome were adequate. A fourth method involves asking disease-specific questions about the care in terms of whether certain laboratory tests were ordered and exams given. The fifth method involves relating the patient outcome to expected outcomes, given different levels of care (e.g., excellent and good).

Undercutting much model-building is the fact that many measures of the process domain are not psychometrically well-developed, while some of the better developed measures are discipline-specific (e.g., physicians) and/or setting-specific. This is taken into account by some authors. For example, in discussing the Intensive Care Unit (ICU) Questionnaire (Shortell et al., 1991) the authors indicate that other services or units can be substituted for ICU without loss of reliability. Typical items measuring physician to physician relationships are "It is easy for me to talk openly with the physicians on this ICU (other unit, specialty, etc)"; "It is easy to ask advice from physicians in this unit." Psychometric characteristics are summarized in Shortell et al. (1991). Similar efforts in the field of health care evaluation have resulted in the measurement of constructs such as conflict management, group environment, team skills, and self-perceived performance. Here we discuss only conflict management and group environment.

Conflict Management

Conflict management provides another theoretical framework for studying the process of quality of care (Rahim & Bonoma, 1979). According to the authors:

> Conflict occurs because one social entity perceives or is made to perceive that he (1) holds behavioral preferences, the satisfaction of which are incompatible with another person's implementation of his preferences; (2) wants some mutually desirable resource which is in short supply, such that the wants of everyone may not be satisfied fully; or (3) possesses values or attitudes which are salient in directing his behavior but which are perceived to be exclusive of the values or attitudes held by the other(s). (p. 324)

In a later publication, the authors present a theoretical model for management of conflict (see Rahim & Magner, 1995), flowing from the work of numerous theorists, dating from 1926 to the present. The conflict management measure resulting from this work assesses five areas (integrating, obliging, dominating, avoiding, and compromising), and has good psychometric properties (Rahim & Magner, 1994, 1995).

Group Environment: Stress and Coping

Stress and coping theory form the basis for the conceptual model used in developing some group environment measures such as the Group Environment Scale (GES) (Moos, 1994). According to this model, the outcome of group participation is influenced by individual demographic factors, personality traits, and individual functioning as reflected in depression, coping skills, and self-concept. Prior and current life stressors as well as the group intervention are posited to influence outcomes. Group environment is posited as a mediating variable influencing performance outcomes. Two of the GES subscales (Anger and Aggression and Task Orientation) are particularly relevant to quality of care delivered to the elderly. Based on the findings of numerous investigators reviewed by Moos (1994), geriatric interdisciplinary teams, which are task oriented groups, are posited to be high on task-orientation and low on anger and aggression. Task-oriented groups include health care teams, staff teams in educational settings, learning groups, and managers. *The Group Environment Scale Manual* summarizes the results of 21 articles (the majority in peer-reviewed journals) providing normative data for the GES. Additionally, numerous other articles provide psychometric and other data regarding the GES. The measure has been used with health care teams in medical rehabilitation (Halstead et al., 1986) and with general medical inpatient teams hospital-based home care team (Farrell, Schmitt & Heinemann, 1988). A recent investigation (Strasser, Falconer, & Marino Saltzmann, 1994) examined interdisciplinary Rehabilitation Treatment Teams.

This discussion of process models has not dealt, specifically, with a determination of quality of care provided in nursing homes, where research relating to the quality of care has generally been relatively less systematic. There have been some carefully designed studies which have found a significant relationship between process variables such as specialized skill levels and positive outcomes. For example, R. L. Kane and colleagues (1989), using a quasi-experimental design, found that the provision of geriatric nurse practitioners was associated with decreased mortality in the experimental group nursing homes as contrasted with comparison group nursing homes. We review, below, some other controlled studies conducted in long-term care settings using the methodology of continuous quality improvement (CQI).

Total Quality Management and Continuous Quality Improvement

Total quality management (TQM) and CQI are included in the discussion of process factors because of their purported relationship to productivity. The approach, as applied by Deming (1989), depends on the direct and ongoing involvement of top administrators, and assumes that all workers, including top management, are involved in the goal of continuous improvement, noting deficiencies as they occur; examination of statistical outliers is used to identify quality problems (Deming, 1965).

Problems in quality may be unique to a system, or external. Comparison of systems of care in terms of outcomes requires that factors which are out of the control of the system (e.g., patient baseline characteristics, such as disease severity) be adjusted (Kritchevsky & Simmons, 1991). The method has been recommended for use in examining quality of care in health care organizations (Laffel & Blumenthal, 1989) and in long-term care delivered to older people (Morley & Miller, 1992). A key feature in improving quality is the standardization of the process of care (Laffel & Blumenthal, 1989); for example, standardizing a protocol for prompting individuals to toilet would be critical in evaluation of programs across settings (Schnelle, Ouslander, Osterweil, & Blumenthal, 1993). Another key element is adequate training in delivery of care; the standard philosophy in medical training: "See one, do one, teach one" is not necessarily conducive to delivery of quality care.

In long-term care settings, there are many hurdles to use of the TQM methodology. Turnover among frontline workers (nursing attendants) as well as management results in lack of continuity (Castle, Zinn, Brannon, & Mor, 1997). Poor pay and overwork among nursing attendants may also act as disincentives (Schnelle et al., 1993). Finally, the long-term care population in both hospitals and nursing homes is highly diverse in terms of needs; it may be difficult to adequately risk-adjust for such differences. For example, it is important to target the individuals who will benefit from a program such as prompted voiding, estimated to reduce incontinence in only 25% to 40% of patients (Schnelle et al., 1993), or the work process evaluated will appear, on average, to have no effect on incontinence outcomes. A general lack of staff resources is a problem in long-term care. One conclusion of the forthcoming IOM report (J. Schnelle, personal communication) on quality of care in long-term care is that staffing is a critical component in the delivery of quality care and that most nursing homes lack resources and expertise to implement these. Although advances have been made over the past 15 years in demonstrating the efficacy of interventions in increasing continence and independence in dressing and mobility, few interventions are continued once the research staff leave; this is in part because of the demands on aid time.

Despite these problems, there is a movement away from quality assurance as the primary evaluative tool in long-term facilities and movement to embrace quality improvement methodology. It is estimated that at least two-thirds of hospitals now use TQM/CQI, as do about one-third of nursing homes, with another third planning to implement the approach (Castle et al., 1997). In part the movement toward TQM is motivated by findings that regulation alone is not adequate to improve quality, that the quality assurance methodology is punitive, and does not involve front-line staff. Finally, there are economic incentives such as alternatives to long-term care and shrinking revenues which will force nursing homes to improve quality in order to be more competitive (Castle et al., 1997). The fact that the Joint Commission for Accreditation of Healthcare Organizations and the Health Care Financing Administration support the quality improvement approach may also have an impact on the adoption of such programs in long-term care settings (see Castle et al., 1997)

Measuring and Modeling Intermediate and Ultimate Outcomes: Consumer Satisfaction, Service Use, Family and Staff Burden, Adverse Events, Health Status and Morbidity, Quality of Life, and Mortality

Overview

Discussed here are two levels of outcome criteria: intermediate and ultimate (see Shaughnessy et al., 1997). Intermediate outcomes may include satisfaction, staff morale, and other factors which can be viewed in some models as intervening variables in the relationship between system, support, environmental and individual characteristics, and ultimate outcomes such as morbidity, mortality, institutionalization and lifetime costs of care. Mitchell and Shortell (1997) review findings related to several outcome measures at both levels: mortality, complications, and other adverse events. Adverse events have been defined as falls, fractures, decubiti, and failure to rescue (death after an iatrogenic complication). In long-term care they also have included factors such as aspiration, agitation, restraints, drug errors, rehospitalization, and deficiencies in regulations (usually defined as failure to document activity) (Mitchell & Shortell, 1997). Others have included various events, such as urinary tract, wound, and respiratory tract infections in the definition. A recent review of the literature on adverse events in relation to mortality, classified events as surgical, nursing care-related, administrative, medical (not related to the disease), and infections (Garcia-Martin et al., 1997). The differences across disciplines in the definition of adverse events contributes to the confusion of outcome-and-process variables.

Mitchell and Shortell (1997) conclude that mortality, complications, and other adverse events are not affected by changes in organizational structure and by the process of the care delivery system. Inter-hospital differences in risk-adjusted mortality were related to unit-level features rather than to facility-level structural features. The authors emphasize the need for study of intermediate-level outcomes, such as turnover and provider satisfaction, as well as ultimate-level resident outcomes. Additionally, failure-to-rescue recently has been suggested as an important quality-of-care outcome. Health-related quality of life has also been proposed as a construct which should be considered as a health care delivery outcome (Murdaugh, 1997). In contrast to hospital settings, nursing home health-related quality of life and quality-of-care outcomes are more broadly defined to include factors such as nosocomial infection, restraint use, catheterization, medication errors, aspiration, and excess functional decline (Cherry, 1991; Johnson-Pawlson & Infeld, 1996). Also modeled are behavioral outcomes such as behavior disorder and suicide attempts, and service-use outcomes, such as rehospitalization. Finally, deficiencies from surveys are used as evidence of quality, although these tend to be narrow, focusing on failure to document rather than on such phenomena as worsening of pressure sores (Johnson-Pawlson & Infeld, 1996; Mitchell & Shortell, 1997). However, the use of the Minimum Data Set (MDS) (Morris et al., 1990) may now allow examination of quality in relation to change in selected health status variables. A critical point is that, as noted by several authors, mortality and morbidity measures are inadequate as measures of medical care and intervention (Aiken et al., 1997; Murdaugh, 1997). For example, Holtzman and Lurie (1996) found that mortality and quality-of-care indices operated in different respective directions in nursing homes.

Development of Quality Indicators

Because many of the efforts to develop quality indicators have used outcome measures, this section is included under Modeling Outcomes; however, we repeat our cautionary note that we do not necessarily view outcomes as quality indicators.

Source of information for quality indicators has long been a topic of study; concern has been raised about the accuracy of diagnoses, the completeness of medical records, and the generally low interrater reliability accompanying interpretation of some diagnostic tests (Rothenberg, Mooney, & Curtis, 1997). Additional concerns regarding administrative data include the manner in which the information was obtained (standardized method or not), the occasion for data collection, and the training and experience of the data collector (Teresi & Holmes, 1992, 1997a). Several recent studies have provided some assistance in determining the accuracy of quality indicators. For example, a recent analysis (Dresser, Feingold, Rosenkranz, & Coltin, 1997) of the use of a chart-review methodology, as contrasted with use of automated data from computerized patient records, claims, and encounter records, shows that for nearly all quality indicators, errors occurred in the direction of underreporting by the automated systems (that is, failing to identify events identified by the chart review). The authors suggest that both chart review (using trained raters and standardized protocols) and automated systems be used in order to improve accuracy. Another analyses of the interrater reliability of quality indicator data abstracted from clinical abstraction centers showed that examining only the reliability of the component parts rather than that of the final quality indicator (usually derived from complex algorithms) resulted in overstatement of reliability (Huff, 1997). While reliability was generally high for the components, the more parts to the indicator and the more complex the logic, the lower the reliability. Further, the use of standardized abstraction criteria improved the reliability considerably over other methods of abstraction using implicit quality criteria used in other investigations.

Shaughnessy et al. (1997) propose outcome-based quality improvement (OBQI), an approach developed for home health care. The approach provides a taxonomy of outcomes which include end results (e.g., improvement in health care status); intermediate results (e.g., changes in compliance); and utilization (e.g., hospital admission). Twenty-five QUIGS (quality indicator groups) are proposed, each of which is comprised of two major categories: acute and chronic conditions. Chronic conditions include, for example, cognitive and mental problems, while acute conditions include the subcategories of rehabilitation, and medical and specialized care (e.g., use of IV therapy.) The QUIG outcomes are condition-specific. One can calculate an improvement or stabilization outcome. Risk-adjusted dichotomous improvement and stabilization, measured using the OASIS (Outcome and Assessment Information Set), can be translated into ratios or proportions to describe and compare across agencies (Shaughnessy et al., 1997). An advantage to this methodology is that many of the OASIS items are appropriate across a continuum of impairment and of care. However, some sections of the instrument require cognitive capabilities beyond those common to a substantial segment of the chronic care population, and others involve considerable rater judgement, with attendant issues of reliability. Finally, the format of the information obtained using the OASIS does not readily lend itself to clinical implementation, and/or monitoring. Examples of definitional inexactitude are found in some areas of the measure. For example, how does one assess inadequate cooling in the midst of winter, the adequacy of sewerage systems, or what constitutes a cluttered (as opposed to soiled) living area? At what time of day are the insects present (cockroaches are apt to appear in force only at night)? Because psychometric properties are as yet unpublished, and the judgement of nurse raters is key, more standardization work is necessary before the instrument can be evaluated.

Most recently, the MDS was used to develop quality indicators for long-term care settings by Arling, Karon, Sainfort, Zimmerman, and Ross (1997), who stratified residents into high- or low-risk groups. The stratification was based on analysis of the MDS risk indicators, using logistic regression in which the quality indicator was the outcome. Separate risk indicators were identified for each quality indicator. The quality indicators selected were a combination of process and outcome variables (prevalence of indwelling catheters, antipsychotic use, pressure ulcers, bladder and bowel incontinence, behavior disorder, and incidence of decline in late loss ADLs).

Another effort to develop a community measure of quality of care is embodied in the MDS-HC (Morris et al., 1997). This measure contains 47% of the nursing home MDS items measuring function, health status, social environment, and service use as well as additional items. The measure, intended for use by clinical professionals, is not a structured questionnaire, but contains items to be coded and 30 clinical assessment protocols, intended for use in care planning and to identify areas for further assessment. With some exceptions, the reported kappas measuring interrater reliability for the nursing home items as applied to the home care samples were adequate to good, ranging from .60 to .87. The average kappa across the new items was .70. The reliability data reported was pooled from five countries, including the United States. Some of the items are also being used to prescreen individuals for different purposes, such as referral, or for targeting for more intensive assessment.

Several issues surface from this work. First is the question of the adequacy of the input data in terms both of coverage and accuracy. Because some of the indicators were to be linked to reimbursement, the issue of gaming must be considered. Kane (1998) points out the inherent potential conflict associated with an outcomes approach to improving care linked to a reimbursement system where decline in certain areas is rewarded by greater reimbursement. He adds that there was a tendency from the outset for nursing home staff to view the MDS as a regulatory device, rather than as a clinical tool. These conflicts and attitudes can work to undermine the potential of the MDS as an instrument for examining quality of care. Second, as the authors point out, the validity of the quality indicators must be investigated, although a recent study (Rantz et al., 1997) provided some evidence that MDS-derived quality indicators were successful in differentiating between poor- and good-quality homes. Finally, as discussed above, there is the problem of use of resident-level outcomes such as decline in ADL as indicators of quality, rather than structural and process variables such as staffing ratios, presence of primary care nursing, and other factors. One effort to link adverse events and health conditions directly to quality was made by Hawes and colleagues (1997) who examined quality indicators such as "residents with inadequate (but some) vision without glasses or contact lens" and "residents with no ostomy and bowel incontinence but no toileting program."

Because the MDS has become the most important assessment and care planning methodology for long-term care populations, and because it ultimately may become the gold standard in terms of developing quality indicators, it has also received continuing scrutiny. For example, while the authors of the MDS have promoted the measure as effective in terms of changes in several outcomes, it is unclear if the changes are the result of instituting the MDS methodology or other factors (Ouslander, 1997), or how the changes are related to the quality-of-care process. It has been speculated that the differences between homes on MDS quality indicators may reflect "paper compliance and not reality" (Schnelle, 1997). These statements are made in light of findings that MDS ratings and chart data did not correlate well with incontinence checks (Crooks, Schnelle, Ouslander, & McNees, 1995), restraint use documentation (Schnelle, Ouslander, & Cruise, 1997) and visual acuity test results (Swanson, 1995). The issues of the accuracy of locally collected MDS data (Teresi & Holmes, 1992) and the accuracy across subgroups such as the cognitively impaired (Phillips, Chu, Morris, & Hawes, 1993) remain to be addressed adequately. Finally, Schnelle (in press) points out that a recent HCFA study showed that lack of staff training in how to perform the MDS assessment was seen as a serious problem by both nursing home staff and survey staff. Staff training is critical if locally collected data are to be used in assessments of quality.

Satisfaction

Consumer and provider satisfaction measures are very popular in the age of marketing managed care. For example, Patrick (1997) has argued that satisfaction measures constitute important process (or intermediate outcome) variables because, while patients cannot judge technical competence, they can respond to the personality of providers, and to the roughness, and quality of care. Satisfaction and attitudes are considered in evaluation research as low level (level 1) outcomes, characterized by reaction. Strengths of the approach are that such measures (often typified as "feel good" measures because the results reflect only general feelings about the object being "evaluated") are generally acceptable to respondents and easy to complete. However, the utility of such measures is debatable, because the literature shows that attitudes often do not predict behavior; e.g., individuals with the same pre- and post-intervention health status may have very different satisfaction ratings (Maciejewski, Kawiecki, & Rockwood, 1997). Such findings result in clinicians' mistrust of satisfaction measures: "Patients may be satisfied with care that is not high quality and can be dissatisfied with quality care" (Cleary & Edgman-Levitan, 1997, p. 1608). Questions also remain about how well satisfaction is measured and sampled. Frequently the measures are highly left-skewed; the point of discrimination is the differentiation being between "good" and "very good" or "very good" and "excellent." In addition, the sampling of patients is frequently poor, for example, physicians with a large panel of patients may be assessed by a few responders who are not representative of either the population of patients in general or of those frequently seen. However, more serious is the failure to link satisfaction to technical quality of care (Maciejewski et al., 1997) or to ultimate outcomes.

Although some studies have reported high correlations between patient and staff (physicians' and hospital employees') *ratings* of quality of care (Chang, Uman, Linn, Ware, & Kane, 1984; Nelson, Larson, Hays, Nelson, 1992), and between patient satisfaction and adverse events (Bindman, Grumbach, Keane, Rauch, & Luce, 1991), other major studies have found no significant or significant *negative* correlations between patient satisfaction and outcomes. For example, the medical outcomes study (Greenfield, Rogers, Mangotich, Carney, & Tarlov, 1995) showed no relationship between satisfaction with care and functional or clinical outcome. Similarly, a study of 25 critical care units found no relation of satisfaction to process or to structural variables, and higher mortality prevalence ratios and lengths of stay among units with high satisfaction (Mitchell, Shannon, Cain, & Hegyvary, 1996). Finally, a review by Hester et al. (1997) suggests that individuals with high rates of pain report high rates of satisfaction, calling into question the appropriateness of satisfaction as an outcome in such studies (see also Lin, 1996).

On the other hand, there is some evidence that process variables such as medication compliance may be related to satisfaction (Bartlett et al., 1984), and that increased satisfaction is associated with introduction of auditing procedures in long-term care (Chambers, Knight, & Campbell, 1996). Additionally, significant multivariate predictors of satisfaction, such as patients being allowed to choose their own physician (Schmittdiel, Selby, Grumbach, & Quesenberry, 1997), can help to inform providers about process indicators which may relate to perceived quality of care.

As discussed above, there are numerous methodological problems inherent in the use of satisfaction as a quality of care index. These have recently been reviewed by Rosenthal and Shannon (1997) and include

1. ceiling effects of the measures;
2. ethnic, age, gender and culture bias across measures (e.g., older patients consistently score higher on satisfaction measures; little is known about ethnic/cultural group differences, although there is evidence of higher satisfaction when there is a match of sociodemographic characteristics of patients and physicians (Cleary & McNiel, 1988);
3. nonresponse bias (non-response has been reported to be as great as 70% in some studies);
4. selection bias (those sampled may not be representative of the patient population served);
5. reporting-source bias (proxies such as family and friends report more dissatisfaction); and
6. bias due to occasion (satisfaction ratings have been found to vary with length of time between the assessment and the target medical care event).

Other problems with the application of a satisfaction criterion to health care is that it is assumed that expectations regarding care are anchored in prior experience; in the absence of prior experience, expectations are formed by other sources, e.g., caregivers or friends (Maciejewski et al., 1997) who may have had different diseases or different baseline functional status. Finally, the use of satisfaction measures among chronic care elderly persons is problematic because cognitive impairment, more prevalent among older persons, influences the capability of many residents to be measured on process and outcome measures (Hayes, Morris, Wolfe, & Morgan, 1995; Teresi & Holmes, 1997a; Teresi, Lawton, Ory, & Holmes, 1994). Because response bias is a serious problem in the administration of satisfaction measures among individuals with cognitive impairment (Zinn, Lavizzo-Mourey, & Taylor, 1993), proxy measures are sometimes used; however, reporting source bias then becomes a problem of concern (Magaziner, 1997; Teresi & Holmes, 1997b). Cleary and Edgman-Levitan (1997) argue that pre-post questions about health-related quality of life, or post questions about actual experiences during an illness episode, may better relate to quality of care than do satisfaction measures.

Examination of consumer satisfaction and expectations must now factor in knowledge of health care obtained through telephone medical information systems and through the Internet (Blumenthal, 1997). However, if misinformation is disseminated, or if the patient learns of experimental protocols unknown to their physician, this may lead to the patient's unwarranted devaluation of the physician. E-mail has become another vehicle for communicating with physicians. While this may reduce the number of phone calls physicians make to patients, it also holds the potential for doubling the number of contacts. This may result in more dissatisfaction, if physicians are so swamped that they are unable to respond in a timely fashion. Again, the issue is whether this dissatisfaction is conceptualized as an indicator or an outcome of quality of care or, for that matter, viewed simply as a result of the information explosion associated with modern technology.

Service Use

Although the medical outcomes literature typically does not include the modeling of service use as an outcome variable, it is included here because, service use can be viewed as an intermediate outcome, particularly for elderly people. Service use could be conceived of as a result of the quality of care delivered. If poor care is delivered to an individual, there is a higher likelihood that the person may need further home or institutional services. For example, the "quicker and sicker" outcome associated with hospitalization of the elderly may apply.

Conceptual Models for the Analyses of Service Use

One model is provided by Golant and McCaslin (1979), who classify services according to dependency level of the population served (preinstitutional vs less disabled, well elderly) and to the area of behavioral function supported (e.g., social role, perception-cognition, health). Using this classification scheme, the authors accounted for 44% of the variance in well-elderly service use and 15% of the variance in use of preventive services. Kethley and Ehrlich (1989) propose another model that classifies service users into two groups: social service clients (who receive the majority of help from social workers and homemakers primarily with respect to instrumental ADL); and health care clients (receiving the highest proportion of help, in basic ADL services, from registered nurses and home health aides).

The most widely used conceptual model for the prediction of service use is the behavioral model based on the work of Anderson and Newman (1973) and Anderson and Aday (1978). This model posits that service use is determined by characteristics of the population at risk and of the health care delivery system. According to the model, the population at risk has predisposing, enabling, and need characteristics. Predisposing characteristics are causally prior, existing before the onset of illness: demographic characteristics (age, gender); social structure variables (education, ethnicity, race); and health beliefs (attitudes toward and knowledge about services). Enabling characteristics refer to resources available to the individual that determine ability to obtain services (income, insurance, community resources). Need variables can include unmet service needs, cognitive impairment, comorbidities, disability. Need can be determined objectively or subjectively. The model has been criticized for the relatively small amount of variance in utilization it explains, but Branch et al. (1981) point out that most analysts have not employed a test of the full model, such as including a focus on more stable/chronic aspects of need. The authors, in a longitudinal study of community-resident elderly, found that different components and different variables within each component explained five different types of service utilization. Wolinsky (1994) has argued that it is not so much the model which is the problem as it is the inadequate measures used in its implementation.

Organizational System, Family and Caregiver Process and Outcomes

A second criticism of the Anderson/Newman model is its failure to include informal and formal supports; Noelker and Bass (1989) expanded the model to include these components. Bass, Looman, and Ehrlich (1992) further expanded the model to include cognitive impairment as a need variable that may be a modifying factor in the relationship of other variables to need (predictors of service use interact with cognitive impairment of the client). Chappell (1994) argues that while need variables (functional disability) have been found to predict service use in many international studies, research must be broadened beyond the Anderson-Newman model to include external factors (availability of alternative services and coordination of services), which may influence use of different models of care (see also Holmes et al., 1989).

Modeling Staff Process and Outcomes

Following the Donebedian (1980) model of structure, process and outcome, the Institute of Medicine report (Institute of Medicine, 1986)) summarized the early research on quality of care in nursing homes. Both environmental structural variables (e.g., Lawton, 1980) and environmental process variables (e.g., Kahana, Liang, & Felton, 1980) such as autonomy and personalized care, have been found to relate to quality-of-life variables such as morale and life satisfaction. Structural variables such as staffing patterns and ratios, as well as process of care variables, have also been found to relate to positive changes in health status (R. A. Kane, Bell, Riegler, Wilson, & Keeler, 1983). Few conceptual models have been proposed with respect to staffing, with the exception of modeling staff burnout, where complex structural equation models have been formulated (e.g., Byrne, 1991, 1994). Overviews of staffing models as applied to chronic care populations are presented in Teresi, Lawton, Ory, & Holmes (1994) and Grant et al. (1998).

Nursing home studies have shown a relationship between higher ratios of total nursing staff (but not RNs) to lower rates of deficiencies measured in part by adverse events, which were weighted by nursing quality-of-care saliency ratings of nurse ombudsmen (Johnson-Pawlson & Infeld, 1996). Use of skilled staff (geriatric nurse practitioners) also has been associated with improved functional status and fewer adverse events (R. L. Kane, Garrand, Skay, et al. 1989; Shaughnessy et al., 1995). Despite evidence of increasing disability among nursing home residents, nursing staff ratios have remained unchanged or even declined (Kanda & Mezey, 1991) and training and support are woefully inadequate (Teresi, Grant, Holmes, & Ory, 1998). Moreover, programs which have been shown to relate to resident and staff satisfaction and better resident outcomes such as primary care nursing (Teresi et al., 1993a; Teresi, 1993b), or ombudsmen programs (Cherry, 1991), are not systematically implemented.

Conceptual Models of Health Status

Several authors have argued that instead of health service use, health status should be modeled (see Mechanic, 1989; Ware, 1987). The rationale is that the major predictor of health services use is health status. For example, Johnson and Wolinsky (1993, 1994) argue for the modeling of health status, assuming that health status can be invariantly measured across gender and ethnic/racial groups. Recently, they have modeled health status based on a model originally proposed by Nagi (1965), which posits that disease directly affects physiological impairment, which affects performance limitations, which, in turn, affects disability. Johnson and Wolinsky advocate a prediction model using more than single equation modeling; specifically, they use structural equation modeling to examine direct and indirect effects as well as the factor structure of health status. The conceptual model posits direct and indirect pathways from disease to disability to functional limitation to perceived health. Johnson and Wolinsky (1993) have expanded the model to include indirect affects, allowing disease to act directly on perceived health, and indirectly through disability and functional limitation. Presumably these pathways lead to service use. In this and other papers on the topic (Wolinsky & Johnson, 1991, 1992), Wolinsky and colleagues have modeled disability disease (measured by individual states or traits such as stroke, atherosclerosis, coronary artery disease, angina, hip fracture, Alzheimer's), which is considered as occurring first in a causal link leading directly to disability (measured by upper and lower body disability), to functional limitation (measured by basic activities of daily living, household, instrumental activities of daily living and advanced [cognitively related] activities of daily living, which are related to cognitive disorder), and to perceived health. Perceived health is measured using three indicators which include subjective self-assessment, the perception of how well one is doing in taking care of his or her health, and one's activity level relative to peers. Indirect effects of disease on perceived health through disability and functional limitation are also posited.

However, others (e.g., Tennstedt, Sullivan, McKinlay, & D'Agostino, 1990) have questioned the assumptions of the health status model, pointing out that it is well known (at least for the mild and moderately impaired) that the family is the key service provider (see for example, Branch & Jette, 1983). Cantor (1979) found that informal help was preferred over formal help except with respect to financial and health problems. Dependent elderly living with a primary caregiver receive more informal care (Soldo & Myllyluoma, 1983) than do women and those living alone, who receive relatively more formal care. Thus, lack of informal supports is perhaps as important as health and disability status as predictors of service use. Moreover, as pointed out by McCaslin (1988) typically a small amount of variance is accounted for by the health status variables. Finally, many models have examined health services exclusively (or aggregated with health and social services). In some studies, health status, while a predictor of health care service use, has not been found to be the major predictor of use of personal care services (see Bass et al., 1992).

Modeling Aspects of Quality of Life

Although some authors (Mitchell & Shortell, 1997) have argued that nursing home studies of quality of care and medical outcomes have suffered from lack of control for case mix, the balance of the evidence shows the opposite. Most large-scale nursing home studies have evidenced considerable methodological skill, using sophisticated measures of health, cognitive, and functional status as covariates. Nursing home studies have included process-focused quality-of-life outcome indicators rather than simply focusing on mortality and adverse events, which may have little meaning for a long-term care population.

Further illustrating this level of sophistication, in 1982, as part of the Kleemeier Lecture Lawton introduced the conception of quality of life as the "good life" which contained four sectors: behavioral competence, objective environment, perceived quality of life, and psychological well-being (Lawton, 1983, 1986). Each component was structurally defined. Behavioral competence included a hierarchy of domains based on complexity or increasing involvement of different levels of the human system extending from the microbiological to the macrosocial level. Biological and functional health, cognitive status, time use, and social behavior can be situated across this hierarchy of complexity. Personal preference and cultural factors play a role in the more complex behaviors. Lawton (1991) defined quality of life as "the multidimensional evaluation by both intra personal and social-normative criteria, of the person–environment system of the individual" (p. 6). Recently Lawton (1997) specified how one might conceptualize quality of life among individuals with communication disorders. The measures of objective quality of life would fall into two categories: attribute ratings and direct behavior observation; the domains include functional health, behavioral symptoms, clinical depression, time-use quality, social interaction, affect states and displays, and environmental quality. Sources of information include the nurse, family, care staff, and researcher.

Psychological Well-Being

Excepting the work of Stewart and Ware (1992), one relatively neglected area in medical outcomes research has been what Lawton terms "The Fourth Sector" of the Good Life, that is, psychological well-being. He divides this sector into three major categories: positive affect, negative affect, and cognitive sense of life satisfaction. Specific constructs include general mental health, self-esteem, and morale. Lawton (1993) and Lawton, Van Haitsma, and Klapper (1996) conceptualize emotional well-being as positive and negative affect, representing an internal state. Recently Shue, Beck, and Lawton (1996) have discussed affect as an important outcome measure in chronic care populations; increased affect may result from interventions aimed at increasing quality of care.

Modeling: Need Covariates: Risk Adjustment, Case-Mix, Comorbidity, Severity

Overview

Recently the issue of comorbidity and risk adjustment has figured widely in quality-of-care research. Conceptual models have been considered separately for disease-specific vs. generic outcomes (see R. L. Kane, 1997). Treatment is treated as a moderator variable in the relationship between clinical factors such as severity, baseline status, comorbidity, and patient characteristics, and outcomes such as cardiac output, complications, and function. There are several condition-specific measures such as the Arthritis Impact Measure Scales (Meenan, Gertman, & Mason, 1980) that recently have been reviewed by Atherly (1997). These measures are specific to the condition studied and may have the advantage of better relating to narrowly defined outcomes such as those used in clinical drug trials. Using the example of arthritis, Atherly (1997) illustrates the need for a conceptual model of the etiology and course of the disease as prerequisite to selection of a measure. For example, a positive change in ambulation may be inferred as the result of an exercise program aimed at reducing the debility associated with arthritis; however, the change may be measuring not arthritis-born debility, but change in global functional ability resulting from the exercise program.

Conceptually, a distinction usually is made between measures of comorbidity and of severity. Comorbidity is used to designate conditions other than the primary target disease studied, and severity is used to measure the degree of impairment associated with the primary or comorbid conditions. Another distinction among risk-adjustment measures relates to whether they focus on the individual, e.g., the Charlson Comorbidity Index (Charlson, Pompei, Ales, & Mackenzie, 1987), the group, e.g., Diagnostic Related Groups (DRGs), or the population (see Rothenberg et al., 1997).

Volicer and Hurley (1997) review several types of comorbidity, some originally proposed by Kaplan and Feinstein (1974). The broad categories are titled "random" and "pathological." Designation as "random" indicates that two conditions exist independently of one another; thus, the prevalence of both occurring at once should be the product of the prevalences of the two diseases. If the prevalence of pathological comorbidity is higher than the product of individual prevalences, then the term "pathological" applies, as the two conditions may be present due to the same causal agent (see Volicer & Hurley, 1997).

The need for comorbidity assessment and one of the first methodologies for risk adjustment came from the work of Kaplan and Feinstein (1974), who developed a comorbidity severity index based on a clinical weighting of salient conditions predictive of mortality associated with diabetic patients. Analyses of 5-year survival data was later used as an outcome variable. In the area of long-term care, R. A. Kane (1981) developed a case-mix methodology, the prognostic adjustment factor (PAF), which predicts a resident's status over time using data from the individual and from other matched individuals. The method examines the outcomes of care which are evaluated by comparing the predicted and actual status of the resident over a specified time period.

Risk Adjustment and Comorbidity

Several recent reviews of other comorbidity risk-adjustment measures frequently used in acute care settings are contained in R. L. Kane (1997), Volicer and Hurley (1997), and Rothenberg et al., (1997). These include the Charlson Comorbidity Index (Charlson et al., 1987), the APACHE (Knaus, Zimmerman, Wagner, Draper, & Lawrence, 1981), and case-mix measures such as the Patient Review Instrument (PRI) and the DRGs.

The Charlson Comorbidity Index, developed to predict mortality, adjusts at the individual level; weights for different medical conditions have been developed using Cox proportional hazards models. The APACHE was developed to predict mortality among ICU patients. The latest version uses 16 physiologic measures such as laboratory values, age, presence of comorbid conditions, and type of ICU admission as indicators. Logistic regression was applied to these measures in order to identify salient factors and to derive weights. Criticisms of these models are that the weights used in these methods may not cross-validate well using other samples or other disease categories. In fact, the evidence indicates that comorbidities differ in terms of saliency across different primary diagnoses (Wray, Hollingsworth, Petersen, & Ashton, 1997), and that disease-specific risk adjustment may be needed.

Among measures developed for the prediction of events other than mortality, the Index of Coexistent Disease (ICED) (Greenfield, Apolone, McNiel, & Cleary, 1993) uses medical records to model functioning after hospitalization. Few interrater reliability data are published. Volicer and Hurley (1997) caution that the measure may be problematic for use with dementia patients because some of the ICED indicators are also indicators of dementia severity, so that if cognitive impairment is an outcome, this would result in overadjusting. The recently published Duke Case-Mix System (DUMIX) (Parkerson, Michener, Yarnall, & Hammond, 1997) is a case-mix measure for use in ambulatory care.

This system uses data relevant to physical health status, perceived health status, severity of illness, age, and gender, collected directly from the patient and from a provider or auditor. Cox models are used to model expected future charges as a function of the patient-specific variables weighted by the group-specific coefficients. Based on the expected charges, the patients are classified into four severity groups. As with other case-mix measures, the DUMIX is vulnerable to gaming; however, as the authors point out, use of two sources of information will help to achieve a more valid classification. The model explained 17% of the variance in future clinic charges which, while modest, is similar to the amount explained using other methodologies.

The validity of risk-adjustment measures as applied to long-term care has received little attention (Arling et al., 1997). This inattention derives in part from the absence of a gold-standard criterion, in part because measures and risk adjustments have focused at the facility, rather than the individual level, and in part because of the lack of adequate individual-level measures contained in administrative data sets, although individual researchers have applied sophisticated comorbidity measures.

Clinical weights derived from judges' ratings also have been used to determine preference, and utility weights assigned to elements of combined scales used in developing quality-adjusted life-years (Maciejewski, 1997). Such weights suffer from rater and selection bias. Judges may not agree on ratings, and they may not be representative of the population of target individuals. A recent comparison (Lenert et al., 1997) of several methods of evaluating preference weights, including visual analogue, standard gamble (selection of increasing acceptable risk of death to avoid life with a particular health state) and paired comparisons (preference for one of two health states) showed inconsistencies among methods in terms of ranked preference ratings. The authors recommend excluding inconsistent ratings from samples used to derive population utility values.

A recent analyses comparing 12 different severity measures used in risk adjustment to compare hospital mortality rates, showed disagreement among the measures in identification of outliers (Iezzoni, 1997). The author concludes that severity measures do not completely account for increased risks, particularly among populations differing in race and socioeconomic status, and that severity-adjusted mortality rates are not likely to discriminate hospitals in terms of quality. Given the experience in acute care, the use of risk-adjustment techniques in long-term care merits close attention.

Comorbidity typically includes measures of disease severity and functional impairment. There has been renewed interest in the performance functional-assessment measures, including those measuring upper body and hand function and lower body strength. For recent reviews of performance-based measures see Duncan & Studenski, 1994; Teresi et al., 1994; Zimmer, Rothenberg, & Andresen, 1997. The areas of biomechanics and human factors present some models for the study of function and may provide more sensitive risk-adjustment measures; however, the tradeoff in terms of skill level required and cost of assessment must be considered.

Methodological and Statistical Considerations
As They Apply to Risk Adjustment

Risk adjustment becomes a critical issue in assessing quality of care because as R. L. Kane (1997) points out, a "level-playing field" is essential for comparisons of programs. While certain issues implicit to the process of risk adjustment are complex, e.g., the calculation of utility or value weights, and the clinical or empirical weighting of medical conditions and severity, the concept of risk adjustment is really no different from most analyses of data collected without the benefit of a randomized controlled trial. Different analytic procedures such as Cox proportional hazards analyses are used to adjust for the covariates which are related to the outcome and compete with the intervention or program evaluated for attribution of impact. Methodological issues salient to risk adjustment are selection bias; identification of the proper subgroups as moderator variables (subgroups which may vary in rates or ratios of the target disease); and the problem of overadjusting for aspects of the disease which are also part of the outcome. Nitz (1997) provides examples: complications of disease which occurred after hospitalization may be part of the outcome; or adjusting for differences in medication practices of cardiac surgeons vs other specialties, when this actually reflects attributes of the physician skills which are part of the intervention.

Evaluation of comorbidity measures, the mainstay of risk adjustment, must take into account numerous factors. These include:

- The purpose for which the measures were developed (prediction of mortality, adverse events, functional decline, reimbursement, service use);
- The types of adjustment variables included (medical condition, severity of conditions, demographic characteristics, functional variables, etc.);
- The source of data (clinician ratings, direct interview, chart review, medical reimbursement records);
- The weights used (clinical vs empirically derived using logistic regression and Cox models);
- The samples on which the weights were developed (elderly outpatients, elderly inpatients, non-elderly, etc.);
- The setting (outpatient, ICU, nursing home);
- The order of the additive equation used to combine scores (constant weight [simple count], exponential, multiplicative, quadratic, or clinical); and
- The timing of the measure of comorbid events (should be measured before the intervention).

The fact that weights are not invariant across populations and subgroups makes them suspect when applied indiscriminately. Another problem with many existing measures is the absence of adequate interrater-reliability studies conducted by neutral outside groups. Additionally, many measures are proprietary without published details of the modeling approach or of the algorithms used in the computation of case-mix indices. They are therefore viewed with suspicion by clinicians as well as by researchers who, without reports in peer-reviewed journals, can neither replicate nor evaluate the results. Finally, many measures were developed as a means to predicting mortality which, as previously discussed, may not constitute an adequate outcome measure.

Overall Limitations of Current Conceptual Models and Instruments, and the Need for an Integrated Approach

Currently, evaluation of quality of care focuses on one component of the care continuum at a time, i.e., a non-integrated approach. However, most theorists agree that integrated outcomes are superior to non-integrated outcomes; patients should be followed in their transitions across the continuum of care (Lamb, 1997; Shaughnessy et al., 1997). As stated by Lamb (1997): The central goal of measuring outcomes across the continuum is to capture performance of the whole continuum on quality, access to care and cost. (p. NS108) It is also argued that selected outcomes must be those which are of interest to those in administration and marketing as well as to researchers, and should reflect not only changes in health and functional status, but in satisfaction, service use, and costs. Lamb posits a model which shows both direct and indirect effects of population characteristics on outcomes through disciplinary mediators (e.g., self-care, environmental variables). Lamb reviews methods for studying these processes including: (1) the single snapshot examining outcomes; (2) the single snapshot examining transition states; (3) the multiple snapshot examining global outcomes; and (4) the multiple snapshot examining population-based outcomes. The first method examines separately elements of the system. Limitation of this approach are that examining the outcomes of one component, e.g., the hospital surgical experience or ICU experience, does not capture service outcomes—related to the immediate service, or to aftercare, e.g., home care, or to how well the services are integrated. The second approach examines transition states between hospital and community; however, there is no examination of the entire system. The third approach examines similar, multiple outcomes across multiple populations of patients such as those with diabetes, stroke, etc. The final method tracks, longitudinally, the outcomes of targeted populations of homogeneous cohorts across multiple sites of care.

Whenever the goal is to apply measures across the continuum of care, floor and ceiling effects will constitute a problem, necessitating the use of proxy measures. There is a substantial literature on the different types of bias associated with the use of such measures. In general, the bias is not in the same direction across domains (for some conditions, e.g., cognition, there is under-reporting of symptomatology by proxies; for others, e.g., function, there is over-reporting); making comprehensive assessment even more complex. Other statistical issues are discussed in the next section.

STATISTICAL MODELING OF QUALITY OF CARE

Statistical issues related to quality of care include adequate measurement and modeling of quality of care outcomes and risk adjustment and dealing with unit-of-analysis issues. Statistical service use and health-status models are usually hierarchical regression, logistic regression, or structural equation models; however, others have used discrete time-hazard function methods to model the probability of admission and discharge (e.g., Greene & Ondrich, 1990). Because of frequently occurring problems with missing data over time, and the need to mix units of analyses (institutions and individuals), random-effects modeling procedures offer attractive alternatives. Markov modeling is also now being used to model transition states in and out of disability (see Teresi, 1994, for an overview of statistical models applied to aging research.)

Modeling Quality-of-Care Outcomes:
Structural Equation Modeling

Path analysis using Structural Equation Modeling (SEM) (Bentler, 1989; Joreskog & Sorbom, 1981; Muthen, 1991) is frequently used in the context of modeling quality-of-life outcomes. The use of multi-equation modeling using a structural-equation approach is a conceptual advance (Johnson & Wolinsky, 1993, 1994). However some caveats regarding such modeling are revisited below.

Caveats

Distribution of the Variables and Model Fit

One consideration in the application of structural-equation modeling to the study of chronic care settings is that symptomatology data may not be normally distributed, possibly resulting in problems in interpreting the goodness-of-fit statistics. Some structural-equation models include extensive tests of violations of the model assumptions and allow for distribution-free estimation methods in the case of data which are not multivariate-normal. However, these methods require larger sample sizes (Bentler & Newcomb, 1992). There are numerous goodness-of-fit tests now available with various software packages. More theoretically based work, e.g., Bentler (1990), linking goodness-of-fit tests to the noncentrality parameter, may provide alternative, less sample size-dependent measures. Additionally, previous experience indicates that a weighted least-squares rather than a maximum likelihood solution may yield better fit in testing models of health status data.

Disattenuation

An added concern is the intrinsic correction for attenuation due to unreliability built into the measurement model for some software (Cohen, Cohen, Teresi, Marchi, & Velez,

1990). When latent variables are measured with differential reliability, this correction can affect the structural-equation estimates by producing disattenuated effects for the latent variable that is measured less reliably. (Disattenuated relationships can result in changes in partial relationships with other variables.) Although it is well-known that measurement error can result in biased regression estimates, artificially inflating the reliabilities of less well-measured variables could lead to erroneous estimates. This issue has recently been revisited in the literature (Bedeian, Day, & Kelloway, 1997).

Specification

Lawton and Lawrence (1994) posit that health is a latent construct measured by numerous indicators. They question whether health can be considered as a generic construct, given the numerous complexities inherent in specifying a health-status model. The authors discuss five overarching conceptual partitions in the operationalization of health: the facets of health; the type of measure (objective vs. subjective); the source (lab reports, self-report, proxy); the scale or metric; and the centrality of the indicator in terms of its tie to biologic health. Lawton (1984) posits that the health construct is defined by three major components: life threat (the risk of mortality); pain and discomfort (usually a subjective domain), and functional ability (competent role functioning). Lawton and Lawrence (1994) view physical health as a second-order factor, measured by two first-order latent factors: objective and subjective health. Physical health relates in a nonrecursive structure to the four sectors of the good life: psychological well-being, behavioral competence, objective environment, and perceived quality of life. Presumably one might view quality of care as causally prior in this model—leading to poor health intermediate outcomes, to poor psychological health, behavioral incompetence, poor quality of life, and to the ultimate outcome of mortality.

In modeling quality-of-care outcomes such as change in health status, there arises the conceptual argument as to whether it is a state or a trait that is being assessed. This is a problem raised by Teresi and Holmes (1994) and relevant to the review of health status measures by Lawton and Lawrence in the 1994 *Annual Review*, which focused on assessment. This translates into the questions: "What is the extent to which indicators of latent variables are generative or not?" and "Are the indicators of health status causes of, or caused by, the latent variable?" Many structural-equation modeling programs are based on the premise that the construct is defined in terms of the indicators on which it has an effect; the latent variable explains the correlations among the observed indicators. Some constructs could be both causal and emergent, depending upon the types of indicators. Cohen and colleagues (1990) discuss the mathematical results which occur when a latent variable is inadequately specified, so that it does not explain a large proportion of each indicator variable (the indicators are not highly intercorrelated). In addition to possible identification problems which can result from misspecification of the causal nature of the latent variable measured, the misspecified variable may have a spuriously low reliability estimate; as discussed above, many structural-equation models will perform a correction for attenuation for less reliably measured variables, frequently resulting in inflated or deflated causal estimates.

Measurement Models

Confirmatory Factor Analysis Using the Measurement Model of Structural Equation Modeling

Factorial invariance is often a goal of confirmatory factor analysis, particularly when applied to different subgroups. A concern is the improper application of factor analyses, yielding variant loadings across samples (Cunningham, 1991). In confirmatory factor analysis, invariance is not necessarily expected, but is a hypothesis to be tested. For example, Horn and colleagues (Horn & McArdle, 1992; Horn, McArdle, & Mason, 1983) contend that exact metric invariance (identical loadings) is scientifically unreasonable. They argue in favor of configural invariance, where the requirement is only that the configuration of zero loadings and the salient loadings remain invariant. Meredith (1993) *has* shown that under rather restrictive conditions, one can expect invariance.

Nesselroade and Thompson (1995) suggest that (a) only covariance matrices be analyzed; (b) factor variance and covariance matrices be allowed to differ across groups; and (c) an oblique solution be applied (factors are not constrained to be fixed or orthogonal). Our experience suggests that weighted least-squares rather than maximum-likelihood solutions may yield better results (better fit) because the data modelled in health status and quality of care are frequently ordinal or dichotomous and non-normal.

We recommend that (a) the measurement model be examined separately (not in the context of the structural equation model); (b) at least four indicators for each latent variable (see also Cohen et al., 1990); and (c) information about which parameter elements are fixed or freed be reported. Other recommendations for the use of exploratory and confirmatory factor analyses in the context of construct validity testing and development of scales can be found in Thompson & Daniel (1996).

Item Response Theory

The methods of modern psychometric theory are now being used to develop and investigate health care measures, and are recommended for use in developing measures of care outcomes. One strong advantage of item response theory (IRT) is the capability to examine differential-item functioning or item bias with respect to population subgroups differing on variables such as ethnicity. A second advantage of IRT is that is provides estimates of standard errors or precision for different points along the measure of the latent attribute, in contrast to estimating only one summary measure of reliability.

The models derived from modern psychometric theory (see Lord, 1980) produce invariant parameters (item difficulty, item discrimination) which are not sample-dependent and which, therefore, are not affected by disorder- or item-prevalence ratio differences. There have been numerous recent advances in IRT (Van der Linden & Hambleton, 1995), and in the methods of Differential Item Functioning (Camilli & Shepard, 1994; Holland & Wainer, 1993). New methods incorporate the capabilities to model polytomous (multiple categories of) responses, including nominal categories, multiple choice, graded responses, and rating scales. Because these models relate item characteristics to the underlying attribute, they take disability (ability) level into account. The most commonly used IRT model defines the conditional probability of passing an item, given standing on the latent attribute, using the cumulative logistic function originally proposed by Birnbaum (Lord & Novick, 1968). An item characteristic curve (ICC) relates item response to an individual's standing on the latent attribute. A detailed explication of the model is beyond the scope of this chapter; however, see Hambleton, Swaninathan, and Rogers (1991); Teresi et al. (1995); and Teresi and Holmes (1994) for reviews.

Statistical Issues in Risk Adjustment

Because of the impracticality of randomized controlled trials (RCTs) in many chronic care settings, particularly in nursing homes, there is a need for statistical control. The problem becomes one of correctly linking the outcome to the appropriate process of care or care interventions after adjusting for the competing individual risk factors that may be causally related to the outcome (Kane, 1998). The mainstay of statistical risk adjustment has been some type of regression analysis. These models have typically evidenced poor fit in terms of explained variance (cumulative R^2) in health care expenditures (see Hogan, 1997). Some models, using different units of analyses (pooled risk groups instead of individuals), explain more variance (Rosenkranz & Luft, 1997), in part an artifact of the unit of analyses used (see Welch, 1997). Recently Stone and colleagues (Stone et al., 1995) introduced a classification tree methodology to model the probability of hospitalization; this uses an interactive approach to determine cut-points on continuous indicators which best discriminate the two target groups, e.g., dead or alive. In this fashion subgroups that are similar on covariates and with the same probability of the outcome are identified. The subgroups comprise the propensity score strata, for which treatment effect differences between groups can be calculated.

Because many residents of nursing homes are on a decline trajectory, both Schnelle (in press) and Kane (1998) call for new methods for linking the individual resident's course to an expected course for such an individual. Statistical models which examine nonliner decline trajectories are beginning to be developed. For example, Liu, Tsai, and Stern (1996) used nonliner growth curves to model the conditional change in functional measures over the time interval since a given measurement. Expanding the model to include unequal time intervals. Liu, Teresi, and Waternaux (in press) modeled change in functional status over adjacent data points with time-varying covariates. These methods may be useful in determining a decline trajectory.

As discussed previously, the methods are only as good as the data supplied (which are only as good as data samples and sources), and there are several recent reviews comparing the use of different types of data in risk-adjustment equations. Wray and colleagues (1997) conclude that while administrative databases have traditionally contained inaccurate diagnostic data, the situation is improving and some databases, e.g., discharge databases contain better-quality data. Primary data collection based on standard abstraction procedures is an alternative widely used; however, evidence indicates that generic risk-adjustment methods are inferior to disease-specific methods using either administrative data sets or primary data collection, and that the two types of data (administrative and primary) yield more comparable findings when disease-specific risk adjustment is undertaken. However, the "primary" method is usually reliant on chart review data, which may be inferior to direct patient-collected data, and frequently does not include outside factors, such as compliance, which may influence analytic results. Wray and colleagues (1997) summarize the findings, suggesting that risk adjustment should be diagnosis- and outcome-specific; comorbidities should be included as should be demographic variables which may act as proxies for unmeasured lifestyle variables. The key comorbidities and demographics themselves may vary across disease states.

Modeling Quality Adjusted Life Year

A different approach to developing severity ratings which takes quality of life into account is the Quality Adjusted Life Year (QUALY). The duration of a health state, life expectancy, and a qualitative value attached to the illness are used in the model (Ganiats, Miller, & Kaplan, 1995). Decision-theory methodology is used to assign weights to health states in order to adjust survival for quality of life. This approach plots the health-related quality of life (HRQL) scores against time and estimates the QUALY as the area under the curve resulting from connecting the points. An average HRQL score is obtained for all interviews at each time point; the mean QUALY for the population is estimated from the averages. A recent analysis (Ganiats et al., 1995) of several approaches to estimating and comparing QUALYs across groups showed that an interview-based approach (estimating both the proportion of subjects surviving and the average health-status score at each timepoint) was preferable. Estimation methods include Kaplan-Meier survival models, used to weight the area under the survival curve by the average HRQL for those still alive, or maximum likelihood estimation of the mean HRQL for those alive at time t_i.

Unit of Analysis Problems

Much of the quality-of-care research addresses problems where mixed units of analysis are encountered. Individuals are nested within sites, hospitals, and programs. For example, repeated measures of health status over time may constitute a level 1 unit, which is nested within patients (level 2), which are nested within hospitals (level 3). The identification of unit of analysis is a key question in quality of care research. Is the unit of analysis the subscriber group (e.g., all enrollees and family members covered under an insurance plan), the individual patient, the individual physician, the office visit, or the episode of care? Or is the unit of analysis the facility, department, or unit? At a more macro level, the unit of analysis could consist of a community or region, a hospital system, or a nursing home chain (Fennell & Flood, 1998).

Hester and colleagues (1997) raise the methodological controversy surrounding making group-level inferences from individual data. To what extent do individuals, when aggregated, represent the unit performance and views? On the other hand, if the physician is the unit of analysis, the issue is how to examine only his or her contribution to an illness episode which involves many health care professionals, laboratory tests, etc. (Palmer & Chapman, 1997). Moreover, the number of patients cared for by any single selected physician may be small and not representative of the population of patients.

The key statistical issue is that most inferential statistics assume that observational units are independent of each other; biased statistical tests result from violations of the assumption. Failure to model the correlation among observations may result in poor estimates of variance and biased underestimates of the standard errors, resulting in Type 1 error. One method used by educational researchers to circumvent this practice was to substitute the mean as the unit of analysis rather than the individual, however, this results in a diminution of statistical power (see Kromrey & Dickinson, 1996). Another manner of treating this problem is to construct nested ANOVA models in such a way that hospitals, for example, constitute levels of a random factor nested within a care process intervention, and patients might be treated as levels of a random factor nested within hospitals.

There are other models, labelled random effects or mixed models in some literature (see Littell, Milliken, Stroup, & Wolfinger, 1996), and hierarchical linear models (HLM) in other literature (see Bryk & Raudenbush, 1992). These models allow for examination of individual-specific (e.g., patients) and group-specific (clusters such as hospital) heterogeneity. These methods avoid treating cluster-specific effects as dummy variables, which can lead to inconsistent estimates of regression coefficients. An example of an application of HLM, modeling level 1 (individual) and level 2 (institutional) characteristics in examining quality of care in Canadian nursing homes is provided by Bravo, De Wals, Dubois, and Charpentier (1999).

Problems in application of traditional multivariate models when data are missing due to unbalanced designs (subjects are measured at different times), incomplete data (subjects are missing from some waves of data), inability to handle unequally spaced data, and inability to model individual differences in slopes (rates of change) have lead to the recommendation of the use of random-effects modeling (Hedeker, Gibbons, Waternaux, & Davis, 1989), of which growth curve analysis and repeated measures can be viewed as special cases (Laird & Ware, 1982). Zeger and Liang (1992) provide an overview of random effects and other modeling techniques for dealing with correlated measures and missing data in longitudinal studies. Most recently variants of such models have been applied to quality-of-life data in clinical trials (Beacon & Thompson, 1996).

Random effects modeling can be used to incorporate modeling of possible differences among subjects not only in baseline values (intercepts) but in rates of change (slopes). For example, using a random effects approach, one can model health status over time as a function of covariates, treating treatment as a group variable, coded 0 and 1. The intercept (b_0), slope (b_1) and standard deviation (σ) is estimated for each subject, and the relationship between the mean slope for outcomes and the mean on other variables determined.

Implications

We have attempted to briefly outline some of the central issues in the measurement and modeling of quality-of-life and care outcomes. In particular, we have attempted to present and promote some of the newer techniques which can be used to circumvent problems which have traditionally bedeviled statistical analysts. In fact, the central point being made in the immediately preceding pages is that it is no longer necessary to avoid certain central issues, e.g., differences in the unit of analysis, because techniques exist with which will help the analyst to deal with such conundrums.

CONCLUSIONS

Hopefully, the content of this chapter reflects the state of the art in modeling issues as they relate to quality-of-care assessment. What many regard as the most "popular" quality-of-care models have been presented and discussed. Particular attention has been given to the differentiation between the process of care and gross outcomes such as mortality or morbidity, which may bear little or no relation to the process of care provision. Clearly, the major sermon being preached is to exercise judicious care in the selection of quality-of-care indicators and criteria and, most particularly, that outcome measures not be permitted to substitute for process measures in the assessment of quality of care.

In this discussion there has been repeated reference to Lawton's work, which simply reflects the extent of his contributions. Specifically, his work has encouraged us to:

- View health measurement in multidimensional terms;
- Go beyond a narrow focus on criteria such as mortality to a broader concern with the quality of life;
- Go beyond focusing on personality and behavior, to include the physical and social environment in the investigative equation;
- Appreciate the importance of person/environment fit;
- Attempt measurement in hard-to-assess populations, for example, communication-disordered, cognitively impaired nursing home residents; and to
- Go beyond the development and application of quality-of-care assessment approaches, to the design and implementation of interventions designed to test the impacts of the process of caregiving.

Quite simply, he has provided much that, over time, many of us have come to take for granted.

REFERENCES

Aiken, L. K., Sochalski, J., & Lake, E. T. (1997). Studying outcomes of organizational change in health services. *Medical Care, 35*(Suppl.), NS6–NS18.

Anderson, R., & Aday, L. A. (1978). Access to medical care in the Unites States: Realized and potential. *Medical Care, 16*, 533–546.

Anderson, R., & Newman, J. F. (1973). Societal and individual determinants of medical care utilization in the United States. *Milbank Memorial Fund Quarterly, 51*, 95–124.

Andresen, E., Rothenberg, B., & Zimmer, J. G. (1997). *Assessing the health status of older adults*. New York: Springer Publishing Company.

Arling, G., Karon, S. L., Sainfort, F., Zimmerman, D. R., & Ross, R. (1997). Risk adjustment of nursing home quality indicators. *Gerontologist, 37*, 757–766.

Ashton, C., Del Junco, D., Souchek, J., Wray, N., & Mansyur, C. (1997). The association between the quality of inpatient care and elderly readmission: A meta-analysis of the evidence. *Medical Care, 35*, 1044–1059.

Atherly, A. (1997). Understanding health care outcomes research. In R. Kane (Ed.)., *Condition-specific measures* (pp. 53–66). Gaithersburg, MD: Aspen.

Bartlett, E. E., Grayson, M., Barker, R., Levine, D. M., Golder, A., & Libber, S. (1984) The effects of physician communication skills on patient satisfaction, recall, and adherence. *Journal of Chronic Disease, 37*, 755–764.

Bass, D. M., Looman, W. J., & Ehrlich, P. (1992). Predicting the volume of health and social services: Integrating cognitive impairment into the modified Anderson framework. *Gerontologist, 32*, 33–43.

Beacon, H. J., & Thompson, S. G. (1996) Multi-level models for repeated measurement data: Application to quality of life data in clinical trials *Statistics in Medicine, 15*, 2717–2732.

Bedeian, A. G., Day, D. V., & Kelloway, E. K. (1997). Correcting for measurement error attenuation in structural equation models: Some important reminders. *Educational and Psychological Measurement, 57*, 785–799.

Bentler, P. M. (1989). *EQS structural equations program manual*. Los Angeles: BMDP Software.

Bentler, P. M. (1990). Comparative fit indexes in structural models. *Psychological Bulletin, 107*, 238–246.

Bentler, P. M., & Newcomb, M. D. (1992). Linear structural equation modeling with nonnormal continuous variables. In J. Dwyer, M. Feinleib, P. Lippert, & H. Hoffmeister (Eds.) *Statistical models for longitudinal studies of health* (pp. 132–160). New York: Oxford University Press.

Bindman, A. B., Grumbach, K., Keane, D., Rauch, L., & Luce, J. M. (1991). Consequences of queuing for care at a public hospital emergency department. *Journal of the American Medical Association, 266*, 1085–1091.

Binstock, R. H., & Spector, W. D. (1997). Five priority areas in long term care. *Health Services Research, 32*, 715–730.

Blumenthal, D. (1997). The future of quality measurement and management in a transforming health care system. *Journal of the American Medical Association, 278*, 1622–1625.

Branch, L., & Jette, A. (1983). Elders' use of informal long-term care assistance. *Gerontologist, 23*, 51–55.

Branch, L., Jette, A., Evashwick, C., Polansky, M., Rowe, G., & Oiehr. P. (1981). Toward understanding elders' health service utilization. *Journal of Community Health, 7*, 80–92.

Bravo, G., De Wals, P., Dubois, M-F., & Charpentier, M. (1999). Correlates of care quality in long-term care facilities: A multilevel analysis. *Journal of Gerontology: Psychological Sciences, 54B*, P180–P188.

Brooks, R. H., McGlynn, E. A., & Cleary, P. D. (1996). Quality of health care: Part 2. Measuring quality of care. *New England Journal of Medicine, 335*, 966–970.

Brooten, D. (1997). Methodological issues linking costs to outcomes. *Medical Care, 35*, NS87–NS95.

Bryk, A. S., & Raudenbush, S. W. (1992). *Hierarchical linear models.* Newbury Park, CA: Sage.

Byrne, B. M. (1991). The Maslach Inventory: Validating factorial structure and invariance across intermediate, secondary, and university educators. *Multivariate Behavioral Research, 26*, 583–605.

Byrne, B. M. (1994). *Structural equation modeling with EQS and EQS/Windows.* Thousand Oaks, CA: Sage.

Camilli, G., & Shepard, L. A. (1994). *Methods for identifying biased test items: Volume 4.* Thousand Oaks, CA: Sage.

Cantor, M. H. (1979). The informal support system of New York's inner city elderly: Is ethnicity a factor? In D. E. Getland & A. J. Kutzik (Eds). *Ethnicity and aging: Theory, research, and policy.* New York: Springer Publishing Co.

Castle, N. G., Zinn, J. S., Brannon, D., & Mor, V. (1997). Quality improvement in nursing homes. *Health care management.* Philadelphia: Hanley and Belfus.

Chambers, R., Knight, F., & Campbell, I. (1996). A pilot study of the introduction of audit into nursing homes. *Age and Ageing, 25*, 465–469.

Chang, B., Uman, G., Linn, L. W., Ware, J. E., & Kane, R. (1984). The effects of systematic varying components of nursing care on satisfaction in elderly ambulatory women. *Western Journal of Nursing Research, 6*, 367.

Chappell, N. L. (1994). Home care research: What does it tell us? *Gerontologist, 34*, 116–120.

Charlson, M. E., Pompei, P., Ales, K. L., & Mackenzie, C. R. (1987). A new method of classifying prognostic comorbidity in longitudinal studies: Development and validation. *Journal of Chronic Diseases, 40*, 373–383.

Cherry, R. L. (1991). Agents of nursing home quality of care: Ombudsmen and staff ratios revisited. *Gerontologist, 31*, 302–308.

Cleary, P., & McNeil, B. (1988). Patient satisfaction as an indicator of quality care. *Inquiry, 25*, 25.

Cleary, P. D., & Edgman-Levitan, P. A. (1997). Health care quality. *Journal of the American Medical Association, 278*, 1608–1612.

Cleary, P. D., Edgman-Levitan, S., Roberts, M. J., Moloney, T. W., McMullen, W., Walker, J. D., & Delbanco, T. L. (1991). Patients evaluate their hospital care: A national survey. *Health Affairs, 10*, 254–267.

Cohen, J., & Struening, E. (1964). Hospital social atmosphere profiles and effectiveness. *Journal of Consulting and Clinical Psychology, 28*, 291–298.

Cohen, P., Cohen, J., Teresi, J., Marchi, P., & Velez, N. (1990). Problems in the measurement of latent variables in structural equation causal models. *Applied Psychological Measurement, 14*, 183–186.

Crooks, V. C., Schnelle, J. F., Ouslander, J. G., & McNees, P. M. (1995). Use of the minimum data set to rate incontinence severity. *Journal of the American Geriatrics Society, 43*, 1363–1369.

Cunningham, W. R. (1991). Issues in factorial invariance. In L. M. Collins & J. L. Horn (Eds.), *Best methods for the analyses of change: Recent advances, unanswered questions, future directions* (pp. 106–113). Washington, DC: American Psychological Association.

Davis, M. A. (1991a). Nursing home ownership revisited: Market, cost and quality relationships. *Medical Care, 3*, 1062.

Davis, M. A. (1991b). On nursing home quality: A review and analysis. *Medical Care Review, 48*, 129–166.

Deming, W. E. (1965). Principles of professional statistical practice. *Annals of Mathematical Statistics, 36*, 1883–1900.

Deming, W. E. (1989). *Out of the crisis*. Cambridge, MA: Massachusetts Institute of Technology, Center for Advanced Engineering Studies.

Donabedian, A. (1980). *Exploration in Quality Assessment and Monitoring: The Definitions of Quality and Approaches to Its Assessment (Vol. 1)*. Ann Arbor, MI: Health Administration Press Vol. 1.

Donabedian, A. (1988). The quality of care: How can it be assessed. *Journal of the American Medical Association, 260*, 1743–1748.

Donabedian, A., Wheeler, J. R. C., & Wyszewianski, L. (1982). Quality, cost and health: An integrative model. *Medical Care, 20*, 975–992.

Dresser, M., Feingold, L., Rosenkranz, S., & Coltin, K. (1997). Clinic quality measurement: Comparing chart review and automated methodologies. *Medical Care, 35*,539–552.

Duncan, P. W., & Studenski, S. (1994). Balance and gait measures. In M. P. Lawton & J. A. Teresi (Eds.), *Annual Review of Gerontology and Geriatrics: Vol. 13. Focus on assessment techniques* (pp. 76–92). New York: Springer Publishing Co.

Farrell, M. P., Schmitt, M. H., & Heinemann, G. D. (1988). Organizational environments of health care teams: Impact on team development and implications for consultation. *International Journal of Small Group Research, 4*, 31–53.

Fetter, R. B., Shin, Y., Freeman, J. L., Averill, R., & Thompson, J. (1980). Case mix definition by diagnosis-related groups. *Medical Care, 18*, 1–53.

Fennell, M. L., & Flood, A. B. (1998). Key challenges in studying organizational issues in the delivery of healthcare to older Americans. In M. G. Ory, J. Cooper, & A. Siu (Eds.), Organizational issues in the delivery of primary care to older Americans [Special Issue]. *Health Services Research, 33*, 424–444.

Frederick/Schneiders, Inc. (1995). *Analysis of focus groups concerning managed care and medicine.* Prepared for Henry J. Kaiser Family Foundation. Washington, DC: Author.

Ganiats, T. G., Miller, C. J., & Kaplan, R. M. (1995). Comparing the quality-adjusted life-year output of two treatment arms in a randomized trial. *Medical Care, 33,* AS245–AS254.

Garcia-Martin, M., Lardelli-Claret, P., Bueno-Cavanillas, A., Luna-del-Castillo, J. D., Espigares-Garcia, M., & Galvez-Vargas, R. (1997). Proportion of hospital deaths associated with adverse events. *Journal of Clinical Epidemiology, 50,* 1319–1326.

Golant, S. M., & McCaslin, R. (1979). A functional classification of services for older people. *Journal of Gerontological Social Work, 1,* 187–210.

Grant, L. A., Potthoff, S. J., Ryden, M., & Kane R. A. (1998). Staff ratios, training and assignment in Alzheimer Special Care Units. *Journal of Gerontological Research, 24,* 9–16.

Greene, V. L., & Ondrich, J. I. (1990). Risk factors for nursing home admissions and exits: A discrete-time hazard function approach. *Journal of Gerontology: Social Sciences, 45,* S250–S258.

Greenfield, S., Apolone, G., McNiel, B. J., & Cleary, P. D. (1993). The importance of coexistent disease in the occurrence of postoperative complications and one-year recovery in patients undergoing total hip replacement. *Medical Care, 31,* 141–154.

Greenfield, S., Rogers, W., Mangotich, M., Carney, M. F., & Tarlov, A. R. (1995). Outcomes of patients with hypertension and non-insulin dependent diabetes mellitus treated by different systems and specialties: Results from the medical outcomes study. *Journal of the American Medical Association, 274,* 1436–1444.

Gurland, B. J., & Wilder, D. E. (1984). The CARE interview revisited: Development of an efficient, systematic clinical assessment. *Journal of Gerontology, 39,* 129–137.

Halstead, L. S., Rintalla, D. H., Kanellos, M., Griffin, B., Higgins, L., Rheinecker, S., Whiteside, W., & Healy, J. E. (1986). The innovative rehabilitation team: An experiment in team building. *Archives of Physical Medicine and Rehabilitation, 67,* 357–361.

Hambleton, R., Swaninathan, H., & Rogers, H. (1991). *Fundamentals of items response theory.* Newbury Park, CA: Sage.

Hawes, C., Mor, V., Phillips, C. D., Fries, B. E., Morris, J. N., Steele-Friedlob, E., Greene, A. M., & Nennstiel, M. (1997). The OBRA-87 nursing home regulations and implementation of the Resident Assessment Instrument: Effects on process quality. *Journal of the American Geriatrics Society, 45,* 977–985.

Hayes, V., Morris, J., Wolfe, C., & Morgan, M. (1995). The SF-36 Health Survey Questionnaire: Is it suitable for use with older adults? *Age and Ageing, 24,* 120–125.

Hedeker, D., Gibbons, R. D., Waternaux, C., & Davis, J. M. (1989). Investigating drug plasma levels and clinical response using random regression models. *Psychopharmacology Bulletin, 25,* 227–231.

Hester, N., Miller, K., Foster, R., & Vojir, C. (1997). Symptoms management outcomes: Do they reflect variations in care delivery systems? *Medical Care, 35,* NS69–NS83.

Hogan, A. J. (1997). Methodological issues in linking costs and health outcomes in research on differing care delivery systems. *Medical Care, 35,* NS96–NS105.

Holland, P. W., & Wainer, H. (1993). *Differential item functioning.* Hillsdale, NJ: Lawrence Erlbaum.

Holmes, D., Teresi, J., Holmes, M., Bergman, S., King, Y., & Bentur, N. (1989). Informal versus formal supports for impaired elderly: Determinants of choice on Israeli kibbutzim. *Gerontologist, 29,* 195–202.

Holtzman, J., & Lurie, N. (1996). Causes of increasing mortality in a nursing home population. *Journal of the American Geriatrics Society, 44,* 258.

Horn, J. L., & McArdle, J. J. (1992). A practical and theoretical guide to measurement invariance in aging research. *Experimental Aging Research, 18,* 117–144.

Horn, J. L., McArdle, J. J., & Mason, R. (1983). When is invariant not invariant: A practical scientist's look at the ethereal concept of factor invariance. *Southern Psychologist, 1,* 179–188.

Huff, E. (1997). Comprehensive reliability assessment and comparison of quality indicators and their components. *Clinical Epidemiology, 50,* 1395–1404.

Iezzoni, L. I. (1997). The risks of risk adjustment. *Journal of the American Medical Association, 278,* 1600–1607.

Institute of Medicine. (1986). *Improving the quality of care in nursing homes.* Washington, DC: National Academy Press.

Johnson, R. J., & Wolinsky, F. D. (1993). The structure of health status among older adults: Disease, disability, functional limitation and perceived health. *Journal of Health and Social Behavior, 34,* 105–121.

Johnson, R. J., & Wolinsky, F. D. (1994). Gender, race and health: The structure of health status among older adults. *Gerontologist, 34,* 24–35.

Johnson-Pawlson, J., & Infeld, D. I. (1996). Nurse staffing and quality of care in nursing facilities. *Journal of Gerontological Nursing, 22,* 36–45.

Joreskog, K., & Sorbom, D. (1981). LISREL: *Analysis of Linear Structural Relationships by Maximum Likelihood and Least Squares Methods.* Upsala,Sweden: University of Upsala.

Kahana, E. (1975). A congruence model of person-environment interaction. In T. O. Byerts, M. P. Lawton, & J. Newcomber (Eds.), *Theory development in environments and aging.* Washington, DC: Gerontological Society.

Kahana, E., Liang, S., & Felton, B. (1980). Alternative models of person-environment fit: Prediction of morale in three homes for the aged. *Journal of Gerontology, 35,* 584–595.

Kanda, K., & Mezey, M. (1991). Registered nurse staffing in Pennsylvania nursing homes: Comparison before and after implementation of Medicare's prospective payment system. *The Gerontologist, 31,* 318–324.

Kane, R. A. (1981). Assuring quality of care and quality of life in long-term care. *Quality Review Bulletin, 7,* 3–10.

Kane, R. A., Bell, R., Riegler, S., Wilson, A., & Keeler, E. (1983). Predicting the outcomes of nursing home patients. *The Gerontologist, 23,* 200–206.

Kane, R. L. (1997). *Understanding health care outcomes research.* Gaithersburg, MD: Aspen.

Kane, R. L. (1998). Assuring quality of nursing home care. *Journal of the American Geriatrics Association*, 46, 232–237.

Kane, R. L., Garrand, J., Skay, C. I., Radosevich, D. M., Buchanan, J. L., McDermott, S. W., Arnold, S. B., & Kepferle, L. (1989). Effects of a geriatric nursing practicioner on process and outcome of nursing home care. *American Journal of Public Health*, 79, 1271.

Kaplan, M. H., & Feinstein, A. R. (1974). The importance of classifying initial comorbidity in evaluating the outcome for diabetes mellitus. *Journal of Chronic Diseases*, 27, 387–404.

Kellam, S. G., Goldberg, S. C., Schooler, N., Berman, A., & Shmelzer, J. L. (1967). Ward atmosphere and outcome of treatment of acute schizophrenia. *Journal of Psychiatric Research*, 5, 145–163.

Kethley, A., & Ehrlich, P. (1989). Benjamin Rose Institute: A model community long-term care system. In Z. Harel, P. Ehrlich, & R. Hubbard (Eds.), *The vulnerable aged* (Vol. 9, pp. 276–294). New York: Springer Publishing Co.

Kleemeier, R. W. (1959). Behavior and the organization of the bodily and the external environment. In J. E. Birren (Ed.), *Handbook of aging and the individual* (pp. 400–451). Chicago: University of Chicago Press.

Knaus, W. A., Zimmerman, J. E., Wagner, D. P., Draper, E. A., & Lawrence, D. E. (1981). APACHE: Acute physiology and chronic health evaluation. A physiologically based classification system. *Critical Care Medicine*, 9, 591–597.

Kritchevsky, S. B., & Simmons, B. P. (1991). Continuous quality improvement. *Journal of the American Medical Association*, 13, 1817–1823.

Kromrey, J. D., & Dickinson, W. B. (1996). Detecting unit of analysis problems in nested designs: Statistical power and type I error rates of the F test for groups-within-treatment effects. *Educational and Psychological Measurement*, 56, 215–231.

Laffel, G., & Blumenthal, D. (1989). The case for using industrial quality management science in health care organizations. *Journal of the American Medical Association*, 262, 2869–2873.

Laird, N. M., & Ware, J. H. (1982). Random effects models for longitudinal data. *Biometrics*, 38, 963–974.

Lamb, G. S. (1997). Outcomes across the care continuum. *Medical Care*, 35, NS106–NS114.

Lawton, M. (1980). Residential quality and residential satisfaction among the elderly. *Research on Aging*, 2, 309–328.

Lawton, M. P. (1965). Personality and attitudinal correlates of psychiatric-aid performance. *Journal of Social Psychology*, 66, 215–226.

Lawton, M. P. (1970). Ecology and aging. In L. A. Pastalan & D. H. Carson (Eds.), *Spatial behavior of older people* (pp. 40–67). Ann Arbor: Institute of Gerontology, University of Michigan.

Lawton, M. P. (1982). Competence, environmental pressure and the adaptation of older people. In M. P. Lawton, P. Windley, & T. Byerts (Eds.), *Aging and the environment: Theoretical approaches* (pp. 33–59). New York: Springer Publishing Co.

Lawton, M. P. (1983). Environmental and other determinants of well-being in older people. *The Gerontologist, 23*, 349–353.

Lawton, M. (1984). Investigating health and subjective well-being: Substantive challenges. *International Journal of Ageing and Human Development, 19*, 211–227.

Lawton, M. P. (1986). Functional assessment. In L. Teri & P. M. Lewinsohn (Eds.), *Clinical assessment and treatment of the older adult* (pp. 39–84). New York: Springer Publishing Co.

Lawton, M. P. (1991). A multidimentional view of quality of life. In J. E. Birren, J. E. Lubben, J. C. Rowe, & D. E. Deutchman (Eds.), *The concept and measurement of quality of life in the frail elderly* (pp. 3–27). New York: Academic Press.

Lawton, M. P. (1993). Quality of life in Alzheimer's disease. *Alzheimer Disease and Associated Disorders, 8*, 138–150.

Lawton, M. P. (1997). Assessing quality of life in Alzheimer disease research. *Alzheimer Disease and Associated Disorders, 11*(Suppl.6), 91–99.

Lawton, M. P., & Goldman, A. (1965). Role conceptions of the psychiatric aide. *Genetic Psychology Monographs, 71*, 311–348.

Lawton, M. P., & Lawrence, R. H. (1994). Assessing health. In M. P. Lawton & J. A. Teresi (Eds.), *Annual review of gerontology and geriatrics* (Vol. 14, pp. 23–56). New York: Springer Publishing Co.

Lawton, M. P., & Teresi, J. A. (1994). *Annual review in gerontology and geriatrics: Focus on assessment* (Vol. 14). New York: Springer Publishing Co.

Lawton, M. P., Van Haitsma, K., & Klapper, J. (1996). Observed affect in nursing home residents with Alzheimer's disease. *Journals of Gerontology, 51B*, P3–P14.

Lawton, M. P., Weisman, G. D., Sloane, P., & Calkins, M. (1997). Assessing environments for older people with chronic illness. *Journal of Mental Health and Aging, 3*, 83–100.

Lenert, L., Morss, S., Goldstein, M., Bergen, M., Faustman, W., & Garber, A. (1997). Measurement of the validity of utility elicitations performed by computerized interview. *Medical Care, 35*, 915–920.

Lin, C. (1996). Patient satisfaction with nursing care as an outcome variable: Dilemmas for nursing evaluation researchers. *Journal of Professional Nursing, 12*, 207.

Littell, R. C., Milliken, G. A., Stroup, W. W., & Wolfinger, R. D. (1996). *SAS system of mixed models*. Cary, NC: SAS Institute.

Liu, X., Teresi J., & Waternaux C. (in press). Modeling the decline pattern in functional measures from a prevalent cohort study. *Statistics in Medicine*.

Liu, X., Tsai, W., & Stern, Y. (1996). A functional decline model for prevalent cohort data. *Statistics in Medicine, 15*, 1023–1032.

Lord, F. M. (1980). Applications of item response theory to practical test problems. Reading, MA: Addison-Wesley.

Lord, F. M., & Novick, M. R. (1968). *Statistical theories of mental test scores (with contributions by A. Birnbaum)*. Reading, MA: Addison-Wesley.

Maciejewski, M. (1997). Generic measures. In R. L. Kane (Ed.), *Understanding health care outcomes research* (pp. 19–52). Gaithersburg, MD: Aspen.

Maciejewski, M., Kawiecki, J., & Rockford, T. (1997). Satisfaction. In R. L. Kane (Ed.) *Understanding health care outcomes research* (pp. 67–89). Gaithersburg, MD: Aspen.

Magaziner, J. (1997). Use of proxies to measure health and functional outcomes in effectiveness research in persons with Alzheimer Disease and related disorders. *Alzheimer Disease and Associated Disorders, 11*, 168–174.

McCasin, R. (1988). Reframing research on service use among the elderly: An analysis of recent findings. *The Gerontologist, 28*, 592–599.

Mechanic, D. (1979). Correlates of physician utilization: Why do major multivariate studies of physician utilization find trivial psychosocial and organizational effects? *Journal of Health and Social Behavior, 20*, 387–396.

Mechanic, D. (1989). Medical sociology: Some tensions among theory, method and substance. *Journal of Health and Social Behavior, 30*, 147–160.

Meenan, R. F., Gertman, P. M., & Mason, J. H. (1980). Measuring health status in arthritis: *The AIMS, Arthritis Rheum, 23*, 146–152.

Meredith, W. (1993). Measurement invariance, factor analysis and factorial invariance. *Psychometrika, 58*, 525–543.

Mitchell, P. H., Heinrich, J., Moritz, P., & Hinshaw, A. S. (1997). Outcome measures and care delivery systems. *Medical Care, 35*, NS1–NS5.

Mitchell, P., Shannon, S., Cain, K., & Hegyvary, S. (1996). Critical care outcomes: Linking structures, processes, organizational and clinical outcomes. *American Journal of Geriatrics Care, 5*, 353.

Mitchell, P. H., & Shortell, S. M. (1997). Adverse outcomes and variations in organization of care delivery. *Medical Care, 35*, NS19–NS32.

Montgomery, R. J. V. (1994). Commentary: Family measures in the special care unit context. *Alzheimer Disease & Associated Disorders, 8*(Suppl.1), S242–S246.

Moos, R. H. (1994). *Group environment scale manual*. New York: Consulting Psychologists Press.

Moos, R. H., & Houts, P. S. (1968). Assessment of the social atmosphere of psychiatric wards. *Journal of Abnormal Psychology, 73*, 595–604.

Moos, R. H., & Lemke, S. (1994). *Group residences for older adults*. New York: Oxford University Press.

Morley, J. E., & Miller, D. K. (1992). Editorial: Total quality assurance: An important step in improving care for older individuals. *Journal of the American Geriatrics Society, 40*, 974–975.

Morris, J. N., Fries, B. E., Steel, K., Ikegami, N., Bernabei, R., Carpenter, G. I., Gilgen, R., Hirdes, J. P., & Topinkova, E. (1997). Comprehensive clinical assessment in community setting: Applicability of the MDS-HC. *Journal of the American Geriatrics Society, 45*, 1017–1024.

Morris, J. N., Hawes, C., Fries, B. E., Phillips, C. D., Mor, V., Katz, S., Murphy, K., Drugovich, M. L., & Friedlob, A. S. (1990). Designing the National Resident Assessment Instrument for nursing homes. *The Gerontologist, 39*, 293–307.

Murdaugh, C. (1997). Health-related quality of life as an outcome in organizational research. *Medical Care, 35*, NS41–NS48.

Muthen, B. O. (1991). Analysis of longitudinal data using latent variable models with varying parameters. In L. Collins & J. Horn (Eds.), *Best methods for the analysis of change: Recent advances, unanswered questions, future directions.* Washington, DC: American Psychological Association.

National Institute of Health Task Force on Medical Rehabilitation Research. (1990). *Report of the Task Force on Medical Rehabilitation Research.* Washington, DC: Author.

Nagi, S. Z. (1965). Some conceptual issues in disability and rehabilitaton. In M. B. Sussman (Eds.), *Sociology and rehabilitation* (pp. 100–113). Washington, DC: American sociological association.

Nelson, E., Larson, C., Hayes, R., Nelson, S., Ward, D., & Batalden, P. B. (1992). The physician and employee judgement system: Reliability and validity of a hospital quality measurement method. *Quality Review Bulletin, 18*–284.

Nesselroade, J. R., & Thompson, W. W. (1995). Selection and related threats to group comparisons: An example comparing factorial structures of higher and lower ability groups of adult twins. *Psychological Bulletin, 117*, 271–284.

Nitz, N. M. (1997). Comorbidity. In R. L. Kane (Ed.), *Understanding health care outcomes research* (pp. 153–174). Gaithersburg, MD: Aspen.

Noelker, L. S., & Bass, D. M. (1989). Home care for elderly persons: Linkages between formal and informal caregivers. *Journal of Gerontology: Social Sciences, 44*, S63–70.

Ory, M., Cooper, J., & Siu, A. (Eds.) (1998) Organizational issues in the delivery of primary care to older Americans [special issue]. *Health Services Research, 33*(Suppl.).

Ouslander, J. G. (1997). The Resident Assessment Instrument (RAI): Promise and pitfalls. *Journal of the American Geriatrics Society, 45*, 975–976.

Palmer, R. H., & Chapman, R. H. (1997). *Quality of care for medicare beneficiaries: Implications of changing health care financing mechanisms.* Washington, DC: American Association for Retired Persons.

Parkerson, G. R., Michener, J. L., Yarnall, K. S. H., & Hammond, W. E. (1997). Duke Case-Mix System (DUMIX) for ambulatory health care. *Journal of Clinical Epidemiology, 50*, 1385–1394.

Patrick, D. L. (1997). Finding health-related quality of life outcomes sensitive to health-care organization and delivery. *Medical Care, 35*, NS49–NS57.

Phillips, C. D., Chu, C. W., Morris, J. N., & Hawes, C. (1993). Effects of cognitive impairment on the reliability of geriatric assessments in nursing homes. *Journal of the American Geriatrics Society, 41*, 136–142.

Rahim, M. A., & Bonoma, T. V. (1979). Managing organizational conflict: A model for diagnosis and intervention. *Psychological Reports, 44*, 1323–1344.

Rahim, M. A., & Magner, N. R. (1994). Convergent and discriminant validity of the Rahim Organizational Conflict Inventory-II. *Psychological Reports, 74*, 35–38.

Rahim, M. A., & Magner, N. R. (1995). Confirmatory factor analysis of the styles of handling interpersonal conflict: First-order factor model and its invariance across groups. *Journal of Applied Psychology, 80*, 122–132.

Rantz, M. J., Popejoy, L., Mehr, D. R., Zwygart-Stauffacher, M., Hicks, L. L., Grando, V., Conn, V. S., Porter, R., Scott, J., & Maas, M. (1997). Verifying nursing home care quality using minimum data set quality indicators and other quality measures. *Journal of Nursing Care Quality, 12*(2), 54–62.

Rosenkranz, S., & Luft, H. (1997). Expenditures models for prospective risk adjustment: Choosing the measures appropriate for the problem. *Medical Care Research and Review, 54*(2), 123–143.

Rosenthal, G. E., & Shannon, S. E. (1997). The use of patient perceptions in the evaluation of health-care delivery systems. *Medical Care, 35*(Suppl.), NS58–NS68.

Rothenberg, B. M., Mooney, C., & Curtis, L. (1997). Measures of severity of illness and comorbidity. In E. Andresen, B. Rothenberg, & J. G. Zimmer (Eds.), *Assessing the health status of older adults* (pp. 92–142). New York: Springer Publishing Co.

Sainfort, F. C., Ramsay, J. D., & Monato, H. (1995). Conceptual and methodological sources of variation in the measurement of nursing facility quality: An evaluation of 24 models and an empirical study. *Medical Care Research Review, 52*(1), 60–87.

Schmittdiel, J., Selby, J. V., Grumbach, K., & Quesenberry, C. P. (1997). Choice of a personal physician and patient satisfaction in a health maintenance organization. *Journal of the American Medical Association, 278*, 1596–1599.

Schnelle, J. F. (1997). Can nursing homes use the MDS to improve quality? *Journal of the American Geriatrics Society, 45*, 1027–1028.

Schnelle, J. (in press). Organization capacity. In Institute of Medicine (Ed.), *Improving the quality of care in long-term care*. Washington, DC: National Academy Press.

Schnelle, J. F., Ouslander, J. G., & Cruise, P. A. (1997). Policy without technology: A barrier to improving nursing home care. *The Gerontologist, 37*(4), 527–532.

Schnelle, J. F., Ouslander, J. G., Osterweil, D., & Blumenthal, S. (1993). Total quality management: Administrative and clinical applications in nursing homes. *Journal of the American Geriatrics Society, 41*, 1259–1266.

Shaughnessy, P., Crisler, K., Schlenker, R. E., & Arnold, A. (1997). Outcomes across the care continuum: Home health care. *Medical Care*, SN115–NS123.

Shaughnessy, P. W., Kramer, A. W., Hittle, D. F., & Steiner, J. F. (1993). Quality of care in nursing homes: Findings and implications. *Health Care Financing Review, 16*, 55–83.

Sheridan, J. F., White, J., & Fairchild, T. J. (1992). Ineffective staff, ineffective supervision, or ineffective administration? Why some nursing homes fail to provide adequate care. *Gerontologist, 32*(3), 334–341.

Shortell, S. M., Rousseau, D. M., Gillies, R. R., Devers, K. J., & Simons, T. L. (1991). Organizational assessment in Intensive Care Units (ICUs): Construct development, reliability and validity of the ICU Nurse-Physician Questionnaire. *Medical Care, 29*, 709–726.

Shue, V., Beck, C., & Lawton, M. P. (1996). Measuring affect in frail and cognitively impaired elders. *Journal of Mental Health and Aging, 2,* 259–271.

Sofaer, S. (1998). Aging and primary care: An overview of organizational and behavioral issues in the delivery of health care services to older Americans. In M. G. Ory, J. Cooper, & A. Siu (Eds.), Organizational issues in the delivery of primary care to older Americans [Special Issue]. *Health Services Research, 33,* (Suppl.), 298–321.

Soldo, B., & Myllyluoma, J. (1983). Caregivers who live with dependent elderly. *Gerontologist, 23,* 605–611.

Speigel, D., & Younger, J. B. (1972). Ward climate and community stay of psychiatric patients. *Journal of Consulting and Clinical Psychology, 39,* 62–69.

Stewart, A. L., & Ware, J. E. (1992). *Measuring functioning and well-being: The medical outcomes approach.* Durham: Duke University Press.

Stone, R. A., Obrosky, S., Singer, D. E., Kapoor, W. N., Fine, M. J., & the Pneumonia Patient Outcome Research Team (PORT) Investigators. (1995). Propensity score adjustment for pretreatment differences between hospitalized and ambulatory patients with community-acquired pneumonia. *Medical Care, 33,* AS56–AS66.

Strasser, D. C., Falconer, J. A., & Martino Saltzmann, D. (1994). The rehabilitation team: Staff perceptions of the hospital environment, the interdisciplinary team environment, and interprofessional relations. *Archives of Physical Medicine and Rehabilitation, 75,* 177–182.

Swanson, M. W. (1995). Care plan assessment of visual status and evaluated vision among nursing home residents. *Optometry and Vision Science, 72,* 151–154.

Tennstedt, S. L., Sullivan, L. M., McKinlay, J. B., & D'Agostino, R. B. (1990). How important is functional status as a predictor of service use by older people? *Journal of Aging and Health, 2,* 439–461.

Teresi, J. (1994). Methodological issues in the study of chronic care populations. *Alzheimer's Disease and Associated Disorders: An International Journal, 8*(Suppl. 1), S247–S273.

Teresi, J., Golden, R., Cross, P., Gurland, B., Kleinman, M., & Wilder, D. (1995). Item bias in cognitive screening measures: Comparisons of elderly white, Afro-American, Hispanic, and high and low education subgroups. *Journal of Clinical Epidemiology, 48,* 473–483.

Teresi, J., Grant, L., Holmes, D., & Ory, M. (1998). Staffing in special and traditional and special dementia care units: Preliminary findings from the NIA collaborative dementia care studies. *Journal of Gerontological Nursing,* 49–53.

Teresi, J., & Holmes, D. (1992) Should the MDS be used as a research instrument? *Gerontologist, 32*(2), 148–149.

Teresi, J., & Holmes, D. (1994). Overview of methodological issues in gerontological and geriatric measurement. In M. P. Lawton & J. A. Teresi (Eds.), *Annual Review Of Gerontology and Geriatrics: Focus on assessment techniques* (Vol. 14, pp. 1–22). New York: Springer Publishing Co.

Teresi, J., & Holmes, D. (1997a). Methodological issues in cognitive assessment and their impact on outcome measurement. *Alzheimer Disease and Associated Disorders: An International Journal, 11*, S6, 146–155.

Teresi, J., & Holmes, D. (1997b). Reporting source bias in estimating prevalence of cognitive impairment. *Journal of Clinical Epidemiology, 50*, 175–184.

Teresi, J., Holmes, D., Benenson, E., Monaco, C., Barrett, V., Ramirez, M., & Koren, M. (1993a). A primary care nursing model in long-term care facilities: Evaluation of impact on affect, behavior, and socialization. *Gerontologist, 33*, 667–674.

Teresi, J., Holmes, D., Benenson, E., Monaco, C., Barrett, V., Ramirez, M., & Koren, M. (1993b) A primary care nursing model in urban and rural long-term care facilities: Attitudes, morale, and satisfaction of residents and staff. *Research on Aging, 15*, 414–432.

Teresi, J., Lawton, M. P., Holmes, D., & Ory, M. (1996). Guest Editorial: Measurement issues in older chronic care populations. *Journal of Mental Health and Aging, 2*, 147–148.

Teresi, J., Lawton, M. P., Holmes, D., & Ory, M. (1997). Measurement issues in older chronic care populations. *Journal of Mental Health and Aging, 3*, 3–4.

Teresi, J., Lawton, P., Ory, M., & Holmes, D. (1994). Overview of measurement issues in chronic care populations. *Alzheimer's Disease and Associated Disorders: An International Journal, 8*(Suppl. 1), S144–S183.

Thompson, B., & Daniel, L. G. (1996). Factor analytic evidence for the construct validity of scores: A historical overview and some guidelines. *Educational and Psychological Measurement, 56*, 197–208.

Trickey, F., Maltais, D., Gosselin, C., & Robitaille, Y. (1993). Adapting older people's homes to promote independence. *Physical and Occupational Therapy in Geriatrics, 12*, 1–14.

Van der Linden, W. J., & Hambleton, R. K. (1995). *Handbook of modern item response theory*. New York: Springer Publishing Co.

Volicer, L., & Hurley, A. (1997). Comorbidity in Alzheimer's Disease. *Journal of Mental Health and Aging, 3*, 5–17.

Ware, J. E. (1987). Standards for validating health measures: Definition and content. *Journal of Chronic Diseases, 40*, 473–480.

Welch, W. P. (1997). Commentary. *Medical Care Research and Review, 54*, 144–147.

Weisman, G. D., Calkins, M., & Sloane, P. (1994). The environmental context of special care. *Alzheimer's Disease and Associated Disorders Journal, 8*, S308–S320.

Wholey, D. R., Burns, L. R., & Lavizzo-Mourey, R. (1997, September). *Dimensions of managed care and the delivery of primary care to the elderly*. Paper presented at the AHCPR-NIA Conference on Aging and Primary Care: An Overview of Organizational Issues in the Delivery of Health Care Services to Older Americans, Washington, DC.

Wholey, D. R., Burns, L. R., & Lavizzo-Mourey, R. (1998). Managed care and the delivery of primary care to the elderly and the chronically ill. In M. G. Ory, J. Cooper, & A. Siu (Eds.), Organizational issues in the delivery of primary care to older Americans [Special Issue]. *Health Services Research, 33* (Suppl.), 322–353.

Wolinsky, F. (1994). Health services utilization among older adults: Conceptual, measurement and modeling issues in secondary analysis. *The Gerontologist, 34,* 470–475.

Wolinsky, F. D., & Johnson, R. J. (1991). The use of health services among older adults. *Journal of Gerontology: Social Sciences, 46,* S345–S357.

Wolinsky, F. D., & Johnson, R. J. (1992). Widowhood, health status, and the use of health services among older adults: A cross-sectional and prospective approach. *Journal of Gerontology: Social Sciences, 47,* S8–S16.

Wray, N., Hollingsworth, J., Petersen, N., & Ashton, C. (1997). Case-mix adjustment using administrative database: A paradigm to guide future research. *Medical Care Research and Review, 54*(3), 326–356.

Zeger S. L., & Liang, K-Y. (1992). Overview of methods for the analysis of longitudinal data. *Statistics in Medicine, 11,* 1825–1839.

Zimmer, J. G., Rothenberg, B. M., & Andresen, E. M. (1997). Functional assessment. In E. Andresen, B. Rothenberg, & J. G. Zimmer (Eds.), *Assessing the health status of older adults* (pp. 1–40). New York: Springer Publishing Co.

Zinn, J. S., Lavizzo-Mourey, R. J., & Taylor, L. M. (1993). Measuring satisfaction with care in the nursing home setting: The nursing home resident satisfaction scale. *Journal of Applied Gerontology, 12,* 452–565.

Zinn, J. S., & Mor, V. (1998) Organizational structure & the delivery of primary care to older Americans. In M. G. Ory, J. Cooper, & A. Siu (Eds.), Organizational issues in the delivery of primary care to older Americans [Special Issue]. *Health Services Research, 33* (Suppl.), 354–380.

6

Family and Nursing Home Staff's Perceptions of Quality of Life in Dementia

Margaret A. Perkinson

Quality of life looms large as a concept of central concern in M. Powell Lawton's body of work. His continuing efforts to define it, measure it, and understand the factors that affect it suggest avenues of further research and practice that promise to enhance the life experience of older adults. His early and continued work to extend this concept to persons with dementia has contributed greatly to the growing interest in understanding the inner world of the Alzheimer's patient. In applying this concept to the study of persons with dementia, Lawton was one of the first to challenge both researchers and practitioners to move beyond the limits of mere custodial care. A growing number of gerontologists now acknowledge the continuation of selfhood in dementia and the demented person's continued potential for communication. In this chapter I will provide a brief overview of some of Lawton's contributions to the understanding of quality of life, focusing on quality of life in dementia, and then turn to current areas of research that have been enriched by his work.

LAWTON'S NOTION OF QUALITY OF LIFE

Lawton defines quality of life as "the evaluation, by both subjective and social-normative criteria, of the behavioral and environmental situation of the person" (Lawton, 1994, p.138). In his discussion of the conceptual framework underlying quality of life, he describes four major sectors that comprise its multidimensional content (Lawton, 1983, 1994). Behavioral competence is the socio-normative or objective evaluation of the individual in dimensions of biological and functional health, cognition, social behavior, and time use. Perceived quality of life is the individual's subjective evaluation of his or her own functioning in any of the behavioral competence dimensions. The quality of the external environment (including home, neighborhood, social networks) and psychological well-being, i.e., the "weighted evaluated level of the person's competence and perceived quality in all domains of contemporary life" (Lawton, 1991, p. 11) comprise the remaining domains.

Lawton's inclusion of both subjective as well as objective evaluations of quality of life, plus his insistence on attending to positive as well as negative features of life, pose special challenges in investigating the quality of life of persons with dementia.

QUALITY OF LIFE IN DEMENTIA

In spite of its significance and implications for practice, it is perhaps not surprising that the study of quality of life in dementia has been relatively neglected. Until rather recently, the medical model has dominated the study of dementia. The person with Alzheimer's Disease or a related disorder was typically reduced to his or her neurobiology (Downs, 1997), and the "death of the self" was assumed for these individuals. However, a growing interest in the psychosocial aspects of dementia has fueled a growing debate over the nature of the self and subjective experience of persons with Alzheimer's Disease or related disorders. Lawton (1994) identified this as a critical area for future research and has done much to advance its study by initiating psychosocial studies of dementia and addressing key conceptual and methodological issues in this field.

His early efforts to improve the quality of life of persons with dementia challenged the conventional wisdom of the day that equated quality dementia care with custodial care. Working with a multidisciplinary team of researchers and practitioners (Lawton, Fulcomer, & Kleban, 1984; Leibowitz, Lawton, & Waldman, 1979), he embarked on one of the first studies of social and behavioral aspects of dementia. Investigating the impact of the physical environment on dementia, Lawton and his colleagues developed the Weiss Institute of the Philadelphia Geriatric Center, a precursor to today's special care units.

In another early project with his PGC colleagues (Brody, Kleban, Lawton, & Silverman, 1971), Lawton turned his attention to "excess disabilities" in dementia (areas of functioning that showed some potential for change), developing a program of individualized assessment and care planning that resulted in some increments of improvement in these areas. These early projects offered the hope that it was possible to maintain or, in some cases, even improve the functioning of people with dementia and thus impact on their quality of life.

In his more recent work in dementia, Lawton has turned his attention to the study of more elusive aspects of quality of life: the subjective or inner states of the demented person and the methodological issues in evaluating these states. Critics of the field (Cotrell & Schultz, 1993; Herskovits, 1995; Lyman, 1989) have maintained that the perspective of the person with dementia has been largely ignored in dementia research, and researchers have made little effort to understand the feelings and preferences of Alzheimer's patients. This may be due in part to the traditional model of dementia that posits a process of "unbecoming" or loss of self, in which victims of dementia are seen as lacking subjective experience. Lawton's recent work represents a significant contribution to the new wave of inquiry into the subjectivity of dementia (Cohen & Eisdorfer, 1986; Downs, 1997; Herskovits, 1995; Kitwood, 1993; Sabat and Harre, 1992). A crucial stance underlying his research is his view that the person with dementia continues to be a human being, an individual whose sense of self continues, however difficult it may be to discern. Our goal, as responsible and humane contributors to the field, should be to identify ways to sustain and encourage the continuation of this sense of self.

In his recent work he confronts the methodological challenges of deciphering the subjective quality of life of persons who have limited ability to give verbal expression to their inner experiences. Expressions of emotion represent neglected but promising indicators of quality of life of the demented. With PGC colleagues, Lawton has developed and refined the Philadelphia Geriatric Center Affect Rating Scale to operationalize these expressions of inner states (Lawton, Van Haitsma, & Klapper, 1996; Lawton et al., 1996). This scale measures both positive states (pleasure and interest) as well as negative states (sadness, worry/anxiety, and anger), relying on direct observation and coding of facial expressions, body movement, and other cues of the demented person. Research at the Philadelphia Geriatric Center (Lawton, 1994; Lawton, Perkinson, et al., 1996), based on extensive observational data and the use of this scale, has demonstrated that even persons with moderate to severe levels of dementia exhibit a variety of emotions and that these emotions are clearly related to the social and physical contexts in which they take place. Recent research by Danner and Friesen (1995), Hallberg, Edberg, Nordmark, Johnsson, and Norberg, (1993), and Jansson, Norberg, Sandman, Ayhlin, and Asplund (1993) support this work, indicating that even severely demented persons experience an awareness of and a reaction to themselves, their condition, and their environment.

As social gerontologist Jay Gubrium (1988, p. 250) suggests:

Even though there may be lack of cognitive ability, there are still messages of the heart, the meanings and intentions that lie behind the gestures and confused speech.

Lawton's research has attempted to decipher these "messages of the heart," to document and understand the expression of emotion in persons with dementia, and thus gain insight into their preferences, wishes, and needs. If researchers and caregivers can discriminate positive and negative states and from these cues infer the preferences, likes, and dislikes of the person with dementia, they will be better able to evaluate the effects of caregiving efforts and interventions. With a heightened sensitivity and awareness of subjective states of persons with dementia, researchers and those involved in dementia care should be better able to identify those settings, events, behaviors, and conditions that tend to precede or provoke expressions of positive and of negative states. Such information should provide increased insight into variation in emotional states and suggest ways to optimize environments so that positive states are more likely to occur. Finally and most importantly, if we can assess the inner states, feelings, and needs of the person with dementia, we will be better able to relate to that individual as a person rather than a diseased entity.

ASSESSING CAREGIVER'S ASSESSMENTS OF QUALITY OF LIFE IN DEMENTIA

Lawton's body of work on quality of life and the assessment of subjective states in dementia has greatly influenced my own research. For several years I collaborated with him and Dr. Kimberly Van Haitsma on the project: "Emotion and Dementia: Its Measurement and Comprehension by Caregivers," funded by the Alzheimer's Association. While the main thrust of this project was to refine the PGC Affect Rating Scale, my role was to provide a more qualitative approach to the assessment of inner states of persons with dementia. As an anthropologist who has focused on issues of dementia and caregiving, I wanted to investigate the process of assessment of subjective states as conducted by experienced lay and paraprofessional caregivers (i.e., family members and nurses' aides). I reasoned that a number of these caregivers, because of their close and continued contact with dementia patients, may have refined effective strategies for interpreting emotion in dementia, perhaps developing heightened sensitivities to nuances of expression or gestures of the demented person. By collecting their narratives of their experiences with persons with dementia, I elicited accounts of these strategies, along with caregivers' general understandings or folk models of dementia. These lay understandings included interpretations of the impact of dementia both on the brain and on the experience and expression of emotion. Ultimately, I wanted to now how the characteristics of the caregiver's folk model of dementia influences the way he or she "reads" a dementia patient. I wanted to identify the specific criteria caregivers used in identifying various emotions and the conceptual models they employed both to understand the impact of dementia and to frame their assessments of emotions.

In my analyses, I relied heavily on the literature of psychological anthropology, especially Holland and Quinn's book *Cultural Models in Language and Thought* (1987) and D'Andrade's essay in that volume, "A Folk Model of the Mind" (1987). Much of this work is devoted to the description and explication of conceptual models, or schemas, mental processing mechanisms that frame experience. As an abstract representation of the components and structures of a particular domain, a schema enables one to interpret experience and selectively focus on those cues or elements of experience identified as relevant within the model.

In their discussion of how knowledge is embodied in cultural models, Quinn and Holland (1987) distinguish between two types of schemas: proposition-schemas and image-schemas. Proposition-schemas "specify concepts and the relations which hold among them" (Quinn & Holland, 1987, p. 25). One proposition is linked to another, often by various causal assumptions.

In contrast, image-schemas may be regarded as gestalts much in the same way that visual images are. Image-schemas may contain both visual and kinesthetic components. They are based on metaphors from the physical world, e.g., physical properties and relationships such as motion and shape that are readily comprehended and can be used to interpret more intangible phenomena. For example, in Lakoff and Kovecses' (1987) analysis of the image-schema of anger, anger is conceptualized as a hot liquid within a container. Such a schema allows one to then think of anger as reaching a boiling point, rising, pressing against its limits, and then exploding. According to Quinn and Holland (1987), image-schemas work through metaphor. Metaphor allows the intangible to be reconceptualized in terms provided by the tangible image conveyed within the image-schema. Through the gestalt provided by the image-schema, multiple relations inherent in the target phenomena may become more easily understandable. The process of mapping from physical domains encompassed in schemas to intangible target domains allows one to "run mental models" to simulate what could happen under various conditions (Collins & Gentner, 1987).

The in-depth interview that I used to elicit informants' schemas of dementia was greatly influenced by D'Andrade's (1987) investigation of folk models of the mind. It consisted of a series of questions that focused on the nature of dementia and its impact on the experience and expression of emotions; the intensity and control of emotions; and the causes or triggers of emotions. I also asked the caregivers to share their perceptions of dementia's effect on thought processes, memory, personality, and social interaction or relationships. The following case studies illustrate two very different schemas of dementia and the mind, elicited from individuals with very different histories of experience with demented persons.

Case #1

Mrs. Steiner was a middle-aged daughter whose mother has resided on the dementia unit a number of years. Although her mother was severely demented and could no longer communicate verbally, the daughter visited her regularly and continued to feel close to her. Her discussion of dementia was based primarily on her understanding of her mother's condition, with occasional references to other residents on the floor, whom she knew on a first-name basis.

Although she felt persons with dementia do have emotions, their experience and expression of those emotions is significantly altered. In her words: "They (emotions) probably are not as sharp as they would be. They don't see the full impact of a bad, I say bad more than a good, happening."

With a decreased ability to perceive and evaluate events and phenomena in his or her environment, the demented person is unable to fully realize their impact or significance. As a result, in the view of this woman, any emotional response would be attenuated or "dulled."

While she was unsure whether her mother still experienced certain complex feelings such as guilt, sympathy, or interest, when asked to comment on a list of emotions the daughter agreed that her mother continued to experience a variety of inner states such as pleasure, anger, depression, contentment, love, hate, dislike, joy, embarrassment, sadness, surprise, boredom, disgust, and mourning.

Even though she retained many of her previous emotions, the daughter felt her mother might not feel and did not express these emotions with the same intensity. Present conditions or past memories that would have previously elicited strong negative emotions now seemed to evoke little response:

> I think my mother's emotions are very much intact with her dementia, and as she was getting to this point, she may have been lessening her acuteness of certain pains that she had experienced earlier in her life. I can see her . . . being less in pain from certain memories, or not talking about it as much.

Her image of her mother's condition was of a deteriorating brain and diminishing senses, that resulted in an inner world that was "a faded, little bit of a cloudy environment, as opposed to being in full command of all of your faculties."

A diminished personality or sense of self accompanied this faded inner world. The daughter's conceptual model included an understanding of the personality and the self as shaped by the social and cultural environment. In her view, the environment is reflected in the self, in what one thinks and how one reacts. If one lacks a full awareness of the environment, one will not react as fully:

> They (persons with dementia) don't have as much personality because they don't have the shaded opinions. They're not as in touch with their environment, you know, the world around them which shapes their personality, their likes, dislikes...as they would have been before. You know, consciousness of monetary things and material things, and decisions, and opinions, and rights and wrongs, and insults and non-insults. You know, these are the things that reflect in a person, the things that we think and how we react to our environment. If she's not getting a full acuteness or awareness of her environment, she's not really going to react.

When asked to explain what caused or provoked certain emotions in her mother, the daughter referred to both internal and external triggers. The internal trigger, an inability to express herself, provoked anger and frustration. The significance of this frustration could only be understood within the context of the mother's past history (or the daughter's version of that history). The daughter described her mother as an extremely well-read and articulate woman, who placed great value on her ability to communicate:

My mother's vocabulary is much bigger than mine. She read everything she could put her hands on. So it was very troublesome and frustrating for her when she could not have a discussion with one of her physicians and really speak with the right words and the right level. All those things are very important to her.

Other triggers of emotion were of a more social nature, and again, were interpreted within the daughter's model of dementia (specifically as it related to social interactions and relationships), and the daughter's rendition of her mother's past preferences.

If she could talk now, I promise you, she would be embarrassed, she would be disgusted at some of the things she was looking at, and she would be critical of some of the people that are walking around like children pulling up their dresses. I mean, up to 6 months ago she thought that was disgraceful. She would point out to me all the different people, "I want to stay away from her. Get away, stop going near us . . ." and just very critical of all the things that she was seeing.

Case #2

A second, contrasting conceptual model was reflected in some of the interviews of the nurses' aides who worked on the dementia floor. The following is based primarily on the interview with Anna, a woman who had worked as an aide for 32 years. Twenty-one of those years were spent on the dementia unit.

Anna also felt that persons with dementia could both feel and express emotions. In contrast to the faded, diminished inner world of the dementia patient described above, however, Anna thought that the residents on the unit tended to be *more* emotional, and those emotions were stronger. Demented persons were less able to control these emotions, and engaged in displays of emotion foreign to their "previous selves":

I think it (dementia) makes them more (emotional) because I think that once upon a time, before these people got that way, some of them were different people. Some things they say, cursing and carrying on, that they never did before.

Nevertheless, she felt many residents fluctuated between "good" and "bad" days, when they were more or less in control.

While Anna felt demented persons generally did not feel emotions such as guilt, sympathy, surprise, or mourning, she agreed with the daughter described earlier that demented persons can feel a wide array of emotions.

Based on her many years of experience working closely with dementia patients, Anna felt she was something of an expert in reading or interpreting residents' emotions and communicating with people who could no longer verbally express themselves.

Anna: You know, when you work with people like that for so long, you really get to know how they feel about things. I sometimes say to Mildred, "You feel okay, Mildred?" and she'll make a frown, I say, "You don't feel good?" and then she'll make a different frown, you know.

Interviewer: So there are different types of frowns?

Anna: Yeah, different types of expressions on her face, as if to say, "Now you know I don't feel good." You know, something like that . . . She might move her mouth, or she might just grunt, and she'll open her eyes. She will let you know she knows what you're talking about.

Anna looked for indicators of intensity of emotion, distinguishing between regular and what she called "half-way" expressions. While a moan or grunt would signal discomfort, the intensity of the communication coupled with knowledge of residents' past habits could cue her to identify specific needs.

A lot of times when they don't feel good like her, she'll moan and groan. You go in there sometimes, she's just moaning and groaning. And sometimes when she just wants a drink, she might moan a little bit, because she was used to drinking a lot at home.

When asked to identify various causes or triggers of emotion, Anna and many of the other aides were more likely than family members to refer to general patterns of emotional display common to many of the residents, such as sundowning:

Maybe towards the afternoon sometimes, some of them get disgusted. I don't know whether they get tired of sitting or they get tired of the noise and, you know, there's a lot of noise out there sometimes.

Another aide suggested that the general movement involved in shift change might also contribute to the increased level of agitation on the floor at that time.

Anna echoed the daughter's observations that certain residents triggered negative emotions in other residents, and agreed with the observations of another aide:

They seem to want to sit there with this person and that person. They'd rather be with one that's demented. They, like, divide themselves up (i.e., according to cognitive ability).

Anna felt that demented residents could recognize others and were aware of other's emotions. They were also sensitive to different social contexts, displaying different emotions or expressive styles and acting in a more dependent manner when family members were present, in contrast to their typical styles with the staff.

But you know, when you get around your children, you want to act like you can't do this because they've got you here and you can't do that. But around us, it is a different ball game. She sits there and she eats with that hand, but if her daughter is around, she won't move it. See? See how smart they are? See?

Anna referred to residents having "good" and "bad" days, when they were more or less in control of their emotions. On the "good" days, the nature of interaction between Anna and a given resident was qualitatively different. A resident might display some level of insight into his or her condition and might reveal and explain their "true" self, their past, and their feelings. At such times residents might apologize for certain behaviors. Anna indicated that her interpretations of a given resident's emotions were modified in light of such a revelation, and she would equate the "real" Mrs. X with the way that resident acted or expressed herself on her "good" day. Anna described a particularly significant example:

So she said, "I want to tell you something. I know I get nasty sometimes, but really that's not the Sarah Jones that used to be." Now listen to this. She says, "I love all of you, especially you. You're my heart. But if I ever say anything to you out of order, please forgive me . . ." This was one of her best days to tell me this, and she picked that day to talk. And everything was perfect. She says, "I was an educated woman. I used to play golf. I used to do all these things. Now I can't do nothing. I get bitter sometimes. It just so happens it falls on you." I hugged her. I said, "Thank you. I'm glad to know that because at least I know who you were." Not that I didn't know, but I wanted her to know that I understood where she was coming from. And she was so happy about it. Even now, if she says something, she'll look at me and she'll say, "You know I didn't mean that." I say, "I know, because you told me one time." But she can really hit you.

These two case studies illustrate two very different ways of thinking about dementia. In the image-schema underlying the daughter's description of her mother's condition, the demented brain is envisioned as deteriorating. This deterioration results in a subjective world that is characterized as "cloudy," a faded, dull blankness. Dementia is seen as a process of inexorable decline. The decline in sensitivity and awareness of the social and physical environment results in the gradual diminishment of the very essence of personhood itself.

The image-schema that structured the nurses' aide's conceptualization of dementia produced a very different picture from that described above. Rather than a process of slow diminishment into nothingness, dementia was seen as an unleashing of wild, uncontrollable urges, behaviors, and emotions that were foreign to the pre-dementia state. Emotions were perceived to grow stronger under the influence of dementia. Dementia did not destroy awareness or sensitivity to social contexts. On the contrary, the aide noted examples of willful (and sometimes successful) manipulation of family members by residents. Although dementia may destroy the ability to communicate verbally, it did not extinguish the ability or desire to communicate through other means. The essence of the person was not seen as fading or eroding. Rather, inner states were seen to fluctuate, with the "real" person continuing on, even though seemingly hidden on "bad" days.

This image of dementia and its effects had definite implications for behavior. It allowed the aide to continue to relate to residents in a humane manner, in spite of occasions of abusive behavior on the part of residents toward her. It also prompted her to attend to nonverbal cues of communication from those who could no longer express themselves verbally.

IMPLICATIONS FOR MODELS OF DEMENTIA CARE

Recent thinking about the nature of the self underscores the significance of lay models of dementia for the quality of life of demented persons. Social constructionist theory posits a core aspect of personhood that is essentially social in nature, constructed within the interaction of a social context (Kitwood, 1993; Sabat & Harre, 1992). The self that is socially and publicly presented is a joint production requiring the cooperation of others to recognize, respond to and confirm it in their actions and reactions in order for that self to come into being. While the neurological impairment characteristic of dementia sets limits, the process of personhood in dementia rests in the interplay between the biological constraints, the personal psychology of the individual, and the social context (Kitwood, 1990; Kitwood & Bredin, 1992). A number of social gerontologists (Bender & Cheston, 1997; Sabat & Harre, 1992) claim the loss of self in dementia is primarily the result of the ways that others view and treat the demented person. A person with Alzheimer's may attempt to construct a particular self, but if his or her partner refuses to cooperate in that constructive process, that self will not come into existence.

Sabat and Harre's (1992) description of the social construction (or destruction) of identity within a nursing home provides a vivid example. An elderly resident refused to join the regularly scheduled bingo game, insisting on strolling around the unit instead. Those who observed him interpreted his behavior as wandering, and viewed him as reclusive and antisocial. After interviewing him, however, the authors found this resident had purposefully chosen not to participate, viewing bingo as a childish diversion that was beneath him. In her ethnographic observations of an adult day care center, Karen Lyman (1988, 1989) noted similar interactions contributing to the loss of personhood. Normal behaviors were consistently interpreted in terms of disease stages once day care participants were labeled as demented.

There are ways to preserve a sense of self among persons with dementia, however. Recent models of dementia care (Bohling, 1991; Jenkins & Price, 1996; Kitwood, 1993) advocate that caregivers employ more active listening skills than those typically required in everyday interactions. In order to facilitate the preservation and maintenance of the self, the caregiver must be actively empathetic, open to the demented person's frame of reference. This includes an open acceptance or provision of "safe space," to allow concerns to emerge without the demented person feeling overwhelmed.

To a greater extent than with nondemented individuals, the person with dementia requires help in defining situations and holding expectations in place. The caregiver should actively collaborate with that person in defining interactions. This would include producing conversational cues that clearly signal the frame of meaning structuring the conversation, and cues that signal frame breaks or changes in the direction of the conversation to new topics (Bohling, 1991). The caregiver also should provide clear feedback, acknowledging and validating the subjective truth of the demented person's experience.

In this approach, caregiving becomes a cooperative and reciprocal engagement in the social construction and maintenance of personhood, rather than a doing to or for a needy patient. This shift in caregiving perspective results in a heightened responsiveness to the needs of the person with dementia, maximizes the demented person's sense of dignity and independence, and helps the caregiver avoid dehumanizing everyday caregiving tasks (Bohling, 1991; Jenkins & Price, 1996).

The caregiver's conceptual model of dementia is obviously crucial to the success of such an approach to dementia care. Caregivers who regard even the most severely demented persons as individuals seek to understand their behaviors, abilities, and expressions by attending to cues and inferring inner states (Jansson et al., 1992). Those who perceive dementia as a disease that extinguishes inner states tend to view the demented as objects. They tend to be less committed to their care, and to focus on custodial aspects of care (Athlin et al., 1990). If health professionals can elicit the schemas of dementia held by the family caregivers and paraprofessionals with whom they work, they will be in a better position to communicate with these people and correct possible misperceptions. By helping caregivers to perceive the potential for personhood in dementia, we can facilitate a more humane approach to care and an enhanced quality of life for persons with dementia.

REFERENCES

Athlin, E., Norberg, A., & Asplund, K. (1990). Caregivers' perceptions and interpretations of severely demented patients during feeding in a task assignment system. *Scandinavian Journal of Caring Sciences, 4*, 147–156.

Bender, M., & Cheston, A. (1997). Inhabitants of a lost kingdom: A model of the subjective experiences of dementia. *Aging and Society, 17*, 513–532.

Bohling, H. (1991). Communications with Alzhemer's patients: An analysis of caregiver listening patterns. *International Journal of Aging and Human Development, 33*, 249–267.

Brody, E. M., Kleban, M. H., Lawton, M. P., & Silverman, H. (1971). Excess disabilities of mentally impaired aged: Impact of individualized treatment. *The Gerontologist, 1*, 124–133.

Cohen, D., & Eisdorfer, C. (1986). *The loss of self: A family resource for the care of Alzheimer's disease and related disorders.* London: W. W. Norton.

Collins, A., & Gentner, D. (1987). How people construct mental models. In D. Holland & N. Quinn (Eds.), *Cultural models in language and thought* (pp. 243–265). Cambridge: Cambridge University Press.

Cotrell, V., & Schulz, R. (1993). The perspective of the patient with Alzheimer's disease: A neglected dimension of dementia research. *Gerontologist, 33*, 205–211.

D'Andrade, R. (1987). A folk model of the mind. In D. Holland & N. Quinn (Eds.), *Cultural models in language and thought* (pp. 63–89). Cambridge: Cambridge University Press.

Danner, D., & Friesen, W. (1995). Are severely-impaired Alzheimer's patients aware of their environment and illness? *Journal of Clinical Geropsychology, 2*, 321–335.

Downs, M. (1997). The emergence of the person in dementia research. *Aging and Society, 17*, 597–607.

Gubrium, J. (1988). Incommunicables and poetic documentation in the Alzheimer's disease experience. *Semiotica, 72*, 235–253.

Hallberg, I., Edberg, A., Nordmark, A., Johnsson, K., & Norberg, A. (1993). Daytime vocal activity in institutionalized severely demented patients identified as vocally disruptive by nurses. *International Journal of Geriatric Psychiatry, 8*, 155–164.

Herskovits, E. (1995). Struggling over subjectivity: Debates about the "self" and Alzheimer's disease. *Medical Anthropology Quarterly, 9*, 146–164.

Holland, D., & Quinn, N. (Eds.). (1987). *Cultural models in language and thought.* Cambridge, England: Cambridge University Press.

Jansson, L., Norberg, A., Sandman, P., Ayhlin, E., & Asplund, K. (1992–1993). Interpreting facial expressions in patients in the terminal stage of Alzheimer's disease. *Omega, 26*, 309–324.

Jenkins, D., & Price, B. (1996). Dementia and personhood: A focus for care? *Journal of Advanced Nursing, 24*, 84–90.

Kitwood, T. (1993). Towards a theory of dementia care: The interpersonal process. *Ageing and Society, 13*, 51–67.

Kitwood, T., & Bredin, K. (1992). Towards a theory of dementia care: Personhood and well-being. *Ageing and Society, 12,* 269–287.

Lakoff, G., & Kovecses, Z. (1987). The cognitive model of anger inherent in American English. In D. Holland & N. Quinn (Eds.), *Cultural models in language and thought* (pp. 195–221). Cambridge, England: Cambridge University Press.

Lawton, M. P. (1983). Environment and other determinants of well-being in older people. *Gerontologist, 23,* 349–357.

Lawton, M. P. (1991). A multidimensional view of quality of life. In J. Birren, J. Lubben, C. Rowe, & D. E. Deutchman (Eds.), *The concept and measurement of quality of life in the frail elderly* (pp. 3–27). New York: Academic Press.

Lawton, M. P. (1994). Quality of life in Alzheimer Disease. *Alzheimer Disease and Associated Disorders, 8,* 138–150.

Lawton, M. P., Fulcomer, M. C., & Kleban, M. H. (1984). Architecture for the mentally impaired elderly: A post occupancy evaluation. *Environment and behavior, 16,* 730–757.

Lawton, M. P., Perkinson, M. A., Van Haitsma, K., Ruckdeschel, K., Seddon, K., & Clunk, L. (1996). *Affect and quality of life in Alzheimer's disease: A guide to the assessment of apparent affect.* Final report submitted to the Alzheimer's Association.

Lawton, M. P., Van Haitsma, K., & Klapper, J. (1996). Observed affect in nursing home residents with Alzheimer's disease. *Journal of Gerontology: Psychological Sciences, 51,* P3–P14.

Leibowitz, B., Lawton, M. P., & Waldman, A. (1979). Designing for confused elderly people: Lessons from the Weiss Institute. *Institute of Architects Journal, 68,* 59–61.

Lyman, K. (1988). Infantilization of elders: Day care for Alzheimer's disease victims. In D. Wertz, *Research in the sociology of health care* (pp. 159–171). Greenwich, CT: JAI Press.

Lyman, K. A. (1989). Bringing the social back in: A critique of the biomedicalization of dementia. *Gerontologist, 29,* 597–605.

Quinn, N., & Holland, D. (1987). Culture and cognition. In D. Holland & N. Quinn (Eds.), *Cultural models in language and thought* (pp. 3–40). Cambridge, England: Cambridge University Press.

Sabat, S. R., & Harre, R. (1992). The construction and deconstruction of self in Alzheimer's disease. *Ageing and Society, 12,* 443–461.

7

Style Versus Substance: The Cross-Cultural Study of Well-Being

Allen Glicksman

For the past 30 years, Powell Lawton has been studying both the substance and measurement of subjective well-being (SWB) (Lawton, 1971, 1972). This term, which at times has been treated as synonymous with other terms such as "life satisfaction," "morale," "happiness," and "psychological well-being," connotes a general state of feeling about self. While there is no precise or completely agreed-upon definition of the term, it is usually assumed that SWB contains some combination of an evaluation of one's current psychological, physiological, material, and social states (Glicksman, 1990). It usually includes both affective and cognitive elements, therefore measuring both emotional status and of a self-evaluation of one's current overall condition. This cognitive element of SWB is measured both in terms of conditions in the past relative to current conditions and the condition of the person conducting the self-evaluation relative to others in the present. SWB is therefore both multidimensional and temporal.

For Lawton, high morale, one related term for SWB, has three elements. First is a positive feeling about oneself and one's worth. Second, there is a feeling that one has a place in the environment and that the environment has value—whether that value is expressed in an acceptance of the environment or in a struggle to change it. Third reflects a sense of realism that tempers the positive outlook. This separates true high morale from pollyannaish fantasy (Lawton, 1971).

The concept of SWB is more general than that of clinical depression. It is not designed as clinical measure, but more as a general gauge of general feelings. SWB is more intertwined with daily events and worldview than clinical states. It responds more to daily events, uplifts as well as hassles, and in general has multiple determinants—general environmental factors, other aspects of well-being (economic and physical), as well as social relations. SWB does share with clinical states of depression a very personal (hence the term subjective) element in how different domains (such as feelings about physical health or income) are evaluated by each individual. As with other mental health states, the same events (such as the loss of a loved one) do not elicit the same responses in every person. Just as most persons who experience events thought to be traumatic do not develop the symptoms of Post-Traumatic Stress Disorder, so it is impossible to predict how specific events will effect the feelings of SWB of any given individual.

But the differences between SWB and clinical states are critical. If SWB is more tied to interaction with the world than more interpsychic states, then it must be more tied into social aspects of life, including attitudes brought to interpret daily events (and interactions) as well as defining of reactions to those events as appropriate or inappropriate forms of behavior. This in turn raises questions about the role of cultural tradition in SWB, since it is through these traditions that such attitudes and values are formed.

Lawton's work in this area is best known through the scales he developed to measure aspects of SWB, most notably the PGC Morale Scale (PGC-MS) and the PGC Affect Scales (PGC-AS; Lawton, 1975). His research into the validity of such scales, not limited to his own scales, continues to the present. His most recent work in this area concerns the impact of level of education on the ability of respondents to understand the meaning of questions designed to measure well-being. This continues a long tradition on his part of understanding the ways in which questions can be easier or more difficult to understand for an older population. For example, one reason the PGC-MS is asked as a series of "Yes/no" questions rather than a Likert scale is Lawton's concern that for the oldest old, a multi-point answer scale might be confusing.

Lawton's interest in patterns of answers and concerns about systematic biases in answer patterns led him to encourage me to investigate a phenomenon he had frequently noticed in analyzing data from his surveys. The pattern he had noticed is that older Jews often report significantly poorer SWB (as measured on these scales) than members of other religious and ethnic groups. This was of special interest because the PGC Morale Scale was standardized in part on a sample of respondents from the York House of PGC, an entirely Jewish population. In fact, it was during this process that the PGC-MS was translated for the first time into another language—Yiddish, for those respondents who had difficulty with the English original.

ETHNICITY AND SUBJECTIVE WELL-BEING

In fact, the PGC-MS has been used among many groups without specific concerns about the sensitivity of the questions to ethnic heritage. Since the development of the PGC-MS in the late 1960s and early 70s, the scale has been used in countless studies with a wide variety of ethnic groups and in many countries. Versions are now available in such exotic languages as Hebrew, Chinese, and as a product of my own research needs, Ukrainian.

It was this use of the scale among so many culturally diverse populations, as well as Lawton's observation that there was a clearly distinct answer pattern among the Jewish respondents, that led me to try to understand the more general role of cultural background in the ways in which persons evaluate and express their sense of SWB, as well as to specifically understand the nature of the patterns found among Jewish respondents. With Lawton's encouragement and mentoring, I completed my doctoral dissertation on the subject of the SWB of older Jews, with a focus on their answer patterns to three scales of SWB, including the PGC-MS (Glicksman, 1990).

Because most research studies in gerontology simply asked about the religion and race of the respondent, and nothing else relevant to their cultural background, there was no way to examine specific ethnic groups and their distinctive cultural heritages. Instead, we could only construct general categories. These general categories (White Catholics, for example), would include persons of many different cultural heritages (here Italians, Irish, and English Catholics among others) all together, even though their cultural heritages are very difference from one another, for example, in terms of expressive style. It would therefore be difficult to compare heterogeneous groups, such as White Catholics, with a relatively homogeneous group such as American Jews, most of whose elderly are either immigrants or children of immigrants from Eastern Europe. This very contrast between homogeneous and heterogeneous groups might alone account for the fact that older Jews were so distinctive in their answer patterns relative to other groups.

While there was little to go on in terms of the gerontological literature, there was certainly evidence in the qualitative studies of middle-aged adult populations that cultural heritage is a significant factor in understanding patterns of mental health status. Classic works in sociology and anthropology, such as *Suicide* by Durkheim (1951) and *People in Pain* by Zborowski (1969) had argued that the rates of mental illness in a population are not governed by the level of oppression that community had experienced (Durkheim) and that the negative emotions sometimes expressed by members of these communities may have more to do with cultural style than real differences in mental health status (Zborowski). In both of these books, the question of the mental health of Jews in particular was considered. Durkheim's conclusion that Jews had lower rates of suicide because of higher levels of communal solidarity and Zborowski's description of Jewish complaining behavior together form a picture of a group where levels of negative affect do not necessarily reflect low levels of SWB. At the same time, their conclusions cannot be taken as proof that the answer patterns of older Jews to questions of SWB will be both unique and worse than that of other groups.

On the other hand, if the pattern of responses from Jewish respondents was really unique and worse than members of other groups we would need to ask why. Are there historical reasons for poorer SWB among Jews, or were we simply looking at cultural difference masquerading as poorer mental health, as in Zborowski? If the latter was the case, then we would need to ask if the scales were of any use at all. Scales designed to measure SWB but that in fact "measured" differences in ethnic heritage would be useless at best, and at worst would provide "data" for those who wish to see certain groups, including Jews, as inferior.

CULTURE AND AFFECT

It seems logical that cultural traditions should affect the way in which persons evaluate and express their sense of SWB. Value systems, which form the base on which various domains such as income and family relations are given weight relative to other domains, emerge from historical experience and cultural systems. For example, a person's depression can be based on failed expectations that emerge from specific value systems that are culturally bound (for example, women should have children; one should make a lot of money). Depression can also reflect a sense of personal isolation that is exacerbated by social factors as described in *Suicide* (Durkheim, 1951). Fundamentally, the roots of personality and style are learned at home, and these values learned at home come from the cultural traditions in the society in which the parents were socialized and live.

Further, appropriate and inappropriate ways of expressing oneself in public are defined by culture as well, through the socialization of children by their parents and the praise or scolding the children receive based on their public behavior. Answer styles are in part defined by culture, so some Jews put a negative twist on a positive answer because of the old fear of the "evil eye" being attracted by good news. Language style can also be expressive. One older Jewish research respondent told a story. When he was a child and went for a cherry soda to the local delicatessen, if the server poured too much cherry syrup into the soda the owner, a Jewish immigrant from Eastern Europe would cry out "Blood, that's my blood being poured out there!" This type of vivid imagery may be an acceptable style in some cultures while considered uncouth and rude in others (not to mention a sign of emotional distress).

There are of course two different ways of looking at this phenomenon. We can see it as cultural style, without imputing a real connection between the style and SWB, or we can say that some cultures provide permission for their adherents to express negative emotions, while others do not. This particular question about the meaning of such expressiveness arises from two sources: Lawton and his thinking about the nature of SWB questions, and the hint from the literature on Jewish expressive behavior. In this way, culturally defined standards, such as the notion that it is boorish to talk about one's health problems in public, seem to be "common sense" learned at home, and not based on values concerning the meaning of suffering that emanate from religious and cultural systems.

The question of whether, independent of cultural style, SWB can be measured to determine how a given individual is feeling, is intimately related to the general question of the connection between culture and SWB. This is not to say that either SWB or depression is simply a product of cultural elements. However, if SWB is even more a product of daily social activity than clinical depression, then how much more so must it have a cultural determinant along with other determinants.

This also leads to another interesting question: Do we need general measures that are independent of culture? If culture is such an important determinant of SWB, then shouldn't it be part of any measure of this domain?

CULTURE AND SUBJECTIVE WELL-BEING:
TWO STUDIES

To understand the relation of SWB to cultural background I decided to test the question raised before: whether Jewish answer patterns are truly distinctive and poorer than other groups. To accomplish this task, as part of my dissertation, I conducted a secondary analysis of the 1968 National Senior Citizens Survey, which asked the PGC-MS questions and also asked extensive questions about ancestry as well as religion and race. This allowed me to construct four groups: Jews of Eastern European heritage, Irish Catholics, Italian Catholics, and Anglo-Presbyterians. These are the same four groups that appeared in *People in Pain* (Zborowski, 1969) and also represent the same religious traditions covered in *Suicide* (Durkheim, 1951). In doing so, I could create four distinct cultural groups based on extensive literature on all four groups. Much of the interpretation of the response patterns of Anglo-Presbyterians to questions of SWB is based on a religious explanation. The Calvinist heritage of this group is called upon to explain their behavior. It suggests that the religious precept that one's response to pain is in fact a measure of how one accepts God's will has been translated into a cultural style of an optimistic attitude and a "stiff upper lip." For this reason, and because the Anglo-Calvinist tradition is at the core of American civilization, the Anglo-Presbyterians were selected for analysis (Ahlstrom, 1975).

The two other groups selected, Irish and Italian Catholics, were also chosen for reasons in addition to their appearance in the two texts already mentioned. The literature on these groups suggested that the expressive style of the Italians would be much like that of the Jews, while the style of the Irish would be much like that of the Anglo-Presbyterians. If these hypothesized relations held true, then two conclusions might be drawn. First, since the historical experience and cultures of these four groups are very unlike each other, there is no reason to think that hypothesized cultural determinants for the behavior of one group (say for the Jews) is likely to be the reason for the similar behavior of a very different group (the Italians). On the other hand, there may be no reason to expect that SWB itself will vary culturally, so if there are distinct patterns among the groups, then some other explanation than real levels of SWB would need to be found to explain the differences (McGoldrick, Pearce, & Giordano, 1982).

The analyses concentrated on the PGC-MS and its three component factors. These factors, Agitation, Loneliness, and Attitude Toward Own Aging, measure three different domains of SWB. In Lawton's original development of the PGC-MS, he described the Agitation factor as symptoms of anxiety as well as dysphoric mood elements. The "Attitude" factor was described as "related to self-perceived change or lack of change as one ages, evaluation of the quality of change" (p. 88). The Lonely factor was described as "acceptance or dissatisfaction with things as they now are" (Lawton, 1975, p. 88).

Though a series of one-way ANOVAs I demonstrated that there were significant differences in the mean scores on two of the PGC-MS factors (Agitation and Loneliness) between the Jewish respondents and the Irish and Anglo-Presbyterians (using the Scheffé test). There were no significant differences on the Attitude Toward Aging factor. The significant differences between the Jewish respondents on the one hand and the Irish and Anglo-Presbyterian respondents on the other on two of the factors certainly confirmed that the Jewish respondents had answer patterns that were distinctive and lower than members of other groups. At the same time however, the lack of any differences between the Jewish and Italian respondents, as well as the lack of any significant differences on the Attitude Toward Own Aging PGC-MS factor, left questions about the nature of this relation. Further, it could not be determined from these analyses whether it was membership in one of these cultural groups that was the deciding factor in determining the scale scores, or whether membership in these groups covaried with other domains that were generally recognized as predictors of SWB.

Using a series of regressions where we controlled for the major predictors of SWB as described in the literature (physical health, socioeconomic status, and positive interactions with friends and family) Jewish status continued to be an independently significant predictor of PGC-MS scores overall and the Agitation factor scores as well. When these analyses were rerun using a larger data set collected at PGC by Lawton, Jewish status was a significant predictor of the overall PGC-MS score and of all three factor scores when controlling for the three domains mentioned above. Clearly, Jewish status had some relation with SWB, or at least with scores designed to measure SWB as compared to the other cultural groups. But what could that relation be? I could not answer the important question of whether these Jewish/non-Jewish differences were a product of real differences in the level of SWB between the Jewish and non-Jewish respondents, or whether they reflected cultural differences in answer styles.

To answer this second question, I developed, again with the mentoring of Lawton, a research project designed to examine the reasons for the differences in answer patterns to SWB questions. This research project was not simply an extension of the dissertation. The evolution of the project also reflected the development of my own thinking. It also was enriched by Lawton's continued research in this area.

I decided that the only way to fully understand the answer patterns for Jews and other ethnic groups to SWB questions was to ask some of the questions in a systematic open-ended manner. In doing so I would be able to understand the reasons for the answers being given to the scale questions, and resolve the question of whether the scales are indeed measuring SWB, cultural differences, or some mixture of the two. By asking the questions first in their traditional close-ended format, and then probing for the reasons that these selected questions were answered in a particular way, I hoped that the open-ended data would provide the needed insight into the reasons for the close-ended answer that the respondent selected. This in turn would provide the data needed to answer two critical questions. First, are the reasons given for negative answers to questions of SWB really signs of low SWB, or is it more cultural style; and second, do the concerns expressed vary systematically by group.

For this project I retained two of the cultural groups from my dissertation: the Jews and the Anglo-Presbyterians. The Jews were selected because they had been the focus of the research initiative from the beginning. The Anglo-Presbyterians were selected because they provided the strongest contrast with the Jews in the analyses conducted for the dissertation and because their tradition is the dominant cultural tradition in the United States. I removed the Irish and Italian Catholics because other than their presence in the earlier studies mentioned, there was no theoretical reason to include them. I replaced them with two groups, each of which allowed me to ask other theoretical questions about the relation between SWB and culture. These two groups are African-American Protestants (mostly Baptist) and Ukrainians of the Ukrainian Greek Catholic faith.

While most work on Jews, including my own, has assumed that distinctive patterns found reflect something about Jewish status, the question has not been asked as to whether something about this generation of older Jews, all born in or children of persons born in Eastern Europe, had anything to do with cultural styles from this region of the world. While prejudice of members of each group toward the other is well documented, questions have not been asked about the possible existence of a common style in expressive behavior. The assumption seems to be that the formal differences between the two groups in terms of culture and faith, as well as the infamous antipathy that some members of each group hold for the other, would negate any chance of common styles in terms of SWB. I wanted to know if there were similarities between the groups. If such similarities exist, then explanations about Jewish behavior would have to be modified to account for their East European origin, and explanations (including my own) that focused entirely on issues internal to the Jewish community and Jewish culture would have to be reevaluated. Further, of the current generation of older Ukrainians and Jews, one would have to assume that the Ukrainians suffered much more, and so if collective suffering is a predictor of lower SWB, then the SWB of the Ukrainians should be lower than that of the Jews. A higher proportion of Ukrainian elders are immigrants to this country, and many came fleeing the devastation of the Second World War. The overwhelming majority of American Jews, although they experienced the Great Depression and are aware of the Holocaust, did not personally experience this last event. Therefore, if level of collective suffering is behind the differences in scores, then the Ukrainians should score lower on these measures than the Jews. Otherwise, if the differences in scores reflect stylistic differences, then it was possible that there would be no significant differences between Ukrainian and Jewish respondents due to their common East European heritage.

The African Americans were selected for similar reasons. The question of whether the scale scores of Anglo-Presbyterians is more a reflection of the Anglo or the Calvinist heritage of these respondents has not been examined in a systematic manner. By bringing a sample of Calvinists by faith but not Anglo by heritage respondents, we can ask where religious tradition ends and cultural style begin in defining answers to SWB questions.

I also made some changes in which scales were used to measure SWB. While retaining the PGC-MS, I replaced the two scales used in the dissertation (the Life Satisfaction Index and the Bradburn Affect Balance Scales) with two more contemporary scales, the Center for Epidemiological Studies Depression Scale (CES-D) and the newly developed PGC Affect Scales (PGC-AS). The CES-D is one of the most popular measures of SWB in use. In theory, it is a clinical scale, with scores over 16 measuring a state of depression. The scale itself is comprised of 20 items that fall into four factors: Somatic Symptoms, Depressive Symptoms, Positive Affect, and Social Interaction. Its widespread use, in various forms (using anywhere from 8 to 11 to all 20 of the items, and changing the four-point scale to a three- or even a two-point scale), justified its use in this study. If there are significant differences by ethnic group in the scale scores, then this is an important factor to consider in analyzing the results of the use of the scale. This second scale represents Lawton's continued thinking about and development of measures of SWB. The PGC Affect Scales (Positive and Negative) measure various emotions. Questions are phrased, "In the past 24 hours, did you feel . . ." and then 10 emotions, from angry to contented, are selected. The time frame can vary. We used 24 hours to distinguish it from the CES-D, where we used "In the last week" as a time frame and from the PGC-MS, where no specific time frame is given.

We are just beginning the analysis of this data collected in the past few years. Therefore, we are not in a position to report on the results of the open-ended questions. However, the preliminary analyses have yielded some interesting results that point not only to answers to questions concerning SWB and cultural background, but also to the importance of Lawton's continued work in this area.

Of the scales used, there were significant differences in the mean scores between Jews and Anglo Protestants on two of the factors on the PGC-MS (Agitation and Lonely) and on two of the factors of the CES-D (Depression and Somatic Symptoms). The two factors of the PGC Morale Scale where ethnic differences were discovered were the same two factors yielding significant differences between white Protestants and Jews in the author's dissertation. Significant differences were also found between the responses of the Jewish respondents and the African-American respondents on the Agitation (PGC-MS) and Lonely factors. There were also significant differences between the Ukrainian respondents and the Protestant respondents (both Anglo and African-American) on the Lonely factor (PGC-MS) and the Somatic Symptoms factor (CES-D).

Two things characterize the differences listed above. The first is that all the differences are between the two East European groups on the one hand and the two American Protestant groups on the other. No matter how much tension has existed with each of these pairs (race hatred between the Anglo and Black Protestants; religious and ethnic hated between Jews and Ukrainians), there are clearly answer patterns that differentiate these two sets of groups. Secondly, the scales which are most sensitive to ethnic differences are those composed entirely or almost entirely of negatively phrased questions. However, the scales which are comprised entirely or almost entirely of positively phrased questions showed no ethnic differences in answer patterns. It is in the scales with the most negatively phrased questions that the real differences lie. The one exception is the Negative PGC-AS. This scale is also characterized by asking about passing emotions rather than ones that might be more trait-like. Perhaps one can excuse a passing feeling of sadness, but not one that seems to stick around.

CONCLUSIONS

What conclusions can we draw from this preliminary analysis? Lawton's own suggestion, when asked about this pattern, was that it is important to look at the nature of the
questions. The scales that allow for negatively phrased questions need permission to
give such answers—they are not socially acceptable. Cultures, by defining appropriate and inappropriate behavior, allow for differences.

Another explanations is that negative answers carry different meanings in different
cultures. What about real differences in SWB? It would seem difficult to make the case
that there are real and significant differences in the levels of SWB without seeing significant differences in the subscales that use positively worded questions. While one
might argue that these scales are measuring other domains, the fact remains that the only
differences found were by this pattern of the wording of the questions. Without cultural
differences in the positive and general social questions, we cannot assume that there are
real differences in SWB by group. Further, we cannot make clinical judgments based on
scale scores.

Also, clearly the most trait-like questions (the PGC-MS) created the most significant
differences, while the fewest differences are in the least trait-like questions—the PGC-
AS. So now we have two dimensions to consider when considering ethnic and cultural
differences: first, the negative/positive nature of the question; second, the extent to which
it is trait or state. Culture then provides context within which one can and cannot express
certain emotions. It is perhaps all right in all the cultures under study to talk about passing feelings, but when emotions, especially negative emotions, are more than a fleeting
state, then talking about them is much more difficult. Perhaps one can excuse oneself a
momentary lapse, while more permanent states can be seen as reflections of character.
One also might wonder if the ability to express negative emotions can be helpful, or
whether they can prevent having an optimistic ideology.

Jews seem to have "permission" for generally more expressive styles than do White
Protestants. There are many reasons for this, some of which reflect specifically Jewish
elements and some of which reflect their East European heritage. For example, as
Judaism has never placed any religious meaning on suffering, only on the relief of suffering, there is no moral onus on complaining. Pain cannot be "donated" as it can be in
Catholicism, or be taken as a test of moral character, as it is in Calvinist Protestantism.
Rather, complaining can serve to let others know that one is in need and provide them
the opportunity to follow a commandment—to relieve the suffering of the afflicted individual. Further, the general East European superstition about the "evil eye" can lead some
people to put everything in negative terms so that good news does not tempt the evil eye
to seek to do damage. For example, one older Jewish woman in an earlier PGC study,
when asked why she does not sleep at night, reported that she worries that her grandchild, who is a student at the Harvard Medical School, works too hard. Certainly this is
an excellent example of the reverse bragging common among those who fear the Evil
Eye or who have learned the style that emerges from that fear. However, on the PGC-
MS, this is a "low morale" answer. Jews have significantly lower scores than White

Protestants on measures of well-being that are primarily phrased in negative terms, but no differences on factors comprised mostly or entirely of questions phrased in a positive manner. Jews therefore have the permission, or perhaps a cultural mandate, to phrase things in either way.

This would all fit nicely into a religious explanation—wherein the Jews have reasons to accept negatively phrased questions and the two Protestant populations do not—were it not for the scores of the Ukrainian respondents. The problem, of course, is that the Ukrainians are like the Jews in their answer patterns.

With the Ukrainians being like the Jews, then it becomes less clear what the explanation is for the behavior. If it is religion, then the Jews should be unlike the Ukrainians as well. The Ukrainians in our sample are almost entirely members of the Ukrainian Catholic Church. As such, they share the faith that pain can be used creatively, that it can be donated to release souls from purgatory and glorify God. We might have to look for an alternative explanation. Could it be that the majority culture (here Russian or Polish) have had a style of talking that was reflected by both Ukrainians and Jews? Certainly other aspects of Jewish culture, such as the distinctive garb of the Hasidim, were borrowed from the Polish nobility. Could the similarity between the two Protestant groups be based more on learning from a majority culture (the African-Americans learning from the Anglo-Americans) than shared religious values? In each case, we are talking about a dominant political culture exercising hegemony over the minority cultures under its sway. These patterns may have as much to do with power and status as any psychic state.

Such a finding could relate to Lawton's concern about class differences in answering questions concerning well-being by pointing to macro-level political issues in defining what constitutes good mental health. This still begs the question of where the values come from, or what will happen when the Jews and Ukrainians have been many generations in the United States, assuming they retain unique ethnic identities. However, if our assumptions are correct, then we can say that the response patterns seen in the answers to questions concerning SWB are influenced by the culture of the world around the respondent, and are not simple intrapsychic measures. Whether this is a bad idea or not depends on the extent to which one assumes that SWB is in part a reaction to the world around us and therefore must be an intimate part of any person's SWB.

Clearly, Lawton's latest attempt to develop a scale has gone beyond his previous attempt in its ability to make one free of certain biases that might affect answering. His current work points to the direction in which this research must move to continue measurement of these domains by scaling.

What can we say about the scales themselves? Are the scales picking up real differences in SWB? The general answer seems to be yes. There is variation on the scales within each group, and as one might expect, most people have generally positive SWB scores. However, it is also probable that one is missing the less extreme cases of SWB. Perhaps many of the lower scores among the East European groups reflect something in addition to, or even instead of, low SWB.

Style therefore plays its part—but so does substance. Lawton's work in both theory and measurement clearly shows the signs of trying to relate the two.

REFERENCES

Ahlstrom, S. (1975). *A religious history of the American people.* Garden City, NY: Image Books.

Durkheim, E. (1951). *Suicide: A study in sociology.* New York: Free Press.

Glicksman, A. (1990). *The psychological well-being of elderly Jews: A comparative analysis.* Doctoral dissertation, Department of Sociology, University of Pennsylvania.

Lawton, M. P. (1971). Morale: What are we measuring? In C. N. Nydegger (Ed.), *Measuring morale: A guide to effective assessment.* Washington, DC: Gerontological Society of America.

Lawton, M. P. (1972). The dimensions of morale. In R. Kastenbaum, D. Kent, & S. Sherwood, (Eds.), *Research planning and action for the elderly: The power and potential of social science* (pp. 144–165). New York: Human Sciences Press.

Lawton, M. P. (1975). The Philadelphia Geriatric Center Morale Scale: A revision. *Journal of Gerontology, 30,* 85–89.

McGoldrick, M., Pearce, J. K., & Giordano, J. (Eds.). (1982). *Ethnicity and family therapy.* New York: Guilford.

Zborowski, M. (1969). *People in pain.* New York: Jossey-Bass.

III

Studies of Affect

8

The Assessment and Integration of Preferences into Care Practices for Persons with Dementia Residing in the Nursing Home

Kimberly Van Haitsma

In recent years there have been increasing calls for a shift in focus away from a purely biomedical and paternalistic approach to Alzheimer's Disease (AD) to an incorporation of the perspective and psychosocial preferences of the dementia patient into both research and practice (Brod, Stewart, & Sands, 1997; Cotrell & Schulz, 1993; Danner & Friesen, 1996; Kasper & Rabins, 1997; Lawton, Van Haitsma, & Klapper, 1994; Logsdon, McCurry, Gibbons, & Teri, 1997; Logsdon & Teri, 1997). Evidence gathered to date suggests that persons with dementia retain the ability to be expressive about their quality of life, preferences for care, and emotions throughout the course of their illness, although the form of expression may change with the level of cognitive impairment (Danner & Friesen, 1996; Hallberg, Edberg, Nordmark, Johnsson, & Norberg, 1993; Lawton, Van Haitsma, & Klapper, 1996; Lawton, Van Haitsma, Perkinson & Ruckdeschel, 1999).

The purpose of the present chapter is to focus on one specific component of an AD individual's perspective, namely, that of the assessment of psychosocial preferences for pleasant events and the incorporation of these preferences into care for individuals at various levels of cognitive impairment. In the early to middle stages of the disease, verbal expression remains the main avenue of communication, and preferences can be assessed through interviews with the person. Later in the disease course, communications regarding preferences must be largely inferred from the person's behavior and observed emotions (Cotrell & Schulz, 1993) or obtained from proxy raters. The challenge for the research and caregiving community is to develop methods and measurements to reliably interpret these communications, train caregivers to utilize these methods effectively, and to incorporate them into the process of care provision in order to enhance overall quality of life. This chapter will present theoretical frameworks relevant to this area of inquiry, review current instruments related to the assessment of preferences, and describe the beginnings of a clinical research program in which two of these instruments were integrated into practice.

THEORETICAL FRAMEWORKS FOR THE ASSESSMENT OF PREFERENCE IN DEMENTIA

As we consider the assessment of preferences in dementia, there are at least two theoretical frameworks that are useful in conceptualizing the surrounding issues. The first is a concept of quality of life (QOL) put forth by M. Powell Lawton (1983, 1991, 1994) and the second is an ecological model of stimulation and retreat also developed by Lawton and colleagues (Lawton & Nahemow, 1973; Lawton et al., 1994).

Lawton conceptualizes four domains of QOL in AD which do not differ from QOL for persons in general. Two domains can be evaluated objectively, by observers using normative criteria: behavioral competence and the objective environment; and two domains are inherently subjective in nature: perceived quality of life and psychological well-being. In determining the subjective aspect of QOL, individuals may be asked to evaluate many aspects of their overall QOL such as housing, social, and leisure activities, activities of daily living, relationships to formal and informal caregivers, and others. Evidence gathered to date suggests that the diagnosis of AD does not, by default, mean that individuals cannot participate in meaningful discussions about their perceived quality of life (Logsdon et al., 1997) or reflect on the quality of their current experiences of being demented (Cohen & Eisdorfer, 1986). The question remains as to how far into the progression of the disease a person can still contribute verbally about his or her experiences in a meaningful way. In an intriguing case study, Danner and Friesen (1996) reported an examination of 10 persons with AD who were severely impaired (mean Mini-Mental Status Examination [MMSE] score of 2.4; Folstein, Folstein, & McHugh, 1975) and found that most were able to volunteer verbally some awareness of their illness, the environment around them, and changes in the way in which care providers reacted to their attempts to communicate. These investigators concluded that "efforts to encourage the severely demented AD patient to communicate and careful attention to the patients' communicative efforts may be more fruitful than previously thought" (p. 333). Clearly, the limits of tapping into a demented individual's subjective quality of life are still open to investigation.

However, when one considers the objective aspects of quality of life for the severely cognitively impaired individual, that is, directly observed behaviors, one finds a much more fully developed conceptual scheme for inferring the subjective state of the person with dementia. Lawton (1994) expanded his definition of QOL to include measurements of positive behavior and directly observed emotional states. He contends that positive behaviors, such as time use and social behavior, and directly observed positive and negative emotional states are "our major key in learning about the preferences of dementia patients and their responses to our interventions" (p. 145). Currently, emotional aspects of QOL in AD are receiving increasing attention (Albert et al., 1997; Hurley, Volicer, Hanrahan, Houde, & Volicer, 1992; Magai, Cohen, Gomberg, Malatesta, & Culver, 1996). These investigators have found evidence to suggest that a range of emotional behaviors and facial expressions can be observed clearly in even severely impaired individuals. Furthermore, Magai and colleagues (1996) found evidence to suggest that fully one third of the end-stage AD patients they studied were able to react to emotionally laden events appropriately (e.g., sadness at the departure of their relative, anger during routine caregiving), suggesting that the "information-processing abilities of at least some dementia patients have been underestimated in past research that relied exclusively on cognitive tests of mental function" (p. 39). Continuing to develop our understanding of the emotional aspect of QOL appears to be a potentially fruitful avenue for ascertaining the likes and dislikes of even severely demented persons.

The second conceptual framework useful to the purpose of this chapter is the ecological model (Lawton & Nahemow, 1973; Lawton, Van Haitsma, & Klapper, 1996). The ecological model as applied to dementia posits that optimal QOL in dementia is brought about by balancing the level of demand placed on the individual by the physical and human environment with the behavioral competence of the demented individual. Decreases in QOL can be brought about by either a stimulating environment, which taxes the remaining coping capacities of the individual, or the obverse of this condition, a boring environment, which fails to provide meaning or interest compatible with remaining capabilities. By definition, this ecological model requires that treatment be individualized for any given person with dementia. What may be an appropriate level of stimulation for one person may be too much or too little for another. By the same token, what may be the appropriate level of stimulation at one point in time for a given individual may be inappropriate at a later date as the individual's condition changes.

On a more concrete level, it follows from this theoretical framework that the characteristics of the stimulation itself must be understood on an individual level. Information about past and present individual preferences becomes highly relevant in this model. Domains of preference can include such areas as social and nonsocial activities, daily routines, personal and instrumental activities of daily living, aspects of the physical environment, the timing or pacing of activities, involvement in care by informal and formal caregivers, types of health care services, and broader personality-related dimensions such as the need for control or privacy, tolerance for change, comfort level with dependence, and preferred ways of coping with emotional distress (Degenholtz, Kane, & Kivnick, 1997; Lemke & Moos, 1989; Logsdon & Teri, 1997; Rader, 1996).

MEASURES OF PREFERENCE IN DEMENTIA

Measures for ascertaining preferences in dementia are slowly emerging as interest in subjective and directly observable aspects of QOL grows in both research and clinical fields. Several extant instruments will be reviewed briefly before turning to focus more extensively on two measures being developed at the Philadelphia Geriatric Center, the Observed Emotion Rating Scale and the Pleasant Events Preference Inventory-Nursing Home Scale.

Pleasant Events Schedule—AD

The Pleasant Events Schedule—AD (PES—AD) is a 53-item checklist of events and activities for mildly impaired AD patients developed by Logsdon and Teri (1997). Items were selected to correspond with two domains, passive–active and social–nonsocial, and are rated according to their frequency, availability, and current and past enjoyment level. Coefficient alpha values ranged from .86 to .95. A 20-item short form that demonstrated good validity also is available. This measure has been used extensively to explore relationships between cognitive impairment, participation in pleasant activities, and depression. The instrument has been field tested with primarily middle-class, Caucasian, AD patients who live in the community with a family caregiver. The instrument was designed to be completed jointly with a caregiver for the purposes of planning daily activity schedules for the demented individual. The PES—AD has not yet been field tested with AD patients completing it independently.

Values Assessment Protocol

The Values Assessment Protocol is a 9-item interview designed for community-dwelling elders receiving in-home long-term care services (Degenholtz et al., 1997). Case managers responsible for treatment planning administered the protocol, which requires elders to make a judgment about whether each item is "very important, somewhat important, or not at all important" when thinking about their care now and in the future. The protocol focuses on a combination of values and preferences that relate to everyday life for those receiving care. Kane and Degenholtz (1997) make a distinction between the assessment of values, which are beliefs about what is desirable and good, and preferences, which refer to "positive choices among one or more options" (p. 20). The nine items are designed to be asked on a value level, and the case manager completing the interview is relied upon to assess preferences in a more open-ended fashion at his/her discretion. The items include assessments of daily routine, activity participation, involvement of family in care, things to look forward to, personal privacy, avoidance of pain and discomfort, freedom versus safety, designation of a decision-maker, and an identity-related item. Case managers at two sites completed a total of 779 value assessments. Unfortunately, no data were available for information about the clients' level of cognitive impairment, other than a comment by the authors that the clients had to be sufficiently cognitively intact in order to be interviewed.

Discomfort Scale

The Discomfort Scale is a 9-item scale developed by Hurley et al. (1992) designed to be used to directly observe indicators of distress in AD patients. The items include noisy breathing, negative vocalization, absence of a look of contentment, sad look, frightened look, frowning, absence of a relaxed body posture, tense look, and fidgeting. The scale demonstrated good reliability, internal consistency, and external validity for 5-minute observation periods.

Adult Behavior Questionnaire

The Adult Behavior Questionnaire is designed to measure five basic emotions: anger, fear, joy, interest, and sadness (Magai & Cohen, 1996). The scale was modeled after a scale which assessed affect in the infant and preverbal child. Two versions are available, a 102-item version for professional caregiving staff, and an 85-item version for family members. The Cronbach's alphas for both versions of the scale were adequate, with the exception of the family Interest subscale, which improved after the elimination of two items.

The following two scales are currently being developed at the Philadelphia Geriatric Center to assess preferences in persons with dementia.

Observed Emotion Rating Scale

The Observed Emotion Rating Scale (formerly the Apparent Affect Rating Scale) is a 5-item scale developed by Lawton and colleagues (1996, in press) to directly observe three negative emotions (anger, anxiety, sadness) and two positive emotions (pleasure, interest) in moderately to severely impaired persons with dementia. Observers are instructed to rate the amount of time they observed each of the five emotions. Several different forms of the scale are available corresponding to different time frames: 5 minutes, 10 minutes, or 2 weeks. Reliability and validity for trained research observers was found to be within acceptable limits (kappa: Pleasure = .80, Interest = .86, Anger = .89, Anxiety =.78, Sadness =.81). A more extensive discussion of the properties of this instrument can be found in Lawton et al. (1996). The scale also has been tested using ratings obtained by activity therapists (ATs), certified nursing assistants (CNAs), and family members. In the study to be described later in this chapter, intra-class correlations between research staff and CNA ratings of 10-minute observational periods were found to be less reliable than those between trained observers, but still indicative of substantial agreement (N = 480 pairs): Pleasure = .85, Interest = .84, Anger = .68, Anxiety = .63, and Sadness =.58.

The Pleasant Events Preference
Inventory–Nursing Home Questionnaire

The Pleasant Events Preference Inventory (PEPI–NH) Questionnaire is a 53-item checklist of events and activities for moderately to severely impaired AD patients being developed by Van Haitsma and Lawton as part of an ongoing study of the psychosocial preferences of demented nursing home patients funded by the Alzheimer's Association/ Tacrine Fund Pilot Research Grant (TRG 95–006) and the Harry Stern Family Center for Innovations in Alzheimer's Care. This scale incorporates many items directly from the PES–AD (Logsdon & Teri, 1997), but eliminates and replaces items which were not suitable for a more severely impaired nursing home population. The scale assesses preferences in six conceptually derived activity categories: Music, Physical Exercise, Sensory Stimulation, Social Interaction, Activities of Daily Living, and Crafts/ Handiwork/ Hobbies. Items are rated according to the person's current and/or past enjoyment of the activity, dislike of the activity, or no preference for the activity. This instrument is designed to be completed through of variety of methods: an interview with the demented resident; as a self-administered questionnaire completed by a family caregiver most knowledgeable about the resident; or as a questionnaire completed by a staff member, usually an Activity Therapist (AT).

THE CURRENT STUDY

The PEPI–NH is being developed as part of a larger, ongoing study designed to examine the impact of the integration of psychosocial preferences into resident care. This study seeks to examine the effectiveness of an intervention designed to enhance the affective and behavioral quality of life for persons residing in a nursing home who suffer from Alzheimer's Disease or a related disorder. The goal of the intervention is a careful assessment and integration of resident preferences into the psychosocial care delivered by a Certified Nursing Assistant (CNA). To achieve that goal, CNAs received training in communicating with persons with dementia (Dementia Communication Skill Training) and in delivering Individualized Positive Psychosocial Interventions (IPPIs). Through a randomized controlled trial, this study seeks to examine the outcomes of this clinical program for both demented residents and CNAs. By random selection, eight nursing home units were designated as either a Dementia Communication Skill Training unit, or a "no training" unit. Within each unit, 20 residents who had a MMSE score of 24 or less were randomly selected to receive a series of 10-minute psychosocial interventions three times a week for 3 weeks, or usual care (no intervention). Further details of the procedures of this study as they relate to the assessment and integration of preferences will be presented in the next section of this chapter.

Sample

A total of 111 nursing home residents were approached for a PEPI-NH interview. Interviews were attempted with residents of all cognitive impairment levels in order to test the limits of assessing preferences in the very impaired. Residents were interviewed regarding their current preferences for activities. Residents also were asked to rate their past preferences for these activities, but those data are not presented here. Out of those approached, 49% ($N = 54$) completed the interview and 51% ($N = 57$) did not. Forty-seven of the non-completers were too cognitively impaired to be interviewed and 10 refused to participate in the interview. A total of 47 female and 7 male nursing home residents completed the interview. Noncompleters had an average MMSE score of 3.28 (SD = 4.94), whereas completers had an average MMSE score of 13.85 (SD = 6.49). More specifically, the cognitive impairment level of completers of the interview was characterized as follows: 30% ($N = 16$) had a MMSE score between 18–24, 41% ($N = 22$) had a MMSE score between 11–17, and 30% ($n = 16$) had a MMSE score of 10 or less. Although the majority of persons with MMSE scores less than 10 were not able to complete the interview, it is noteworthy that over a quarter of the interviews were completed by persons who were extremely cognitively impaired. This study found that these individuals consistently were able to respond to questions about their likes and dislikes either verbally or nonverbally (nodding, smiling, shaking their head, or frowning).

Administration of the Questionnaire

The staff member begins by asking the resident about his or her past preferences for the listed activities. We discovered that in asking about past preferences for activities, the resident is generally able to give more detailed responses. When asked about current preferences, many residents will simply respond to the perceived lack of availability of the activity (e.g., "They don't have that here") or their inability to perform the activity in traditional ways (e.g., "I can't see the needlepoint anymore"). A resident was judged to be unable to complete the interview if he or she did not respond at all or perseverated in responding either "yes" or "no" in a logically impossible manner to more than four items in each category.

PEPI–NH questionnaires also were completed by the AT on the resident's unit and by the family member most familiar with the resident. Activity therapists were asked to rate only the resident's current preferences for the activities, while family members were asked to rate the resident's current and past preferences for the activities.

Psychometric properties. The internal consistency (Cronbach's alpha) of each category was as follows: Music (3 items) =.42, Physical Exercise (6 items) = .65, Sensory Stimulation (8 items) =.48, Social Interaction (15 items) =.41, ADLs (16 items) =.72, and Crafts/Handiwork/Hobbies (7 items) = .51. We also were interested in the level of agreement between residents' self-report and proxy raters' report of preferences. A total of 53 (98%) PEPI–NH questionnaires were completed independently by both an activity therapist (AT) assigned to the resident's home unit and a resident. A total of 30 (56%)

family members independently completed the PEPI–NH regarding the resident's current preferences. The most common reasons for failing to complete the questionnaire were: nonreturn of the questionnaire, no family, or family members refusing to complete the form because they "didn't know family member well enough." Intra-class correlations were averaged across all categories of activities. The average intra-class correlations were as follows: between resident and AT =.15; between resident and family member =.28. These very low correlations suggest that proxy raters may be a poor substitute for asking the resident directly about preferences. The current study viewed the resident's responses as the "gold standard" for selecting preferred activities, while family and staff ratings were used only in the absence of such data.

Table 8.1 displays the percentage of 54 nursing home residents with dementia who endorsed liking, disliking, or having no preference for PEPI-NH current pleasant activities. Percentages were rounded to the nearest whole number. Overall, persons clearly were much more likely to endorse "liking" things, than "disliking" or having "no preference" for an activity. In examining categories, the most preferred activity type by the entire sample was Social Interaction (mean of 74% of sample endorse this category as liked). There was no clearly disliked category of activities.

Several specific items stand out as being endorsed as liked by 90% or more of persons, including such activities as Listening to Music, Visits by Children, and Receiving Cards or Letters. The most frequently disliked items by 40% or more of the sample were Being Left Alone, Making a Bed, Dusting, Wood-working, and Making Collections. Examining group preference responses may assist a unit or long-term care community in the overall design of activity programming for a given group of individuals with dementia. However, group preference data serves only as a stepping stone to the ultimate goal in obtaining preference data, namely, the integration of an individual's preferences into a plan of care.

INTEGRATION OF PREFERENCE INSTRUMENTS INTO PRACTICE: AN EXAMPLE IN THE NURSING HOME

Integrating assessment of the preferences of a demented individual into practice is highly desirable because of its relevance to the individualization of care and the potential for enhanced QOL. The provision of individualized care and balancing opportunities for stimulation and retreat rely heavily on the ability of the caregiver to accurately and comprehensively assess the likes and dislikes of the care-receiver. The instruments reviewed above are one avenue for providing this information to the caregiver. However, the integration of preferences into everyday care is inherently more difficult in the institutional setting, where a variety of conditions conspire to obstruct the process. These conditions include but are not limited to: the fact that formal caregivers lack a historical relationship with and knowledge about the demented individual; the demands of providing care to a large number of individuals; and the level of cognitive impairment of the caregivee, which frequently distorts reactions that may signal preferences or aversions.

The following example is presented as one way in which the knowledge of preferences could be integrated into clinical practice in the nursing home setting. Many other methods of accomplishing this goal are most certainly possible. The method presented here is not meant to suggest that this process is an ideal one. Rather, by sharing this attempt, it is hoped that the reader will be provoked into thinking about the benefits and challenges in attempting such a task in an institutional environment.

Setting

The setting for this study was a large, urban, not-for-profit 550-bed nursing home on the East coast. A total of eight units were selected (out of twelve) with an aim of including a range of residents with cognitive impairment from mild to severe. The average dayshift staff ratio for these units was one Certified Nursing Assistant (CNA) for every nine residents. This ratio increased to one CNA to every 12–13 residents for the evening shift. Each unit had a day-time professional staff complement of one RN Nurse Manager (NM), one or two Licensed Practical Nurses, a half-time Activity Therapist, a half-time Social Worker, a consulting Dietitian, and a consulting psychologist. The payor mix was 77.5% Medicaid, 5.6% Medicare, 16.8% private pay, and .1% HMO.

Selection of residents for intervention. For the purposes of the study, only residents who scored 24 or less on the MMSE were eligible for participation. In addition, residents were excluded who had resided on the unit for less than 1 month, were acutely medically ill, spoke English very poorly, or who were slated for imminent transfer off the unit. No resident was considered too cognitively impaired to participate in the program. Staff on the unit expressed significant reservations about performing the psychosocial interventions with persons who were the most cognitively impaired. Staff clearly expressed a belief that the program would be more helpful for the more cognitively intact or "those who know what is going on." However, we felt it was important that the program be tested across the full spectrum of dementia. Ideally, the selection of residents would be done by the care planning team with an equal openness to "testing the limits" with residents in their care.

Intervention Delivery

The interventions were delivered 3 days a week for 3 weeks, always on a Monday, Wednesday, and Thursday. Time of day for the intervention was generally either 10 am, 2 pm, or 4 pm. These times were selected for ease of fit into a combination of CNA and resident activity schedules. To select among these three times for a given resident, the care team considered such things as regular therapy or doctor appointments, family visits, nap times, times of greatest need for attention or stimulation, times of greatest need for comfort or retreat, and group activities. In general, these times worked well for residents and staff alike. However, one Nurse Manager did express the belief that intervention periods should be completely flexible to individual resident need, such as while

Table 8.1 Percentage of 54 Nursing Home Residents with Dementia Who Endorsed Liking, Disliking, or Having No Preference for Current Pleasant Events

Event	Percentage like	Percentage dislike	Percentage no preference
Music			
Playing instrument	35	28	37
Singing	56	27	17
Listening	96	4	0
Average percentage for category	*62*	*20*	*18*
Physical exercise			
Walking	59	22	19
Exercise	56	26	18
Dancing	61	18	21
Watching dance	80	10	10
Playing sports	28	37	35
Watching sports	59	14	27
Average percentage for category	*57*	*21*	*22*
Sensory Stimulation			
Hugging	63	22	15
Holding hands	74	12	14
Getting back rub	45	33	22
Sitting close	68	14	18
Hand massage	42	30	28
Smelling flowers	84	8	8
Listening to nature	87	13	0
Touching fabrics	56	26	18
Average percentage for category	*65*	*20*	*15*
Social Interaction			
Being left alone	40	46	14
Watching people	76	10	14
Joking	80	12	8
Looking at photos	86	6	8
Visits by children	92	6	2
Animals	62	25	13
Meeting new people	86	10	4
Group socializing	69	22	9
Writing cards	40	33	27

Table 8.1 *(continued)*

Event	Percentage like	Percentage dislike	Percentage no preference
Receiving cards	92	4	4
Talking on phone	63	16	21
Reminiscing	73	14	13
Told you're loved	71	4	25
Being read to	46	39	15
Going to movies	59	14	27
Average percentage for category	*74*	*17*	*14*
ADL			
Putting on makeup	50	28	22
Getting a manicure	80	18	2
Wearing bright colors	58	23	19
Brushing own hair	76	4	20
Having hair brushed	55	20	25
Dressing up	73	10	17
Receiving compliments	73	10	17
Making bed	34	42	24
Dusting	24	43	33
Decorating	46	38	16
Eating snacks	72	16	12
Keeping tidy	69	17	14
Organizing closets	46	28	26
Sorting drawers	44	28	28
Folding clothes	56	24	20
Average percentage for category	*57*	*24*	*20*
Crafts/Handiwork/Hobbies			
Working on crafts	47	28	25
Sewing	43	26	31
Painting, drawing	30	39	31
Woodworking	13	65	22
Making collections	25	41	34
Houseplants	51	27	22
Gardening	65	30	5
Average percentage for category	*39*	*37*	*24*

waiting to eat breakfast, change of shift, or after eating dinner. Barriers to such complete responsiveness to resident need included such things as staff lunch and break periods, rigidly set food tray delivery times, an institutional policy prohibiting the use of staff overtime, and the reduction of the number of available staff on the evening shift.

Selection of Preferred Intervention
for a Given Individual

A pool of 31 Individualized Positive Psychosocial Intervention protocols have been developed to correspond with activities listed in the PEPI-NH. These protocols provide the CNA with concrete and consistent instruction in the delivery of these activities and contain all necessary materials to conduct the activity. The most common protocols selected for implementation have included: Sing-Along, Active Listening to Music, Reminiscing About Housework, Stretching, Making a Memory Book, Making a Greeting Card, and Beauty Time.

The selection of the intervention for a given resident began with the administration of the PEPI–NH questionnaire to residents selected for the study, a mailing of the PEPI–NH to a family member who knew the resident well, and the completion of the questionnaire by the resident's AT. As noted previously, not all residents were able to complete the questionnaire (49% completed) and not all family members returned the questionnaire (response rate: 56%). However, all available data from the PEPI–NH was pooled and discussed at an initial meeting of researcher, NM, AT, and CNA. At this meeting, information (if available) was prioritized in the following way: resident self-report of preferences, AT ratings of resident current preferences, and family member ratings of resident preferences. These preferences were discussed in light of the cognitive, emotional, physical, and social strengths and deficits of the resident. The two most preferred activities were selected which best matched each resident's current needs for stimulation or retreat. The two selected IPPI protocols were then brought for consideration to the interdisciplinary care planning team, including a CNA. The team then selected one intervention to be implemented by a CNA.

Assignment of Residents to CNAs

A single CNA was assigned as a primary interventionist for a given resident for the entire 3 weeks of intervention to ensure consistent implementation of the IPPI and the opportunity for the development of a relationship between the two. Each CNA had a partner designated to conduct the IPPI in his/her absence (e.g., sick days, vacation days, etc.). The matching of CNA with the resident was left entirely up to the Nurse Manager of the unit. The method of matching was highly diverse and included: asking CNAs to select whom they preferred, assigning CNAs alphabetically to residents, requesting that researchers make the assignments, or assigning the residents based on the current 1-month case assignment of the CNA. In general, the optimal methods of pairing CNAs to residents appeared to be those that facilitated maximal CNA choice. When allowed to do so, the CNAs usually chose residents they especially liked, making the intervention process more enjoyable for both resident and CNA.

Training of CNAs in Intervention Delivery

After the first unit, CNAs were enlisted to help orient each successive unit's staff to the program. CNAs responded very positively to their role as trainer in the orientation process, and their presence appeared to significantly enhance the "buy-in" of the orienting unit. Once interventions were selected and CNAs assigned to residents, the CNAs had to be trained in the intervention protocol. Protocols contained specific instructions in how to introduce, conduct, and terminate the intervention. CNAs were trained in two stages. First, each CNA and his or her partner watched an AT deliver the intervention with their assigned resident. After the session, the AT and a researcher reviewed the steps of the protocol with the CNA. For the second stage, CNAs delivered the intervention while being observed by the AT and the researcher. Once again, protocol steps were reviewed and constructive feedback was given to the CNA. It was emphasized to the CNAs that small changes in resident behavior and affect were the goal of the intervention, lest they inaccurately assume that performance expectations were unrealistically high. Between the fourth and seventh intervention session, the CNA was again observed and given performance feedback by the clinical researcher (a clinical psychologist).

In order to complete this training in the absence of a research presence, it would be necessary to designate a staff member in the facility who would be responsible for overseeing the program. In addition, nursing supervisory personnel would have to be substituted for the researcher in the above CNA training process. The person providing feedback to the CNA should be skilled in giving feedback, as many of the CNAs directly or indirectly expressed a great deal of anxiety about being watched or not "doing it right," and insecurity about being "corrected" in how they delivered the intervention.

It also should be noted that the ATs varied in their ability to be a trainer and role model for CNAs. Several ATs were enthusiastic, skilled in suggesting ways of approaching the residents, and creative in suggesting variations on how to individualize the content of the protocol to fit a resident's special needs (e.g., hearing or visual impairment). However, other ATs were less enthusiastic about being placed in a training role with the CNAs, had a stilted communication style, and were reluctant to make suggestions to the CNAs. Clearly, the skills of each person involved in the training process need to be carefully considered before launching a clinical program such as this.

Training of CNAs in the Assessment of Residents Emotional Reaction to Intervention

In addition to training in the delivery of the IPPI, the CNAs also were trained to assess the residents' emotional reactions to the interventions using the Observed Emotion Rating Scale. Some difficulties in using this scale with staff have been noted in previous publications about this instrument (Lawton et al., 1999). The process of training staff to use this instrument as an ongoing assessment tool to assess resident emotional responses to interventions requires further investigation.

CNAs were instructed to complete the OERS at the cessation of each intervention period. Positive and negative emotional responses were tracked over time to assess whether the intervention was achieving the goal of providing a balance between stimulation and retreat (i.e., eliciting predominantly positive emotion). Ideally, based on the resident's emotional response, the care planning team could make recommendations regarding the frequency or quality of the intervention, the need for a different intervention strategy or maintenance of the current one, or a method for enhancing monitoring and communication regarding the resident's functioning.

Training for the use of the OERS was incorporated into the training for the intervention itself. In the first training session, researchers met with CNAs to introduce the instrument and explain the criteria. This process was especially difficult with CNAs who had English as a second language. Currently, there is a videotape available that provides many visual examples of the emotion criteria (available through Terra Nova Films, 1998) which should help to alleviate some of these difficulties in the initial training session. Researchers then had a practice session with the CNA, observing residents engaged in a typical "down time" on the unit and providing feedback on the CNA's scoring. In the next OERS training session, the CNA rated the resident's response after watching the AT deliver the intervention and was given feedback. The CNA also rated the resident's response after his or her first attempt at delivering the intervention and again was given feedback regarding his or her performance. Thereafter, the CNA rated the resident's response after each intervention and was given periodic feedback between the fourth and seventh session of intervention with a given resident.

The rating of observed emotion was viewed as a key method for assessing the resident's preferences in the moment. Positive emotions served as a powerful reinforcer to the CNA delivering the intervention. It was seen as concrete evidence that the CNA was doing something right and good for the resident. In addition, as an outcome measure, the OERS assisted in determining whether the intervention selected from the PEPI-NH was indeed a good fit with the resident's current needs. Interventions which consistently provoked more negative emotion than positive from the resident were changed to try to find a more appropriate fit with the resident's preferences.

While the majority of the CNAs readily understood the criteria and mechanics of the rating scale, difficulties were encountered in several areas. Some CNAs had little difficulty in selecting the emotion being displayed, but did have problems estimating the duration of the emotional response. This problem was somewhat allayed by the researchers counting off the intervals of time during the training period. Several CNAs mentioned that they ignored the number of seconds and simply substituted relative duration descriptors such as "rarely," "somewhat," "a lot," along the 5-point continuum. A small number of CNAs appeared to have difficulty in understanding the basic concept of rating apparent emotion. These individuals struggled with focusing on the subtle, nonverbal cues that make up these emotional responses in demented individuals. Motivation to learn the concept did not appear to be a mitigating factor. These individuals missed many expressions of emotion, and when they did rate an emotion, appeared to be unable to articulate why they rated the person the way they did or gave rationales that were not clearly emotional in nature. At times, CNAs needed to be reminded to base their rating on the emotions observed during the current session, rather than responding according to the resident's "typical" emotion. Relatedly, CNAs' ratings occasionally appeared to be biased by the context within which the observation took place. That is, if a pleasant, lively event such as a birthday party were underway in another part of the room, a CNA might assume that a resident would be experiencing a positive emotion.

In terms of difficulties in rating particular emotions, Interest proved to be a challenging emotion to rate for very severely impaired individuals. The hallmark of this emotion is generally considered to be tracking and angle of gaze (Lawton et al., 1996). However, severely demented individuals may often have a fixed gaze or sit with their eyes closed, but may nonetheless respond to their environment, indicating a subtle form of engagement with the world around them. The resident may move in response to a CNA question by nodding, raising eyebrows, or reaching out a hand. In a similar vein, the resident may respond to the CNA by increasing the rate or volume of incoherent speech, perhaps indicating an attempt to communicate with the CNA. As a result of this experience, these criteria have been added to the OERS to make it more sensitive to emotional expression in the most severely demented individuals.

From a research perspective, difficulties in rating observed emotion are easily remedied by identifying poor raters from the outset and removing them from the rating pool. From a clinical perspective, the inability to reliably rate observed emotion becomes a much more complex issue. Intensive training minimized difficulties with the structural aspects of the process (e.g., problems reading descriptors on the scale, estimating the duration of an emotion, or extremely subtle and fleeting emotion cues). However, the inability to correctly perceive observed emotion was a more intractable problem. This particular issue deserves further study. Do persons who have difficulty in perceiving observed emotion have more problems in interacting with persons with dementia? In missing emotional cues, do they find themselves trying to manage behavioral difficulties that others who are more skilled do not encounter? Do they quit at a higher rate than those more skilled at reading nonverbal emotional responses? The answers to these questions and others would have high applicability for the selection and training of staff who work with persons who have dementia.

Management Issues in Intervention Implementation

Several management issues arose in the course of implementation on the units, including difficulties in obtaining support from supervisory nursing staff who did not espouse a psychosocial model of treatment, "pulling" of CNAs from the unit on scheduled intervention days, and chronic difficulties in working short-handed, which created significant pressure to drop the psychosocial interventions in order to complete basic daily ADL tasks. Many of these difficulties were resolved with consistent support from upper-level management who remained committed to incorporating resident psychosocial preferences into day-to-day care provision, and many initially reluctant supervisory staff were won over by watching the residents respond to the interventions.

Each NM was interviewed after 3 months of the program to solicit his or her reactions. Responses of the NM to the program ranged from grudging support, i.e., "The CNAs didn't dread it as much as I thought they would", to outright praise, e.g., "It gave the CNAs a chance to get to know the residents on a deeper level, rather than superficial, like just getting them washed up," and "It helped the CNAs to see the resident in a different light, their hidden talents, and delighted them with a positive response to their efforts." One NM who began the program with an air of beleaguered tolerance became transformed into an ardent supporter who continued the program after the researchers left the unit.

Complaints about the program from NMs centered around the amount of supervision time it took to get the program up and running, even with research staff support, for example, "I just had to keep on answering the same questions from the CNAs over and over because everything was new." Other NMs related difficulties in motivating CNAs to do something which was not previously part of their job description and which was perceived as being added to an already burdened schedule. Many expressed feeling overburdened themselves, and stressed the difficulties in "keeping everyone in line" and having a hard time finding the "fine line between authority and nurturing" with the CNAs. Suggestions for improvements from these managers included increasing the amount of lead time before beginning the interventions to allow the staff to accommodate to the changes in routine and increasing the amount of training by encouraging CNAs to participate in small group activities with the ATs to give them more exposure to working with the residents in a psychosocial capacity.

CNAs' Reactions to the Intervention Program

The vast majority of the CNAs on each unit were extremely helpful and cooperative in the process of ascertaining preferences and implementing interventions with the residents. We found these individuals to be cheerful, warm, creative in their approaches to the resident, willing to "follow" the resident's lead, and attentive to even minute changes in the resident's emotional state. When asked about their impressions of the program after its conclusion, reactions were positive and varied including:

1. Enjoyment in watching the residents' responses, connecting with them on an emotional level, and implied emotional benefits to their own well-being; "I liked watching the expressions, the smiles and the excitement of the residents;" "[For some residents] it made their memories come alive;" "It keeps us in touch with the resident emotionally;" "I enjoyed the closeness of getting to know the whole person;" "I liked getting to know them on a personal level";

2. Gaining knowledge about the resident that they did not have before, "It helps you to learn what you don't know about the resident through quality time;" "It gives you more

time to study the resident and react now through what you learned;" "Different people have different behaviors, and I was able to learn strategies to handle people better;" "I didn't know Sadie could still talk!" "You know what they are thinking, what they like, and what they used to do"; and

3. A recognition that their attentions made a difference to the residents, "They loved the attention;" "It made them feel important, like someone cares;" "They got undivided attention;" "Just us talking to them affected them the most—the eye to eye contact."

Unfortunately, a small number of CNAs (usually no more than 1–2 on a unit) were not so enthusiastic about the prospect of changing how they did their jobs and incorporating resident preferences into their care routine, even if it was only for 10 minutes out of their day. These persons usually were indirect in expressing their dissatisfaction with the program by consistently being unavailable or late for the scheduled intervention, having poor eye contact with the resident, discontinuing the intervention at the first sign of resident resistance, or suddenly being very busy with pressing things to do for other residents, even when another CNA had been designated to attend to these residents for the 10-minute period. When interviewed, these CNAs expressed a belief that the psychosocial time was

1. Not a part of their job with the residents; "The Activity Therapist should be doing these;" "Someone else should do it, not CNAs";

2. Focused on a few residents to the detriment of others; "To do this you have to deny some residents to cater to one";

3. Unhelpful to many residents; "It didn't affect them at all," "Some people [residents] didn't want to do it"; or

4. A significant disruption to their routine; "It was OK for the residents but not for me;" "It interfered with our lunch break schedule."

CNA suggestions for improving the program included: (a) allowing the duration of the intervention to increase or decrease according to resident need; (b) giving the CNA more discretion in selecting the intervention to be implemented; (c) including more residents in the program, especially more cognitively capable ones; and (d) doing more of the interventions on evenings and weekends when there is more time.

DISCUSSION

This chapter reviewed two theoretical frameworks relevant to the assessment and incorporation of individualized preferences into the care of persons with dementia, examined several current instruments available to assist in the assessment of preferences, and described a clinical research program in which two of these instruments were integrated into practice in the institutional environment.

The pioneering work of M. Powell Lawton in conceptualizing subjective and objective aspects of quality of life for persons with dementia has provoked the development of assessment instruments which measure both domains. In the subjective QOL realm, many investigators have demonstrated the importance of continuing to attempt assessment of self-reported preferences, thoughts, and feelings from demented individuals (Cotrell & Schulz, 1993; Danner & Friesen, 1996; Magai-Cohen, 1999). The question remains as to how far into the severity of the dementing condition an individual can reliably verbally report his or her preferences.

The piloting work done with the sample of individuals described here suggests that a small, but clinically significant, proportion of persons with severe dementia (MMSE score between 4–10) can still meaningfully respond when asked about their preferences for enjoyed activities. This question is clearly open to future empirical investigation. In the objective QOL realm, advancements made in the measurement of observed emotion are key to the ascertainment of preferences in the severely cognitively impaired individual. A growing number of investigators have developed reliable and valid measures for the rating of observed emotions, which can be fruitfully utilized in individualizing care to the person with dementia.

For the individual with dementia, the combination of utilizing an assessment of verbally expressed preferences and the subsequent observation of his or her response to a preferred intervention is a powerful one. Each method of assessment informs the other as they are woven into the practice of delivering care. Tools such as the PEPI-NH and the OERS and others can significantly contribute to the staff's knowledge of initiating and monitoring the incorporation of preferences into the care of a given individual.

Furthermore, the ecological model delineated by Lawton also can serve as a practical descriptive framework for guiding the process of incorporating preferences. This chapter attempted to describe but one method for applying the ecological model in the long-term care institutional environment. The attempt outlined in this chapter highlighted the complexity involved in the selection of persons to receive preferred interventions, training in intervention delivery, the assessment of preferences in a population with advanced dementia, and the management issues involved in both professional and non-professional staff. Many other methods of assessing and implementing preferences could be used within the ecological framework, some of which have been developed in non-geriatric realms. An excellent review and critique of methods of assessing preferences in persons with developmental disabilities highlights the use of interviews, questionnaires, pictorial presentations, technological apparati, and direct observation (Kearney & McKnight, 1997). Many of these methods have significant potential for modification and application in geriatric populations with dementia. Some examples of these methods include pair-wise assessments, in which the person is presented with two stimuli and asked to choose one, or measuring approach toward a specific item. Many of these methods remain untapped in the domain of ascertaining preferences in dementia.

The importance of asking questions regarding preferences of the person with dementia is further highlighted by the lack of concordance between a demented individual's self-report and the report of staff and family proxies. The source of the disagreement is less than clear. Many investigators have pointed to the dementia- related language dysfunction in expressing and comprehending speech as the source of the difficulty. While this is most certainly part of the explanation for the lack of concordance between self-report and proxy report, it is clearly not the whole picture. This is especially true when considering information about specific aspects of preferences for everyday living. We were struck by how often family members, in particular adult children, would tell us that they did not know intimate details of their relative's preferences for everyday activities. Many family members had never lived with their relative, and/or had never inquired about many domains of preference. While it has become increasingly popular and accepted to document and discuss preferences in the medical treatment realm, that is, in regard to living wills and medical advanced directives, the same documentation and discussion has not yet gained favor in the psychosocial preference realm. Ideally, the individual him or herself would have the opportunity to discuss his or her psychosocial preferences with a family member prior to becoming too significantly impaired to do so. A structured interview such as the one developed by Degenholtz, Kane, & Kivnick (1997) is one example of a technique which can provide documentation of an individual's preferences and make the need for proxy assessments less critical later on in the disease process.

Once the ability to verbally communicate one's preferences is lost, the reliance on ascertaining preferences through emotional expression appears to be a viable alternative. Our experience in training nursing home staff to read emotional expressions in dementia suggests that this process is hardly a straightforward one. The ability to accurately discern emotional expression and then to use this information in formulating a plan of care is an extremely complex task that requires considerable interpersonal skill and practice. Future research is needed to determine ways of detecting persons who are skilled in this ability, how to effectively train persons who are not as skilled in reading emotion, and optimal methods for incorporating individualized preferences into the planning of care for persons with dementia.

REFERENCES

Albert, S., Del Castillo-Castaneda, C., Sano, M., Jacobs, D., Marder, K., Bell, K., Brandt, J., Albert, M., & Stern, Y. (1997, November). *Decline in expression of emotions with progression of Alzheimer's Disease.* Paper presented at the 50th annual meeting of the Gerontological Society of America, Cincinnati, OH.

Brod, M., Stewart, A., & Sands, L. (1997, November). *The conceptualization of quality of life in dementia.* Paper presented at the 50th annual meeting of the Gerontological Society of America, Cincinnati, OH.

Cohen, D., & Eisdorfer, C. (1986). *The loss of self.* New York: W.W. Norton.

Cotrell, V., & Schulz, R. (1993). The perspective of the patient with Alzheimer's Disease: A neglected dimension of dementia research. *Gerontologist, 33*, 205–211.

Danner, D., & Friesen, W. (1996). Are severely-impaired Alzheimer's patients aware of their environment and illness? *Journal of Clinical Geropsychology, 2*, 321–335.

Degenholtz, H., Kane, R. A., & Kivnick, H. Q. (1997). Care-related preferences and values of elderly community-based LTC consumers: Can case managers learn what's important to clients? *Gerontologist, 37*, 767–776.

Folstein, M., Folstein, S., & McHugh, P. (1975). Mini-mental state: A practical method for grading the cognitive state of patients for the clinician. *Journal of Psychiatric Research, 12*, 189–198.

Hallberg, I., Edberg, A., Nordmark, A., Johnsson, K., & Norberg, A. (1993). Daytime vocal activity in institutionalized severely-demented patients identified as vocally disruptive by nurses. *International Journal of Geriatric Psychiatry, 8*, 155–164.

Hurley, A., Volicer, B., Hanrahan, P., Houde, P., & Volicer, L. (1992). Assessment of discomfort in advanced Alzheimer patients. *Research in Nursing and Health, 15*, 369–377.

Kane, R. L., & Degenholtz, H. (1997). Assessing values and preferences: Should we, can we? *Generations, 21*, 19–24.

Kasper, J., & Rabins, P. (1997, Novermber). *Reliability and validity of a scale to measure quality of life in Alzheimer's Disease patients.* Paper presented at the 50th annual meeting of the Gerontological Society of America, Cincinnati, OH.

Kearney, C. A., & McKnight, T. J. (1997). Preference, choice, and persons with disabilities: A synopsis of assessments, interventions, and future directions. *Clinical Psychology Review, 17*, 217–238.

Lawton, M. P. (1983). Environment and other determinants of well-being in older people. *Gerontologist, 23*, 349–357.

Lawton, M. P. (1991). A multi-dimensional view of quality of life. In J. Birren, J. Lubben, J. Rowe, D. Deutchman, (Eds.), *The concept and measurement of quality of life in the frail elderly* (pp. 3–27). New York: Academic.

Lawton, M. P. (1994). Quality of life in Alzheimer Disease. *Alzheimer Disease and Associated Disorders, 8*, 138–150.

Lawton, M. P., & Nahemow, L. (1973). Ecology and the aging process. In C. Eisdorfer, M. P. Lawton, (Eds.). *Psychology of adult development and aging* (pp. 619–674). Washington, DC: American Psychological Association.

Lawton, M. P., Van Haitsma, K., & Klapper, J. (1994). A balanced stimulation and retreat program for a special care dementia unit. *Alzheimer Disease and Associated Disorders, 8*(S1), S133–S138.

Lawton, M. P., Van Haitsma, K. S., & Klapper, J. A. (1996). Observed affect in nursing home residents. *Journal of Gerontology: Psychological Sciences, 51B*(1), P3–P14.

Lawton, M. P., Van Haitsma, K., Perkinson, M., & Ruckdeschel, K. (1999). Observed affect and quality of life in dementia: Further affirmations and problems. *Journal of Mental Health and Aging, 5*, 69–81.

Lemke, S., & Moos, R. H. (1989). Personal and environmental determinants of activity involvement among elderly residents of congregate facilities. *Journal of Gerontology, 44*, S139–S148.

Logsdon, R., McCurry, S., Gibbons, L., & Teri, L. (1997, November). *Quality of life in AD: A community based longitudinal investigation.* Paper presented at the 50th annual meeting of the Gerontological Society of America, Cincinnati, OH.

Logsdon, R. G., & Teri, L. (1997). The Pleasant Events Schedule-AD: Psychometric properties and relationship to depression and cognition in Alzheimer's disease patients. *Gerontologist, 37*, 40–45.

Magai, C., & Cohen, C. (1998). Attachment style and emotion regulation in dementia patients and their relation to caregiver burden. *Journal of Gerontology Series B-Psychological & Social Sciences, 53B*, 147–154.

Magai, C., Cohen, C., Gomberg, D., Malatesta, C. & Culver, C. (1996). Emotional expression during mid- to late-stage dementia. *International Psychogeriatrics, 8*, 383–395.

Rader, J. (1996). Assessing the external environment. In E. M. Tornquist (Ed.), *Individualized dementia care: Creative, compassionate approachesx* (pp. 47–82). New York: Springer Publishing Co.

Terra Nova Films. (1998). *Recognizing and responding to emotion in persons with dementia.* [A training videotape produced by the Philadelphia Geriatric Center; 1 (800) 779–8491].

9

Opportunities for Redefining Late Life Depression *Ab Initio*

Ira R. Katz

I first spoke with Powell Lawton in 1982 before I came to Philadelphia, to make sure that the opportunity to work with him could be part of the package included with providing psychiatric services to the residents of the Philadelphia Geriatric Center. I expressed my interest in depression from clinical, biological, and psychopharmacological perspectives, and my hope that research on frail elderly patients with extensive medical comorbidity could provide insight into the biological processes leading to depression. In what, from our current perspective, was clearly the language of the time, I spoke about the possibility that biological markers could help to characterize clinical depressions in complex geriatric patients. In contrast, Powell spoke from a more enduring position about the value of research based upon detailed behavioral observations, and told me about his wish to explore day-to-day variability in affect as a way to understand the changes in emotional experience that occurred with aging and with chronic disabling disease.

Although knowledge about depression in older people with chronic disease, disability, and frailty has expanded significantly since that time (Katz & Alexopoulos, 1996; Lebowitz et al., 1997; Rubinstein & Lawton, 1997; Schneider, Reynolds, Lebowitz, & Friedhoff, 1993), there are a number of key questions about the definition of the syndrome of depression that remain unanswered. From the broadest of perspectives, we have learned that standard (*Diagnostic and Statistical Manual of Mental Disorders* [DSM–IV]; American Psychiatric Association, 1994) approaches to the diagnosis of major depression identify patients with increased rates of functional and cognitive decline, greater pain complaints, poorer nutritional status, and decreased survival. Moreover, we know that these patients respond, at least over the short term, to treatment with the standard antidepressant medication nortriptyline, but not to placebo. However, there have been long-standing concerns about the reliability of the diagnosis of major depression among older patients with significant medical illness. In addition, there has been increasing awareness that many, if not most, of the clinically significant depressions of late life do not meet standard diagnostic criteria for major depression, and that minor or subsyndromal depressions are also significant in terms of their association with adverse outcomes.

In the past, there had been hopes that it might be possible to define readily accessible biological measures that could discriminate between physically healthy adult patients with a depressive disorder, those with other psychiatric disorders, and normals, and that it might be possible to apply these markers as tools to facilitate the identification and characterization of depressive syndromes in more complex populations, such as the elderly and those with significant medical or neurological illnesses. Candidate measures included the dexamethasone suppression test, the thyrotropin releasing hormone–thyroid stimulating hormone, measures of imipramine or paroxetine binding and monoamine oxidase activity in platelets, and others. It is still possible to debate about whether this approach was ever promising or reasonable. However, it is clear that it has not helped to clarify the recognition or diagnosis of depression in late life. Our own approaches to exploring this area did, in fact, identify peripheral biochemical measures that were associated with depression among the residential care elderly including plasma levels of albumin and transferrin (Katz, Beaston-Wimmer, Parmelee, et al., 1993). However, these are biochemical indicators of protein-calorie subnutrition, probably a reflection of appetite disturbances and self-neglect in those with depression (Katz & DiFilippo, 1997). For clinicians, these findings have provided significant information on the morbidity associated with depression, but for those who may be interested in using physiological parameters to define syndromes, they merely underscore the complexity of the task. Biology is, it appears, unlikely to provide a shortcut toward the definition of depression in the frail elderly. Understanding depression must, therefore, be viewed as a problem in the evaluation of experience and behavior.

The DSM-IV diagnosis of major depression is based on affective symptoms, such as depressed mood and loss of pleasure; ideational symptoms, such as worthlessness, guilt, and thoughts of death; somatic symptoms, such as decreased appetite, fatigue, and sleep disturbance; and behavioral symptoms, such as psychomotor agitation or retardation. One recurring question concerns the value of somatic symptoms for diagnosis in patients with coexisting medical illness. This has led to the development of specialized methods for screening for depression for the elderly that avoid the use of somatic items (e.g., using the Geriatric Depression Scale; Yesavage, Brink, Rose, et al., 1983), and the use of a series of defined strategies for dealing with ambiguities in the origin of these symptoms (e.g., inclusive, exclusive, etiological, and substitutive strategies; Cohen-Cole & Stoudemire, 1987; Rapp & Vrana, 1989). These issues are of great practical importance in identifying those individuals who are to be treated. They do not, however, represent fundamental questions about how depression is defined. Instead, they assume that standard approaches derived from clinical experiences on young and healthy patients remain valid, and they are concerned with pragmatic approaches to dealing with the nuisance created by ambiguous symptoms.

More significant questions about the diagnosis of late life depression are those that have been discussed using the term "masked depression." These include two related concerns. The first is about whether the structure or profile of depressive symptoms may be different in the elderly relative to younger patients; the second is about whether older individuals with significant depression are less likely to complain of affective changes or endorse symptoms of dysphoria or anhedonia in the context of research or clinical assessments. Because help-seeking in mental health care settings requires that the patient or others experience suffering and identify a problem, questions about the frequency of masked or other atypical presentations of depression cannot be answered through studies of patients seen in psychiatric clinical samples. However, the methods for ascertainment of symptoms in epidemiological studies are, of necessity, more structured and less able to probe for subtle or complex presentations of problems than clinical evaluations.

Evidence suggesting that substantial numbers of older patients may have a clinically significant depressive syndrome without significant ideational symptoms comes from epidemiological findings that older individuals with depression express less guilt but more somatic symptoms than younger adults (Gurland, 1976). Other studies have demonstrated that older individuals with depression are less likely to respond to structured diagnostic interviews by endorsing items asking if they were distressed by either dysphoria or loss of pleasure or interests (Gallo, Anthony, & Muthen, 1994). Moreover, they found that "nondysphoric depression" observed in community samples can lead to disability and other adverse outcomes (Gallo, Rabins, Lyketsos, Tien, & Anthony, 1997.

This line of inquiry reinforces concerns about the possibility that current approaches to assessment may systematically underestimate rates of depression in the elderly. However, current problems are not limited to those that may lead to false negatives in case recognition and diagnosis. There are also concerns that decreases in motivation and initiative resulting from neuropsychological impairments in frontal systems can be confused with depression and can lead to false positives in diagnosis. This may be the basis for much of the difficulties that may occur in distinguishing between mild to moderate degrees of depression and the changes in behavior that may occur as the earliest signs of Alzheimer's Disease and related dementias (Katz & Parmelee, 1997). However, apathy and related symptoms could also, in principle, occur as a consequence of age-related changes in frontal systems or as a result of (clinical or subclinical) cerebrovascular disease.

The tools that are most likely to be able to disentangle these complex problems are not biological, but behavioral markers for depression. The value of a fine structured approach to behavior and its variability over shorter as well as longer periods of time is becoming increasingly obvious to those in the behavioral sciences. However, for those in biomedical research in general, and, more specifically, for those in the clinical neurosciences, these methods could represent significant new advances. This promise can be illustrated by following the progress that Powell Lawton and his colleagues have made in the evaluation of multiple repeated measures of affect in the elderly. Briefly, this line of work has demonstrated that major components of the variability that occurs from day to day in emotions can be characterized with brief measures of positive and negative affect that are somewhat independent of each other, and that there are significant relationships between daily affects and daily events (Kleban, Lawton, Nesselroade, & Parmelee, 1992; Lawton, DeVoe, & Parmelee, 1995; Lawton, Kleban & Dean, 1992;

Lawton, Kleban, Dean, Rajagopal, & Parmelee, 1992; Lawton, Kleban, Rajagopal, Dean, 1992). In studies comparing frail older patients with controls, individuals with major depression were found to vary considerably from day to day with respect to negative affect, but they were low and relatively invariant in their reports of positive affect. In contrast, normals varied significantly from day to day in positive affect, but were low and invariant in negative affect (Lawton, Parmelee, Katz, et al., 1996). These findings suggest that all subjects experience relatively good and relatively bad days, but that the nature of the day-to-day variability differs between normals and those with major depression. Perhaps most significantly, these findings suggest that the most consistent affective symptom of major depression in elderly patients may be anhedonia, the relative absence of positive affect, rather than dysphoria, the increased intensity of negative affects. In this, they recall earlier formulations that anhedonia is the cardinal symptom of "endogenomorphic" depression (Klein, 1974). Moreover, they suggest that a multiple repeated measures approach to the detection and measurement of anhedonia is feasible.

Other work by Powell Lawton and his colleagues has extended their methods for the assessment of affect to evaluate the affect of older patients with cognitive impairment through direct observation of facial expression, body movement, and other cues that do not depend on self-report (Lawton, Van Heitsma, & Klapper, 1996). Moreover, they have developed and applied direct observation of behavior for characterizing the spontaneous behaviors of older individuals in residential care in terms of behavior streams (Lawton, 1994). This method, based on multiple repeated periods during which one resident's behavior is directly observed and coded with respect to time use and social behaviors, can serve to determine the balance within an individual between engagement in voluntary activities, purposeful actions, and interactions with others versus null behaviors.

Taken together, these conceptual and methodological advances establish the feasibility of a fundamental, unbiased reevaluation of depression in the frail elderly in which multiple repeated measures of negative and positive mood, together with reports of daily events and naturalistic observations of spontaneous behaviors, can be used to define states of dyphoria and anhedonia, and to evaluate their relationship to apathy, decreases in spontaneous behaviors, and neuropsychological impairments. From a conceptual perspective, such an approach is necessary to evaluate the associations between affective and motivational symptoms, and in probing their relationships with other depressive symptoms on one hand, and impairments in executive functions on the other. From a more pragmatic point of view, such studies may be necessary to improve the identification of those who should be treated for depression.

These questions are increasingly relevant in light of recent research on the pathogenic mechanisms that may lead to late life depression. The literature in this area distinguishes between major depressions in older patients that are recurrences of disorders with their initial onset earlier in life (early onset depressions) and those that began for the first time when patients were older (late onset depressions). Evidence is accumulating that these subtypes differ in pathogenic mechanisms. Early onset depressions appear to be characterized by an increased history of depression among first-degree relatives, consistent with a genetic predisposition, while late onset depressions, instead, are characterized by other factors, most prominently an increased presence of chronic medical or neurological illness. More recently, these findings have been augmented by observations by a number of investigators that late onset major depressions are associated with an increased prevalence of subcortical and deep white matter hyperintensities present on magnetic resonance imaging scans of the brain (Krishnan, Hays, & Blazer, 1997). Neuroimaging research has demonstrated that these lesions occur in the context of risk factors for cerebrovascular disease such as hypertension, cardiac disease, diabetes, and peripheral vascular disease, and that they are most likely to represent silent and subclinical vascular disease with ischemic lesions in white matter or subcortical gray matter regions. Other research has demonstrated that the white matter lesions of the type that characterize vascular depression can disrupt connections between areas of the cerebral cortex (Leuchter et al., 1994) and that, above critical thresholds, they are associated with impairments in frontal systems and neuropsychological tests that probe executive functions (DeCarli et al., 1995; Lesser et al., 1996; Sultzer, Mahler, Cummings, et al., 1995). These findings have led to a model for late onset vascular depressions as a subtype of major depression, in which the path to illness flows from the presence of diseases that compromise the cerebral circulation through subclinical cerebrovascular disease marked by subcortical and deep white matter hyperintensities on magnetic resonance imaging to psychiatric symptoms. Clinical studies have suggested that patients with vascular depression have features that distinguish them from other late life depressions including more retardation, less guilt feelings, greater lack of insight, anhedonia, and neuropsychological findings including decrements in verbal fluency and naming (Alexopoulos et al., 1997; Krishnan et al., 1997).

One model explaining many of these findings is that white matter lesions can lead to decreased activity of the neural systems underlying positive affect and positive affective (hedonic) responses to daily events. This could occur if these lesions disrupted the ascending, predominantly dopaminergic fibers subserving reinforcement and intracerebral self-stimulation that originate in the brain stem and ascend to limbic regions (Self & Stein, 1992; Stein, Xue, & Belluzzi, 1993). Moreover, it could lead to anhedonia without significant dysphoria or depressive ideations. In spite of the intuitive strength of the association between depression and decreased activity of reinforcement systems, there has been little research in this area over the past decade, possibly because it has proven difficult to conduct quantitative research on the relationship between antidepressant drug administrative and changes in the parameters characterizing the responses of experimental animals to electrical stimulation of these systems. In fact, models based upon these systems have served to guide research on substance abuse more than affective disorders. There has, however, been a suggestion that neuronal systems underlying reinforcement may be dysfunctional in one type of late life depression: that associated with the neurodegenerative disorder Parkinson's Disease. In patients with Parkinsonism complicated by major depression, administration of the stimulant (and dopamine-releasing) medication methyphenidate led to less "activation plus euphoria" than in others with Parkinson's disease or those with major depression alone (Cantello et al., 1989). In this study, the effects of methylphenidate was discussed as a probe of the activity of "hedonic synapses," those aminergic neural systems that regulate reinforcement and pleasure, and the conclusion was that depression occurs when the process of neurodegeneration extends to include these neurons.

Another model is based on suggestions that depression can result from damage to neural circuits linking the frontal cortex, basal ganglia, and thalamus. Dysfunction of striato–pallido–thalamo–cortical pathways could lead to depression by direct damage to in- or outflow paths involving the frontal cortex, or impairment of dopaminergic, noradrenergic, or serotonergic pathways that regulate the activity of frontal systems, and/or disruption of descending prefrontal controls of brainstem serotoninergic systems. Evidence in favor of this model comes from findings on the anatomic distribution of subcortical and white matter lesions (Krishnan, 1993) and from functional neuroimaging research that links depressions in a number of brain diseases to decreased frontal activity (Mayberg, 1994). According to this model, older patients' lack of complaints related to affective symptoms could be related to decreased insight as a component of impaired executive functions.

Findings on the clinical features of vascular depression as a subtype of late life major depression reinforce those derived from epidemiological studies. They suggest the hypothesis that states of decreased positive affect, decreased positive affective responses to potentially pleasurable events, and decreased motivation or initiative can occur in older individuals, often without insight or distress, and that they may be associated with neuropsychological deficits in tests that evaluate executive functions. These clinical features may characterize the core features of late life depression, or a prodromal state. It is possible that the evolution of this state to the full syndrome of major depression in which these symptoms are complemented with dysphoria, ideational, behavioral, and somatic symptoms may occur primarily in those with vulnerable personalities, those without adequate social supports, or those who experience severe psychosocial stress. Alternatively, a more deterministic model might suggest that the development of a complete major depression may occur when underlying vascular pathology progresses to reach a critical threshold. If these symptoms are, in fact, precursors of major depression, they may be appropriate targets for preventive interventions. Moreover, in light of suggestions that patients with vascular depression may respond to pharmacological treatments for depression more slowly and less completely, it is important to evaluate the extent to which the clinical features under discussion here are, in fact, alleviated with standard treatments for major depression. If they remain as residual symptoms, they may be appropriate targets for rehabilitation.

Until now the field of geriatric psychiatry has, of necessity, borrowed its definitions of pathology from what was learned in younger and healthier patients. Although, as discussed above, current DSM-IV based approaches to diagnosis do, in fact, identify patients that benefit from treatment, even among the oldest old and those with significant comorbid conditions, there must be both conceptual and pragmatic concerns that some patients with significant depression are missed, while others may be treated unnecessarily. Powell Lawton's methods make it possible to take a new look at the within- and between-individual variability in affect and spontaneous behaviors in older individuals, and to characterize the cross-sectional and longitudinal associations of both anhedonia and apathy. Such an ab initio look at the core features of depression can serve to define the depressive syndromes of late life in a way that responds to the clinical realities of this population.

REFERENCES

Alexopoulos, G. S., Meyers, B. S., Young, R. C., Kakuma, T., Silbusweig, D., & Charlson, M. (1997). Clinically defined vascular depression. *American Journal of Psychiatry, 154*, 562–565.

American Psychiatric Association. (1994). *Diagnostic and statistical manual of mental disorders* (4th ed.). Washington, DC: American Psychiatric Press.

Cantello, R., Aguggia, M., Gilli, M., Delsedime, M., Chiardo Cutin, I., Riccio, A., & Mutani, R. (1989). Major depression in Parkinson's disease and the mood response to intravenous methylphenidate: Possible role of the "hedonic" dopamine synapse. *Journal of Neurology, Neurosurgery & Psychiatry, 52*, 724–731.

Cohen-Cole, S., & Stoudemire, A. (1987). Major depression and physical illness. Special considerations in diagnosis and biological treatment. *Psychiatric Clinics of North America, 10*, 1–17.

DeCarli, C., Murphy, D. G., Tranh, M., Grady, C. L., Haxby, J. V., Gillette, J. A., Salerno, J. A., Gonzales-Aviles, A., Horwitz, B., Rapoport, S. I., & Schapiro, M. B. (1995). The effect of white matter hyperintensity volume on brain structure, cognitive performance, and cerebral metabolism of glucose in 51 healthy adults. *Neurology, 45*, 2077–2084.

Gallo, J. J., Anthony, J. C., & Muthen, B. O. (1994). Age differences in the symptoms of depression: a latent trait analysis. *Journal of Gerontology: Psychological Sciences, 6*, P251–P264.

Gallo, J. J., Rabins, P. V., Lyketsos, C. G., Tien, A. Y., & Anthony, J. C. (1997). Depression without sadness: functional outcomes of nondysphoric depression in later life. *Journal of the American Geriatrics Society. 45*, 570–578.

Gurland, B. (1976). The comparative frequency of depression in various age groups. *Journal of Gerontology, 31*, 283–292.

Katz, I. R., & Alexopoulos, G. S. (1996). The diagnosis and treatment of late life depression: Consensus update conference. *American Journal of Geriatric Psychiatry, 4*, supplement.

Katz, I. R., Beaston-Wimmer, P., Parmelee, P., Friedman, E., & Lawton, M. P. (1993). Failure to thrive in the elderly: Exploration of the concept and delineation of psychiatric components. *Journal of Geriatric Psychiatry and Neurology, 6*, 161–169.

Katz, I. R., & DiFilippo, S. (1997). Neuropsychiatric aspects of failure to thrive in late life. In R. Verdug (Ed.), *Failure to thrive in older people*. Philadelphia: Saunders.

Katz, I. R., & Parmelee, P. (1997). Assessment of depression in patients with dementia. *Journal of Mental Health and Aging, 2*, 235–252.

Kleban, M. H., Lawton, M. P., Nesselroade, J. R., & Parmelee, P. (1992). The structure of variation in affect among depressed and nondepressed elders. *Journal of Gerontology, 47*, P190–P198.

Klein, D. F. (1974). Endogenomorphic depression: A conceptual and terminological revision. *Archives of General Psychiatry, 31*, 447–454.

Krishnan, K. R. (1993). Neuroanatomic substrates of depression in the elderly. *Journal of Geriatric Psychiatry & Neurology, 6*, 39–58.

Krishnan, K. R., Hays, J. C., & Blazer, D. G. (1997). MRI-defined vascular depression. *American Journal of Psychiatry, 154*, 497–501.

Lawton, M. P. (1994). Quality of life in Alzheimer disease. *Alzheimer Disease & Associated Disorders, 8* (Suppl 3), 138–150.

Lawton, M. P., De Voe, M. R., & Parmelee, P. (1995). Relationship of events and affect in the daily life of an elderly population. *Psychology & Aging, 10*, 469–477.

Lawton, M. P., Kleban, M. H., & Dean, J. (1993). Affect and age: cross-sectional comparisons of structure and prevalence. *Psychology & Aging, 8*, 165–175.

Lawton, M. P., Kleban, M. H., Dean, J., Rajagopal, D., & Parmelee, P. A., (1992). The factorial generality of brief positive and negative affect measures. *Journal of Gerontology, 47*, P228–P237.

Lawton, M. P., Kleban, M. H., Rajagopal, D., & Dean, J. (1992). Dimensions of affective experience in three age groups. *Psychology & Aging, 7*, 171–184.

Lawton, M. P., Parmelee, P. A., Katz, I. R., & Nesselroade, J. (1996). Affective states in normal and depressed older people. *Journal of Gerontology, Series B, Psychological Sciences & Social Sciences, 51*, P307–P316.

Lawton, M. P., Van Haitsma, K., & Klapper, J. (1996). Observed affect in nursing home residents with Alzheimer's disease. *Journals of Gerontology: Psychological Sciences & Social Sciences, 51*, P3–P14.

Lebowitz, B. D., Pearson, J. L., Schneider, L. S., Reynolds, C. F., Alexopoulos, G. S., Bruce, M. L., Conwell, Y., Katz, I. R., Meyers, B. S., Morrison, M. F., Mossey, J., Niederehe, G., & Parmelee, P. (1997). Diagnosis and treatment of depression in late life: Consensus statement update. *JAMA, 278*, 1186–1190.

Lesser, I. M., Boone, K. B., Mehringer, C. M., Wohl, M. A., Miller, B. C., & Berman, N. G. (1996). Cognition and white matter hyperintensities in older depressed patients. *American Journal of Psychiatry, 153*, 1280–1287.

Leuchter, A. F., Dunkin, J. J., Lufkin, R. B., Anzai, Y., Cook, I. A., & Newton, T. F. (1994). Effect of white matter disease on functional connections in the aging brain. *Journal of Neurology, Neurosurgery & Psychiatry, 57*, 1347–1354.

Mayberg, H. S. (1994). Frontal lobe dysfunction in secondary depression. *Journal of Neuropsychiatry & Clinical Neurosciences, 6*, 428–442.

Rapp, S. R., & Vrana, S. (1989). Substituting nonsomatic for somatic symptoms in the diagnosis of depression in elderly male medical patients. *American Journal of Psychiatry, 146*, 1197–1200.

Rubinstein, R., & Lawton, M. P. (1997). *Depression among the frail elderly*. New York: Springer Publishing Co.

Schneider, L. S., Reynolds, C. F., Lebowitz, B. D., & Friedhoff, A. J. (1993). *Diagnosis and treatment of depression in late life: Results of the NIH Consensus Development Conference.* Washington, DC: American Psychiatric Press.

Self, D. W., & Stein, L. (1992). Receptor subtypes in opioid and stimulant reward. *Pharmacology & Toxicology, 70,* 87–94.

Stein, L., Xue, B. G., & Belluzzi, J. D. (1993). Cellular targets of brain reinforcement systems. *Annals of the New York Academy of Sciences, 702,* 41–60.

Sultzer, D. L., Mahler, M. E., Cummings, J. L., Van Gorp, W. G., Urkin, C. H., & Brown, C. (1995). Cortical abnormalities associated with subcortical lesions in vascular dementia: Clinical and positron emission tomographic findings. *Archives of Neurology, 52,* 773–780.

Yesavage, J. A., Brink, T. L., Rosen, T. L., Lum, O., Huang, V., Adey, M., & Leiser, V. O. (1983). Development and validation of a geriatric depression scale. *Journal of Psychiatric Research, 17,* 31–49.

IV

Personal and Human Development

10

A Stage Theory Model of Adult Cognitive Development Revisited

K. Warner Schaie and Sherry L. Willis

S ome 20 years ago, K. Warner Schaie (1977–1978) formulated a stage theory of cognitive development that included three adult stages, based on findings from research on adult intellectual development. In introducing this model, he suggested that his previous empirical work on psychometric intelligence had generally shown that the largest differences in cognitive function between young and old are on the whole not ontogenetic in nature. Instead, the largest age differences were often found when individuals were compared who belonged to generations differing in the asymptotic level of acculturated materials acquired in young or middle adulthood (Schaie, 1974). Nevertheless, even if these changes over age within individuals on measures validated for the young are relatively modest until advanced old age, this does not necessarily mean that the young and the old are cognitively alike. Indeed, simple observation required the admission, if only in terms of face validity, that there ought to be some qualitative age-related changes. Hence, Schaie and colleagues (Willis & Schaie, 1986, 1993) concluded that the processes which have been documented for the acquisition of cognitive structures and functions in childhood and during the early adult phase may not be altogether relevant for the maintenance of functions and reorganization of structures required to meet the demands of middle age and later life.

As will be discussed in this chapter, we now believe that there is indeed continuity from childhood into old age with respect to the basic processes and complex skills measured in the context of psychometric intelligence (Schaie, Willis, Jay, & Chipuer, 1989). But we also believe that these processes, in adulthood, represent only the *necessary* conditions for adequate cognitive functioning. As Schaie surmised in 1977–78, there are thought to be additional processes that would enhance explanations of qualitative and quantitative changes in cognitive function occurring throughout the adult lifespan. Schaie began to articulate an alternative model for adult cognitive development which might provide a blueprint for the development of new descriptive strategies. He did not elect to posit more complex post-formal stages of thought as have been proposed by writers such as Commons et al. (1990), Labouvie-Vief (1992), or Sinnott (1984, 1996) that imply further changes in cognitive structures per se. Instead, influenced by work of sociologists and anthropologists (e.g., Berry & Irvine, 1986; Kohn & Schooler, 1983; Lowenthal et al., 1975; Riley, 1994) his model explicitly addressed contextual demands that impact adult cognitive functioning. Before proceeding it needs to be made clear that we are talking exclusively about the process of normal cognitive aging. No effort is made to speculate on how the occurrence of dementia might affect the progression of cognitive changes.

In this chapter we will expand the original model by specifying two additional adult stages. We then provide a rationale for the necessity of maintaining performance, at least above minimal threshold levels, on the psychometric abilities so important in youth and young adulthood. We will also consider the importance of certain cognitive styles and personality in the maintenance of adult cognitive functioning. Finally, we will consider the role of cooperative modes of cognitive performance; that is, the role and support of a partner in problem-solving efforts.

THE 1977–78 ADULT STAGE MODEL

The Achievement Stage

Schaie began with the observation that Piaget's childhood stages describe primarily increasing efficiency in the acquisition of new information (cf. Flavell, 1963). He doubted that adults progress beyond the powerful methods of science (formal operations) in their quest for knowledge. Therefore, if one is to posit adult stages, they should not be further stages of acquisition, but instead they should reflect different uses of intellect. For example, in young adulthood, people typically switch their focus from the acquisition to the application of knowledge, as they use what they know to pursue careers and families. This was called the achieving stage. It represents most prominently the application of intellectual skills in situations that have profound consequences for achieving long-term goals (such as those involving decisions about career and marriage).

The situations described above, of course, are not the hypothetical ones posed on educational tests or encountered in classroom studies, nor are they the problems of childhood whose solutions are closely monitored by parents and society. Instead, they are problems adults must solve for themselves, and the solutions must be integrated into a life plan that extends far into the future. The kind of mental abilities exhibited in such situations is similar to that manifested in scholastic tasks, but it requires more careful attention to the possible consequences of the problem-solving process. Attending to the context of problem solving is similar to health-care decision making, where the conse-

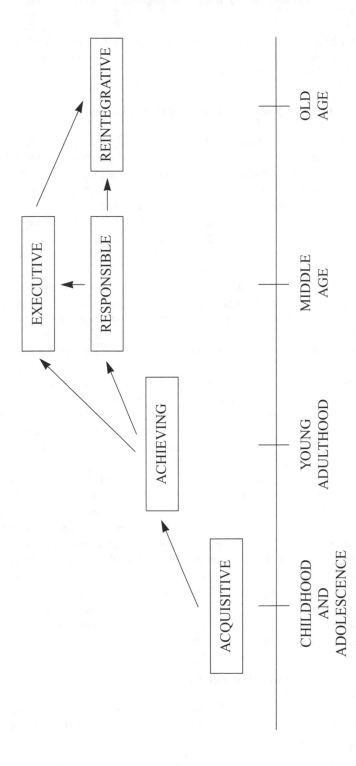

Figure 10.1 Schema depicting the original 1977–79 cognitive stage model.

From K. W. Schaie (1977–1978). Toward a stage theory of adult cognitive development. *Journal of Aging and Human Development, 8,* 133. © 1978 Banwood Publishing Company, Inc. Reproduced with permission.

quences of a particular decision can involve the maintenance or termination of one's life (Lawton, 1997; Smyer, Schaie, & Kapp, 1996). Figure 10.1 provides a schematic depicting the original 1977–78 stage theory model.

The Responsible and Executive Stages

Young adults who have mastered the cognitive skills required for monitoring their own behavior and, as a consequence, have attained a certain degree of personal independence will next move into a stage that requires the application of cognitive skills in situations involving social responsibility. Typically, the responsible stage occurs when a family is established and the needs of spouse and offspring must be attended to. Similar extensions of adult cognitive skills are required as responsibilities for others are acquired on the job and in the community (Hagestad & Neugarten, 1985).

Some individuals' responsibilities become exceedingly complex. Such individuals— CEOs of business firms, presidents of academic institutions, officials of churches, government officials, and people in a number of other positions—need to understand the structure and the dynamic forces of organizations. They must monitor organizational activities not only on a temporal dimension (past, present, and future), but also up and down the hierarchy that defines the organization. They need to know not only the future plans of the organization, but also whether policy decisions are being adequately translated into action at lower levels of responsibility. The number of individuals requiring this level of thinking is larger than might be thought. They are found among the approximately 25% of both men and women in the labor force who are in the professional job category which often involves executive responsibilities (Department of Labor, 1992). Attainment of the executive stage, as a variation on the responsible stage, depends on exposure to opportunities that allow the development and practice of the relevant skills (Avolio, 1991; Avolio & Waldman, 1990; Smith, Staudinger, & Baltes, 1994).

It should be noted that the executive stage is not narrowly age-based. Although it usually begins in late midlife, there are exceptions of persons taking leadership roles in their late 30s and early 40s. By the same token, while for most persons the executive stage will end in their early 60s, there are some who continue on into their 70s and 80s. Noteworthy examples of the extension of the executive stage may be found among Supreme Court justices and church leaders. Indeed, as life expectancy has increased, and in the case of the United States, mandatory retirement by reason of age has been abandoned or delayed, the executive stage may be prolonged into old age for many professionals. It should also be noted that persons with executive experience are being called out of retirement with increasing frequency to serve as professional consultants, or to cover vacant positions on an interim basis in periods of economic expansion or political change.

The Reintegration Stage

In the later years of life, beyond the age of 70 or 75, the need to acquire vast domains of substantive knowledge declines even more. The necessity of monitoring decisions in terms of long-term consequences also decreases, because the future appears more short-term. Executive monitoring is less important, because frequently the individual has retired from the position that required such an application of intelligence. What, then, is the nature of cognitive functioning in an elderly adult? Schaie (1977–1978) suggested that there is a transition from the childhood question "What should I know?" through the adult question "How should I use what I know?" to the question of later life "Why should I know?" This final stage, reintegration, corresponds in its position in the life course to Erikson's (1963, 1984) stage of ego integrity. The information that elderly people acquire and the knowledge they apply is, to a greater extent than earlier in life, a function of their interests, attitudes, and values (Dittman-Kohli, 1990; Wong, 1989). It requires, in fact, the reintegration of all of these. The elderly are less likely to "waste time" on tasks that are meaningless to them. They are unlikely to expend much effort to solve a problem unless that problem is one that is frequently faced in their lives, or that involves a one-time decision that is of critical importance to them (see also Berg, Klaczynski, Calderone, & Strough, 1994).

TWO ADDITIONAL STAGES

The Reorganizational Stage

Since the original stages were formulated, we have learned a lot about the differentiation of our older population into distinct life stages. In the research literature, distinctions are now commonly made between the young-old, the old-old, and the oldest old (or very-old; Suzman & Riley, 1985). This differentiation is informed by the fact that today's young old are distinguished from the middle-aged primarily by the fact that the vast majority of persons in this life period are no longer engaged in the world of paid work.

A major effort must now be expanded in reorganizing one's life such that the earlier engagement with family raising and job responsibilities, characteristic of what we call the responsible or executive stages, is replaced by an effort to substitute meaningful pursuits for these activities. In addition, activities are directed towards planning how one's resources will last for the remaining 15 to 30 years of post-retirement life characteristic for most individuals in industrialized societies (Brandstädter & Renner, 1990; Brim, 1992; Smith, 1996). These activities include active planning for that period in life when one may expect dependence upon others in order to maintain a high quality of life in the face of increasing frailty. Such efforts may involve changes in one's housing arrangements, or even one's locality of residence, as well as making sure of the eventual availability of both familial and extrafamilial support systems. In this context it may become increasingly important to make or change one's will, to execute advanced medical directives, or to provide durable powers of attorney, as well as to create trusts or other financial arrangements that will protect resources for use during the final years of life or for the needs of other family members (Lawton, 1997; Smyer et al., 1996).

While some of these activities continue to require the cognitive characteristics of the responsible stage, we think that the objectives involved are generally far more centered to current and future needs of the individual rather than the needs of their family or of an organizational entity. Prior to retirement, most persons' time and resources are devoted primarily to the world of work and to raising family. Efforts must now be initiated to reorganize one's time and resources to substitute a meaningful environment, often found in leisure activities, volunteerism, and involvement with their larger kinship network. Eventually, however, these activities are also engaged in with the finitude of life in clear view, for the purpose of maximizing the quality of life during the final years and often with the objective of not becoming a burden for the next generation (Lawton, 1997). Because of the unique objective of these demands upon the individual, we believe that we can recognize an almost universal process occurring at least in the industrialized societies, and believe designation of a separate stage termed the reorganizational stage is warranted.

The cognitive skills required for the reorganizational stage require the maintenance of high levels of cognitive competence as measured by psychometric intelligence. However, for the successful older individual, cognitive competence is increasingly exercised within the parsimonious principles of optimization and compensation (P. B. Baltes, 1987; Baltes & Baltes, 1990; M. M. Baltes, & Carstensen, 1996; Dittman-Kohli & Baltes, 1990). In addition, we would expect that maintenance of flexible cognitive styles will be important in being able to restructure the context and content of one's life upon retiring from the world of work. This flexibility is also needed in making provisions that require relinquishment of control over one's resources to others and the partial surrender of one's independence (Schaie, 1984, 1996).

Unless a person reaches early old age in poor health and in a dependent condition, the reorganizational stage becomes a necessary intermediate phase before the transition into the reintegrative stage can occur. Once these tasks have been accomplished, the maintenance of cognitive skills may become less critical, although it remains an important prerequisite for retaining support systems and exerting some control over one's life. Nevertheless, feelings of personal efficacy (Lachman & Leff, 1989), locus of control (Bandura & Jourden, 1991), and effective states (Lawton, Kleban, Rajagopal, & Dean, 1992) may now play an increasingly important role and socioemotional concerns may become more prominent (Blanchard-Fields, 1996). That is, perhaps already beginning as part of the reorganizational stage, we now see a selective reduction of interpersonal networks in the interest of reintegrating one's concern in a more self-directed and supportive manner (Carstensen, 1993; Fredrickson & Carstensen, 1990). Such efforts are likely to involve a reduction in information-seeking activities while increasing the importance of emotional regulation involved (Carstensen, Gross, & Fung, 1997).

The Legacy-Leaving Stage

As more and more older persons reach the end of their life in advanced old age in relative comfort and often with a clear mind, albeit a frail body, once the reintegrative efforts have been successfully completed, and perhaps temporally overlapping with it, there is yet one other stage that might be suggested. We are here concerned with the cognitive activities engaged by many of the very old in anticipation of the end of their life. We would like therefore to postulate a final legacy-leaving stage, which is of importance in the cognitive development of many, if not all, older persons.

This stage may well begin by the self- or therapist-induced effort to conduct a life review (Butler, Lewis, & Sunderland, 1991). For the highly literate and those successful in public or professional life (in fact, for all who think that their life is worth writing about and of potential interest to others) it will often include writing or revising an auto-biography (Birren, Kenyon, Ruth, Schroots, & Swensson, 1995).

Obviously maintenance of long-term memory and verbal skills is required to complete such an autobiographical task. But the reflection involved also include judgments that are informed by the socioemotional importance of the events and other actors to be included in the autobiography. But there are other more mundane legacies to be left. Women, in particular, wish to put their remaining effects in order, and often distribute many of their prized possessions to friends and relatives, or create elaborate instructions for distributing them. Not uncommon is a renewed effort to provide oral history or explain family pictures and heirlooms for the next generation. Last but not least, directions are given for funeral arrangements, occasionally including donation of one's body for scientific efforts, and there may be a final revision of one's will. All of these activities require cognitive competencies, and all of them involve exercising these competencies within a socioemotional and interpersonal relationship context.

The suggested time-line for the revised stage model is provided in Figure 10.2. It should once again be stressed that what we think is important is the sequential process of these developmental stages; not the precise chronological age at which they occur, which may be quite variable in different societies and for individuals at different levels of intellectual competence and personal engagement.

ROLE OF BASIC ABILITIES IN ADULT COGNITION

One of the themes revisited in this paper is the role in later stages of adult cognition of those basic mental abilities that are particularly salient during the acquisition stage. Some have contended that there is little relationship between the basic abilities traditionally studied in early phases of cognitive development and the cognitively demanding tasks pursued in middle and later adulthood (Berg & Klaczynski, 1996; Sternberg & Wagner, 1986).

Hierarchical Relationships

We have suggested, however, that a hierarchical relationship exists between these more basic forms of intelligence and the complex cognitive tasks involved in the achieving and responsible stages (Willis, 1991; Willis & Schaie, 1993, 1996). Similar to Berry and

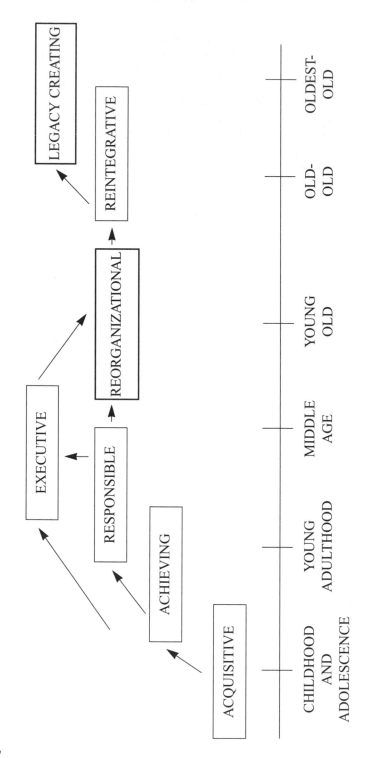

Figure 10.2 Schema depicting the revised cognitive stage model.

Irvine (1986), we propose that the cognitive processes and abilities that seem to dominate the acquisition phases are universal across cultures. When nurtured and directed by a particular society or at a particular stage of life, these processes and abilities develop into cognitive competencies that are manifested in daily life as the bases for cognitive performance in adulthood. In other words, the basic abilities and processes represent genotypic forms of intelligence that are relatively context- or culture-free. On the other hand, everyday competencies, as represented in activities of daily living, are phenotypic expressions of intelligence that are context- and age-specific.

The particular activities and behaviors that serve as phenotypic expressions of intelligence will vary with the age of the individual, that person's social roles, and the environmental context. The relative salience of a particular ability in the performance of everyday tasks is determined in part by the historical and environmental context. For example, as computer-based technologies become more pervasive in all areas of life in Western society, the basic ability of inductive reasoning is becoming increasingly salient in many areas of the adult experience, including work, leisure, social communication, and health care.

Mental Abilities and Instrumental Activities

The relation of basic mental abilities, such as reasoning, memory, and verbal ability, to adult work tasks such as report writing, scheduling, and supervision that occur in the responsible and executive stages seems intuitively plausible. The question arises, however, whether these basic abilities remain relevant to the tasks that older adults perform once they leave the work force, during the reorganizational and reintegrative stages. There are considerable individual differences in what types of activities older adults engage in during these phases, when priorities are shifting. Nevertheless, there are certain domains of tasks that are considered essential for maintenance of independent living. These tasks become increasingly important to almost all adults during later adulthood. Seven task domains have been identified as critical for independent living: Management of finances, transportation, taking medications, telephone usage, meal preparation, shopping for necessities, and housekeeping (Lawton & Brody, 1969).

In our research on the concurrent relationships between the basic mental abilities and performance of cognitively demanding tasks in these activity domains, we have found that over half of the individual differences variance in older adults performance on everyday tasks can be accounted for by mental ability performance (Willis, 1996; Willis & Schaie, 1994). Because different psychometric abilities exhibit different patterns of age-related change in later adulthood (Schaie, 1990), we were particularly interested in the specific abilities that were related to everyday task performance.

Cattell (1971) has differentiated between two broad domains of mental abilities. Crystallized abilities (e.g., verbal, social reasoning) are said to reflect acculturated influences, such as level of schooling. In healthy older adults, crystallized abilities remain stable, on average, showing little or no decline until old-old age or in close proximity to death (Bosworth, 1997; Schaie, 1996). In contrast, fluid abilities (e.g., inductive reasoning, spatial orientation) are said to be impacted by neurological assaults and to exhibit earlier patterns of decline beginning on average in the mid-60s. Thus, older adults' performance on cognitively demanding everyday activities would be expected to show different patterns of developmental change, depending on whether such activates are more closely related to fluid or crystallized abilities.

In our own research both fluid and crystallized abilities have been found to account for substantial proportions of variance in everyday task performance, although a somewhat greater portion of variance was accounted for by fluid abilities (Diehl, Willis, & Schaie, 1995; Schaie, 1996). In our hierarchical model of ability-everyday competence relationships, basic mental abilities have been hypothesized to be the salient antecedents of performance on cognitively demanding tasks in later stages of cognitive development. Thus, lagged rather than concurrent relationships needed to be examined. Fluid ability at the first occasion of measurement was found to predict everyday task performance 7 years later (Willis, Jay, Diehl, & Marsiske, 1992). Everyday task performance predicted abilities at the second occasion significantly less well. Therefore, our hypothesis that adequate performance on basic abilities represents necessary, although not sufficient, antecedents of subsequent everyday task performance was supported.

An association between basic abilities salient in the acquisitive phase and everyday tasks of concern during later cognitive stages, such as reorganizational stage, has been observed not only when the abilities were represented within the psychometric ability framework, but also when basic cognitive processes were represented within a clinical diagnostic framework. Our recent work indicates that processes such as time, orientation, word fluency, short-term memory, and executive functioning are also associated with performance of tasks of daily living (Willis, Dolan, & Bertrand, 1999).

One of the most notable differences between phenotypes of intellectual functioning as represented during the acquisitive and later stages is the level of complexity of the types of tasks involved. That is, many cognitively demanding tasks in the acquisitive phase focus on or represent a single mental ability or process. For example, traditionally, schooling has involved a series of classes or courses, each focusing largely on a single cognitive domain (e.g., math, reading.) In post-secondary education, as training for the achievement phases becomes foremost, the courses focus on more complex substantive domains and skills (e.g., accounting, personnel management). Our research and that of others indicates that the more complex cognitive tasks more common to the later stages seldom represent a single basic mental ability. The tasks are complex, in part, because they require the application of *multiple basic abilities*. As noted earlier in the chapter, the complexity of cognitive functioning in the later stages is not only due to the fact that multiple cognitive abilities are involved, but also because the individual must determine when and how social and emotional knowledge as well as personal experience needs to be incorporated into the problem solution (Blanchard-Fields & Abeles, 1996; Willis & Schaie, 1993).

Personal Knowledge and Problem Solving

The role of prior experience in problem solving in later adulthood has become a topic of increasing interest (Meyer, Russo, & Talbot, 1995; Leventhal & Cameron, 1987). The rich and vast experiences acquired over a lifetime would seem to serve older adults well in making decisions and solving problems in the later years. The utility of this vast store of prior experience, however, depends on the older adult's judgment of when and how to apply this knowledge base.

Sinnott (1989) has described age-related modes of problem solving, A youthful style is characterized by a "bottom-up" approach; the young lack relevant knowledge and compensate by gathering large amounts of information and focusing on data rather than on prior experience. In contrast, the old style represents primarily a "top-down" approach. Older adults are seen as applying somewhat indiscriminatory and extensive knowledge acquired through a lifetime of experience. Procedural knowledge or heuristics developed through prior experience are sometime used with little consideration of whether these procedures are relevant to the problem at hand. Sinnott states (1989, p. 96) that the old style is suited for "rapid, low energy-demand solutions done by the experienced solver with many available structures of knowledge. It was top-down in style with little attention to data, probably because of poor memory capacities." The mature style is characterized as the optimal approach and is said to be more evident in midlife. [It suggests a balance of the bottom-up and top-down as most efficacious.]

Support for Sinnott's old style is found in our recent error analyses of older adults' solutions to everyday tasks (Willis et al., 1999). Subjects provided answers based on prior life experiences with seemingly little consideration or awareness of whether solutions relevant to prior problems remained appropriate for the present situation. With regard to the relationship between basic abilities and subsequent cognitive stages, we have found, as Sinnott suggests, that errors based on inappropriate use of prior experience are associated with poorer memory performance among the elderly. Perhaps inappropriate use of prior experience is a compensatory mechanism that is employed when the older adult is faced with a situation that appears superficially similar to past activities, but the older adult lacks the memory resources or psychological energy to determine whether the critical features (procedural knowledge) of the current problem and prior experience are sufficiently relevant.

PERSONAL CONTROL AND COGNITIVE AGING

Personal control is defined as an individual's beliefs or attitudes regarding the extent to which outcomes or performance are due to his or her own doing, as opposed to forces outside the self (Levenson, 1975). Those who believe that their own actions are responsible for outcomes are said to have an internal control orientation. In contrast, those who believe that outside forces such as fate or powerful others are responsible for outcomes in their life are said to have an external orientation. Of particular concern in this chapter are beliefs about one's own intellectual functioning in the later years.

What does the elder believe about the locus of control over cognitive aging? Longitudinal research conducted by Lachman and Leff (1989) and in our laboratory (Willis et al., 1992) indicate that age-related increments do occur in external control orientations in the elderly. With increasing age, elders ascribe greater control over cognitive aging to circumstances beyond their own efficacy. In particular, there is an increasing belief in the role of powerful others as a source of control. The older adult reports that a significant other in their life (doctor, adult child, minister) is better able to make decisions regarding their affairs than they are. Findings on age-related change in internal control (belief in self-efficacy) are less consistent, with some studies reporting stability while others actually find an increase with age (Lachman & McArthur, 1986).

While in self-efficacy research there has been limited attention to the individual differences perspective, two categories of correlates/predictors of control orientation have been reported. First, Rodin, Timko, and Harris (1985) have reported that with aging health factors, particularly vision and hearing, are significant predictors of internal control beliefs regarding cognition in old age (Willis, Marsiske, & Diehl, 1991). Second, level of performance on psychometric abilities has been found to be a long-term predictor of control beliefs in both Lachman's and our own research. Specifically, psychometric abilities predict subsequent level of control beliefs. In contrast, control beliefs have not been shown to be significant predictors of later intellectual functioning (Lachman & Leff, 1989; Willis et al., 1992).

COOPERATIVE MODES OF COGNITION

A final topic of concern in revisiting the cognitive stage model is the role of shared cognition during the later stages. We hypothesize that cognitive functioning is increasingly likely to involve other individuals, either because of the increasing frailty or limitations of the individual, or because the substantive focus of cognitive tasks takes on a greater social focus in later life (Baltes & Staudinger, 1996; Blanchard-Fields & Abeles, 1996). In the early acquisition phase the focus is on the individual's development of specific mental abilities. Academic performance in Western society focuses largely on individual achievement rather than on group products. Thus, most theories of intellectual development during the early years are concerned with the individual per se.

Social Interaction and Problem Solving

As the individual joins social groups in the achievement phase as a part of work or family development, decision making and productivity become more social in nature. The influence of social interactions in carrying out cognitively demanding tasks continues in the responsible and executive phases. When adults aged 19 to 80 years were asked how they went about solving fundamental life problems, the most frequent reply was that they consulted others (Staudinger & Baltes, 1985). Seeking the advice of others was in fact reported as the most common source mode at all ages. In old age, advice seeking may take the form of locating the locus of control in powerful others (Levenson, 1975). By delegating control to others, proxy control allows the elderly person to maintain earlier goals through the assistance of others (Bandura, 1982).

Research in social psychology on the role of social interaction in relation to cognition has provided some interesting findings (Staudinger, 1996). In general, social interaction is conceived as providing a supportive context for cognitive activities. Studies at younger ages suggest that the mere presence of others may impact cognitive functioning. The individual is more likely to be alert and persistent in cognitive-type tasks when these tasks are performed in the presence of others. Prior social interaction is also likely to influence the subsequent performance of the individual. The group may offer alternative solutions to a problem or require the individual to rethink an approach to a problem. In group problem solving, the strengths of various members of the group can compensate for the particular ability limitations of individual members (Steiner, 1972).

Zajonc (1960) proposed a theoretical formulation called *cognitive tuning*. When the individual is forced to verbalize or communicate certain information to others, this results in a greater differentiation (breadth, number of categories), complexity (depth, subdivisions), unity, and organization of one's own knowledge. However, social interaction per se is not sufficient to facilitate or enhance individual cognition significantly. The best approach is a combination of social interaction combined with individual reflection and problem solving. The individual formulates the problem and speculates on alternative solutions, then considers the problem with a group, and finally reflects on the individual and group's ideas regarding problem solutions (Osborne, 1957; Staudinger & Baltes, 1985).

Social Relationships and Life Review

Thus far, we have considered only the effect of social interaction on cognition with respect to problem solving and decision making. However, there are also research findings that social interaction can be facilitative in the reintegration stage when the focus may be on reflection on one's life, achievements, and disappointments. In the early life stages it has been shown that identity formation is mediated through feedback by others. The life review process suggests that interaction with others is important also in the reintegrative stage (Butler et al., 1991; Kenyon, Mader, & Ruth, 1999; Whitborne, 1986). Interaction with others, particularly with those who have known the individual for many years, can help provide different perspectives on the personal past and facilitate insight into the alternative interpretations of one's life experiences and accomplishments (Herzog & Markus, 1999; Markus & Herzog, 1991). Interaction with others, however, can also lead to negative and overly critical appraisals of one's life. Thus, the tendency of older adults to be selective in social contacts may reflect not only a decrease in psychological energy or need for emotional intimacy, but also represent the elder being judicious in whom they select to review the past with them.

SUMMARY

A more fine-grained understanding of the many faces of old age has led us to the conclusion that more than a single stage is required to describe adequately the contextually demanding cognitive development occurring in the last third of life. We therefore added a reorganizational stage which covers the period of transition from the world of work and primary family responsibilities to the more self-centered content and context of early old age. We also added a legacy creating stage to account for the cognitive aspects of end-of-life pursuits designed to pass on one's material and intellectual treasures to one's descendants.

Given two decades of relevant research since the original cognitive stage model was presented, we further felt an obligation to explicate more strongly our feelings about the lasting importance of basic cognitive skills as necessary, albeit not sufficient, bases for effective cognitive functioning at all life stages. Nevertheless, we also felt the need to give recognition to the increasing importance of socioemotional variables, as well as the as yet under-researched aspects of cooperative cognitive functioning in late life, and we attempted to relate these aspects to our model.

Acknowledgment

An earlier version of this chapter was presented at the 1997 World Congress of Gerontology in Adelaide Australia. Preparation of this work was supported by research grant R37 AG08055 from the National Institute on Aging.

REFERENCES

Avolio, B. J. (1991). Levels of analysis. In K. W. Schaie (Ed.), *Annual review of gerontology and geriatrics* (Vol. 11, pp. 239–260). New York: Springer Publishing Co.

Avolio, B. J., & Waldman, D. A. (1990). An examination of age and cognitive test performance across job complexity and occupational types. *Journal of Applied Psychology, 75*, 43–50.

Baltes, M. M., & Carstensen, L. L. (1996). The process of successful ageing. *Ageing and Society, 16*, 397–422.

Baltes, P. B. (1987). Theoretical propositions of life-span developmental psychology: On the dynamics between growth and decline. *Developmental Psychology, 23*, 611–626.

Baltes, P. B., & Baltes, M. M. (1990). Psychological perspectives on successful aging: The model of selective Optimization with compensation. In P. B. Baltes & M. M. Baltes (Eds.), *Successful aging: Perspectives from the behavioral sciences* (pp. 1–34). New York: Cambridge University Press.

Baltes, P. B., & Staudinger, U. M. (Eds.) (1996). *Interactive minds: Life-span perspectives on the social foundation of cognition.* New York: Cambridge University Press.

Bandura, A. (1982). Self efficacy mechanisms in human agency. *American Psychologist, 37,* 122–147.

Bandura, A., & Jourden, F. J. (1991). Self-regulatory mechanisms governing social-comparison effects on complex decision making. *Journal of Personality and Social Psychology, 60,* 941–951.

Berg, C. A., & Klaczynski, P. A. (1996). Practical intelligence and problem solving: Searching for perspectives. In F. Blanchard-Fields & T. Hess (Eds.), *Perspectives on cognitive change in adulthood and aging* (pp. 323–357). New York: McGraw-Hill.

Berg, C. A., Klaczynski, P. A., Calderone, K. S., & Strough, J. (1994). Adult age differences in cognitive strategies: Adaptive or deficient? In J. Sinnott (Ed.), *Interdisciplinary handbook of adult life-span learning* (pp. 371–388). Westport CT: Greenwood.

Berry, J., & Irvine, S. (1986). Bricolage: Savages do it daily. In R. Sternberg & R. Wagner (Eds.), *Practical intelligence* (pp. 271–306). New York: Cambridge University Press.

Birren, J. E., Kenyon, G. M., Ruth, J. -E., Schroots, J. F., & Swensson, T. (Eds.) (1995). *Aging and biography: Explorations in adult development.* New York: Springer Publishing Co.

Blanchard-Fields, F. (1996). Social cognitive development in adulthood and aging. In F. Blanchard-Fields and T. Hess (Eds.) *Perspectives on cognitive change in adulthood and aging* (pp. 454–487). New York: McGraw Hill.

Blanchard-Fields, F., & Abeles, R. (1996). Social cognition and aging. In J. E. Birren & K. W. Schaie (Eds.), *Handbook of the psychology of aging* (4th ed., pp. 150–161). San Diego: Academic Press.

Bosworth, H. B. (1996). *Terminal drop and terminal change in the Seattle Longitudinal Study.* Doctoral dissertation, Pennsylvania State University, University Park, PA.

Brandstädter, J., & Renner, G. (1990). Tenacious goal pursuit and flexible goal adjustment: Explication and age-related analysis of assimilative and accommodative strategies of coping. *Psychology and Aging, 5,* 58–67.

Brim, O. G. (1992). *Ambition: How we manage success and failure throughout our lives.* New York: Basic.

Butler, R. N., Lewis, M., & Sunderland, T. (1991). *Aging and mental health: Positive psychosocial and biomedical approaches* (4th ed.). New York: MacMillan.

Carstensen, L. L. (1993). Motivation for social contact across the life-span: A theory of socio-emotional selectivity. In J. Jacobs (Ed.), *Nebraska symposium on motivation: Developmental perspectives on emotion* (pp. 209–254). Lincoln, NE: University of Nebraska Press.

Carstensen, L. L. , Gross, J. J., & Fung, H. H. (1997). The social context of emotional experience. In K. W. Schaie & M. P. Lawton (Eds.), *Annual review of gerontology and geriatrics* (Vol. 17, pp. 325–352). New York: Springer Publishing Co.

Cattell, R. B. (1971). *Abilities: Their structure, growth and action.* Boston: Houghton-Mifflin.

Commons, M., Armon, C., Kohlberg, L., Richards, R., Grotzer, T., & Sinnott, J. (Eds) (1990). *Adult development: Models and methods in the study of adolescent and adult thought*. New York: Praeger.

Department of Labor, Bureau of Labor Statistics. (1992). *Employment and earning, 39*.

Diehl, M., Willis, S. L., & Schaie, K. W. (1995). Practical problem solving in older adults: Observational assessment and cognitive correlates. *Psychology and Aging, 10*, 478–491.

Dittmann-Kohli, F. (1990). The construction of meaning in old age: Possibilities and constraints. *Aging and Society, 10*, 279–294.

Dittmann-Kohli, F., & Baltes, P. B. (1990). Toward a neofunctionalist conception of adult intellect. In C. Alexander & E. Langer (Eds.) *Higher stages of human development: Perspectives on adult growth* (pp. 54–78). New York: Oxford University Press.

Dittmann-Kohli, F., Lachman, M. E., Kliegl, R., & Baltes, P. B. (1991). Effects of cognitive training and testing on intellectual efficacy beliefs in elderly adults. *Journal of Gerontology: Psychological Sciences, 46*, P162–164.

Erikson, E. H. (1963). *Childhood and society*. New York: Norton.

Erikson, E. H. (1984). Reflections on the last stage—and the first. *Psychoanalytic Study of the Child, 39*, 155–165.

Flavell, J. H. (1963). *The developmental psychology of Jean Piaget*. Princeton, NJ: Van Nostrand.

Fredrickson, B. L., & Carstensen, L. L. (1990). Choosing social partners: How old age, and anticipated endings make people more selective. *Psychology and Aging, 5*, 335–347.

Hagestad, G. O., & Neugarten, B. L. (1985). Age and the life course. In R. Binstock and E. Shanas (Eds.) *Handbook of aging and the social sciences* (2nd ed., pp. 35–81). New York: Van Nostrand-Reinhold.

Herzog, A. R., & Markus, H. M. (1999). The self-concept in life-span and aging research. In V.L. Bengtson & K.W. Schaie (Eds.), *Handbook of theories of aging* (pp. 227–252). New York: Springer Publishing Co.

Kenyon, G., Ruth, J. E., & Mader, W. (1999). Elements of a narrative gerontology. In V. L. Bengtson & K. W. Schaie (Eds.), *Handbook of theories of aging*. New York: Springer Publishing Co.

Kohn, M. L., & Schooler, C. (1983). *Work and personality: An inquiry into the impact of social stratification*. Norwood, NJ: Ablex.

Labouvie-Vief, G. (1992). A neo-Piagetian perspective on adult cognitive development. In R. J. Sternberg & C. A. Berg (Eds.) *Intellectual development* (pp. 197–228). New York: Cambridge University Press.

Lachman, M. E., & Leff. R. (1989). Perceived control and intellectual functioning in the elderly: A 5-year longitudinal study. *Developmental Psychology, 25*, 722–728.

Lachman, M. E., & McArthur, L. (1986). Adulthood age differences in causal attributions for cognitive, physical and social performance. *Psychology and Aging, 1*, 127–132.

Lawton, M. P. (August, 1997). *Quality of life in health and illness*. Invited address at the annual meeting of the American Psychological Association, Chicago.

Lawton, M. P., & Brody, E. M. (1969). Assessment of older adults: Self-maintaining and instrumental activities of daily living. *Gerontologist, 9*, 179–185.

Lawton, M. P., Kleban, M. H., Rajagopal, D., & Dean, J. (1992). Dimensions of affective experience in three age groups. *Psychology and Aging, 7*, 171–184.

Levenson, H. (1975). Additional dimensions of internal-external control. *Journal of Social Psychology, 97*, 303–304.

Leventhal, H., & Cameron, L. (1987). Behavioral theories and the problem of compliance. *Patient Education and Counseling, 10*, 117–138.

Lowenthal, M. F., Thurnher, M., & Chirboga, D. and Associates. (1975). *Four stages of life*. San Francisco, CA: Jossey-Bass.

Markus, H. M., & Herzog, A. R. (1991). The role of self-concept in aging. In K. W. Schaie (Ed.) *Annual review of gerontology and geriatrics* (Vol. 11, pp. 110–143). New York: Springer Publishing Co.

Meyer, B. J. F., Russo, C., & Talbot, A. (1995). Discourse comprehension and problem solving: Decisions about the treatment of breast cancer by women across the life-span. *Psychology and Aging, 10*, 84–103.

Neugarten, B. L. (1969). Continuities and discontinuities of psychological issues into adult life. *Human Development, 12*, 121–130.

Osborne, A. F. (1957). *Applied imagination* (rev. ed.), New York: Scribner.

Riley, M. W. (1994). Aging and society: Past, present and future. *Gerontologist, 34*, 436–446.

Rodin, J., Timko, C., & Harris, S. (1985). The construct of control: Biological and social correlates. In M. P. Lawton (Ed.) *Annual review of gerontology and geriatrics* (Vol. 6, pp. 3–55). New York: Springer Publishing Co.

Schaie, K. W. (1974). Translations in gerontology—from lab to life: Intellectual functioning. *American Psychologist, 29*, 802–807.

Schaie, K. W. (1977–78). Toward a stage theory of adult cognitive development. *Journal of Aging and Human Development, 8*, 129–183.

Schaie, K. W. (1984). Midlife influences upon intellectual functioning in old age. *International Journal of Behavioral Development, 7*, 463–478.

Schaie, K. W. (1990). Intellectual development in adulthood. In J. E. Birren & K. W. Schaie (Eds.), *Handbook of the psychology of aging* (3rd ed., pp. 291–309). New York: Academic Press.

Schaie, K. W. (1996). *Intellectual development in adulthood: The Seattle Longitudinal Study*. New York: Cambridge University Press.

Schaie, K. W., Willis, S. L., Jay, G., & Chipuer, H. (1989). Structural invariance of cognitive abilities across the adult life span: A cross-sectional study. *Developmental Psychology, 25*, 652–662.

Sinnott, J. D. (1984). Postformal reasoning: The relativistic stage. In M. L. Commons, F. A. Richards, & C. Armon (Eds.), *Beyond formal operations: Late adolescent and adult cognitive development* (pp. 298–325). New York: Praeger.

Sinnott, J. D. (1989). A model for solution of ill-structured problem: Implications for everyday and abstract problem solving. In J. D. Sinnott (Ed.), *Everyday problem solving: Theory and applications* (pp. 72–99). New York: Praeger.

Sinnott, J. D. (1996). The developmental approach: Post formal thought as adaptive intelligence. In F. Blanchard-Fields & T. Hess (Eds.), *Perspectives on cognitive change in adulthood and aging* (pp. 358–383). New York: McGraw Hill.

Smith, J. (1996). Planning about life: Toward a social interactive perspective. In P. B. Baltes & U. M. Staudinger (Eds.), *Interactive minds: Life-span perspectives on the social foundation of cognition* (pp. 242–275). New York: Cambridge University Press.

Smith, J., Staudinger, U. M., & Baltes, P. B. (1994). Occupational settings facilitative of wisdom-related knowledge: The sample case of clinical psychologists. *Journal of Consulting and Clinical Psychology, 62*, 989–1000.

Smyer, M., Schaie, K. W., & Kapp, M. B. (Eds.) (1996). *Older adults' decision making and the law*. New York: Springer Publishing Co.

Staudinger, U. M. (1996). Wisdom and the social-interactive foundation of the mind. In P. B. Baltes & U. M. Staudinger (Eds.), *Interactive minds* (pp. 276–315). New York: Cambridge University Press.

Staudinger, U. M., & Baltes, P. B. (1985). *Interactive minds: A facilitative setting for wisdom-related performance?* Manuscript. Berlin, Germany: Max-Planck-Institute for Human Development and Education.

Steiner, I. D. (1972). *Group process and productivity*. New York: Academic Press.

Sternberg, R., & Wagner, R. (Eds.) (1986). *Practical intelligence: Origins of competence in the everyday world*. New York: Cambridge University Press.

Suzman, R., & Riley, M. W. (1985). Introducing the "oldest old." *Milbank Memorial Fund Quarterly: Health and Society, 63*, 177–185.

Whitborne, S. K. (1986). *The me I know: A study of adult identity*. New York: Springer Verlag.

Willis, S. L. (1991). Cognition and everyday competence. In K. W. Schaie (Ed.), *Annual review of gerontology and geriatrics* (Vol. 11, pp. 80–109). New York: Springer.

Willis, S. L. (1996). Everyday cognitive competence in elderly persons: Conceptual issues and empirical findings. *Gerontologist, 36*, 595–601.

Willis, S. L., Dolan, M., & Bertrand, R. (1999). Problem solving on health-related tasks of daily living. In D. C. Park, R. W. Morrell, & K. Shifren (Eds.), *Processing of medical information in aging patients: Cognitive and human factors perspectives* (pp. 199–219). Hillsdale, NJ: Erlbaum.

Willis, S. L., Jay, G. M., Diehl, M., & Marsiske, M. (1992). Longitudinal change in prediction of everyday task competence in the elderly. *Research on Aging, 14*, 68–91.

Willis, S. L., Marsiske, M., & Diehl, M. (1991, November). *Activities of daily living, control beliefs, and perceived need for assistance*. Paper presented at the annual meeting of the Gerontological Society of America, San Francisco, CA.

Willis, S. L., & Schaie, K. W. (1986). Practical intelligence in later adulthood. In R. Sternberg & R. Wagner (Eds.), *Practical intelligence: Origins of competence in the everyday world* (pp. 236–270). New York: Cambridge University Press.

Willis, S. L., & Schaie, K. W. (1993). Everyday cognition: Taxonomic and methodological considerations. In J. M. Puckett & H. W. Reese (Eds.), *Life-span developmen-*

tal psychology: Mechanisms of everyday cognition (pp. 33–53). Hillsdale, NJ: Erlbaum.

Willis, S. L., & Schaie, K. W. (1994). Assessing competence in the elderly. In C.E. Fisher & R.M. Lerner (Eds.), *Applied developmental psychology* (pp. 339–372). New York: MacMillan.

Willis, S. L., & Schaie, K. W. (1996). Psychometric intelligence and aging. In F. Blanchard-Fields & T. Hess (Eds.), *Perspectives on cognitive change in adulthood and aging* (pp. 293–322). New York: McGraw Hill.

Wong, T. P. (1989). Personal meaning and successful aging. *Canadian Psychology, 30,* 516–525.

Zajonc, R. B. (1960). The process of cognitive tuning in communication. *Journal of Abnormal and Social Psychology, 61,* 159–167.

V

Caregiving

11

Caregiving Research: Looking Backward, Looking Forward

Rachel A. Pruchno

In their article "A Two-Factor Model of Caregiving Appraisal and Psychological Well-Being," Powell Lawton and his colleagues (Lawton, Moss, Kleban, Glicksman, & Rovine, 1991) present a model of caregiving dynamics in which objective stressors, caregiver resources, and subjective appraisals of caregiving (operationalized as caregiving satisfaction and burden) predict both positive affect and depression. This conceptualization and model test is a significant departure from the traditional emphasis on the negative effects of caregiving that has characterized the caregiving literature, and marks an important beginning in caregiving research. It highlights the salience of expanding knowledge about the positive as well as negative dimensions of the caregiving experience. By doing so, the article also suggests the importance of expanding knowledge about the caregiving experience in multiple directions, while maintaining a solid anchor within traditional psychosocial theory. Building on this important paper, the remainder of this chapter will concisely review where caregiving research has been and suggest new directions for future development.

WHO ARE TODAY'S CAREGIVERS?

An understanding of today's caregivers requires knowledge about the people for whom care is provided. While family caregivers may be adults of any age, the discussion that follows focuses on situations in which the caregivers themselves are middle-aged or older. The care-receivers discussed range from young children (as in the case of grandmothers as caregivers) to frail, older people with chronic disabilities.

Children and Spouses

Most of the caregiver literature has focused on caregivers for older people. These studies find that the vast majority of caregivers are women, with most related to care recipients as either daughter or wife. Estimates provided by Stone, Cafferata, and Sangl (1987) suggest that in 1982 approximately 2.2 million family caregivers provided assistance to noninstitutionalized disabled elderly persons having one or more ADL limitations. The majority of these caregivers were women (72%), with adult daughters comprising 29% of all caregivers and wives constituting 23% of this population. The remaining 20% of female caregivers included daughters-in-law, sisters, granddaughters, and other female relatives.

Spouses are the first-line of defense when it comes to caregiving (Stoller, 1983). Frail older people who are cared for by spouses are likely to be more impaired and in greater need of long-term care than are those assisted by other informal caregivers (Hess & Soldo, 1985). Studies focusing on spouse caregivers reveal that although women do not necessarily provide more hours of care than do men, they tend to provide more intimate types of care, have more frequent contacts, and more often have to deal with disruptive and aggressive behaviors (Wright, Clipp, & George, 1993). When men do care for an impaired spouse, they are more likely to receive outside sources of assistance than their female counterparts (Johnson & Catalano, 1983).

In the absence of a spouse, an adult daughter usually assumes responsibility for caring for a disabled parent (Horowitz, 1985a). Although sons do participate in parent care (Coward, 1987), they typically become primary caregivers only when there is not an available female sibling (Horowitz, 1985b). Of the caregiving sons surveyed by Horowitz (1985b), 88% were either only children, had only male siblings, or were the only child geographically available. Moreover, when sons were identified as the primary caregiver, they were more likely than daughters to rely on their spouses for additional support, less likely to provide as much overall assistance to their parents, and less likely to help with "hands-on" tasks such as bathing and dressing. Dwyer and Coward (1991), in a multivariate analysis, found that even after controlling for a variety of factors known to influence the relationship between gender and the provision of care to impaired elders (age, gender, and level of impairment of the elder; marital status, age, employment status and proximity of the adult child), daughters were 3.22 times more likely than sons to provide ADL assistance and 2.56 times more likely to provide IADL assistance.

Parents As Caregivers

When a child suffers from a chronic condition such as a developmental disability or mental illness, the lives of his/her parents are forever altered. As parents of chronically disabled children enter old age, they face not only the health problems and social changes experienced by their age peers, but they also must confront the challenges associated with the needs of their aging child. As time passes, the situation ensues in which there is increased likelihood that the older adult child may require care from very old parents who themselves may require care (Brunn, 1985; Cohler, Pickett, & Cook, 1987). Because of differences in life expectancy between men and women, as well as the tendency for the current cohort of women to have assumed the primary role of lifelong caregiver, mothers of chronically disabled adult children are more likely than fathers to find themselves in the role of primary caregiver (Seltzer, 1985).

Parenting cognitively or affectively disabled adult children within the community are relatively new phenomena in our society for very different reasons. In terms of cognitively disabled adults, the medical and technological advances of the past few decades have resulted in the expectation that large numbers of severely mentally retarded children will not only survive childhood, but will live to adulthood and old age (Janicki & Wisniewski, 1985). Although lifespan projections for the retarded population are currently unavailable (Seltzer & Seltzer, 1985), Walz, Harper, and Wilson (1986) estimate that over 40% of mentally retarded people will survive to age 60. Family care is the dominant residential arrangement for people with mental retardation. According to Fujiura and Braddock (1992) fully 85% of persons with mental retardation live with their families, many for their entire lives.

The trend towards deinstitutionalization has resulted in parents, especially mothers, having caregiving responsibilities for their severely disabled adult children suffering from severe mental illness, including schizophrenia (Cohler et al., 1987; Lefley, 1987). From the mid-1950s to the early 1960s the number of people with mental illness in state and county mental hospitals dropped from more than 550,000 to 120,000 (NIMH, 1985). Patients were frequently released from psychiatric hospitals without adequate systems of community support, leaving families responsible for their care (Hatfield, 1987). Fully 85% of the known caregivers for people with mental illness are parents, most of whom are in their late 50s and 60s (Lefley, 1987). Relatives of persons with mental illness shoulder significant caregiving responsibilities, often with inadequate assistance from mental health and human service agencies .

Grandparents As Caregivers

That grandparents, especially grandmothers, frequently assume caregiving roles has been documented in the case of divorce (Ahrons & Bowman, 1982; Cherlin & Furstenberg, 1986), drug addiction (Minkler & Roe, 1993), and adolescent pregnancy (Burton & Bengtson, 1985; Flaherty, Facteau, & Garner, 1987). Yet the phenomenon of grandparents raising grandchildren has only recently attracted the attention of social scientists (Burton, 1992). According to the 1991 U.S. Bureau of the Census, 3.2 million children under the age of 18 live with their grandparents (Minkler & Roe, 1993). Although the prevalence of grandmothers living with grandchildren is highest in the African American community (12% of all Black children in America live with a grandparent, compared with 5.8% of Hispanic children and 3.4% of White children) (US Bureau of the Census, 1991), the past decade has witnessed an exponential growth in the number of both Black (increasing by 24%) and White (increasing by 54%) children living with their grandparents. Although the age at which an individual becomes a grandparent can range from

30 to 110, most people become grandparents near the age of 45 (Hagestad, 1985). One recent estimate places nearly half of grandparents at less than age 60, one-third at less than age 55, and one -fifth at age 70 or older (Schwartz & Waldrop, 1992).

The reports that do exist indicate that grandmothers living with grandchildren are beset with a myriad of problems. Thinking that their childrearing days were over, many grandmothers now find themselves playing an unexpected parenting role. This new role may come at a time in their lives when their peers are facing issues such as the empty nest, retirement, and widowhood. Furthermore, the experience of assuming primary care of a grandchild can be complicated by the reason care is required. Hence, a child's death, addiction to drugs, or desertion can affect the way in which the caregiver role is experienced. In addition to the challenges of providing day-to-day care to grandchildren, concerns often include securing adequate medical coverage for their grandchildren, making painful decisions about attaining legal custody of their grandchildren, and struggling with a host of other family problems.

THE IMPACT OF CAREGIVING ON MENTAL HEALTH

Children and Spouses

The problems faced by caregivers are complex and multifaceted. Within the realm of studies focusing on caregivers of disabled older people, the broad consensus is that the demands associated with the caregiving role are stressful, disruptive, and have significant mental health consequences. Sainsbury and Grad de Alarcon (1970) found that the emotional health of 63% of family members who provided community care to elderly patients with various psychiatric diagnoses had been affected as a result of caregiving. More recent studies have documented even higher rates of emotional distress characterizing caregivers of demented elders. More recently Schulz, O'Brien, Bookwala, and Fleissner (1995), summarizing the state of the knowledge base regarding psychiatric and physical morbidity among caregivers of dementia patients, conclude that regardless of the depression instrument used, results consistently indicate that elevated rates of depression characterize caregivers. Rabins, Mace, and Lucas (1982), for example, report that 87% of family caregivers of an older person suffering from Alzheimer's disease experienced chronic fatigue, anger, and depression. In other studies of family caregivers of Alzheimer's victims, as many as 81% of respondents met DSM criteria for major depression and 50% experienced symptoms of disturbance at a psychiatrically significant level (Drinka & Smith, 1983; Gilleard, Belford, Gilleard, Whittick, & Gledhill, 1984).

For caregivers of stroke and heart patients, the rate of depression appears to be slightly lower, ranging from 11 to 37% in several studies (Schulz, Tompkins, & Rau, 1988; Wade, Legh-Smith, & Hewer, 1986; Young & Kahana, 1989). Rates as high as 47% were reported in a study of caregivers of elders with severe cardiac disease (Gallagher, Wrabetz, Lovett, DelMaestro, & Rose, 1989).

More recent work using standardized depression scales such as the Beck or CES-D indicates that 28 to 55% of caregivers are clinically depressed (Stommell, Given, & Given, 1990; Tennstedt, & McKinlay, 1989; Miller, 1987), while approximately 30% of caregivers used psychotropic medications (Cohen et al., 1990; Gallagher, Rose, Rivera, Lovett, & Thompson, 1989; Clipp & George, 1990). Comparable rates for the general community population are 14 to 16% for depression and 20% for psychotropics (Blazer & Williams, 1980; Clipp & George, 1990). Using subjects from a central registry of AD patients and their families rather than volunteers from support groups or mental health clinics, Neundorfer (1991) found a depression rate of 25%. It appears that although depressive symptomatology has been frequently documented, the majority of caregivers do not become clinically depressed.

One of the most studied questions in this area has been identifying those caregivers who are at greatest risk for negative mental health consequences. Research consistently indicates that there is a greater negative impact for caregiving women than for caregiving men. These findings hold across a number of studies of caregivers to demented and frail elders (Barusch & Spaid, 1989; Dura, Haywood-Niler, & Kiecolt-Glaser, 1990; Fitting, Rabins, Lucas, & Eastham, 1986; George & Gwyther, 1986; Gilleard et al., 1984; Pruchno & Potashnik, 1989). Comparisons of husbands and wives as caregivers indicates that husbands are less likely than wives to demonstrate clinical depression. Cohen et al. (1990), for example, reported that 24% of caregiver husbands and 49% of caregiver wives were clinically depressed, while Gallagher et al. (1989) reported rates of 21% for husbands and 52% for wives. These findings suggest that female caregivers are more adversely affected by their role than are male caregivers, a pattern than holds among caregivers of physically impaired, stroke, heart disease, and cancer patients (Biegel, Sales, & Schulz, 1991; Schulz et al., 1988; Tennstedt, Cafferata, & Sullivan, 1992; Young & Kahana, 1989).

Level of depression as measured by standardized scales is highest for wives, followed by daughters, then other female caregivers, then sons, and then husband caregivers (Gallagher et al., 1989). Daughters suffer more severe mental health consequences than sons when they are the principal caregiver (Horowitz, 1985b), when they are local siblings of the main caregiver (Brody, Hoffman, Kleban, & Schoonover, 1989), and when they are siblings who live at a geographic distance from the parent and the main caregiver (Schoonover, Brody, Hoffman, & Kleban, 1988). Suggesting that a contrast of the strains experienced by sons and daughters of nursing home residents is an excellent test of gender differences in the effects of parent care because the institutionalized parent receives the same kind of care and treatment from nursing home staff whether the family "responsible other" is a son or a daughter, Brody et al. (1989) found that the gender differences characterizing caregiving effects when older parents are being cared for in the community continue to occur between adult sons and daughters when their parents live in nursing homes.

Parents and Grandparents

In general, much less in known about the mental health consequences experienced by older people providing care to their chronically disabled children and about the effects experienced by older people providing care to their grandchildren. Seltzer and Krauss (1989), studying older women providing in-home care for an adult child with mental retardation, found that despite the long duration of their caregiving roles, many of the mothers seemed to be resilient, optimistic, and able to function in multiple roles. The women were substantially healthier than other noncaregiving women their age, had better morale than caregivers of elderly persons, reported no more burden than family caregivers for elderly residents, and less stress than parents of young children with retardation (Krauss & Seltzer, 1993). Similarly Kazak (1989), comparing levels of psychological distress, marital satisfaction, family adaptability, and cohesion in families with mentally retarded institutionalized adult children with that in nonclinical families who had no mentally or physically disabled children, found that the groups were similar to one another on all outcome measures.

Greenberg, Selzer, and Greenley (1993) contrasted the mental health consequences as experienced by mothers of adult children with a developmental disability with that of mothers of adult children with mental illness. They found that the mothers of the adults with mental illness reported considerably higher levels of burden and poorer relationships with their children than did the mothers of adults with mental retardation. Similarly, Pruchno, Patrick, and Burant (1996) found that mothers of adult children with schizophrenia experienced more depression, more negative affect, lower levels of life satisfaction, and lower levels of positive affect than did mothers of adult children with developmental disabilities.

Studies of the problems and needs of caregivers of family members with chronic mental illness indicate that caregiving burdens are longstanding and pervasive and that families often experience feelings of worry, guilt, resentment, and grief (Biegel, Song, & Chakravarthy (1994). Thompson and Doll (1982), in their study of lower- and working-class caregivers of present and former patients of treatment groups, found that three quarters of families reported being adversely affected by the patient in one or more ways. Almost half of the families were experiencing "moderate" levels of burden, with over one quarter experiencing "severe" burdens. Half the families reported the following burdens: financial hardship, interference with family routines, neglect of the caregiver's responsibilities to other family members, and strained relationship with neighbors. Almost three quarters of families reported feeling chronically overloaded and strained. Similar findings have been reported by Hatfield (1978) and Kreisman, Simmons, and Joy (1979).

Those few studies that have addressed the issue of mental health of grandmothers helping to raise grandchildren highlight the negative effects that often result. Shore and Hayslip (1990), for example, found that those grandparents who had assumed parental responsibilities had reduced scores on three out of four measures of psychological well-being. Burton (1992) found that caring for grandchildren generated considerable stress for grandparents, with 86% of the grandparents she studied reporting feeling depressed or anxious most of the time.

PREDICTORS OF RISK FOR MENTAL HEALTH PROBLEMS: A SUMMARY OF FINDINGS

Although the relationship between caregiving and mental health has been studied for close to 40 years, conclusive statements about caregiving that hold up across studies are limited to the following.

1. Caregiving is burdensome. In general, people who are caregivers to older relatives, adult children with disability, patients infected with HIV, and grandparents caring for young grandchildren experience turmoil in their lives. They report feeling trapped, not having enough time to themselves, that their social lives have suffered, that their health has suffered, and that they are tired, isolated and alone.

2. Caregivers frequently have mental health problems. Beginning with work by Grad de Alarcon and Sainsbury (1963), caregiving research has documented that caregivers experience increased levels of depression, anxiety, insomnia, and excessive irritability. However, not all family caregivers experience mental health problems. One of the most pressing challenges faced by scholars of family caregiving during the past several years has been that associated with identifying predictable and consistent variation in the caregiving experience. Studies contrasting the stress experienced by spouses and adult children of disabled older people consistently indicate that caregiving is more stressful for spouses than for adult children (George & Gwyther, 1986; Gilhooly, 1984). Within the realm of studies focusing on caregivers of the mentally ill, Hoenig and Hamilton (1966) report that parents are less able than spouse caregivers to tolerate family members with mental illness. Evidence regarding living arrangement indicates that shared residence creates the highest levels of stress for caregivers (Brody, Kleban, Hoffman, & Schoonover, 1988; Deimling, Bass, Townsend, & Noelker, 1989; George & Gwyther, 1986; O'Connor, Pollitt, Roth, Brook, & Reiss, 1990) . Although relatively few caregiving studies have addressed the issue of race, those that have contrasted Black and White caregivers indicate that White caregivers report higher levels of burden and depression and less caregiving satisfaction than do Black caregivers (Bulger, Wandersman, & Goldman, 1993; Lawton, Rajagopal, Brody, & Kleban, 1992; Mui, 1992). An exception to this finding is work by Morycz, Malloy, Bozich, and Martz (1987) who found no racial differences in the amount of caregiver burden .

3. The greater the caregiving burden, the worse the depression. That is, the burdens associated with the caregiving role affect the more global mental health of individuals.

Beyond these consistent findings, our understanding about the processes by which caregivers become burdened and depressed is still in its infancy. A great deal of attention has been paid in the literature to the relationship between patient characteristics and distress experienced by the caregiver. At best, the evidence is contradictory. Several studies focusing on caregiving for elderly relatives report that neither severity of impairment, nor frequency of disruptive behavior, nor duration of caregiving have significant relationships to depression or caregiver well-being in dementia situations (Boss, Caron, Horbal, & Mortimer, 1990; Cattanach & Tebes, 1991; Deimling & Bass, 1986; Dura et al., 1990; Fitting et al., 1986; George & Gwyther, 1986). On the other hand, studies by Barusch and Spaid (1989), Novak and Guest (1989), and O'Connor et al. (1990) found positive relationships between extent of patient impairment and caregiver burden and depression. Haley and Pardo (1989) suggest the importance of examining multiple dimensions of behavior and find that while cognitive impairment may steadily increase over time, other stressful behavioral symptoms peak at various stages of dementia.

Studies that have contrasted different caregiving experiences highlight the complexity of the relationship between characteristics of the care-receiver and outcomes experienced by caregivers. Clipp and George (1993), for example, found that Alzheimer's disease caregivers were significantly more compromised across multiple dimensions of emotional health than were caregivers whose spouses had cancer. These differences remained after controlling for duration of caregiving and illness symptoms. In their study of mothers of mentally retarded adult children Seltzer and Krauss (1989) found that child's physical health predicted mother's life satisfaction and burden, while level of retardation predicted neither life satisfaction nor burden. Studies focusing on caregivers of mentally ill family members are more consistent in their findings regarding patient characteristics and caregiver distress. Research by Biegel et al., (1991), Doll (1976), Potasznik and Nelson (1984), Thompson and Doll (1982), Bulger et al., (1993), Noh and Avison (1988) and Biegel et al. (1994) indicates that greater patient distress and more frequent behavioral problems are linked to higher caregiver burden.

Other variables that have not been linked consistently to level of caregiver mental health include patient gender (Biegel et al., 1991, 1994; Doll, 1976; Noh & Avison, 1988 report no relationship, while Cook and Pickett 1985 found that caregivers of female clients had higher levels of burden); age (Biegel et al., 1991, 1994; Doll, 1976; Noh & Avison, 1988 report no relationship; Cook & Pickett, 1985, found that caregivers of older clients had higher levels of burden), socioeconomic status (Bulger et al., 1993, and Hoenig & Hamilton, 1966 find that lower-class caregivers report experiencing less burden, while Noh & Avison, 1988, and Biegel et al., 1994, report no relationship between family income and burden).

Several theories have been advanced regarding the impact of social support on caregiver mental health. There seems to be some, albeit not strong, evidence for the moderator hypothesis of social support. Within the literature focusing on caregivers for impaired elders, increasing levels of social support seem to buffer caregiver strain, but only for caregivers of cognitively impaired, not functionally impaired elders (Bass, Tausig, & Noelker, 1989; Haley, Levine, Brown, & Bartolucci, 1987; Haley, Lenne, Brown, Berry, & Hughes, 1987). For caregivers of functionally impaired elders, Bass et al. (1989) and Tennstedt et al. (1992) report that high levels of support actually had detrimental emotional consequences.

Among caregivers of the mentally ill, there has been support for the moderator hypothesis. Potasznik and Nelson (1984) found that the less caregivers were satisfied with their social support network, the greater their levels of burden. Biegel et al. (1991) found that caregivers who felt they were not getting sufficient help from their families had higher levels of burden. A later study (Biegel et al., 1994) replicated this finding and also indicated that lack of support from the formal network predicted greater caregiving burden. On the other hand, Noh and Avison (1988) in their study of spouse caregivers found no relationship between caregiver's social support and burden.

Coping strategies, representing behaviors or cognitive actions caregivers can use to deal with problems or with consequences of problems, are one aspect of the situation over which caregivers may exert control. Consistent evidence among caregivers of disabled elderly people suggests that emotion-focused coping strategies, including intraspychic, wishfulness, and acceptance are related to poor mental health (Haley Lenne, Brown, & Bartolucci, 1987; Kramer, 1993; Neundorfer, 1991; Pagel, Becker, & Coppel, 1985; Pruchno & Resch, 1989). The relationship between problem-focused coping and mental health outcomes is less clear, with some studies reporting no relationship (Kramer, 1993; Pruchno & Kleban, 1993; Pruchno & Resch, 1989), whereas others reported that problem-focused coping was associated with better mental health outcomes (Haley, Lenne, Brown, & Bartolucci, 1987; Pratt, Schmall, Wright, & Cleland, 1985). Contrasting the effects of coping strategies on the level of depression experienced by mothers of adults with mental retardation and mental illness Seltzer, Greenberg, and Krauss (1995) report that for the mothers of mentally ill adults emotion-focused coping strategies were associated with higher levels of depressive symptomatology. There was no indication, however, that either problem-focused or emotion-focused coping buffered the effects of stress in these mothers. For mothers of adults with mental retardation a very different picture emerged. Use of problem-focused coping strategies was associated with significantly lower levels of depressive symptoms. There were no buffering effects for problem-focused coping. Similarly, for the emotion-focused coping strategies, there were significant relationships with depressive symptoms, but no evidence that the use of emotion-focused coping buffered the effects of caregiving stressors.

There are several explanations for why these inconsistent findings characterize the literature. Included are:

1. Many of the early studies of caregivers, be they of caregivers to older people, to adult children with disabilities or health problems, or to grandchildren, relied on very small heterogeneous samples. As such, findings may vary from study to study because the people studied differ dramatically from one another both within and across studies.

2. Many of the more recent large-scale studies test theoretical models that differ from one another. Using sophisticated structural modeling techniques, these studies examine effects that are partialled differently as a function of the variables included in the model. As such, findings may vary from study to study because of the variables included in the model.

3. There is a great amount of variability inherent in the caregiving experience. As such, there may be many pathways to both positive and negative mental health for caregivers.

MISSING LINKS AND FUTURE DIRECTIONS

The past several decades have witnessed exponential growth in the number of studies seeking to examine the mental health effects experienced by family caregivers. These studies provide important information about the demands associated with caregiving and the effects that caregiving has on the mental health of caregivers. Nonetheless, most of the extant studies are based on small, nonrepresentative samples and frequently focus on a particular age group or disability. The next generation of caregiving studies needs more large-scale studies that include samples that more accurately represent the populations from which they derive.

An important step for future research is to transcend boundaries between specific health conditions or disabilities that create the need for caregiving and identify both a set of common predictors of mental health problems and a set of predictors that are unique to specific caregiving situations. Following the lead taken by Lawton and his colleagues (1991), the caregiving literature would benefit from a more concerted effort than it has seen to specify and test models and hypotheses across a wide variety of caregiving situations. At the very least, published articles should include bivariate correlation matrices that would enable results to be contrasted across studies. Interpretation of results across studies would also increase if researchers began to implement studies having more standardized measures. The time is ripe for a consensus conference on caregiving in which the leading researchers agree on a theoretical framework and set of measures that could be used in the next generation of caregiving studies. In combination these efforts have the potential to add volumes to our knowledge about the caregiving experience.

The selective recruitment of caregivers into studies remains a significant problem for our understanding of the caregiving experience. Most studies to date have relied on broad outreach efforts seeking people involved in various caregiving experiences. These efforts result in a science largely based on input from volunteer participants. This design precludes an understanding of the limits of generalizability of study findings, as well as understanding of any bias that the sample may comprise. While one solution to this problem is to encourage studies that include both caregivers and noncaregivers, the extent of the problem of selective refusal would remain unknown. An alternative strategy would be to invite participation in a study or to randomly invite people to participate in a study who are members of a more well-defined population about which some information exists. An example might be sampling through a health maintenance organization, large hospital system, registry of people involved in support group, or other infrastructure that contains at the very least demographic information about its members. In this vein, contrasts could be made between people who volunteer to participate and those who refuse.

The next generation of caregiving studies needs to be more concerned with the way in which mode of data collection affects results. With most of the current generation of caregiving studies conducted using personal interviews, issues such as bias due to the presence of interviewer, and the way in which interviewers influence responses set has not been adequately addressed. This issues is particularly salient with regard to estimating rates of depressive symptomatology within a population. Preliminary work from my study of grandparents raising grandchildren suggests that compared with people responding to a self-administered questionnaire, those participating in a phone interview consistently scored as having lower levels of depressive symptomatology and higher levels of psychological well-being.

It is important to note that there are significant caregiving roles filled by middle-aged and older family members that have as yet received little research attention. Included are grandparents raising grandchildren, family members caring for their relatives with AIDS, and women caught in the middle of two generations—those women providing care for their aging parents as well as for their own young children. A more complete understanding of the caregiving experience awaits forays into these caregiving populations.

Despite the fact that caregiving roles have the potential to span several decades of an individual's life, we have little knowledge about either the cumulative effects of this role or the ways in which the role develops and changes over periods of time longer than 1 or 2 years. The few longitudinal studies that do exist (e.g., Bass et al., 1989; Pruchno, Kleban, Michaels, & Dempsey, 1990; Rabins, Fitting, Eastham, & Zabora, 1990; Vitaliano, Russo, Young, Teri, & Maiuro, 1991) focus on changes occurring over relatively short time periods. In order to understand the full impact that the caregiving role has on the mental health of family caregivers, longer-term longitudinal studies are needed.

Lacking from the current knowledge base is a good understanding about the ways in which race and ethnicity influence the caregiving process. Although several studies have contrasted the caregiving experience as reported by Black and White caregivers, with most finding that Black caregivers experience fewer mental health problems, relatively little effort has been spent on examining reasons for these differences. Even less attention has been paid to the ways in which ethnicity influences the caregiving role and the consequences that ensue. Inclusion of minority women in caregiving studies will require development of creative strategies for recruitment, staffs that include multiracial interviewers, and sensitivity to definitions of family.

Finally, although older women do provide most of the care that is required by aging spouses, disabled parents, chronically disabled adult children, and grandchildren whose parents are unable to care for them, the effects that the caregiving role has on the mental health of other family members must not continue to be neglected. Research by Stone et al. (1987) and Tennestedt, McKinlay, & Sullivan (1989) has documented the roles played by secondary caregivers, yet little attention has been paid to understanding the effects that caregiving may have on the mental health of these secondary caregivers. These secondary caregivers are generally the husbands and children of the primary caregivers. In order for the effects of caregiving to be understood, it is important that the "webs" connecting the lives of family members be incorporated into future research.

In summary, during the past 40 years, research has only scratched the surface regarding our understanding of the caregiving experience. Caregiving touches a wide variety of social and psychological arenas, and has the potential to teach us much about the human experience. The lead taken by Lawton et al. (1991) to expand our understanding to the more positive aspects of mental health motivates thought about other areas for expansion. Caregiving research has learned a great deal from Powell Lawton. His research and creativity will carry us a long way into the future.

REFERENCES

Ahrons, C. R., & Bowman, M. E. (1982). Changes in family relationships following divorce of adult child: Grandmother's perceptions. *Journal of Divorce, 5*, 49–68.

Barusch, A. S., & Spaid, W. M. (1989). Gender differences in caregiving: Why do wives report greater burden? *Gerontologist, 29*, 667–676.

Bass, D. M., Tausig, M. B., & Noelker, L. S. (1989). Elder impairment, social support and caregiver strain: A framework for understanding supports effects. *Journal of Applied Social Sciences, 13*, 80–93.

Biegel, D. E., Sales, E., & Schulz, R. (1991). *Family caregiving in chronic illness.* Newbury Park, CA: Sage.

Biegel, D. E., Song, L., & Chakravarthy, V. (1994). Predictors of caregiver burden among support group members of persons with chronic mental illness. In E. Kahana, D. E. Beigel, & M. L. Wykle (Eds.), *Family caregiving across the lifespan* (pp. 178–215). Thousand Oaks, CA: Sage.

Blazer, D., & Williams, C. D. (1980). Epidemiology of dysphoria and depression in an elderly population. *American Journal of Psychiatry, 137*, 439–444.

Boss, P., Caron, W., Horbal, J., & Mortimer, J. (1990). Predictors of depression in caregivers of dementia parents: Boundary ambiguity and mastery. *Family Process, 29*, 245–254.

Brody, E. M., Hoffman, C., Kleban, M. H., & Schoonover, C. B. (1989). Caregiving daughters and their local siblings: Perceptions, strains, and interactions. *Gerontologist, 29*, 529–538.

Brody, E. M., Kleban, M. H., Hoffman, C., & Schoonover, C. B. (1988). Adult daughters and parent care: A comparison of one-, two- and three-generation household. *Home Health Care Services Quarterly, 9*, 19–45.

Brunn, L. C. (1985). Elder parent and dependent adult child. *Social Casework, 66*, 131–138.

Bulger, M., Wandersman, A., & Goldman, C. R. (1993). Burdens and gratifications of caregiving: Appraisal of parental care of adults with schizophrenia. *American Journal of Orthopsychiatry, 63*, 255–265.

Burton, L. M. (1992). Black grandparents rearing children of drug-addicted parents: Stressors, outcomes, and social service needs. *Gerontologist, 32*, 744–751.

Burton, L. M., & Bengtson, V. L. (1985). Black grandmothers: Issues on timing and continuity of roles. In V. L. Bengtson & J. F. Robertson (Eds.), *Grandparenthood* (pp. 61–78). Beverly Hills, CA: Sage.

Cattanach, L., & Tebes, J. K. (1991). The nature of elder impairment and its impact on family caregivers' health and psychosocial functioning. *Gerontologist, 31*, 246–255.

Cherlin, A. J., & Furstenberg, F. F. (1986). *The new American grandparent: A place in the family, a life apart.* New York: Basic.

Clipp, E. C., & George, L. K. (1990). Psychotropic drug use among caregivers of patients with dementia. *Journal of American Geriatrics Society, 38*, 227–235.

Cohen, D., Luchins, D., Eisdorfer, C., Paveza, G., Ashford, J. W., Gorelick, P., Hirschman, R., Freels, S., Levy, P., Semla, T., & Shaw, H. (1990). Caring for relatives with Alzheimer's disease: The mental health risks to spouses, adult children, and other family caregivers. *Behavior, Health, and Aging, 1*, 171–182.

Cohler, B. J., Pickett, S. A., & Cook, J. A. (1987, April). *The psychiatric patient grows older: Issues in family care.* Paper presented at NIMH Conference on the Chronically Ill, Orlando, FL.

Cook, J. A., & Pickett, S. (1985, April). *Feelings of burden among parents residing with chronically mentally ill offspring.* Paper presented at Annual Meeting, National Association of Social Work, Chicago, IL.

Coward, R. T. (1987). Factors associated with the configuration of the helping networks of noninstitutionalized elders. *Journal of Gerontological Social Work, 10*, 113–132.

Deimling, G. T., & Bass, D. M. (1986). Symptoms of mental impairment among elderly adults and their effects on family caregivers. *Journal of Gerontology, 41*, 778–784.

Deimling, G. T., Bass, D. M., Townsend, A. L., & Noelker, L. S. (1989). Care-related stress: A comparison of spouse and adult-child caregivers in shared and separate households. *Journal of Aging and Health, 1*, 67–82.

Doll, W. (1976). Family coping with the mentally ill: An unanticipated problem of deinstitutionalization. *Hospital and Community Psychiatry, 39*, 1296–1300.

Drinka, T., & Smith, J. (1983). Depression in caregivers of demented patients [Special Issue]. *Gerontologist, 23*(116).

Dura, J. R., Haywood-Niler, E., & Kiecolt-Glaser, J. K. (1990). Spousal caregivers of persons with Alzheimer's and Parkinson's disease dementia: A preliminary comparison. *The Gerontologist, 30*, 332–336.

Dwyer, J. W., & Coward, R. T. (1991). A multivariate comparison of the involvement of adult sons versus daughters in the care of impaired parents. *Journal of Gerontology, 46*, S259–S269.

Fitting, M., Rabins, P., Lucas, M. J., & Eastham, J. (1986). Caregivers for dementia patients: A comparison of husbands and wives. *Gerontologist, 26*, 248–252.

Flaherty, S., Facteau, L., & Garver, P. (1987). Grandmother functions in multigenerational families: An exploratory study of Black adolescent mothers and their infants. *Maternal Child Nursing Journal, 16*, 61–73.

Fujiura, G. T., & Braddock, D. (1992). Fiscal and demographic trends in mental retardation services: The emergence of the family. In L. Rowitz (Ed.), *Mental retardation in the year 2000* (pp. 203–217). NY: Springer Publishing Co.

Gallagher, D., Rose, J., Rivera, P., Lovett, S., & Thompson, L. W. (1989). Prevalence of depression in family caregivers. *Gerontologist, 29*, 449–456.

Gallagher, D., Wrabetz, A., Lovett, S., DelMaestro, S., & Rose, J. (1989). Depression and other negative affects in family caregivers. In E. Light & B. Lebowitz (Eds.), *Alzheimer's disease treatment and family stress: Directions for research* (pp. 218–231). Washington, DC: National Institute of Mental Health.

George, L. K., & Gwyther, L. P. (1986). Caregiver well-being: A multidimensional examination of family caregivers of demented adults. *Gerontologist, 26*, 253–259.

Gilhooly, M. L. M. (1984). The impact of caregiving on caregivers: Factors associated with the psychological well-being of people supporting a dementing relative in the community. *British Journal of Medical Psychology, 57*, 35–44.

Gilleard, C. J., Belford, H., Gilleard, E., Whittick, J. E., & Gledhill, K. (1984). Emotional distress amongst the supporters of the elderly mentally infirm. *British Journal of Psychiatry, 145*, 172–177.

Grad de Alarcon, J., & Sainsbury, P. (1963). Mental illness and the family. *Lancet, 1*, 544–549.

Greenberg, J. S., Seltzer, M. M., & Greenley, J. R. (1993). Aging parents of adults with disabilities: The gratifications and frustrations of later-life caregiving. *Gerontologist, 33*, 542–550.

Hagestad, G. (1985). Continuity and connectedness. In V. L. Bengtson & J. F. Robertson (Eds.), *Grandparenthood* (pp. 31–48). Beverly Hills, CA: Sage.

Haley, W. E., Levine, E. G., Brown, S. L., & Bartolucci, A. A. (1987). Stress, appraisal, coping, and social support as predictors of adaptational outcome among dementia caregivers. *Psychology and Aging, 2*, 323–330.

Haley, W. E., Levine, E. G., Brown, S. L., Berry, J. W., & Hughes, G. H. (1987). Psychological, social, and health consequences of caring for a relative with senile dementia. *Journal of the American Geriatrics Society, 35*, 405–411.

Haley, W. E., & Pardo, K. M. (1989). Relationships of severity of dementia to caregiving stressors. *Psychology and Aging, 4*, 389–392.

Hatfield, A. B. (1978). Psychological costs of schizophrenia to the family. *Social Work*, 355–359.

Hatfield, A. B. (1987). Families as caregivers: A historical perspective. In A. H. Hatfield & H. Lefley (Eds.), *Families of the mentally ill: Coping and adaptation* (pp.). New York: Guildford.

Hess, B., & Soldo, B. J. (1985). Husband and wife networks. In W. J. Sauer & R. T. Coward (Eds.), *Social support networks and the care of the elderly: Theory, research, and practice* (pp. 67–92). N.Y. Springer Publishing Co.

Hoenig, J., & Hamilton, M. W. (1966). The schizophrenic patient in the community and his effect on the household. *Journal of Social Psychiatry, 12*, 165–176.

Horowitz, A. (1985a). Family caregiving to the frail elderly. In C. Eisdorfer (Ed.), *Annual review of gerontology and geriatrics* (Vol. 5, pp. 194–246). New York: Springer Publishing Co.

Horowitz, A. (1985b). Sons and daughters as caregivers to older parents: Differences in role performance and consequences. *Gerontologist, 25*, 612–617.

Janicki, M. P., & Wisniewski, H. M. (1985). *Aging and developmental disabilities: Issues and approaches.* Baltimore, MD: Paul H. Brookes.

Johnson, C. L., & Catalano, D. J. (1983). A longitudinal study of family supports to impaired elderly. *Gerontologist, 6*, 612–618.

Kazak, A. E. (1989). Family functioning in families with older institutionalized retarded offspring. *Journal of Autism and Developmental Disorders, 19*, 501–509.

Kramer, B. J. (1993). Expanding the conceptualization of caregivers coping: The importance of relationship-focused coping strategies. *Family Relations, 34*, 383–391.

Krauss, M. W., & Seltzer, M. M. (1993). Current well-being and future plans for older caregiving mothers. *Irish Journal of Psychology, 14*, 47–64.

Kreisman, D., Simmons, S., & Joy, V. (1979). Rejecting the patient: Preliminary validation of a self-report scale. *Schizophrenia Bulletin, 5*, 220–222.

Lawton, M. P., Moss, M., Kleban, M. H., Glicksman, A., & Rovine, M. (1991). A two-factor model of caregiving appraisal and psychological well-being. *Journal of Gerontology, 46*, P181–189.

Lawton, M. P., Rajagopal, D., Brody, E., & Kleban, M. H. (1992). The dynamics of caregiving for a demented elder among black and white families. *Journal of Gerontology, 47*, S156–S164.

Lefley, H. P. (1987). Aging parents as caregivers of mentally ill adult children: An emerging social problem. *Hospital and Community Psychiatry, 38*, 1063–1070.

Miller, B. (1987). Gender and control among spouses of the cognitively impaired: A research note. *Gerontologist, 27*, 447–453.

Minkler, M., & Roe, K. M. (1993). *Grandmothers as caregivers: Raising children of the crack cocaine epidemic.* Newbury Park, CA: Sage.

Morycz, R. K., Malloy, J., Bozich, M., & Martz, P. (1987). Racial differences in family burden: Clinical implications for social work. *Journal of Gerontological Social Work, 10*, 133–154.

Mui, A. C. (1992). Caregiver strain among black and white daughter caregivers: A role theory perspective. *Gerontologist, 32*, 203–212.

National Institute of Mental Health. (1985). *Mental health, United States, 1985.* Washington, DC: U.S. Government Printing Office.

Neundorfer, M. M. (1991). Coping and health outcomes in spouse caregivers of persons with dementia. *Nursing Research, 40*, 60–65.

Noh, S., & Avison, W. R. (1988). Spouses of discharged psychiatric patients: Factors associated with their experience of burden. *Journal of Marriage and the Family, 50*, 377–389.

Novak, M., & Guest, C. (1989). Caregiver response to Alzheimer's disease. *International Journal on Aging and Human Development, 28*, 67–79.

O'Connor, D. W., Pollitt, P. A., Roth, M., Brook, C. P. B., & Reiss, B. B. (1990). Problems reported by relatives in a community study of dementia. *British Journal of Psychiatry, 156*, 835–841.

Pagel, M. D., Becker, J., & Coppel, D. B. (1985). Loss of control, self-blame, and depression: An investigation of spouse caregivers of Alzheimer's disease patients. *Journal of Abnormal Psychology, 94*, 169–182.

Potasznik, H., & Nelson, G. (1984). Stress and social support: The burden experienced by the family of a mentally ill person. *American Journal of Community Psychology, 12*, 589–607.

Pratt, C., Schmall, V., Wright, S., & Cleland, M. (1985). Burden and coping strategies of caregivers to Alzheimer's patients. *Family Relations, 34*, 27–33.

Pruchno, R. A., & Kleban, M. H. (1993). Caring for an institutionalized parent: The role of coping strategies. *Psychology and Aging, 8*, 18–25.

Pruchno, R. A., Kleban, M. H., Michaels, J. E., & Dempsey, N. P. (1990). Mental and physical health of caregiving spouses: Development of a causal mode. *Journal of Gerontology, 45*, P192–P199.

Pruchno, R. A., Patrick, J. H., & Burant, C. J. (1996) Mental health of aging women with children who are chronically disabled: Examination of a two-factor model. *Journal of Gerontology: Social Sciences, 51B*(6), S284–S2196.

Pruchno, R. A., & Potashnik, S. L. (1989). Caregiving spouses: Physical and mental health in perspective. *Journal of the American Geriatrics Society, 37*, 697–705.

Pruchno, R. A., & Resch, N. L. (1989). Coping with caregiving: Mental health effects. *Psychology and Aging, 14*, 454–463.

Rabins, P., Mace, N., & Lucas, M. J. (1982). The impact of dementia on the family. *Journal of the American Medical Association, 248*, 333–335.

Rabins, P. V., Fitting, M. D., Eastham, J., & Zabora, J. (1990). Emotional adaptation over time in care-givers for chronically ill elderly people. *Age and Ageing, 19*, 185–190.

Sainsbury, P., & Grad de Alarcon, J. (1970). The psychiatrist and the geriatric patient: The effects of community care on the family of the geriatric patient. *Journal of Geriatric Psychiatry, 1*, 23–41.

Schoonover, C. B., Brody, E. M., Hoffman, C., & Kleban, M. H. (1988). Parent care and geographically distant children. *Research on Aging, 10*, 472–492.

Schulz, R., O'Brien, A. T., Bookwala, J., & Fleissner, K. (1995). Psychiatric and physical morbidity effects of dementia caregiving: Prevalence, correlates, and causes. *Gerontologist, 35*, 771–791.

Schulz, R., Tompkins, C. A., & Rau, M. T. (1988). A longitudinal study of the psychosocial impact of stroke on primary support persons. *Psychology and Aging, 3*, 131–141.

Schwartz, J., & Waldrop, J. (1992). The growing importance of grandparents. *American Demographics, 14*, 10–11.

Seltzer, M. M. (1985). Informal supports for aging mentally retarded persons. *American Journal of Mental Deficiency, 90*, 259–265.

Seltzer, M. M., Greenberg, J. S., & Krauss, M. W. (1995). A comparison of coping strategies of aging mothers of adults with mental illness or mental retardation. *Psychology and Aging, 10*, 64–75.

Seltzer, M. M., & Krauss, M. W. (1989). Aging parents with adult mentally retarded children: Family risk factors and sources of support. *American Journal on Mental Retardation, 94*, 303–312.

Seltzer, M. M., & Seltzer, G. B. (1985). The elderly mentally retarded: A group in need of service. *Journal of Gerontological Social Work, 8*, 99–119.

Shore, R. J., & Hayslip, J. B. (1990, August). *Predictors of well-being in custodial and noncustodial grandparents.* Paper presented at American Psychology Association, Boston, MA.

Stoller, E. P. (1983). Caregiving by adult children. *Journal of Marriage and the Family, 45*, 851–858.

Stommel, M., Given, C. W., & Given, B. (1990). Depression as an overriding variable explaining caregiver burdens. *Journal of Aging and Health, 2*, 81–102.

Stone, R., Cafferata, G. L., & Sangl, J. (1987). Caregivers of the frail elderly: A national profile. *The Gerontologist, 27*, 616–626.

Tennstedt, S., Cafferata, G. L., & Sullivan, L. (1992). Depression among caregivers of impaired elders. *Journal of Aging and Health, 4*, 58–76.

Tennstedt, S. L., & McKinlay, J. B. (1989). Informal care for frail older persons. In M. G. Ory & K. Bond (Eds.), *Aging and health care* (pp. 145–166). New York: Routledge.

Tennstedt, S. L., McKinlay, J. B., & Sullivan, L. M. (1989). Informal care for frail elders: The role of secondary caregivers. *Gerontologist, 29*, 677–683.

Thompson, E. H., & Doll, W. (1982). The burden of families coping with the mentally ill: An invisible crisis. *Family Relations, 31*, 379–388.

US Bureau of the Census. (1991). *Current Population Reports: Marital status and living arrangements: March 1990.* Washington, DC: Government Printing Office.

Vitaliano, P. P., Russo, J., Young, H. M., Teri, L., & Maiuro, R. D. (1991). Predictors of burden in spouse caregivers of individuals with Alzheimer's disease. *Psychology and Aging, 6*, 1–12.

Wade, D. T., Legh-Smith, J., & Hewer, R. L. (1986). Effects of living with and looking after survivors of a stroke. *British Medical Journal, 293*, 418–420.

Walz, T., Harper, D., & Wilson, J. (1986). The aging developmentally disabled person: A review. *Gerontologist, 26*, 622–629.

Wright, L. K., Clipp, E. C., & George, L. K. (1993). Health consequences of caregiver stress. *Medicine, Exercise, Nutrition and Health, 2*, 181–195.

Young, R. F., & Kahana, E. (1989). Specifying caregiver outcomes: Gender and relationship aspects of caregiving strain. *Gerontologist, 29*, 660–666.

12

Appraisals of Dependence Versus Independence Among Care-Receiving Elderly Women

Sandra Litvin

The efforts of Powell Lawton toward understanding later life have come in many areas: measurement, affect, Alzheimer's disease, to name but a few. In addition, Powell Lawton's work has also been critical in developing an understanding of the caregiving process. In recent years, as part of this effort, gerontologists have examined the problems and issues of middle-generation family caregivers to impaired elderly (see Aneshensel, Pearlin, Mullan, Zarit, & Whitlatch, 1995; Brody, 1990, for reviews). Crucial contributions toward understanding caregiving have come through the identification of important caregiver processes and concepts, as well as distinctive caregiver perspectives. Lawton, Kleban, Moss, Rovine, and Glicksman (1989), for example, reassessed "caregiving burden" through an examination of responses of numerous caregiving daughters concerning their feelings regarding parental care, and expanded the concept into a more general one termed "caregiving appraisal." Caregiving appraisal refers to all cognitive and affective caregiver assessments of both potential stressors and one's ability to cope with them. Lawton posited that, rather than merely discussing caregiving in terms of its potential burden and rather than merely assuming stress, caregiving demands are an instance of *subjective* appraisal, which could potentially reflect many possible responses to a potential stressor. It is no exaggeration to say that dissemination of studies such as this have resulted in the contemporary development and refinement of a national consciousness about family caregiving as a normative life course role.

Caregiving research focuses largely on the experiences of caregivers. Care-receivers have gained attention largely with respect to their need for assistance and not necessarily in terms of how care receiving affected their identities, a sense of who they are, and their sense of well-being. It is a great irony that relatively little attention has been given to the elders themselves (Brubaker, Gorman, & Hiestand, 1990). The irony, of course, is that, as Horowitz stated in her 1985 review of family caregiving, while gerontologists study old age, they have opted to study the nonelderly in caregiving research, perhaps falling prey to the stereotype that frail elders cannot speak for themselves at all.

There are surprisingly few studies focusing on the perspectives of care-receivers within the caregiving process (Robison, Moen, & Dempster-McClain, 1995, for review). It appears that there is an unquestioned assumption that although middle-generation caregivers appraise their own situations as stressful, because of situations that can lead to "role strain," care-receivers do not suffer in a similar manner (Krause, 1991). Surprisingly, in the current decade, there has been little expansion in our understanding of the perspectives of frail elderly persons. In 1983 Lawton delivered the Kleemeier Lecture in which he focused on the environment of frail older persons. He recognized that older persons play significant proactive roles regarding their environments, and he advocated that the opportunity for self-management would be most beneficial in enhancing positive affect in elderly persons. He discussed what he termed "the good life" for elderly persons, a construct that included perceived competence, well-being, quality of life, and the objective environment. He concluded that some people can maintain psychological well-being even while facing the demands of physical illness and its behavior concomitants.

Lawton suggested that even if a person loses control over the management of his or her affairs of daily life, there may be some adaptive value in looking at the brighter side of things. Lawton concluded that the world is full of older people who live in very stressful or very deprived environments, yet they manage to remain satisfied with life and/or experience a sense of well-being. Others, in contrast, may retain higher competence levels, but are chronically dissatisfied.

This observation on the part of Powell Lawton has led, in part, to the research described in this chapter. The research reported here addressed the following questions: Why do some frail older persons who receive assistance from their daughters see themselves as "care-receivers," while others tend to view themselves as "independents" who only receive assistance when needed? In addition, does defining oneself as a care-receiver (as opposed to someone who receives help when needed) have positive or negative connotations or both? For example, elderly persons may appraise the caregiving environment as contributing to an enhancement of their lives, or they may see a need for assistance as undermining their ability to maintain their self-esteem. What are the determinants of identifying oneself as a "care-receiver," rather than as someone who receives help once in a while? From the perspective of elderly persons, is the "care-receiver" identity one that denotes a sense of helplessness and or perceived declines in well-being? Are objective measures of impairment consistent with a subjective evaluation of one's identity (care-receiver or independent)? Is the relationship quality between mother and daughter, as care-receiver and caregiver, an influential predictor of care-receiving status, or is care-receiving status mostly contingent on social structural factors? Based on particular characteristics, can we correctly predict who will be classified as "care-receivers" and who will be classified as "independents"?

SOME THEORETICAL COMPONENTS OF CARE-RECEIVER IDENTITY

We have framed this research in part within Lazarus' stress model (Lazarus & Folkman, 1984), a model used by Lawton to examine caregiving appraisal. A stressor has been defined as an event or situation that has the potential for creating stress (Pearlin & Schooler, 1978). Major sources of stress, or possible stressors, include characteristics of the impaired person, characteristics of family relationships, and certain behaviors. According to the stress model, stressors arouse the appraisal process. The appraisal process also defines the external situation as a stressor or nonstressor. The assessment of the person's ability to cope with the stressor determines the impact of the stressor. For example, the necessity for one to accept care would not in itself be a stressor. It is the subjective appraisal of this entity that determines whether the situation is seen as positive, negative, or neutral. Lawton has noted that one of the major ways of coping is an attempt to adapt to the situation by reinterpreting the meaning of either the stressor or the larger situation in which it occurs. Therefore, it may be beneficial to the person to look at both the positive and negative aspects of any potentially threatening situation.

In the case of a frail elderly person with an increasing need to depend on others for help, changes may occur in relationships with a primary caregiver. The result of such changes may be in shifts in power and role status. Family members struggle with balancing the autonomous wishes of the frail elderly against concerns for personal safety. In some cases, the loss of autonomy may be stressful for the elderly person. In other instances, elders may adapt to the changing situation and easily permit the shift of power in order to gain from a sense of security and met needs. Such changes may be accompanied by a change in self-perception.

We propose that there is a major difference between seeing oneself as a care-receiver versus viewing oneself as an independent who receives help only when needed. Clearly, persons who see themselves as care-receivers are those who have adapted to the care-receiving role.

METHODS

Sample and Design

We conducted both quantitative and qualitative interviews with 400 spouseless frail elderly mothers age 70 and over about their experiences in receiving care from their middle-aged daughters. They were cognitively able to answer the interview questions determined by an initial telephone screening, and thereafter by several items tapping into cognitive ability (some mild impairment was expected, such as repeating oneself, etc.).

They all lived in the community (as opposed to nursing home or assisted living environments). In order to be eligible for the study, participants had to have a primary caregiving daughter (that is, a daughter on whom the care-receiver depended the most for assistance with at least two activities of daily living).

Most participants were obtained from individuals responding to publicity about the research through advertisements in regional, neighborhood, and ethnic newspapers; publicity flyers in public places; and direct contact with churches, synagogues, and other voluntary organizations, as well as public information lectures at senior centers and informant referrals of friends.

Procedures and Measures

The main question asked of all the elderly persons, and the one that is most critical to the discussion in this chapter, permitted the division of the sample into two groups, "Care-receivers" and "Independents." The question went as follows: "When you think of your need for assistance, do you: (1) see yourself as a care-receiver or as (2) someone who gets help once in a while?"

The means for the two response groups were compared on their sociodemographic characteristics, functional capacities, and well-being measures. Because there were significant differences between groups on particular sociodemographic characteristics, these variables were used as covariates in further analyses conducted to determine the unique influential predictors of care-receiving status. In addition, a classification analysis indicated the probabilities of correctly classifying cases into the two groups (Care-receivers vs. Independents) based on the predictors.

Variables Examined

Sociodemographic Factors

The demographic variables used in the analysis included: living arrangement (independent or with daughter), number of children who helped other than caregiving daughter, and whether or not daughters worked outside the household. Other variables of significance (considered from empirical findings) included: care-receivers' age, education, financial security, daughters' marital status, and hours of help provided by daughters, but they did not retain their significance when included in the multivariate analysis with the other characteristics.

The Instrumental Activities of Daily Living Scale (IADL), of the Lawton, Moss, Fulcomer, and Kleban (1982) Multilevel Assessment Instrument (MAI) was used as an indicator of functional capacity. (Other health measures, for example, the Personal Maintenance Activities Scale, subjective health status, a count of health conditions, and cognitive impairment, shared variance with the IADL.)

Appraisals of Care-Receiving

In order to assess the influence of specific psychological appraisals on care receiving, several composites were developed. These were as follows: First, care-receivers' perceptions of a sense of control over their lives were examined through three items that focused on competence in problem solving; well-being as a function of personal control; and well-being of the respondent as a function of both the respondent's and her daughter's control. Second, nine items were formed into a composite in examining the reversal of the roles of mothers and daughters, such as the act of transferring a mother's control over some events to her daughter in the caregiving context; the need to check with a daughter before making one's own plans; feelings of powerlessness, constraint, and dependency; any perceived overabundance of care provided by daughter; perceived dictation or control of activities that are dictated by daughters' plans and needs; and, a lack of decision-making ability because of daughter's interference. Third, respondent's fulfillment of needs was examined by a composite score developed from three items that ascertain the degree of balance between needs and care, including care-receiver's participation in decision making in health matters; degree of cooperation between a mother and a daughter in the caregiving process; and the perceived ability of daughter to figure out what mother needs.

In addition, two strongly associated items were combined to assess how satisfied the care-receivers were with their interactions with family and friends. We also examined differences between groups in depression (CES-D) and caregiving satisfaction.

Relationship Quality and Depression

A composite score of five items tapped care-receiver's perceptions of the quality of her relationship with her daughter. Components here included perceived quality of the relationship, as well as perceived closeness, negotiability, and ease of communication between mother to daughter.

In addition, the 20-item Center for Epidemiologic Studies Depression Index (CES-D; Radloff, 1977) was used to examine qualities of depressive states among care-receivers.

FINDINGS AND RESULTS

Sociodemographic Characteristics of Care-Status Groups

A description of all measures used and analysis of variance (ANOVA) comparisons are shown in Table 12.1. Approximately 38% of the elderly mothers perceived themselves as "Care-receivers," whereas 62% saw themselves as merely receiving assistance from their daughters when the need arose ("Independents"). The average age for both groups was 80 years. They had, on average, completed 10 years of education, and for the most

Table 12.1 Characteristics of Frail Elderly Women: One-Way ANOVA Based on Two Care-Receiving Status Groups

Variables ($df = 1,399$)	Total sample ($n = 400$)	Care receivers (A) ($n = 152; 38\%$)	Independents (B) ($n = 248; 62\%$)	Significant group differences	F
Mother's characteristics					
Elder's age (range = 70–100)	80.08	80.61	79.76		ns
Years of education (range = 2–20)	10.29	10.27	10.331		ns
Financial security (low score = secure; range: 1–3)	1.72	1.83	1.72		ns
Living arrangement (Person in household range: 1 = alone	1.34	1.46	1.27	A>B	15.68**
2 = shared)		53.9%	73.0%		
		46.1%	27.0%		
Living with daughter Who is primary helper (range: 1 = yes:	1.72	1.59	1.80	B>A	22.13**
2 = no:		41.4%	20.2%		
		58.6%	79.8%		
Daughter's characteristics					
Daughter's age (range: 20–74)	51.02	50.60	51.27		ns

(continued)

Table 12.1 (continued)

Variables (df = 1,399)	Total sample (n = 400)	Care receivers (A) (n = 152; 38%)	Independents (B) (n = 248; 62%)	Significant group differences	F
Living children other than primary caregiving daughter (range: 1 = yes; 2 = no)	1.23	1.16	1.27	B>A	6.84**
Hours a week daughter spends helping (range: 1–88)	7.93	11.68	7.88	A>B	25.14**
Daughter perceived as caregiver as opposed to someone who helps (1 = caregivers; 2 = helpers)		1.02 97.4% 2.6%	1.69 30.6% 69.4%	B>A	20.79**
Daughter's work status (1 = work; 2 = not working)	1.31	1.41	1.25	A>B	11.24**
Instrumental activities of daily living (8 = low ability; 24 = high ability)	20.54	19.06	21.45	B>A	62.20**
Personal care (7 = unable; 21 = does all)	20.54	20.27	20.70	B>A	9.09**

Variable					
Cognitive Impairment (range 7–35; high = good)	7.52	7.30	7.65	B>A	15.88**
Number of health Conditions (range: 0–14)	5.38	5.94	5.04	A>B	9.44**
Self-rated health (range: 3 = poor; 10 = good)	9.08	8.58	9.38	B>A	21.57**
Mother's Mental Status					
Role reversal (range: 9–43; high = greater reversal)	18.14	21.09	16.32	A>B	45.76**
Balance of needs (range: 3–15); high = better perceived balance)	9.86	10.83	9.26	A>B	28.43**
Perceived sense of control over care decisions (range: 3–12; high = loss of control)	5.17	5.70	4.83	A>B	12.21**
Satisfaction with family life and friendships (range: extremely satisfied =10; to extremely dissatisfied = 2)	8.77	8.70	8.81		*ns*
CES-D (depression, 0 = low; 60 = high; range = 0–48)	9.07	9.81	8.62		*ns*
Quality of relationship with Daughter (high score = good quality)	17.48	18.02	17.15	A>B	7.87**

Table 12.2 Predictors of Care-Receiving Status: Logistic Regression Based on Two Groups of Elderly Women

			Variables in the equation on step 1				
Variable	B	S.E.	Wald	df	Sig	R	Exp(B)
Living arrangements	-3.433	.1325	6.7118	1	.0096	-.0946	.7094
Number of children	.9682	.3048	10.0905	1	.0015	.1240	2.6333
Daughter's work status	.3327	.1230	7.3123	1	.0068	.1005	1.3948
IADL	.2441	.433	31.8054	1	.0000	.2379	1.2765
Constant	-5.9539	1.0072	34.9425	1	.0000		

Chi-Square	df	Significance
78.678	4	.000

			Variables in the equation on step 2				
Variable	B	S.E.	Wald	df	Sig	R	Exp(B)
Living arrangements	-.2810	.1378	4.1569	1	.0415	-.0694	.7550
Number of children	1.0404	.3189	10.6457	1	.0011	.1390	2.8304
Daughter's work status	.3380	.1283	6.9442	1	.0084	.1051	1.4021
IADL	.1875	.0451	16.9845	1	.0000	.1829	1.2040
Sense of balance	-.1022	.0509	4.0334	1	.0446	-.0674	.9028
Sense of control	-.0390	.0524	.5542	1	.4566	.0000	.9618
Role reversal	-.0437	.0211	4.2877	1	.0384	-.0715	.9573
Constant	-2.7762	1.2462	4.9625	1	.0259		

Chi-Square	df	Significance
19.540	3	.0002

Table 12.2 *(continued)*

		Variables in the equation on step 3					
Variable	B	S.E.	Wald	df	Sig	R	Exp(B)
Living arrangements	-.2986	.1398	4.5644	1	.0326	-.0774	.7418
Number of arrangements	-.2986	.1398	4.5644	1	.0326	-.0774	.7418
Number of children	1.0299	.3229	10.1757	1	.0014	.1382	2.8007
Daughter's work status	.3234	.1298	6.2079	1	.0127	.0991	1.3818
IADL	.1817	.0459	15.6915	1	.0001	.1788	1.1993
Sense of balance	-.0613	.0535	1.3103	1	.2523	.0000	.9406
Sense of control	-.0546	.0531	1.0578	1	.3037	.0000	.9468
Role of control	-.0554	.0221	6.2883	1	.0122	-.1001	.9461
Relationship quality	-.1082	.0443	5.9719	1	.0145	-.0963	.8975
Constant	-.8962	1.4756	.3688	1	.5436		

Chi-Square	df	Significance
6.347	1	.0118

part, both groups reported that they perceived themselves to be financially secure. Of the 152 elderly persons who perceived themselves as care-receivers, about 41% lived with their primary helper daughters, compared with only 20% of the 248 elderly persons who coresided with their daughters ($p < .001$). "Care-receivers" reported getting an average of 11 hours help from daughters compared to 7 hours for "independents" ($p < .001$). The "Care-receivers" almost unanimously (97%) perceived their daughters as "caregivers" as opposed to someone who merely assists them in their activities of daily living, compared with only 31% of the "Independents" who saw their daughters as caregivers.

Daughters averaged 51 years of age (range 20–74). The daughters of "Care-receivers" were less likely to work for pay (59%) compared to the Independents (75%) ($p < .001$).

In summary, there was substantial diversity in the sociodemographic characteristics of the two groups of elderly mothers and their daughters. The "Care-receivers" shared households more frequently than the "Independents," were likely to have another living child or children other than the caregiving daughter, and their daughters provided more hours per week of help than did the daughters of the "Independents." The "Care-receivers" also tended to see their daughters as "caregivers" rather than persons who helped, compared to those who perceived themselves as "Independents."

Health Characteristics of Care-Status Groups

In examining differences in perceived health status of elderly mothers, we found that those who defined themselves as "care-receivers" were in fact more limited in instrumental activities of daily living than their "independent" counterparts ($p < .001$). "Care-receivers" had greater limitations in their ability to conduct personal maintenance tasks than the "independents" ($p < .01$). On average, they were more cognitively impaired than their counterparts ($p < .001$). In addition, they had a greater number of health conditions ($p < .001$), and perceived themselves to be in poorer health than did the elderly women who rated themselves as "Independents" ($p < .001$).

Perceived "Care-Receiver" or Someone Who Just Gets Help?

A next question to be addressed is this: Do psychological appraisals differ between "Independents" and Care-receivers"? Again, appraisals include such constructs as role reversal, sense of control over life, control of health care decision making, the perceived balance between needs and assistance received from one's daughter caregiver, and the perceived quality of relationship with that caregiving daughter. "Care-receivers" reported significantly greater role reversal with daughters compared to "Independents" ($p < .001$). They also reported having less control over care when compared to the "Independents" ($p < .001$). On a positive note, however, "Care-receivers" reported that their needs were generally fulfilled by their caregiving daughters ($p < .001$). Interestingly, they also reported a better quality relationship with their daughters than did the "Independents" ($p < .01$). And, there were no significant differences found in ratings of informants' satisfaction with family life and friends or in their reports of depression between the two groups.

Logistic Regression Analysis

To gain a better understanding of the determinants of defining oneself as a "Care-receiver" or as an "Independent," a logistic regression analysis was performed in order to find the most influential factors in predicting care-receiving status. Results are given in Table 12.2. In an initial procedure, only covariates that retained significance were entered into the regression analysis. The variables were entered in the following manner. The sociodemographic and health variables were entered first (living arrangement, number of children other than caregiving daughter, daughters' work status, and the constraints in one's instrumental activities of daily living [IADL]. The psychological and control variables (perceived balance of needs and assistance, sense of control over one's own health decisions, and role reversal) were entered thereafter. A measure of the quality of relationship with daughter was the final entry in the regression analysis. The variables were entered in this manner so that we could determine the importance of relationship between a mother and daughter (caregiver and care-receiver) quality as a predictor of defining one's care status after the influence of all other variables was controlled.

Initially, the first set of variables were all significant, with severity of IADL impairment, not surprisingly, being the most influential predictor of defining oneself as "Care-receiver" ($p < .001$). Having more children other than caregiving daughter who helped, was the second most influential predictor of Care-receiver status ($p < .001$); and thereafter, mothers whose daughters did not work for pay ($p < .01$) provided the remaining explanation.

As noted, three variables were next entered into the analysis focusing on psychological and control appraisals. These included perceived balance between needs and assistance provided, perceived role reversal, and sense of control over health care decisions. Two of the three variables attained significance: balance of needs and assistance, and perceived role reversal. Sense of control over health care decision making lost its unique contribution. As in the bivariate analysis above, "Care-receivers" felt that caregivers were providing a good balance between needs and assistance, but by the same token also reported greater role reversal than did the "Independents."

The final step in the analysis was to enter the composite representing the quality of the mother–daughter relationship. This absorbed the variance in the balance of needs and assistance composite, suggesting that those daughters who provided the appropriate balance of care for mothers' needs also had a better relationship quality with their mothers. In this final equation, quality of relationship was the third most important predictor of Care-receiving status ($p < .01$; $R = .10$) after IADL ($p < .001$; $R = .18$), and having children other than caregiver ($p < .001$; $R = .14$).

Finally, a classification analysis was performed to determine how the predictors used in the analyses affected the likelihood of knowing which persons would define themselves as Care-receivers. Overall, results indicated that 72.61% of the care-receivers were correctly classified as either "Care-receivers" or "Independents."

DISCUSSION

The goal of this chapter was to identify the key variables affecting the way in which frail elderly persons identify their care receiving status. The findings raise some important issues in caregiving from the perspective of those receiving care. As was expected, those who defined themselves as care-receivers were significantly more limited in their functional capabilities. In addition, the "Care-receivers" had more children aside from their caregiving daughters. On average, the caregiving daughters for the elderly "Care-receivers" were not working outside the home. Although "Care-receivers" experienced greater levels of role reversal, feeling their daughters now managed their lives, they also felt well taken care of, reporting that daughters had a good comprehension of their needs. They reported significantly better quality relationships than those elderly persons who defined themselves as "Independents."

The findings can have various interpretations and point again to the need for further exploration of self-identity in later life. Mothers who defined themselves as "Care-receivers" had living children other than the primary caregiver. One could argue that elderly persons who have more than one child may feel more secure in the belief that they have others on whom to depend, whether this belief is true or not. Therefore, seeing oneself as a care-receiver may be associated with a larger care support network, even if one person is only telephoning. "Care-receivers" also reported that there was a good balance between their needs and the fulfillment of those needs. There is, however, a cost to this measure of security. For example, self-defined "Care-receivers" reported greater role reversal, with the perceived shift in power going from mothers to their caregiving daughters. Results indicate that "Care-receivers" are aware that this shift is occurring. They appear to adapt to the situation because they understand that this basic support allows them to remain as independent in the community as is possible. As a result, negotiations and compromises between mother and daughter occur so that relationship quality remains at a high level. Because these elders are more secure, they give priority to maintaining a good relationship with caregivers over any need to retain control over daily decisions.

The "Independents" were less likely to report an adequate balance between their needs and their level of assistance compared to "Care-receivers." "Independents" had fewer children, and thus they may feel that their daughters cannot or do not meet all their needs. It should be underscored that the daughters of the "Independents" were more likely to be working outside the home than were the daughters of "Care-receivers." There was thus less time to undertake the provision of care. The dissatisfaction resulting from a negative assessment of fulfillment of needs may have contributed to a poorer quality of relationship, or the evaluation of the relationship may rest to some extent in the sheer fulfillment of needs. While "Independents" reported more control over their lives and less reversal of roles, they lacked the higher sense of emotional satisfaction of the self-defined "Care-receivers."

In line with Lawton's conclusions on caregiving appraisal, this research has clearly shown that it should not be automatically assumed that receiving care is a stressor to all persons needing assistance with activities of daily living. The findings are supportive of Lawton's belief that there is adaptive value in looking at the various aspects of one's current life situation. It is a matter of subjective appraisal that reflects all degrees of subjective response including positive, neutral, and negative components. In this research, for example, defining oneself as an "Independent" appears to have some negative aspects. While feeling greater autonomy and more control over one's health decisions, the "Independents" reported unfulfilled needs, and did not have the same relationship quality with their daughters as did the "Care-receivers." These findings suggest that the absence of children other than primary caregiving daughter is far more of a constraint on elderly persons than the families' control over the elderly person's life.

By contrast, the positive aspects of defining oneself as a "Care-receiver" are that, on average, the infirm parent feels well taken care of and experiences a better relationship with the caregiving daughter, which appears to outweigh the negative aspects of giving up a degree of control.

This study was just the first step in understanding the experiences of frail elderly persons who see themselves as "Care-receivers" as opposed to persons who receive help when needed. The next step would be to evaluate the adaptation strategies of care-receivers. The use of qualitative data collected from respondents to explore the meaning of independence would greatly enhance the quantitative findings. It would also be beneficial to see how elderly persons' self-identity changes over time as functional limitations increase, and what life event triggered the change.

REFERENCES

Aneshensel, C. S., Pearlin, L. I., Mullan, J. T., Zarit, S. H., & Whitlatch, C. J. (1995). *Profiles in caregiving: The unexpected career*. New York: Academic Press.

Brody, E. M. (1990). *Women in the middle: Their parent-care years*. New York: Springer Publishing Co.

Brubaker, E., Gorman, M. A., & Hiestand, M. (1990). Stress perceived by elderly recipients of family care. In T. H. Brubaker (Ed.), *Family relationships in later life* (pp. 184–201). Newbury Park, CA: Sage.

Horowitz, A. (1985). Family caregiving to the frail elderly. In M. P. Lawton, & G. L. Maddey (Eds.), *Annual review of gerontology and geriatrics* (Vol. 5, pp. 194–246). New York: Springer Publishing Co.

Krause, N. (1991). Stress and isolation from close ties in later life. *Journal of Gerontology: Social Sciences, 46*, S183–S194.

Lawton, M. P. (1983). Environment and other determinants of well-being in older people. The Robert W. Kleemeier Memorial Lecture. *Gerontologist, 23*, 349–357.

Lawton, M. P., Kleban, M. H., Moss. M., Rovine, M., & Glicksman, A. (1989). Measuring caregiving appraisal. *Journal of Gerontology: Psychological Sciences, 44*, P61–P71.

Lawton, M. P., Moss, M., Fulcomer, M. C., & Kleban, M. H. (1982). A research and science-oriented multilevel assessment instrument. *Journal of Gerontology, 37*, 91–99.

Lazarus, R., & Folkman, S. (1984). *Stress, appraisal and coping*. New York: Springer Publishing Co.

Pearlin, L. I., & Schooler, C. (1978). The structure of coping. *Journal of Health and Social Behavior, 19*, 2–21.

Radloff, L. (1977). The CES-D Scale: A self-report depression scale for research in the general population. *Applied Psychological Measurement, 1*, 385–401.

Robison, J., Moen, P., & Dempster-McClain, D. (1995). Women's caregiving: Changing profiles and pathways. *Journal of Gerontology: Social Sciences, 50B*, S362–S373.

VI

Community and Program Development

13

If You Want to Understand Something, Try to Change It: An Essay Honoring Powell Lawton

George L. Maddox

Inscribed on the tomb of Karl Marx in Highgate Cemetery, London, is the admonition, to paraphrase, "The point of history is not to discuss it but to change it." The analog of this sentiment is, in fact, axiomatic in experimental and clinical sciences: If you want to understand something, try to change it. Behavioral and social scientists, particularly those who love the relative isolation and security of ivied towers, want to understand purposive social change—but usually at a safe physical and emotional distance. In a world in which leaders typically aspire to make a difference either in the world of ideas or the world of action, only a few aspire to live in and contribute to a world where leaders are expected to translate ideas into purposive action. Powell Lawton has been one of the rare leaders over a long career in gerontology who has moved easily and well in both worlds. His work in gerontology is among the best known in the national and international academy of scholars, although most of his career of research, teaching, and service has been at the Philadelphia Geriatric Center following his doctorate from Columbia in 1952. A full decade elapsed before "Aging" began to appear in the titles of his publications. But once his research on aging settled in, Powell Lawton has continued to be a prolific publisher of quality research, of well-edited books, and of edited publications in aging on issues related to mental health, on the fit between individuals and the milieus in which they live, on housing for older adults, and on a variety of methodological issues in research. What is particularly remarkable over his long career is that his interest in and his publications about testable, implementable ideas about aging has been sustained. Powell Lawton remains today in full intellectual flight almost a half century after his doctorate. In the first half of 1997, for example, he had five edited books in press; and, in peer-reviewed journals, he had six articles under review and three in press.

One can imagine that, if younger scholars in gerontology seeking their place in the sun sent Powell Lawton a 75th birthday greeting, it might well be "Lighten up, Powell."

This prolific scholar has found time to be a leader in the development of gerontology organizations both in his chairmanship of Division 20 (Aging and Development) of the American Psychological Association and in his presidency of the Gerontological Society of America. Within the GSA he was honored with the prestigious Kleemeier Award for Excellence in Research and in Division 20, APA, with the Distinguished Contribution Award.

THE SUBSTANCE OF A DISTINGUISHED CAREER IN RESEARCH

From a broad range of substantive interests pursued over a long career, three facets of Lawton's work in aging are notable for me. First, he appreciated the importance of putting older adults in a social context; and the milieu of particular practical interest was often housing or other planned living environments. Second, his interest in the environmental context of aging helped to counter in behavioral and social scientific research the tendency in biological and individual psychological research to focus gerontological research primarily or exclusively on the individual in isolation. Third, in Lawton's work, substantive significance is melded well with methodological sophistication and interest in applied intervention research.

When Jim Wiley and I wrote the opening chapter in the first edition of the *Handbook of Aging and the Social Sciences* (Maddox & Wiley, 1976), we identified several of the important themes and issues in the history of gerontology found in Lawton's research and which are the focus of his interest. Wiley and I noted, for example, that gerontology in its early years was decidedly practical, understood the importance of social context, and believed in the possibility of modifying the experience of aging through purposive programmatic and policy interventions. The biological determinism which was so seductive in the 1970s in gerontology was, we felt, missing the mark. The best of contemporary biology, we concluded, was beginning to stress less what biology made necessary in human life and to stress more about what biology makes possible. The enormous cognitive capacity of human beings transforms them from automatons potentially into active agents capable of constructing as well as reacting to environments. The environments in which aging occurs matter.

Therefore, Wiley and I were also struck by the very unproductive discussions of the Age/Period/Cohort issue, particularly the concept of cohort. The concept of cohort had, in our view, been imported rather unreflectively into gerontology from demography. "Cohort" refers most appropriately to a category of persons born about the same time who are exposed to and presumably interact with a succession of defined environments at specified points in history. Gerontologists, quite often, were not bothering to define with evidence either the relevant environments to which cohorts were exposed, or the nature of their personal exposure. The unsatisfactory default position was to identify a specific chronological year or an era (World War II, the Depression) and make broad assumptions about the presumed environment identified. Lawton, by professional inclination and training an environmental psychologist, appreciated the value of conceptualizing a person whose defined needs interact with defined environmental demands and opportunities (see Lawton, 1980). The fitting of these "needs" of individuals and the "presses" of environments within some tolerable range predicts the success or failure of behavioral outcomes (Lawton & Nahemow, 1973). For most older adults, most of the time, person-context fitting falls within a tolerable range. When frailty occurs in later life, compensatory fitting may be necessary, and, if necessary, possible. The potential modifiability of living environments was obviously related to Lawton's concept of purposive person-milieu fitting and explains his persistent interest in housing policy and housing design; living arrangements are an obvious opportunity for the appropriate fitting of needs and resources for frail older adults. Lawton did not attempt to specify in detail rules for adjusting mis-fitting of individuals and milieus, through it was clear that he believed compensatory adjustments to be possible. The details of such adjustments are probably appropriately left to clinical judgment in everyday life.

Both as a clinician by training and an environmental psychologist by preference, Powell Lawton was by inclination action-oriented, as were many of the pioneers in social gerontology. But his interest in interventions to demonstrate the modifiability of the experience of aging never over-rode a commitment to soundly designed research. He, with his colleague Elaine Brody (Lawton & Brody, 1969) will also be remembered, for example, for their contribution to their conceptualization and measurement of morale in later life and for their conceptualization and measurement of Instrumental Activities of Daily Living (IADL). His publications over a period of four decades testify to his practical concern for the health and well-being of older adults and how he translated that concern into useful research and ultimately to purposive beneficial interventions.

REAFFIRMING THE INTERACTION OF PERSONS AND CONTEXTS

The initial focus of gerontology in the 1950s and 1960s was on older adults whose experiences and behavior could be modified through purposive modification of the societal contexts in which they live. This contextual view of aging processes and purposive beneficial interventions gave way in the 1970s to a seductive, simplistic view of aging which stressed intrinsic, inevitable, deterministic biological processes. The observed heterogeneity of older adults was subordinated to a preference for discovering the universal biological determinants of aging. Even in the social and behavioral sciences, the search for universal laws of aging led to a preference for large-scale social surveys in which persons and environments were facilely translated into collections of variables generated by general linear models. This translation was driven in large part by the popularity in behavioral and social science of research involving large representative samples of populations about which generalizations justifiably might be made. This dominant strategy, and its related data analytic procedures, important as they were for the advancement of gerontology, exacted two very large costs for gerontologists. Persons became synthetic collections of variables, and lost their status as active agents who respond selectively to and were capable of modifying their environments; and social contexts and milieus were noted but not measured. Periods in Age, Period, Cohort (APC) analyses were, as noted, typically designated by no more than the notation of a year or a broad era. Survey research analysis did not give substance to milieus primarily because sampling strategies made this difficult, often impossible. Gerontologists became aware of these issues (Maddox & Campbell, 1985; Maddox & Wiley, 1976) and tried unsuccessfully to compensate with large samples of panelists followed longitudinally though rarely in socially defined contexts, and with limited attention to qualitative studies of defined subjects interacting in defined environments (see Campbell, 1995).

Researchers in aging in the 1980s often seemed to lose touch with older adults as persons; they also lost touch with the everyday worlds in which adults grew older. Students interested in the aging of individuals and populations in recent years have spoken to me often about learning gerontology with minimum opportunity to get to know older persons. This is a predictable risk in an educational environment that values predominantly or solely as a teaching device in gerontology the secondary analysis of large-scale social survey data. It becomes possible to write about aging and the aged without getting to know either personally. This outcome is particularly a risk in sociology, which is the only social sciences discipline interested in human aging without a companion discipline focused on translating scientific findings into purposive interventions intended to modify the experiences and processes of aging.

Powell Lawton himself never lost touch with older adults, and the everyday worlds in which they live. One can sense also that the pendulum has swung a bit in social gerontology, at least, away from exclusive interest in secondary analysis of social survey data. The limitations of such strategies are better understood today and there is a new interest in studies that keep individuals as active agents in research design as well as retain an interest in the milieus in which they interact. My impression is that most contemporary students in gerontology will prefer a career in a field in which actively engaged older persons and recognizable social context are evident, a field that can include humanistic qualitative scholarship as well as positivistic research.

SHARED PERSPECTIVES IN GERONTOLOGY

Although Powell Lawton and I are identified with different disciplines, we quite evidently share a number of personal values and perspectives about aging people and societies and about the objectives of gerontology. We both want gerontology to make a difference in the lives of older adults. This is hardly a surprise. We are from the same age cohort that was exposed to the Great Depression, World War II and the civil rights movement, followed by social and economic opportunities that made our cohort among the most favored in human history. We acknowledge our privileged position and have used our opportunities to maintain an interest in social activism.

Powell and I are members of a second and much smaller cohort of individuals from the 1950s who were attracted to gerontology when the discipline was in its formative years. We did not simply inherit gerontology; we helped make it what it was becoming. And, for better or worse, we have grown older doing gerontology. We owed substantial debts to a small number of pioneers in the field, but we were substantially self-taught.

My early experience in and commitment to gerontology has been laid out in some detail in my Kleeimeier Research Award lecture (1985) and does not need repeating in detail here. A review of the essential points in that account, however is appropriate here because it will reveal why I have found a complementary perspective in the career of Powell Lawton so attractive.

My sociological perspective on aging persons and populations led me to focus first on contextual issues which structure human development and aging. Societies, from a sociological perspective, are large-scale experiments in the allocation of social and economic resources to individuals over their life course. Demographic and epidemiologic research have documented, for example, the dramatic differences in life expectancy observed in more and less developed societies. These differences are explained primarily by differential socioeconomic advantage of individuals in access to resources, not by their innate biological characteristics. Change the availability and distribution of resources, and both life expectancy and well-being are also changed responsively. Similarly, within societies, differential socioeconomic, sexual and ethnic location of individuals predict substantially different outcomes in development, aging, and survival. Aging well is not simply a matter to be predicted from genetic or biological analysis.

The demonstrated importance of differential social location of individuals for their well-being and survival had for me three important implications of observed human diversity to be followed in my research. One implication was to focus not on the elderly, but on the extraordinary degree of differentiation among older adults. In research on large populations of aging persons, measures of central tendency are obviously attractive. Averages and modes are useful ways to simplify observed distributions in complex arrays of data. But central tendencies are neither more important nor more instructive than measures of variance, such as standard deviation. One of my early inquiries into the data of the Duke Longitudinal Studies was to document not only the substantial variance in the array of individual performance on many physiological, psychological, and social indicators in later life, but also the persistence of that variance. Older adults did not simply become more alike with age (Maddox & Douglas, 1973). I recall vividly a conversation with the great biological gerontologist Nathan Shock about why, in his reporting of data, he tended to use regression lines without reporting associated standard deviations. He responded simply, "I should have; it was an oversight." It followed for me that, if the observed differentiation among older adults was explained to a substantial degree not by biology but by circumstance of birth in socially stratified societies, modifiability in the allocation of social and economic resources would be a possibility for changing the experience and outcome of aging. One might imagine moving persons below the regression at least to the observed mean through strategic interventions at the individual or social level.

The evidence of persistent variation in older populations has been reinforced by the repeated documentation of significant within-cohort differentiation within older populations. My research on such variances illustrates the importance of such differentiation for understanding the experience and processes of aging (Maddox & Clark, 1992; Maddox, Clark & Steinhauser, 1994). For example, using a large panel ($N = 11,000$) from a single cohort (1906–1911) in the Social Security Administrations Longitudinal Retirement History Study, we traced the trajectories of functional impairment for over a decade. Three predictions from the existing research literature were soundly confirmed: Impairment levels and trajectories of women as compared with men, and of African Americans compared with others and of of lower-SES persons compared with others confirmed that the prevalence of impairment was significantly higher for women, African Americans, and lower-SES persons.

The complexity of these within-cohort differences was indicated further by analyses of comparisons of men and women and of African Americans and others when socioeconomic status (e.g., income and education) were controlled. Unexpectedly, the sex and ethnic differences initially observed in this large longitudinal panel essentially disappeared. Further longitudinal analysis confirmed that SES variables are powerful predictors of functional status outcomes, as epidemiologists have long maintained in their research on health and well being. Such research also sends a warning that sex and ethnicity are variables which need clearer specification in health research. Sex, for example, is often a control variable which is treated as though it is only a biological indicator or only a social designation. It may be either or both. Since longevity is demonstrably longer for women than for men and sickness patterns are known to be sex-linked, one should not rule out sex as a biomedical predictor. But sex also designates a social component, often designated as "gender;" and clearly observed gender differences reflect both the assignment of social roles and rules of stratification that assigns basic societal resources differentially to men and women.

What was clear from this finding about male/female differentiation was that their different experience reflected to an important degree the consequences of societal choices regarding the allocation of resources to men and women. Societies do appear to be large natural experiments in consequences of the differential allocation of resources over the life course using inherited characteristics such as sex and ethnicity.

Intuitively, the next intellectual steps for me appeared obvious. The ways in which societies go about allocating resources by age or sex or ethnicity are theoretically modifiable. One thinks immediately of the useful axiom of experimental and clinical sciences: If you want to understand something, try to change it. One, of course, should be appropriately cautious in applying such a grand axiom. There are obvious practical and ethical limitations in interventions into the lives of older persons by gerontologists, even when intentions are presumed to be good. Nevertheless, the axiom at a minimum breaks the mindset that views observed aging experience and process as somehow biologically determined and hence universal and inevitable. From this perspective, the socioeconomic conditions which eventually limit the education, job opportunities, income, and pensions of women are socially determined and, hence, potentially modifiable.

The evidence-based conclusion that some aging processes and the experience of aging are modifiable is, therefore, one of the significant rediscoveries of gerontological and geriatric research. I refer to the idea of modifiability of the course of aging as a rediscovery because pioneers in gerontology had a clear inclination to be interventionists. All clinicians tend to be interventionist by inclination and training, but they are not necessarily optimistic about the effectiveness of their interventions. The pioneers in social gerontology tended to be very optimistic about the beneficial effects of resource reallocation on behalf of older adults. They tested their optimism through support for major resource allocation projects such as social security, Medicaid/Medicare, and improved housing for older adults. The health and welfare of older adults has been considerably improved by such purposive social interventions. One of the most convincing indications that interest in interventions into processes of aging is now widespread is found in the plan for aging research developed early in the 1990s by the Institute of Medicine/National Academy of Sciences for the National Institute of Aging (Lonergan, 1991; Maddox, 1994). In all areas of science, the agency research plan concluded, the case has clearly been justified in all disciplines for more field trials and purposive interventions to test the limits of our capacity to modify the experience and processes of aging in beneficial ways.

Science has a distinctive role in making a case for the possibility and efficiency of various interventions. But science has a very limited role in determining the social and political desirability and viability of particular interventions. Such determinations are primarily in the realm of political processes which generate public policy to reflect societal values and preferences.

Historically, major institutions of higher education have tended to distance themselves from involvement in public policy processes, except of course, public policy processes that involve their own organizational well-being. One consequence of this principled distancing for gerontological research in universities is that academics tend to know more about beneficial interventions in aging than they actually attempt to implement. Gerontologists, like other academics can sometimes be radical critics of the status quo but without a clear political agenda of any kind.

Late in my career and in my early retirement, I have been attracted to developing a Long-Term Care Resources Program in Duke Center for Aging and Human Development whose principal objective is to translate good ideas about aging well into action. This program, has provided opportunities to explore how the development of community leadership and community planning of resource utilization can assist many frail older individuals to age at home. The ideas sought for implementation are not my ideas only. They come from exploring the marketplace of ideas found among older adults in the communities where the implementation has to occur. Few people would doubt that beneficial outcomes are possible. To return to the opening theory of this essay, the point is not to understand that aging at home is feasible, the point is to make aging well at home possible and probable. Duke's LTC Resource Program is now extensively involved in leadership development through internships for undergraduates and graduate and professional students in settings where they are matched with mentors who know the territory of an aging society and are busily creating new opportunities which will facilitate aging well. The newest venture in leadership development for our program offers opportunities for older, retired individuals who are still intellectually and physically in full flight to create plans for improving their capacities to be effective leaders.

As I have experienced the satisfaction of exploring how to translate good ideas in gerontology into useful actions in an aging society, I have discovered one of the reasons why Powell Lawton is such an optimistic person. Translating gerontological ideas into action is not only possible and useful. It is also enjoyable.

REFERENCES

Campbell, R. (1995). Longitudinal data sets in aging. In G. Maddox (Ed.), *The encyclopedia of aging* (2nd ed., pp. 573–575). New York: Springer Publishing Co.

Lawton, P. (1980) *Environment and aging*. Belmont, CA: Wadsworth.

Lawton, P., & Brody, E. (1969). Assessment of older people: Self-maintaining and instrumental activities of daily living. *Gerontologist, 9*, 179–185.

Lawton, P., & Nahemow, L. (1973). Ecology and the aging process. In C. Eisdorfer & P. Lawton (Eds.), *Psychology of adult development and aging* (pp. 619–674). Washington, DC: American Psychological Association.

Lonergan, E. D. (1991). *Extending life, enhancing life: A national research agenda on aging*. Washington, DC: Institute of Medicine/National Academy Press.

Maddox, G. (1987). Aging differently. *Gerontologist, 27*, 557–64.

Maddox, G. (1994). Social and behavioral research on aging: An agenda for the United States. *Aging and Society, 14*, 97–107.

Maddox, G., & Campbell, R. (1985) Scope, concepts, and methods in the study of aging. In R. Binstock & E. Shanas (Eds.). *Handbook of aging and the social sciences* (pp. 3–31). New York: Van Nostrand Reinhold.

Maddox, G., & Douglas, E. (1973) Aging and individual differences: A longitudinal analysis of social, psychological, and physiological indicators. *Journal of Gerontology, 29*, 555–563.

Maddox, G., & Wiley, J. (1976). Scope, concepts , and methods in the study of aging. In R. Beinstock and E. Shanas (Eds.), *Handbook of aging and the social sciences* (pp. 3–34). New York: Van Nostrand.

Maddox, G. L., & Clark, D. O. (1992). Trajectories of functional impairment in later life. *Journal of Health and Social Behavior, 33*, 114–128.

Maddox, G. L., Clark, D. O., & Steinhauser, K. (1994). Dynamics of functional impairment in later adulthood. *Social Science and Medicine, 38*, 925–936.

14

Community Planning and the Elderly

Robert Newcomer with Carrie Griffin

Powell Lawton's writing in person–environment relations spans three decades, and includes at least seven books and three dozen journal articles. Among this work are empirical studies, theory development, and public policy and design recommendations. Books and articles published in the 1990s by others continue to reference this work. Powell's legacy in person– environment relations stems from several sources. He was one of the pioneers in this area of study. His projects were theory-based and addressed issues of continuing concern. He innovated in both conceptualization and measurement. He continues to publish empirical work and to synthesize his prior work into theoretical and practical applications. Powell's influence has not been limited to writing. He has helped organize and implement housing design training programs, lectured in several design and planning graduate programs, collaborated with numbers of people in research and publications, and worked with other major figures in the field of housing for the elderly. References to his person–environment work are most pervasive in studies of the influence of housing design on resident adjustments and housing satisfaction, but fields as diverse as housing economics, social geography, and demography have used his concepts to examine and understand trends in migration and relocation, the aging of neighborhoods, and the attraction of residents into varieties of specialized housing.

The purpose of this chapter is to discuss Powell's influence on community planning. To understand his contributions in this area, it is informative to see his work in the context of the public policy issues being addressed and emerging during the formative period of the 1960s and 1970s. Foremost among the community planning concerns during the 1960s were urban renewal, the extension of the federally financed interstate highway system to include the building of major highway systems across urban areas, the "war on poverty", and the construction of low-income housing. Urban renewal programs were being used to remove dilapidated housing and commercial and industrial buildings as part of an effort to revitalize urban centers, and to help enable the purchase of land for highway construction. Model cities and the more comprehensive "War on Poverty" social programs directed (at least conceptually) more attention and resources to the identification and amelioration of social conditions contributing to poverty and the decline of urban neighborhoods. These programs included the development of community advocacy groups, job training and job placement programs, and efforts to end discrimination in housing and employment opportunities. Complementing these events was the development of low-income housing projects. The need for this housing was stimulated both by the destruction of low-income housing resulting from urban renewal and highway construction, and from a recognition that many in the society were paying rents well in excess of 25% of their income.

All of these programs placed their principal emphasis on minority and low-income communities, sometimes working with local government, sometimes bypassing it. Not all programs were equally valued by the affected communities. Minority communities and others protested the destruction of their neighborhoods and housing. Cities and the nonminority neighborhoods that might be affected by the relocation of those displaced by the urban programs, or who were likely to be sites of low-income housing, expressed concern that large low-income housing projects would have adverse effects on the racial mix of neighborhood schools, property values, and the racial mix of a neighborhood itself. Such arguments helped spawn a number of studies to evaluate these impacts and the adoption of policies intended to assure more equitable distribution of the projects. Local communities also exercised a more direct accommodation: they often opted to support subsidized housing for the elderly as an alternative to housing for low-income families. Many communities were drawn to this housing because elderly residents seemed to be more acceptable to neighborhoods. This, along with national housing programs and tax policy, helped accelerate the development of specialized housing for the elderly. Nonprofit groups, such as churches, were another source of interest in developing low income housing both to serve their members and as a public good.

Another trend that both contributed to these public policies and resulted from them was the changing racial and age structure in many communities and their neighborhoods. The typical pattern was for nonminority populations (usually those with children) to move to suburban areas, with their housing being taken by minority residents. Suburbanization was facilitated by highway construction, and stimulated by the relocation of commercial and industrial job centers to larger and less expensive suburban locations. The evolution of neighborhoods from a predominance of one racial or ethnic group to another were not new phenomena, but the rate of these changes was accelerated by urban renewal, highway construction, and school busing intended to achieve racial integration of schools.

A final trend arose from the emerging experience of low-income housing projects that had been built a decade or so earlier. These had combined aged and non-aged residents. In these projects, especially the very large ones, crime and violence was growing and many of the elderly occupants frequently expressed concern about personal safety.

In short, public policies of the mid-1960s into the early 1970s, while attempting to address concerns of low-income minority populations, had both direct and indirect effects on the elderly. The elderly were among those relocated due to urban renewal and the destruction of low-income housing. They were among those affected by the changing age and racial mix of neighborhoods, because older nonminority residents were less likely to leave, and consequently would find themselves in transforming neighborhoods. City and transportation planners were generally not prepared to address these issues. Identifying the special needs and potential problems of an aging population, and meeting these needs, was not included in the theoretical and pragmatic training and practice of these professions. Among the major concepts affecting the design and physical organization of communities were the principles of access to work, shopping, and recreation (but for those of working age and their children); and the notion that neighborhoods should be organized to facilitate children walking to schools and parks. How cities changed in terms of the age-mix of neighborhoods had been observed, but most theory about how cities change in land use were based on urban economics, and the idea that the use of land was determined by its "highest and best" use. Simply, this means that the use of the land was determined by the price someone was willing to pay for it. Price was a function of the desirability of the location for the prospective use.

The problems resulting from urban renewal programs were chronicled in books such as *The Federal Bulldozer* (Anderson, 1967), *The Death and Life of Great American Cities* (Jacobs, 1961), and *The Urban Villagers* (Gans, 1962). Such work took issue with urban renewal and urban highway construction and the resulting obliteration or subdivision of neighborhoods and other social support networks within communities. A much smaller and less heralded group began to look specifically at the elderly population and how they were affected by all these changes. Among these investigators were Powell Lawton, Frances Carp, Sandra Howell, Eva Kahana, Lee Pastalan, Irving Rosow, and Sylvia Sherwood. Working as collaborators and in parallel, these and other investigators began to develop a research-based understanding of physical design and how this could influence the life quality of low-income elderly housing project residents, as well as the effects on elderly residents in low income minority neighborhoods. More importantly, this generation of investigators helped establish training programs and other venues so that design and planning practitioners could acquire, apply, and expand this knowledge. From this narrow beginning there eventually grew work that looked at transportation, neighborhood use, the changing age-mix of neighborhoods, and a vast understanding of the specialized housing needs of individuals with varying levels of functional and cognitive ability.

Powell Lawton was not necessarily the originator of these processes, but he was at every critical juncture in the evolution and extension of environmental design for the elderly over the past quarter century. He was an innovating empirical researcher, theorist, training program organizer, friend to both established and aspiring researchers in this field, design consultant, and mentor. A few of his publications in this area are included in the references to illustrate the breadth of the subjects addressed, the number of collaborators, and the time span of his interest and writing. A consistent theme is understanding the relationship between design and other environmental features and resident well-being. This work includes micro-settings of individual facilities (e.g., Lawton,

1985a, 1985b; Lawton, Brody, & Turner-Massey, 1978; Lawton & Cohen, 1974b; Lawton & Simon, 1968), as well as neighborhoods (e.g., Lawton & Cohen, 1974a; Lawton, Kleban & Singer, 1971; Lawton, Nahemow, & Tsong-Min-Yeh, 1980). Among the topics addressed are issues in the measurement of environments and individual ability, the role of services and social areas in housing settings, how needs change over time, and even neighborhood reactions to elderly housing. These research-based findings have been translated into books on community planning (e.g., Lawton & Hoover, 1981; Lawton, Newcomer, & Byerts, 1976; Newcomer, Lawton, & Byerts, 1986), housing management (Lawton, 1975, 1980b), housing design (Altman, Lawton & Wohlwill, 1984; Lawton, 1980), and theory (Lawton, Windley, & Byerts, 1982).

I had originally intended to summarize the more recent person–environment work that has a derivative link back to Powell, but for reasons outlined earlier this is much too daunting a task, and one that would surely be underrepresentative of these many connections. Instead, I will use my relationship with him to illustrate the multiple levels and manner of his influence.

I first met Powell in 1970 when he visited the University of Southern California as part of an Administration on Aging funded training program located there in Environmental Design. This was a program for graduate students in either Architecture or City Planning. The program was funded to encourage these professions to direct more attention to the aged and the long-term care population. Our mentors were Louis Gelwicks, AIA and Eric Pawley, AIA. Our activities included visiting continuing care retirement communities; low-income housing projects; nursing homes; and the then-emerging retirement communities of the Southern California area. On these site visits we would tour the facility, talk to residents and administrators, and develop a critique of the design, and evaluate the features and functions as these enhanced the living situation.

This was an exciting time for us. We were entering a new specialty area in our professions, the nursing home and elderly housing industries were growing rapidly, and the opportunities for advancing knowledge and contributing to innovation seemed boundless. This excitement was further stimulated by a visiting scholars series in our program. The scholar would be on campus for a week, where they would put on one or more seminars for the whole Gerontology Center (later to be known as the Andrus Gerontology Center), have a jovial dinner hosted by Lou Gelwicks and his wife Jeannie (attended by the architecture and planning graduate students), and then be available to each student in the training program to consult on our research projects and to tour housing and long-term care facilities with us commenting on design, service, policies, and other features.

Through this series I had the opportunity to meet Sandra Howell, Francis Carp, Leon Pastalan, Kermit Schooler, and M. Powell Lawton. The work brought to our attention was directed to a very basic understanding of buildings and how interior layout affected behavior patterns: how the location and furniture arrangements of a common room affected their use; why residents congregated into entrance lobbies or around nursing stations; how the location of something as simple as mail boxes and laundromats affected opportunities for social contacts among residents; and how one's sense of privacy was affected by the ability to have private rooms or to control private space.

The experience of retirement communities and continuing care retirement communities (CCRCs) was raising additional issues for investigation. Principal among these was whether and how to segregate residents by physical and cognitive status, how to effectuate the relocation of residents from one level of care to another, and the consequence this would have for the individual and the other residents. Powell's work at the Philadelphia Geriatric Center, and elsewhere in Philadelphia had already begun to address these issues. His analysis of Strawberry Mansion (Lawton et al., 1971), relocation adjustments (Lawton & Yaffe, 1970), and the role of privacy (Lawton & Bader, 1970) were illuminating and insightful. Even more impressive was Powell's ability to step back and reflect on his work (and that of others) and to formulate theoretical perspectives to help guide inquiry into these and a host of other design and planning questions. The most important of these for me was the simplifying formulation of person–environment transactions that he and Lucille Nahemow articulated (1973).

Briefly stated, this framework postulated that the individual seeks to obtain a match between the demands for capable behavior arising from the environment and their ability. A match between ability and demand produces life satisfaction and optimum performance. Mismatches, where demands exceed ability, produce stresses and inadequate performance in that setting; demands below ability produce under stimulation, boredom, and even an erosion of ability.

Embedded in this simple framework is a factorial complexity of situations. Among other things, this framework recognizes that both environment and individual attributes simultaneously operate on many levels. Individual ability includes physical and cognitive functioning, as well as economic resources, educational background, and social skills. Environmental features include physical features, social components like roles and norms, and consideration of the congruence of the individual and the prevailing population modal attributes such as race, income, and physical and mental ability. A third general feature of the framework is that it is based on a relative scale rather than absolutes. In other words, the environmental demands that define excessive and understimulation are relative to the individual's capability. As ability declines, other things being equal, an individual's adaptive range declines. Conversely, as ability increases, so does the adaptive range. A presumptive goal of supportive programs and design would be to recognize an individual's ability and to adjust the salient environmental demand so that it is within the individual's adaptation range.

Being a theory, it was not necessary to operationally define what the adaptive range was, or what identified excessive or under stimulating environmental demand. Powell's initial work was directed to measuring individual and environmental dimensions and the life satisfaction or morale thought to result from successful adaptation. He left for others the task of operationally defining adaptive range as it might apply in varied settings and circumstances.

As a city planning student, my interests were oriented to broader settings than building interiors and space plans, which was the more typical focus of research at that time. I was concerned with how the services and features of buildings affected the use made of the neighborhoods in which they were located, and, conversely, how neighborhoods affected use of the buildings themselves. Physical ability and stamina were among the parameters that might influence where one goes and what they do, as were neighborhood features like distance and fear of crime. Thomas Byerts (an architectural student), Archie MacDonald (a social work student), and I began to explore this issue, examining the use of MacArthur Park near downtown Los Angeles. The park is located in a neighborhood of boarding houses, retirement hotels, and inexpensive apartments. At that time there was a high density of low-to moderate-income elderly living in these units. Tom's interest was in mapping how the elderly (mostly men) used the microspaces in the park: the card playing and shuffleboard areas, park benches along the park entrance and lakeside pathways, and the more private and remote areas. Archie's and my interest was in understanding who used the park, where they were coming from, and why they were coming.

Using a combination of observation and interviews (both in the park and in one residential hotel), we began to come to the conclusion that the men were drawn to the park for different reasons. Private spaces in the park were used by those who had limited ability to control or obtain privacy in their residence. The active spaces, like those used for card playing were often a work-substitute setting used to get out of the house during the day. The observational settings, at the entrance and elsewhere, were used as opportunities for social interaction often by people who felt isolated in their living units (McDonald & Newcomer, 1973).

Our collaboration illustrated what we expected, a relationship between settings and buildings. While this work was influenced by Powell, it was conducted in isolation from him. This changed with Powell's national study of low-income housing projects for the elderly. Tom, who was a year ahead of me in school, graduated and took a position with Powell as an interviewer, spending the better part of a year touring low-income housing facilities and conducting in-depth interviews with the residents about their health and cognitive status, their interests and activities, and a variety of social relationships. Facility level data was also obtained on the services and features available on-site. Through this work, Tom began to form a lifelong friendship with Powell. Their relationship developed further after Tom assumed a position with the Gerontological Society to head up their project on environmental design. Among the goals of this program was to influence architectural education programs across the nation. Powell was very active in this endeavor.

Meanwhile, I was beginning to design my dissertation and to explore with Powell the possibility of doing a follow-up survey with his National Housing Study sample. The purpose was to obtain data on the use of neighborhood services (e.g., convenience stores, hair dressers, libraries, churches, and doctors) and to assess how use patterns were affected by distance, the service options available in the housing project, and various individual and environmental attributes, such as perceptions of environmental barriers and safety. Use of a service and the constellation of services and activities inside and outside the housing projects were, for my purposes, demonstrative illustrations of adaptation. Distance and safety were examples of environmental demand; individual characteristics included functional ability and various demographics, as well as such attributes as familiarity with the neighborhood, social networks, and activity preferences. This endeavor, in short, attempted to operationalize the Lawton-Nahemow person–environment framework, attempting to predict activity patterns within a range of adaptation defined by individual ability, geographic distance, and other environmental features.

Powell's assistance took several forms. He paid for my travel to Philadelphia to orient me to his project's database. He also turned over a contact list for all his study respondents, and then permitted me to send a supplemental mail questionnaire to his sample. All of this was given to me with no conditions. I can still remember his answer to my question about co-authorship on the publications. "Don't worry about that. Publish your own papers. I'll probably be writing about some other issue from these data."

Where did this work go? It led to a publication (Newcomer, 1976) and integration into several book chapters (e.g., Pollack & Newcomer, 1986), but more importantly, it laid the foundation for further work. This took several forms. For 3 years I continued at the Andrus Gerontology Center, assuming the position held by my mentor Lou Gelwicks, who had returned to private practice as an architect-planner in housing and long-term care. There I began working with my own students, most particularly Victor Regnier, Richard Eribes, and Harold Kendig, to further study the concept of a cognitive neighborhood and its relationship to convenience and other service uses, and to one's living situation. This integration of architectural and planning consideration, although perhaps simplistic now, was an important concept then. Low-income housing projects for the elderly were often placed where land was of low cost, even though the area surrounding the site might be dilapidated or lacking neighborhood services located within a convenient distance. Nonprofit institutions, such as churches, fared little better in being sensitive to these issues. They often used donated land to build housing projects, but typically this land was more likely to be adjacent to the church and not convenient to services. Nursing homes were no better. Here, priority was to place these convenient to hospitals and in locations that did not affect nearby residential property values. The needs of the patients (i.e., the residents) and their visitors was not considered. Newly constructed housing, especially the retirement communities and even large continuing care retirement complexes, by necessity needed large parcels of vacant land. Usually, these were outside of established neighborhoods and isolated, at least at a pedestrian scale, from convenience services. Victor Regnier carried this work forward further in his own publications (e.g., Regnier, 1973; Regnier & Gelwicks, 1981; Regnier & Pynoos, 1987) and in his design work.

Work such as Victor's and mine helped influence zoning codes and local site design criteria so that they encouraged the location of elderly housing projects near convenience shopping and other amenities. Over the years both Victor and I have been consultants to environmental impact studies evaluating the appropriateness of a site and project relative to the likely residents and their neighborhood use needs.

Another extension of these studies and of Powell's influence came from planning work done with Lou Gelwicks and his firm. A basic part of most of Lou's projects was estimating the market demand for the proposed housing facility. Basic to this work was an understanding of the decision-making process used by a prospective tenant, or the assumptions made by their family members, in selecting a particular housing facility.

Were they matching their ability to the resources offered by the project and its neighborhood, including the services that could be brought into the housing unit? Would the
facility be in a position to meet the needs of the most likely residents? Did the facility
and its management want to serve the needs of its most likely applicants? What would
be the consequence on the eventual resident mix if certain types of residents (e.g., those
with higher or lower cognitive and functional ability) were disproportionately attracted
(or not attracted)?

Lou and I approached these market analysis questions through surveys of both existing project residents and prospective clients. The funding for this work came from project contracts, not grants, but we were able to refine survey instruments and sampling
designs to generate an increment of insight into who would likely be attracted with the
offering or exclusion of particular services and facilities. Lou and his firm, Gerontological
Planning Associates, worked with numerous clients throughout the 1970s and 1980s
employing these basic methods of market research. This work has been used by a number of nonprofit corporations and such large for-profit groups as the Marriott
Corporation. No doubt other firms have used variations on these procedures, and the
market demand assumptions that derive from the data analysis.

By the mid-1970s I had moved out of the housing and long-term care planning field
into area agencies on aging and the planning of community service programs for the
elderly. As part of an effort to integrate these human service issues with the physical
design work of my immediate past, Powell Lawton, Tom Byerts, and I collaborated on
our first book: *Community Planning for the Elderly* (Lawton et al., 1976). This book was
a clear step beyond the interior design applications of Powell's earlier work. It was written for the multidisciplinary groups responsible, in one way or another, for planning the
environments of older people, whether these be represented by physical, social, or service dimensions. The book provided a comprehensive overview of the assets, liabilities,
and needs of the elderly, and explored the issues that could be considered in the planning of communities, housing, services, and institutions. The readings exemplified then-
existing knowledge about the interrelationships between human behavior and physical
and social environments. Each service or program was viewed as a discrete aspect of the
environment, but we did not focus on the relationships or interactions among services.

My work in human services planning throughout the mid-70s into the mid-1980s
broadened my understanding of federal and state long-term care policies, and how services financing and regulations influence both the supply and demand for services. Such
work was at a macro scale relative to my earlier interests, but any consideration of who
was using a community service and who was going into institutional care would bring
me back to basic issues, such as what influences choice to enter and leave a particular
environment. This could be a physical environment, or one created by financial and practice incentives and disincentives to service access. Though much of my research and
writing through the mid-1980s was directed to state policy effects on long-term care service supply, an underlying issue remained—namely, many incentives were developing
for assisting the elderly to remain at home or in relatively independent settings. All such
policies made an implicit assumption about a matching of need with resources. Adequate

matches permit people to remain in the least restrictive settings; uncertain proportions of the population remain in poorly matched settings. In an effort to better focus on this issue, Powell, Tom, and I again collaborated on a book, *Housing an Aging Society* (Newcomer et al., 1986). The compiled work was selected to respond to two major trends in the aging field. First, the range of housing alternatives was developing as a component of the system of care, i.e., housing was becoming recognized as both a residence and as a service component. Second, and most striking, was the acknowledgment of this fact by professionals outside the housing field. Housing specialists on the other hand were mainly preoccupied with the traditional concerns of financing, affordability, and design. The resulting book was developed to communicate information about housing issues across the health, housing, and human service professions, and in particular to raise the awareness of housing specialists to the changing health and social service milieu, and the consequences this had for a range of housing types. The content covered a wide range of housing types (e.g., retirement communities, supportive living arrangements, hotels, rooming houses, shared housing, and independent housing); the factors influencing choice and availability; and the consequences for lifestyle and activity patterns known to be associated with these alternative living arrangements. This book, much more than the earlier book, emphasized the influences of demography and public policy. Finally, this book brought more attention to neighborhoods and neighborhood quality (e.g., safety), housing site considerations, and continuing market force influences on the displacement of aged households (in this case, the conversion of apartments and single family homes into condominiums).

By the completion of this book, my research interest in housing and community planning had begun to focus on two subgroups: those living in the community with functional frailty, and those living in supportive housing (e.g., residential care facilities, assisted living, and continuing care retirement communities). Holding constant the physical and cognitive functional status of residents, what factors, such as IADL and ADL support, home modifications, or changes in health status were most contributory to a resident's shift from being able to remain in their current environment? And, recognizing that adaptation to an environmental situation is multifactorial, which elements could be brought into equilibrium (e.g., ADL task needs) and which ignored (e.g., social contacts with friends and family)? This interest was approached directly in 1989 as part of the evaluation of the Social Health Maintenance Organization. We supplemented the close out interview with the frail population participating as demonstration clients in Long Beach, California. These individuals were defined as frail based on the presence of two or more limitations in the instrumental activities of daily living (IADL, e.g., shopping, grooming, house keeping) (a measure developed by Powell Lawton and Elaine Brody) or one or more limitations in activities of daily living (ADL, e.g., bathing, dressing, toileting, eating, and transferring). Many of these individuals had been known to us for up to 3 years. All had been interviewed semi-annually after first being identified as frail. The supplemental questions sought to gain an understanding of the housing modifications, services and support received, and the various considerations that had influenced the client's ability to remain in their own homes or the home of a relative over the many months following the onset of their frailty. If the client had relocated into other housing, assisted living, or a nursing home during the tracking period, we also asked about the factors most contributing to their decision to move. This work was supported by the Robert Wood Johnson Foundation in connection with planning for long-term care insurance and the types of benefits that might be included in coverage and relative to the potential interest of the public in using reverse annuity mortgages and other financial incentives to remain in independent housing.

Many of these individuals had made modifications to their homes, such as through the installation of grab bars or ramps, or obtained housekeeping services or other assistance. These were largely seen by the respondents as being helpful, but not essential, to remaining in their homes. Relocation into nursing homes was generally determined by a need for nursing services. Where people started from was an important confounding factor. Folks coming from low-income housing largely entered nursing homes as their next environmental adaptation. People coming from other forms of rental housing may have made more than one move in an effort to find an environment more appropriate to their capabilities. People coming from their own homes had a wider range of options for obtaining a match with their levels of need, using relatives or supportive housing, in addition to nursing homes.

These patterns reflected personal preferences to a large extent, but the options available were constrained by public policy. For example, constrained public funding for residential care (i.e., reliance on Supplemental Security Income and an optional state supplemental payment for such housing) limited the per-day rent available for low-income persons. Consequently, this limited the supply and access to units by those needing income-subsidized assisted living. Fire and safety codes and state licensing requirements similarly limited the types of frailty that could be supported in non-family households. At this time, home health care and other forms of skilled care could not even be provided to residential care occupants. In short, this work, although derived as part of the evaluation of a health care delivery program, illustrated the interaction between person–environment adaptation and public policy (Connolly, Newcomer, & Philips, 1992).

A second set of studies has examined environmental influences on behavior and choice among persons living in supportive housing (in this case, continuing care retirement communities or CCRCs). Over 10 years I was able to get two projects funded, both by the Robert Wood Johnson Foundation, to look at this issue. The first study collected health and functional status data on CCRC residents and prospectively tracked their nursing home, personal care, hospital, physician, and emergency room use over 12 months (Newcomer & Preston, 1994). The starting assumption was that the presence of nurses and other staff on site, and the ability to provide personal care, special meals, and in-room meals would reduce the use of nursing homes and lower the use rates of health services. CCRC residents from two facilities were matched with a sample of persons of similar age using the same medical group practice. Persons with functional disability, particularly in ADLs, but even such IADLs as shopping and meal preparation, not surprisingly were more likely to be living in their own housing units if they were in CCRCs than if they lived in the community. There they would most likely live with other family members. In other words, for both groups, a self-selection balance had been achieved. One year did not yield enough transitional events to examine the process of how balance was achieved, nor did we examine the relative satisfaction of the two groups.

We were able to identify some outcomes arising from the match between personal needs and environmental supports. Hospital and emergency room use was lower in the CCRC group, although nursing unit use was substantially higher, as was physician use. About half of the CCRC nursing unit use consisted of short-term stays associated with ambulatory surgery and podiatry treatments. It was somewhat surprising that the two CCRCs varied substantially from one another in the likelihood of personal care housing use, both short-term and permanent relocations. This appeared to be associated with the relative supply of these alternative beds—if beds were available, they were likely to be used. While this is a physical design issue, it is also a management decision. Retaining the more frail in their "independent units" creates a resident mix that is more integrated with respect to frailty. While this may serve the desires of any particular resident to remain with their friends and in their own unit, the frailty mix may narrow the pool of applicants to the facility. On the other hand, a management practice of relocating the frail into personal care units may give the facility a reputation of not supporting their residents and of being too quick to place residents in personal care or nursing units. Powell Lawton had been studying similar issues in the early 1970s.

Exploration of the relationship between facility bed mix and management preference for supporting continuation of the frail in independent apartment units was the subject of a second study, this one using a database with a longer time horizon and a larger sample of CCRCs (Newcomer, Preston & Roderick, 1995). American Baptist Homes of the West (ABHoW), which had rental payment records on their residents going back up to 25 years, asked us to help them track the transition from independent to personal care and to nursing units, and to calculate the number of days in each level of care. Available data included information on the facility unit mix, and whether it was a high-rise or not. Resident data were limited to age, gender, marital status, and Medicaid eligibility status. The expected relationship was not found; namely, the presence and use of personal care units did not reduce the likelihood of or number of lifetime days in nursing units. Rather, personal care days were a substitute for days in independent living. Consistent with our earlier two-site study, being in a high rise delayed the use of personal care transfers over the transfer rates in low-rise complexes. This finding seems to be explained by the greater ability of residents to get to meals in a high-rise, and by the relative ease of delivering supportive services by the facility.

My colleagues on this last project (Steve Preston and Susan Schock Roderick) and I are presently embarked on a follow-on to this study, again working with ABHoW. This time we are tracking cases forward from 1989 through 1996, a period when the facility collected annual resident assessments as part of screening eligibility for long-term care insurance coverage. We have also used more sensitive measures of resident transfers than rental records. In this case, there are daily census logs in each of the eight facilities. The logs reveal if the resident is in the unit, or temporarily located in a nursing unit, personal care unit or hospital on a particular day. Through these data we will be testing the rate of change in resident functional and health status, and the relationship this may have on the type of living unit being used, the rate of transfer between levels of care, and the short-term use of hospital and nursing homes. Service programs that better monitor changes in health status are expected to reduce the amount of health care use, and to be associated with long stays in independent housing. These questions have a direct link to Powell Lawton's person–environment framework.

Powell's continuing influence on me is not limited to studies of housing. The major work during the past 12 years of my career has been in studying the interface between acute and long-term care. This work includes evaluations of the Social Health Maintenance (S/HMO) demonstration, and the Medicare Alzheimer's Disease Demonstration. Among other things, both projects examined how caregivers and clients adjust to changing functional and health conditions and the consequence of these adaptations for health care use. These adjustments include activity patterns, use of home-based services, changes in primary caregivers, and changes in living arrangements. These familiar themes, although influenced in the analytical modeling by health economics and health behavior theory, have a connection back to my early training and its association with Lawton. I have continued to use his person–environment framework as a conceptual cornerstone to assure that all the dimensions of environmental adaptation are being addressed. Among the practical applications coming out of this work is the identification of the need to monitor certain risk factors (like chronic health conditions and behavioral problems), and conditions (like caregiver relationships) that can precipitate a change in status or living situation; and an estimate of the relative rates of living arrangement change and health care cost that result when the match between individual capability and environmental demand is not maintained.

Powell Lawton's multifaceted influence on community planning and housing has been illustrated through the case example of my work—both the collaborations with him and my own endeavors. The extension of person–environment studies and their applications for the elderly owes much to many individuals, such as Leon Pastalan at the University of Michigan; Jon Pynoos and Victor Regnier at the University of Southern California; and Paul Windley at University of Wisconsin, who have directed training programs in environmental design for the elderly. These programs extend Powell's work and that of many others (including their own). Additionally, there have been a large number of researchers touched in personal ways, such as I was by Powell, who continue to work in this area. Among these are such individuals as Sandra Newman, Beth Soldo, and Steven Golant—among many many others. Philip Sloan and Les Grant are among those who have worked with Powell most recently in extending his basic person–environment concepts to special care units in nursing homes and residential care facilities for those with dementia. Finally, there are others, such as Rudolf Moos, who continue to work in the area of environmental measurement and classification. The collective endeavors of all these individuals (and many more) have helped form and test basic assumptions and approaches in community planning and design for the elderly. Powell Lawton has been a mentor and/or a friend to most of these investigators, a touchstone reminding us of why these are important issues, and a role model for personal and scientific integrity. Thank you, Powell.

REFERENCES

Altman, I., Lawton, M. P., & Wohlwill, J. F. (Eds.). (1984). *Elderly people and the environment*. New York: Plenum.

Anderson, M. (1967). *The federal bulldozer*. New York: McGraw-Hill.

Connolly, L., Newcomer, R., & Philips, D. (1992). *Adaptions made to cope with functional limitations: A survey of California services*. Sacramento, CA: Assembly Office of Research.

Gans, H. J. (1962). *The urban villagers: Group and class in the life of Italian-Americans*. New York: Free Press of Glencoe.

Jacobs, J. (1961). *The death and life of great American cities*. New York: Random House.

Lawton, M. P. (1970). Institutions for the aged: theory, content, and methods for research. *Gerontologist, 10*, 305–312.

Lawton, M. P. (1975). *Planning and managing housing for the elderly*. New York: Wiley.

Lawton, M. P. (1980b). *Social and medical services in housing for the aged* [DHHS Publication No. (ADM) 80–861]. Rockville, MD: Department of Health and Human Services, Public Health Service, Alcohol, Drug Abuse, and Mental Health Administration.

Lawton, M. P. (1980a). *Environment and aging*. Monterey, CA: Brooks/Cole.

Lawton, M. P. (1983). Environment and other determinants of well-being in older people. *Gerontologist, 23*, 349–357.

Lawton, M. P. (1985a). The elderly in context: Perspectives from environmental psychology and gerontology. *Environment and Behavior, 17*, 501–519.

Lawton, M. P. (1985b). The relevance of impairments to age targeting of housing assistance, *Gerontologist, 25*, 31–34.

Lawton, M. P. (1986). *Environment and aging* (2nd ed.). Monterey, CA: Brooks/Cole.

Lawton, M. P. (1988). Three functions of the residential environment. *Journal of Housing for the Elderly, 5*, 35–50.

Lawton M. P., & Bader, J. (1970). Wish for privacy for young and old. *Journal of Gerontology, 25*, 48–54.

Lawton, M. P., Brody, E. M., & Turner-Massey, P. (1978). The relationships of environmental factors to changes in well-being. *Gerontologist, 18*, 133–137.

Lawton, M. P., & Cohen, J. (1974a). Environment and the well-being of inner-city residents. *Environment and Behavior, 6*, 194–211.

Lawton, M. P., & Cohen, J. (1974b). The generality of housing impact on the well-being of older people. *Journal of Gerontology, 29*, 194–204.

Lawton, M. P., & Hoover, S. L., (Eds.). (1981). *Community housing choices for older Americans*. New York: Springer Publishing Co.

Lawton, M. P., Kleban, M. H., & Singer, M. (1971). The aged Jewish person and the slum environment. *Journal of Gerontology, 26*, 231–239.

Lawton, M. P., & Nahemow, L. (1973). Ecology and the aging process. In C. Eisdorfer & M. P. Lawton, (Eds.), *The psychology of adult development and aging* (pp. 619–674). Washington, DC: American Psychological Association.

Lawton, M. P., Nahemow, L., & Teaff, J. (1975). Housing characteristics and the well-being of elderly tenants in federally assisted housing. *Journal of Gerontology, 30,* 601–607.

Lawton, M. P., Nahemow, L., & Tsong-Min-Yeh. (1980). Neighborhood environment and the well-being of older tenants in planned housing. *International Journal of Aging and Human Development, 11,* 211–227.

Lawton, M. P., Newcomer, R., & Byerts, T. (Eds.). (1976). *Community planning for an aging society* (pp.). Stroudsburg, PA: Dowden, Hutchinson and Ross.

Lawton, M. P., & Simon, P. (1968). The ecology of social relationships in housing for the elderly, *Gerontologist, 8,* 108–115.

Lawton, M. P., Windley, P. G., & Byerts, T. O. (Eds.) (1982). *Aging and the environment : Theoretical approaches.* New York: Springer Publishing Co.

Lawton, M. P., & Yaffe, S. (1970). Mortality, morbidity and voluntary change of residence by older people. *Journal of the American Geriatrics Society, 18,* 823–831.

McDonald, A., & Newcomer, R. (1973). Differences in perception of a city park as a supportive or threatening environment. In D. Gray & D. Peligrino (Eds.), *Reflections on the recreation and park movement* (pp. 256-261). Dubuque, IA: W. C. Brown and Company.

Newcomer, R., Connolly, L., & Philips, D. (in press). Housing modifications and moves among functionally impaired elderly. Publication pending *Journal of Housing for the Elderly* .

Newcomer, R., Lawton, M. P., & Byerts, T. (Eds.) (1986). *Housing an aging society.* New York: Van Nostrand Reinhold.

Newcomer, R., & Preston, S. (1994). Relationship between acute care and nursing unit use in two continuing care retirement communities. *Research on Aging, 16,* 280–300.

Newcomer, R., Preston, S., & Roderick, S. (1995). Assisted living and nursing unit use among continuing care retirement community residents. *Research on Aging, 17,* 149–167.

Pollack, L., & Newcomer, R. (1986). Neighborhoods and the aged: Knowledge and intervention. In R. Newcomer, M. P. Lawton, & T. Byerts (Eds.), *Housing an aging society* (pp. 119–126). New York: Van Nostrand Reinhold.

Regnier, V. (1973). *Neighborhood cognition of elderly residents.* Monticello, IL: Council of Planning Librarians.

Regnier, V., & Gelwicks, L. E. (1981). Preferred supportive services for middle to higher income retirement housing. *Gerontologist, 21,* 54–58.

Regnier, V., & Pynoos, J. (Eds.). (1987). *Housing the aged: design directives and policy considerations.* New York: Elsevier.

15

Research As a Resource for Planning and Practice

Avalie R. Saperstein and Abby Spector

P owell Lawton's pioneering work on quality of life has had a significant impact on planning and implementation of services for older people living in institutional settings as well as in the community. His multidimensional view of well-being has led to the development of assessment instruments that have become standard parts of gerontological practice, and helped shape the service delivery systems and facilities that have proliferated nationwide since the 1960s.

This chapter explores how Lawton's work has influenced the evolution of community and institutional services for one provider, Philadelphia Geriatric Center (PGC), over a 30-year period. It focuses on two of Lawton's major contributions to the field. The first is his work on quality of life, which has laid the foundation for assessment, service planning, and facility design. The second is his commitment to applying scientific knowledge and methods to the "real world", where professionals plan and deliver services to the aging and their families. The chapter highlights how his research methods have been incorporated into clinical practice and facility planning, and examines why his approaches have been so successful in building bridges between researchers and service providers.

PGC's experience is just one example of Lawton's wide-ranging influence on the field. It illustrates how researchers and professionals can collaborate to create and implement new ideas that result in better quality of life for older people and their families.

HISTORICAL CONTEXT

When Lawton began his work on quality of life and aging in the 1960s, the field of gerontology was in its infancy. At the time, there had been relatively little research examining the needs and characteristics of older people, especially those living in the community.

Aside from nursing homes, there were few if any services dedicated to meeting the special needs of older people and their families. There were no area agencies on aging, and no programs such as case management, adult day care, or geriatric medical services. The community resources that were available—such as homemaker or family counseling agencies—served the general population, and typically offered just one type of service rather than multidisciplinary interventions aimed at meeting the needs of the whole person.

In this context, Lawton came to PGC and founded one of the first gerontological research institutes in the United States. Here, he began to formulate the concepts of quality of life and well-being, which were to be the focus of his career. Also, he began a close partnership with PGC clinicians, most notably, Elaine Brody, and administrators, such as the late Arthur Waldman. This dynamic collaboration provided a forum where researchers and professionals—clinicians, planners and administrators—could generate and test new ideas. When Lawton first arrived, PGC was a nursing home; as it grew to a multiservice agency with a full continuum of care that it is today, his theories and concepts helped shape virtually every new program as it emerged.

ASSESSMENT

One of Lawton's most significant contributions lies in his pioneering work on assessment of older persons. Begun in the 1960s, this body of work focused on developing a conceptual model of quality of life, defining the key elements, and developing tools to measure it. Lawton views quality of life as multidimensional, taking into account a wide variety of objective and subjective components of human experience. His model identifies the most important factors that contribute to an older person's well-being. It focuses on four dimensions or sectors: behavioral competence (which includes health, function, cognition, time use and social behavior); psychological well-being; perceived quality of life; and the objective environment, which refers to an individual's physical and social context.

When Lawton applied this framework to assessment, he concentrated on defining the domains and elements within each sector, and developing scientifically reliable and valid methods to measure them. Far from working alone, he was influenced by, and, in turn, influenced, clinical and research colleagues at PGC and other institutions. In fact, Lawton built explicitly on tools that already had been designed by such researchers as Sidney Katz at The Benjamin Rose Institute.

Lawton has made many contributions to the field of assessment. However, from a service provider's standpoint, his most significant innovation was to underscore the necessity of a multidimensional approach to evaluate well-being, and to broaden the array of factors that should be considered. Lawton added important new domains in cognition, psychological status, function, and environment. Furthermore, he was an early advocate of using subjective as well as objective measures to evaluate quality of life. Lawton's ideas and techniques deeply influenced service planners and practitioners at PGC. His multidimensional approaches gave us new tools to measure service needs, and led us to create new solutions to address those needs. By integrating his assessment instruments into daily practice, we were able to capture key information about clients' lives, and design interventions more effectively at the individual level as well as for aggregate populations.

Most importantly, when Lawton framed quality of life and assessment multidimensionally, we began to recognize that we should also plan and organize services multidimensionally. This concept had a dramatic effect on PGC's service system, which was evolving rapidly at the time. We were incredibly fortunate to have Lawton as a willing partner when we began to translate his theories into practice through the design of a spectrum of community services.

COMMUNITY SERVICES

In-Home Services

PGC's first community program, called In-Home Services, provides an excellent example of this collaboration. The program began in 1974 as a federally funded research and demonstration project to study the service needs and preferences of older adults living in the community, as well as to test an intervention that was an early form of case management. Lawton was the research consultant on the project, which offered him a unique laboratory in which to test his evolving ideas on assessment. The project incorporated Lawton's instrumentation, and translated his multidimensional view of well-being into a service intervention that could meet clients' needs comprehensively.

As the first step in the study, all subjects received a broad-based assessment. In line with Lawton's work, the interview protocol incorporated objective and subjective measures for the domains of health status, psychological status, cognition, ability to carry out activities of daily living, social participation, family and friendship networks, financial resources, and environmental factors. Eventually, many of the items and scales used in the protocol became part of the nationally known Multilevel Assessment Instrument (MAI).

Following the assessment, a subset of those surveyed received the project intervention. Subjects in the experimental group, who expressed a need for services, were assigned to community service workers. These paraprofessionals used the assessment tool as the basis to create a service plan, and link clients with formal and informal resources that would meet their needs across the relevant dimensions.

The project yielded several important findings. First, from a scientific standpoint, it validated Lawton's measures with a large sample of community-dwelling older people. Also, it demonstrated that a research-based multidimensional assessment tool could be used effectively for clinical purposes. The instrument provided community service workers with rich data about their clients' needs and circumstances.

Second, the project confirmed that many older people have multiple simultaneous needs, which can best be met through multidimensional service solutions. Approximately 15% of community residents age 60 or older had at least one service need, and a significant percentage had needs across several domains. We saw clearly that clients with complex problems could be served most effectively by a model that started with a comprehensive assessment, followed by the formulation of a multidisciplinary service plan, arranging and coordinating the full range of services an individual might need, and reassessment at appropriate intervals. This model, which was also evolving at a small number of sites across the country, came to be known as service or case management.

The assessment and service management techniques piloted in the project have had a broad impact. At the state level, the project was a prototype for the community case management program instituted across the Commonwealth of Pennsylvania. In 1977, the Department of Aging adopted PGC's assessment and service management model for its area agencies on aging across the state. As Pennsylvania's community-based long-term care initiatives expand, state-funded agencies continue to use the multidimensional assessment and service delivery approaches inspired by Lawton's work. In addition, on the local level, PGC's In-Home Service Program served thousands of older people and their families living in the ethnically and economically diverse area surrounding the agency during its 20-year existence.

Growing Complement of Community Programs

In the 1970s and 1980s, Lawton's concepts continued to influence the burgeoning community programs at PGC. Although he did not directly design the services, each reflects his way of thinking and his methods. The programs incorporate Lawton's multidimensional assessment techniques and focus on meeting the needs of the "whole person". Also, they employ case management and interdisciplinary team strategies that grew naturally from multifaceted concepts of quality of life and well-being. The programs include:

- A consultation and diagnostic center, which opened in 1975, as one of the nation's first comprehensive geriatric asssessment services in the United States.
- An adult day health center which opened in 1979 as one of the first such programs in the Philadelphia metropolitan area. Although medical day care is not subsidized in Pennsylvania (public subsidies for social day care are available), the center offers health and rehabilitative services, along with activities, to older adults with physical and cognitive impairments.
- A Medicare certified home health agency that began in 1979 and serves older people living in the community who need skilled nursing and rehabilitative care.
- A geriatric medical ambulatory care practice begun in 1982. It pioneered the concept of coordinated primary and specialty medical care by physicians trained in geriatric medicine and working as a team with a social worker, nurse, psychologist, nutritionist, and other professionals.

- A counseling and support program for caregivers, which began in 1983 as a research and demonstration project, and continues today as an ongoing program. It serves families seeking counseling, information, or referral who are caring for elderly relatives with physical or cognitive impairments.

As another important outcome of a multidimensional way of thinking, PGC saw the importance of organizing its new services into a true continuum of care. That is, it was not enough simply to add individual new programs, but they must be tied together in an accessible and coordinated system that would meet an older person's comprehensive needs. As we designed each new program, we attempted to integrate it with others to the extent possible, within the constraints of a fragmented public and private financing system for health care and social services.

As just one example, a family might enter PGC's service system through the Counseling for Caregivers Program, which would provide information, training, and support to family members caring for an aging relative. Eventually, the older person might be linked to the adult day health care center, where he or she could participate in therapeutic activities and, as part of the day, receive geriatric medical services at the clinic, or use bathing and beauty shop services in the nursing home, on the same campus. Thus, through a single point of entry, the client family could gain access to coordinated caregiver support services, respite care, a therapeutic day program, and personal care and health services, all with the seamless ease of "one-stop shopping".

Lawton's work on quality of life and assessment have had an incalculable influence on PGC. At the most fundamental level, the agency's mission embraces a biopsychosocial philosophy. Across the continuum of care, virtually every PGC program, including nursing home and retirement counseling facilities, as well as community services incorporates a multidimensional perspective on aging and assessment, as well as the holistic intervention strategies that grew out of these concepts. Over the years, Lawton's theories have enabled the organization to understand the needs of the aging comprehensively, and provided the conceptual framework for professionals to design services and facilities consonant with those needs.

COLLABORATION BETWEEN RESEARCHERS AND PROFESSIONALS

Lawton's research theories and findings have shaped the content of community services at PGC, but they have had an equally important impact on the way we do our work. As a result of Lawton's influence, we have learned to integrate research methods into clinical practice and planning, and collaborate closely with researchers in our daily work to enhance our understanding of the needs of each new cohort of the aging and their families, evaluate our interventions, and continuously improve our services.

Over the years, through exposure to research, professionals have learned how scientific methods can help them achieve their goals—whether in individual clinical practice, for aggregate planning, performance improvement, or funding purposes. Although Lawton's influences are many, we will highlight just a few of the most important research methods that we have incorporated into clinical practice and facility planning. In the 1960s, when Lawton arrived, the PGC environment was ripe for this approach. The agency has a long-standing history of innovation, and a pioneering spirit that has led to the continuous development of new programs.

Research Methods Are Useful in Clinical Practice

Starting with our work on the In-Home Services Program in the early 1970s, and continuing to the present day, we have incorporated research methods into clinical practice. These approaches include the use of structured interviews with our clients, as well as a reliance on data collection and analysis for service planning, program evaluation and continuous quality improvement.

For clinicians involved in direct service delivery, one of the most important techniques involves the use of structured interviews. Through their experience using tools such as the MAI, clinical staff learned the value of structured interviews and quantitative scales to understand their clients' situations, perceptions, and needs. In the early 1970s, when we first began using these techniques, clinicians typically were schooled in open-ended interviewing approaches. Naturally, some were skeptical about quantitative, research-based methods, which they saw as cold and esoteric. Yet, clinicians soon found that standardized tools could help them collect the critical information about their clients systematically and efficiently, without having to worry about overlooking important questions. The tools were user-friendly for clinicians and clients, and actually simplified the data collection task instead of complicating it. Also, clinicians saw that using carefully worded questions with proven reliability and validity could make it easier to identify, compare, and prioritize client needs, and measure change after an intervention.

At the same time, clinicians found that structured interviews could have therapeutic value for clients, and when administered properly, were not the impersonal experiences that some had feared. Clients, especially those in crisis, often perceive their situations as confusing and overwhelming. Structured interviews can give them the opportunity to examine their circumstances more objectively, to differentiate their problems, and to highlight their strengths and resources. Questions can prompt solutions, and help clients reframe feelings and situations so that they seem more manageable.

From a program management standpoint, systematic data collection and analysis ·became a routine part of our community programs from the start. The ability to quantify information is critical for service planning and resource allocation decisions as well as for program evaluation. Through our experience with In-Home Services, and the other community programs that followed, we found that we could use the same documentation tools to collect information for clinical, administrative, and research evaluation purposes. Armed with aggregate data, we could describe the size and characteristics of our client population, analyze how resources were being used, identify unmet needs, evaluate the impact of our interventions, and target our services more effectively. Also, with high quality data, we could demonstrate the value of our programs more convincingly to funders, such as the federal government, private foundations, and individual philanthropists.

One of the most important research tools that we borrowed for our clinical programs were consumer satisfaction surveys. Now a standard practice in most health care and social service programs, consumer satisfaction studies were relatively uncommon in the early years of aging services. We learned about their significance during a project called "A Controlled Study of Respite Service for Caregivers of Alzheimer's Patients," a 3-year research and demonstration initiative that began in 1983, and eventually became the ongoing Counseling for Caregivers Program. The study examined the effects of offering respite services to family members caring for dementia patients. For a variety of reasons, the project could document only limited improvement in outcomes—for example, the rate of institutionalization showed a modest decline, but caregivers' mental health was unchanged. Nevertheless, caregivers consistently told us that they valued respite services and found them helpful—important information for clinicians, planners, and policy makers that could only be captured through client satisfaction data. Ever since, client satisfaction surveys, which are a very "do-able" form of research in clinical settings, have become a routine feature of our programs.

PGC is committed to continuously evaluating and improving its programs based on objective scientific information. One recent example relates to PGC's congregate housing and the dilemmas created by aging in place. The York House apartments were built in the 1960s for seniors who were independent but seeking retirement housing with social activities, group dining, and housekeeping services. By the 1990s, the resident population had grown older, and the level of frailty had increased. This is a common issue in senior housing, where sponsors are faced with decisions about how they will respond to residents' changing needs. Staff recognized the need to enhance the York House service package, but wanted to understand residents' problems more precisely before formulating possible solutions.

Lawton provided valuable assistance. He helped the York House team design a study that would measure residents' needs accurately and efficiently. Lawton created a brief assessment instrument that our home health agency staff could administer to a representative sample of residents. When the data were analyzed, the study found that almost all residents had at least one chronic illness, 60% had some degree of mental impairment, a substantial number needed assistance with personal care, and an unexpected proportion were without viable families or social supports. As a result, many residents were at risk of institutionalization or leading a marginal existence. Based on the findings, we recommended that York House should add a social worker to the staff who could help residents and families problem-solve and obtain the support they need. Also, we suggested establishing an interdisciplinary team with weekly meetings to coordinate and monitor care, as well as instituting a special training program for housekeeping and dining room staff in order to enhance their effectiveness with frail elders. These changes would require investment of new resources.

York House leadership presented the findings and recommendations to the board of directors. Impressed with the quality of the data and the analysis, the board approved the request to allocate additional funds to York House for new services. Seven years later, it is clear that the study findings accurately represented the problems of York House residents and led to design of an effective set of interventions. The study illustrates how research methods can be used to solve a facility's operational problems. A simple design, requiring little additional outlay of resources, can have a powerful impact on service delivery and resident quality of life. Yet, this is only one example of the close collaboration between researchers and professionals.

PROMOTING EXCHANGE BETWEEN
RESEARCHERS AND PROFESSIONALS

There is no doubt that Lawton's work has deeply influenced clinicians, practitioners, and planners as well as other researchers, and they have influenced him. What is it about his work that creates this synergy? There are many answers.

Perhaps the most important elements are the humanistic focus and methods of his work. For most of his career, Lawton has concentrated on enhancing well-being, a mission that resonates with clinicians, administrators, and researchers. Furthermore, his work incorporates the subjective as well as the objective. As reflected in the Lawton Morale Scale, MAI and many research studies, he values how older people feel about their lives, including their environments, their health, and many other dimensions. Like a good clinician, Lawton listens to human experience, combining quantitative and qualitative methods in his work.

In fact, Lawton makes it clear that he places great importance on the experience of professionals as well as research subjects. He seeks out clinicians and administrators to hear about their clients' situations. Often, he formulates clinical observations into questions that can be researched systematically. It is not uncommon for clinicians to see their words and observations reflected in an interview protocol, or to trace the shape of their input after Lawton has related the ideas to a research theory or method. Lawton joins with professionals so that they feel that they are on a common mission, each with unique contributions to the process.

Another important factor is Lawton's common-sense and flexible approach to research methods. As demonstrated by the study of aging in place at York House, he understands the constraints inherent in service environments, and is willing to help professionals determine how they can apply research methods to answer key questions—within the limits of the available staff and funding. He is able to help service providers modify scientific methods and standards so that they meet the needs of the "real world." Service programs do not operate in controlled environments, nor do they have the resources to measure and evaluate their results according to the highest scientific standards. Instead, they must find efficient and practical methods to study clients' problems and evaluate the effects of new interventions.

On another level, Lawton's work resonates with clinicians because he explores solutions to improving quality of life that are based on common sense, easy to provide and, often, low-tech. He validates the "small" things an older person can to do make a difference in quality of life. One of the best illustrations comes from the 1985 study, "A Housing Quality Component for In-Home Services." This project examined the competency level of older people living in ordinary housing, and the adaptations they could make to create a safer, more personal, functional, accessible and legible home environment. According to the study, one of the most significant ways to improve the life of a chronically impaired older person is to bring the central functions of daily life into the person's sphere of control. As another illustration, Lawton currently is involved in projects that teach certified nursing assistants to read the emotions of persons with advanced dementia. Nursing assistants, who are the primary caregivers in nursing homes, learn to gauge voice tone and touch to create more effective and satisfying one-to-one interactions with frail residents.

As a related factor, Lawton listens to and validates providers' needs. He is willing to assist in developing grant proposals, creating clinical tools, and translate research findings into language and content that is useful to professionals.

As a result of his approach, virtually all PGC programs have benefited from Lawton's involvement. Lawton has been effective in building close collaboration between PGC researchers, administrators, and clinicians. As they worked together, natural barriers broke down, and both sides found the partnership enriching and productive.

Facility Design

In addition to the influence on community services, Lawton's theories and methods have had a dramatic impact on the design of long-term care facilities at PGC and across the nation for more than a quarter century. In the 1960s and 1970s, Lawton's concept of the "good life" guided the pioneering design of the Weiss Institute—the first nursing facility in the country built specifically for persons with Alzheimer's Disease. In the 21st century, Lawton's ideas will continue to shape nursing home design at PGC; his theories provide the conceptual framework for the agency's new facility, which is scheduled to open by 2002. Equally important, through his work on the Weiss Institute and the new site, Lawton has taught us a process for facility design that integrates the latest research findings and techniques to generate further innovations that benefit residents, their families, and staff.

The Weiss Institute

The 10-year planning process for the Weiss Institute began in the mid-1960s, a time when little was known about the needs of the aged with dementia. Residents with "senility" were seen as incurable, and unable to benefit from therapeutic intervention. Along with other nursing home residents, they were housed in facilities that typically resembled hospital wards and offered little stimulation. The units were large and had a uniform decor and design, usually with a large nursing station at the entrance, a simple day room, and multiple-occupant resident rooms aligned repetitively along double-loaded corridors. The care was primarily custodial, with little activity or variety.

Despite the lack of formal research on dementia at the time, Lawton and others on the PGC planning team suspected that conventional nursing units were not meeting the needs of cognitively impaired residents, and might actually increase the level of disorientation, confusion, and dependence. To remedy this problem, the group adopted the goal of designing a building that would actively promote the health and well-being of residents with dementia. They embarked on a research and planning effort that ultimately would break the mold in nursing home design, and create a dramatically new physical and behavioral environment more in tune with the needs of Alzheimer's patients and their families.

The planning process for the new building was characterized by a spirit of openness, creativity, and a willingness to experiment and learn through trial and error. Documents from the early phases discuss the need to "inquire, investigate and try" new concepts as well as to "abandon old programs" in the face of new knowledge. The planning team sought input from a wide variety of sources. Conferences were held where experts from the new fields of gerontology, geriatrics and environmental psychology, as well as more established disciplines, summarized the existing literature and contributed cutting-edge ideas. In addition, PGC board members and staff from all levels—from certified nursing assistants to administrators—gave their recommendations for the design of the new facility and its services. Also, consumers—including current and prospective nursing home residents and their relatives—were asked to share their needs and preferences during focus groups.

As a result of this input and his own emerging theories, Lawton proposed that PGC should create a "prosthetic environment"; that is, a setting that would compensate for the physical, cognitive, psychological, and social deficits experienced by dementia patients. The concept contrasted sharply with the prevailing view of dementia as an irremediable and hopeless condition. In addition to defining the facility's major goal, the planning team identified six more specific objectives derived from Lawton's theory of the "good life." The objectives were to: enhance sensory functioning; increase autonomy in performing activities of daily living; enhance cognitive functions, especially memory orientation; increase meaningful use of time; increase social interaction; and enhance the sense of self. From the outset, research was integrated into the program in order to inform and evaluate the facility's efforts to achieve its goals.

The building that resulted is a 120-bed skilled nursing facility for the aged with moderate to severe Alzheimer's disease and other dementias. It contains many innovations that have since been replicated by nursing home and assisted living sponsors nationwide. Here we highlight just a few of the critical elements.

In contrast to the traditional nursing home design, the Weiss Institute has an open layout with a large central activity area surrounded by private and semi-private rooms (for

40 residents) on three sides. This arrangement enhances orientation by allowing residents to see most of the unit, as well as staff, from almost any point. Also, the layout fosters social interaction among residents, and makes it easy for them to join in with or observe others involved in formal or informal activities. The nursing station is accessible to residents and allows them to be monitored readily by staff. Finally, the decor helps to orient residents, whose bedrooms, door frames, and other important areas are color-coded to promote recognition and wayfinding.

Post-occupancy research at the Weiss Institute confirms the benefits of the design for a cognitively impaired population. The studies involved direct observation of the residents in their new and old quarters, staff ratings of resident behavior, a mental status test, and a survey of family members and staff. The data show that residents exhibited less pathological behavior, more participation in enriching activity, and a greater rated degree of interest in their new surroundings. Also, they showed a greater angle of gaze and less fixed staring—a sign that the environment was stimulating. Furthermore, both family and staff rated the building favorably. One of the most striking findings from the research was that the rate of visiting doubled in the Weiss Institute as compared to the previous facility.

PGC's New Facility

Twenty-five years after the Weiss Institute opened, PGC once again is planning a new nursing home intended to "push the envelope" in therapeutic design for older people with dementia. The new nursing home will be located on a suburban site, which will replace PGC's current urban campus shortly after the turn of the century. In addition to the nursing home highlighted here, the site will contain an assisted living residence, a campus "Main Street," and a host of medical and social service programs for older people and their families living in the general community.

The context for planning new facilities has changed dramatically in the past quarter century. In the years since the Weiss Institute was built, the field of long-term care has become increasingly sophisticated, with a growing scientific literature on dementia care and dementia-friendly design. The challenge for sponsors of new facilities is to sift through the available information, incorporate the best of existing knowledge, and identify the areas where still further innovation is needed. In addition, the profile of the client population is shifting. With advances in medicine and technology, new home and community-based care alternatives, and the trend toward managed care financing, the resident population in nursing homes is becoming frailer, sicker and more physically and cognitively disabled than ever before.

Despite these changes, Lawton's theories and approaches still provide the important guideposts for facility design. Once again, we are drawing upon Lawton's concept of the "good life", and the principles that emanate from it, as the framework for our new design. Our overall aim for the new facility is the same as for the Weiss Institute: To create a prosthetic environment that will promote a positive quality of life for the most severely impaired aged. The specific objectives for our new facility draw heavily on Lawton's original goals. The guiding principles for the philosophy of care, physical design and organizational structure of the new nursing home are:

Resident goals:
- Maximize dignity, privacy and choice
- Preserve personal continuity and links to family, friends, and community
- Promote health and well-being
- Support functional independence
- Infuse Jewish values, meanings, and observance
- Create a positive social milieu
- Ensure safety and security
- Integrate nature and the outdoors

Organizational goals:
- Maximize staff quality and efficiency
- Maintain a commitment to research and inquiry
- Use technology creatively
- Adapt to changing needs

To design a facility that meets these objectives, we are replicating many aspects of the planning process used so successfully for the Weiss Institute effort. Once again, we have assembled an interdisciplinary design team, with PGC board members, administrators, clinicians, researchers, and consulting architects—committed to a spirit of innovation. To catalyze the creative process, we are seeking diverse input—through a continuous review of the scientific literature and consultations with leading experts in the fields of gerontology, architecture, sociology, nursing, social work, and occupational therapy, as well as through site visits and interviews with sponsors of cutting-edge long-term care facilities across the country. Through focus groups and other forums, we speak to the "users" of the new facility—including family members of current and potential nursing home residents as well as a cross-section of PGC staff. The PGC board of directors and other community leaders are involved through committees concerned with virtually every aspect of campus planning.

Although our new nursing home is still in the conceptual design phase, the team has made preliminary decisions about the nature and scale of the facility. The design of the 324-bed nursing home will incorporate many of the prosthetic features employed in the Weiss Institute, such as color-coded decor to promote wayfinding, decentralized units that are smaller than the norm to bring services and activities within easy reach of highly impaired residents, and traffic patterns and communal spaces designed to promote stimulation and social interaction.

Also, our facility will build upon work begun in the Weiss Institute to make nursing home environments more truly homelike. In addition to nursing stations, activity spaces, and resident bedrooms, the design for nursing units in the Weiss Institute called for living areas, dining areas, and kitchenettes—spaces that were important departures from the traditional institution of the day. As we plan our new facility, we intend to push this concept further, and reinterpret it in line with today's consumer expectations, the available knowledge, new technology, and more flexible regulations. The fact that we can make more significant movement on this issue now is a mark of true progress.

The heart of the new design is the resident household, where small groups of older people will live in units that resemble typical suburban homes, with conventional living rooms, dining rooms, dens, and porches or patios. Most daily activities, including recreation and dining, will be decentralized and occur in the household, where severely impaired residents can participate fully. The emphasis is on creating as normal and noninstitutional an environment as possible, with familiar activities, freedom of choice, one-to-one attention, family involvement, and a focus on strengths, enjoyment, and abilities, not disability. To minimize noise and distraction, and highlight the homelike atmosphere, most service traffic will be kept discreetly out of the household mainstream.

Reflecting Lawton's influence, and the Weiss Institute precedent, we are recording our design decisions in a functional program. This document is a useful tool for several reasons. First, it requires us to be clear and specific about our goals, and the way they will be operationalized through architecture, interior decor, and virtually every aspect of the organization of resident life and services. Also, the document provides an efficient mechanism to keep the design team in synch through a complex planning process involving players at many sites. In addition, it provides a detailed guide for our architects, interior designers, and others involved in creating the facility. It leads directly into a research process to evaluate the success of our new facility. Finally, it provides a record of our thinking and design choices so they can be re-examined in the future.

Planning documents from the Weiss Institute have been tremendously useful to us in our new design initiative. Throughout the current design process, we find ourselves reviewing the Weiss Institute records, and deliberating over many of the same dilemmas that were the source of discussion in the 1970s. As we compare our current functional program with the earlier effort, we see that we are examining the same questions about centralization and decentralization of resident services, the mix of private and semiprivate rooms, the pros and cons involved in family style or tray service for meals, and the extent to which staff should be able to observe residents during the day, evening, and night. It may be that every generation faces similar design questions, but the solutions change in light of new knowledge, new technology, and new consumer perceptions. Innovations become possible by re-examining these fundamental issues.

Once our new facility is open and fully occupied, we plan to conduct a research evaluation just as we did with the Weiss Institute. The purpose is to determine whether our strategies and innovations prove effective in improving resident, family, staff, and organizational outcomes. Although the research has not been designed yet, we anticipate that it will incorporate direct observation of residents, using techniques developed by Lawton for his studies of Alzheimer's special care units and affect among dementia patients. Also, family and staff satisfaction surveys will be key components. By conducting a systematic study—that reveals our successes and our failures—we hope to advance our own ability to plan still better facilities in the future, as well as add more broadly to the growing knowledge base in the field of dementia care.

CONCLUSIONS

Many of the practices discussed in this chapter have become standard procedure for today's providers of services to the elderly, but they were not standard and often did not exist in the time frame we are discussing. Multidimensional assessment is standard, as is multidimensional service provision. Assessment instrumentation is systematic, incorporating scales and other valid and reliable measures. Data are collected in standardized ways. Evaluation is an integral part of most programs. Subjective data, especially in the form of client satisfaction surveys, are highly regarded and used extensively as an important measure of program impact. The concept of dementia-friendly design has become widespread. In a substantial way, Lawton propelled PGC clinicians and service providers in many of these changes, resulting in the creation of cutting-edge PGC programs, which in turn influenced the service world. In another way, his work was a powerful voice in the tumult of change occurring on a national scale, in some situations pioneering, and in others, reinforcing the direction to understand and achieve an older person's "good life."

As professionals, when all is said and done, we often find that it is not providing the person with a meal or a new medication that makes the difference. We are often still left struggling to find that magic subjective ingredient that will make people feel better about themselves and their situations. The clinical process and Lawton's work coalesce. Both are seeking the magic ingredient and do so by searching the environment, behavioral competencies, social participation, and other factors. Inherent in this inquiry and subjective measures is a basic respect for the individual and for her experience.

16

Outcomes Research in Mental Disorders of Late Life: Alzheimer's Disease As Example

Barry D. Lebowitz

W hy don't our treatments ever work as well in actual practice as they do in clinical trials? And why don't treatment effects enhance overall functioning?

These are questions that have bedeviled individual patients and their clinicians for many years. More recently, researchers and policy makers have had to address these concerns as well. The answers to the questions is actually reasonably clear. Moreover, the solution that allows us to address these questions is actually available to us within the work of M. Powell Lawton.

Most treatment studies are done with a very specific purpose in mind: to gain approval or acceptance of a particular therapeutic modality. In a shorthand way, and borrowing from the area of pharmacotherapeutics, this type of consideration is appropriately referred to as a "regulatory" one. For studies done in accordance with this regulatory model, the inclusions and exclusions are typically so limiting, the conditions of treatment delivery are so optimized, and the outcomes so narrowly defined that generalization or application is virtually impossible.

Research following the regulatory model is specifically geared to the legal requirements of drug approval and registration. Although there is no equivalent to the Food and Drug Administration (FDA) for psychotherapy, the methodology of the regulatory model has been adopted in that field as well. In that circumstance, it is essential that pure disease entities are isolated and that dimensions of outcome are limited to the direct symptomatic measures of that disease. So as to prevent administrative or delivery problems from masking the effect of the treatment, clinicians are typically specially selected and trained. Intrusions such as the administrative requirements of a health care plan or third-party payer are minimized and the treatment is provided in optimal form, often in an academic health center. Specific measures are taken to assure compliance of the clinician with the protocol and adherence of the patient with the procedures and treatments. The conclusion of such a study becomes the gold standard of what is possible under closely controlled or ideal situations.

Research supported for regulatory purposes, particularly that supported by the drug companies themselves, will, of necessity, conform to the regulatory model. This is the case regardless of whether the site of the study is an academic health center or a community treatment facility and regardless of whether the coordination of the study is done directly by the sponsor or by an intermediary (contract research organization, or CRO). It is worth noting that this CRO type of arrangement has not (yet) been adopted by those doing clinical psychotherapeutic or behavioral research. This model has also been carried over into research that has no industrial sponsorship, even to research on mental disorders that has been directed to government agencies or foundations.

There is a need in the field to adopt a public health model of treatment studies. The opportunity is certainly there. In a public health model, exclusion criteria are minimal (and based only on concerns for safety). Age, gender, and comorbidity are no longer the basis for exclusion, but rather present important dimensions to assure sample representativeness and clinical generalizability. Questions of modifications of treatment (e.g., dosing strategy and duration) for these subgroups in the population are easily addressed within a more flexible approach to providing the actual treatment. Outcomes are broadly construed, to include performance, relationships (family, interpersonal, etc.), function, disability, quality of life, morbidity, mortality, institutionalization, and health care resource use. Settings are widely selected from a full range of academic and nonacademic institutions, specialty and primary care, and public and private facilities. Sample sizes are sufficiently large as to assure adequate power. Residual symptomatology and excess disability are addressed through a formalized approach to short- and long-term rehabilitation within the context of the treatment itself.

For the most part, a public health model of treatment research builds upon the many strengths of the scientific contributions of M. Powell Lawton and his collaborators. Investigators in the mental disorders of late life have, typically, expanded the scope of their treatment studies beyond the traditional regulatory approach. In particular, studies addressing questions of function and disability in older persons with complex patterns of comorbidity and impairments have long been part of the common practice in our field. Many of us adopt the Lawton approach to the conceptualization and measurement of function as part of the standard package of instrumentation in clinical and epidemiological studies in general and in treatment studies in particular. Nursing homes, primary care settings, and other facilities outside the academic health center have traditionally been used as sources for geriatric patients; and nowhere has the potential for developing the nursing home as a research center been better demonstrated than at the Philadelphia Geriatric Center. Quality of life is seen as almost an essential part of any intervention study; here, again, Lawton and his colleagues have provided us with a standard.

Consequently, the public health model of intervention studies is readily compatible with treatment research with older persons. Other areas of treatment research will have more adjustments to make in order to accommodate a public health approach; I expect that investigators in those other areas will be looking to our field, and to the work of M. Powell Lawton for leadership and for guidance in selecting the most appropriate and efficient approaches to design and measurement.

In all areas of health care, interventions research has become increasingly focused on the application of treatment in everyday practice. This represents a broadening of attention to concerns of effectiveness as distinct from the strict concern with efficacy that had characterized an earlier generation of studies.

Formally speaking, efficacy studies define optimal treatment outcomes for narrowly selected patients treated under rigidly controlled and ideal conditions. With a primary focus on symptomatology, the assessment of efficacy is based upon the degree to which the level of symptomatology is reduced or eliminated (Lohr, 1988; Scott, 1993). In an efficacy trial, treatment is provided by specially selected and trained clinicians who provide optimal treatment and who expend substantial resources to assure compliance and to minimize dropout. The classic efficacy trial is used to define the gold standard of the best outcome under ideal circumstances. Because of the tight standard of control required in efficacy studies, the policy and practice relevance of these trials will always be limited (Wells, Sturm, Sherbourne, & Meredith, 1996).

Effectiveness studies, on the other hand, bring us into the world of actual practice with time-pressured clinicians taking care of large numbers of patients with uncertain clinical presentations, complex comorbidities, and varying degrees of interference with ideal levels of compliance. The exclusive focus on symptomatology is expanded to include outcomes related to issues of function, disability, morbidity, mortality, resource use, and quality of life. The classic effectiveness trial is used to assess the expected outcome under usual circumstances of practice (DeFriese, 1990).

In contrast to the elegantly crafted efficacy trial, an effectiveness trial is going to be bigger in size, simpler in design, broader in terms of inclusions and narrower in terms of exclusions, and more representative with respect to settings of care. These settings will not be limited to academic health centers or tertiary care institutions, but will include primary care, community settings, and long-term care institutions. Unlike efficacy trials, in which specially trained clinicians carry out state-of-the-art assessment and treatment, effectiveness trials are carried out in settings of usual practice where there is a broad range of clinician expertise and experience with the disorder under study. Outcome measures will typically extend beyond symptomatology to include function, disability, morbidity, mortality, health care and other resource use, family burden, institutionalization, and quality of life. Effectiveness studies are not simply administrative or financial analysis of administrative data collected in large and naturalistic databases, but are broadly inclusive of clinical, family, and organizational factors (Dickey & Wagenaar, 1996).

To illustrate the benefit of the transition from a regulatory to a public health approach, or from efficacy to effectiveness, I will use the case of treatment studies in the area of Alzheimer's disease (AD), an area to which Lawton and his colleagues have made significant and substantial contribution.

THE NATURE OF ALZHEIMER'S DISEASE

Alzheimer's 1907 report (1987) presented a complex clinical report of a patient with significant disturbances in cognition, behavior, and affect. The multidimensional nature of this disorder has been acknowledged by the Agency for Health Care Policy and Research (Costa, Williams, Somerfield et al., 1996); the American Academy of Neurology (1994); the American Psychiatric Association (1997); and in the Consensus Statement of three national organizations (Small et al., 1997).

The cognitive aspects of AD are well understood. Progressive loss of memory and executive function, coupled with progressive increases in aphasia and apraxia, have been considered the hallmarks of the disease. The correlation of these with the neuropathological signs of AD has been established as well. More recently, a substantial body of clinical neuroscience research has documented the underlying pathophysiology of the noncognitive symptoms of AD such as depression, psychosis, and circadian disruption (Finkel, 1996). Consequently, when treatment strategies for AD are considered, it is no longer sufficient to limit the focus to cognitive enhancement alone. The non-cognitive behavioral and affective symptoms of AD must be incorporated into any approach addressing the disease.

ASSESSMENT OF TREATMENT EFFICACY

There are four different approaches to the assessment of efficacy for an proposed intervention for AD (Leber, 1996). In theory, we can conceptualize approaches that:

- Prevent the occurrence of AD;
- Prolong the time to AD onset;
- Slow or reverse the progression of AD; and
- Manage the symptoms of AD.

Considerable effort is being expended at the basic science level to identify agents that could prevent or delay the onset of AD or could reverse its progression. This work is very speculative and is, by and large, still in the prediscovery stage of basic science. At this point, the best body of clinical trials information is derived from approaches to symptomatic management by means of cognitive enhancers (Anand & Enz, 1996; Anand & Gharabawi, 1996; Kalaria & Giacobini, 1997; Knapp, Knopman, & Solomon, et al., 1994; Rogers et al., 1996); conventional and newer antipsychotics (Goldberg & Goldberg, 1997; Salzman, Vaccaro, Lieff, et al., 1995; Schneider, Pollock, & Lyness, 1990), antidepressants (Pollock, Mulsant, Sweet et al., 1997), and other agents such as vitamin E, selegiline (Sano et al., 1997), non-steroidal anti-inflammatories, estrogen, and natural products and nutriceuticals such as ginkgo biloba. It is possible that some of these may slow progression of AD as well. A full review of treatments is beyond the scope of this paper but is available elsewhere (American Psychiatric Association, 1997; Small et al., 1997). Nonetheless, the general conclusion one can draw is that approved cognitive enhancers in the U.S. (tacrine and donepezil) have modest efficacy with respect to cognition in some patients with AD of mild or moderate severity. Antipsychotics generally produce modest improvement in behavioral symptoms such as psychosis and agitation. Data on antidepressants are suggestive, but remain limited.

Limits on Generalizability

The data on treatment efficacy are derived from clinical trials which conform to the highest standards of methodological rigor. They are randomized, placebo-controlled, double-blind trials with firm and exact inclusion and exclusion criteria. The cognitive enhancer trials, for example, typically exclude any patient with psychiatric or neurologic symptoms or substance abuse and require the patient to be generally physically healthy and to be living with a caregiver. Applying these criteria to a large, statewide database resulted in an estimated eligibility for clinical trials of less than 10% of AD patients (Schneider, Olin, Lyness, & Chui, 1997). The resulting sample of trial-eligible patients was not clinically representative of the range of AD patients in terms of symptomatology or severity. In addition, the resulting sample was not demographically representative of the AD patient population, with a preponderance of younger, high-income, highly educated, White men.

It is, therefore, no great surprise that treatment trials are difficult to do, samples are difficult to attain, and that results are not generally transferable to the typical kinds of patients who seek treatment from their doctors.

The Measurement of Outcomes:
A Regulatory Approach

In U.S. efficacy trials done for regulatory purposes of drug approval and registration in AD, the design includes a measure of cognitive function. In the U.S., that has typically been the cognitive subscale of the Alzheimer's Disease Assessment Scale, or ADAS-COG (Mohs, Rosen, & Davis, 1983) and a measure of global functioning (a Clinical Global Impression of Change, or CGIC (Schneider & Olin, 1996). A growing number of trials have been focused on behavioral aspects of AD. A variety of scales have been used to assess non-cognitive or behavioral disturbance in AD trials (Finkel, 1996). There is no consensus standard in this aspect of treatment. Some investigators advocate a unitary behavioral perspective (e.g., specific studies for wandering, screaming, etc.). Others recommend a more syndromal view (e.g., psychosis, depression, delirium, circadian disruption) as a target for intervention. Still others recommend a global, all-inclusive view (e.g., behavioral disturbance).

The Instrument Development Project of the Alzheimer's Disease Cooperative Study in the U.S. has developed and tested a variety of new instruments that could be used in combination with established approaches to the assessment of efficacy. A useful report on this work was published as a special supplement to the journal *Alzheimer's Disease and Associated Disorders* (Ferris & Mackell, 1997).

The regulatory approach to treatment of AD is best captured in a recent editorial in the *New England Journal of Medicine* (Drachman & Leber, 1997). In commenting on a report of a selegiline/vitamin E trial (Sano et al., 1997) the authors raise the important issue of whether endpoints such as function, mortality, and institutionalization properly represent fundamental aspects of the disease process of AD. In the regulatory sense, the answer is clear: they do not. AD is a disease of cognition deterioration and behavioral disturbance. A treatment for AD must address this aspect of symptomatology in order to be considered, truly and in law, a treatment for AD.

On the other hand, from the public health perspective, the focus on function, disability, and institutionalization and other dimensions is entirely appropriate and necessary as part of a broader view of treatment effectiveness. In the remainder of this paper, several aspects of outcomes assessment are addressed.

THE EXPANSION OF OUTCOMES

Institutionalization and Nursing Home Placement

In 1993 there were 1.8 million patients in nursing homes in the United States. The societal and familial impact of nursing home care is enormous. The costs of care exceeded $60 billion; nearly half came from the direct personal expenditures of patients and their families, with the remainder coming from insurance or medical assistance (Medicaid). The financial burden of the nursing home is only part of the picture, however. Nursing home placement typically comes at the end of a long and difficult period of caregiving by the family. The burden of this caregiving in terms of stress, depression, and quality of life have been definitively documented (Light, Niederehe, & Lebowitz, 1994). When the burden of caring for an AD patient exceeds the capacity of the family, placement in a nursing home or other long-term care facility is usually required. The signal events precipitating nursing home placement are behavioral disturbance and incontinence—it is, therefore, no great surprise that over half the patients in nursing homes have AD.

It is only the rare (and very wealthy) family that can afford to provide the care necessary for an AD patient; institutional care will be required for virtually all AD patients who survive to the end stage of the disease. It would be in everyone's interest to forestall institutionalization until it was absolutely necessary and to prevent premature use of this costly resource. From the public health perspective, delay in institutional placement of even a few months could have significant positive impact.

Use of nursing home placement as an outcome in AD intervention trials is increasing. Mittelman et al. (1996) demonstrated clear benefit in terms of significant delay in institutional placement for AD patients whose family caregivers were randomized to a counseling type of intervention. The delay in nursing home placement, a difference of over 300 days between treatment and control conditions, is of great importance and deserves serious attention.

Sano and colleagues (1997) suggest that selegeline or vitamin E treatment of the patient could have impact on risk of institutional placement, but unavoidable methodological problems with the study make conclusion somewhat difficult (the randomization failed to create comparable groups in terms of cognitive impairment).

In an interesting series of reports, long-term, high-dose tacrine use was shown to have significant impact on risk of institutional placement (Knopman et al., 1996; Smith Talwalker, Gracon, & Sriramo, 1996). These reports were based on open data on AD patients maintained on the drug after the conclusion of the regulatory-oriented clinical trial. Because of the open, naturalistic aspect of the report, it is impossible to determine whether this is a true drug effect. Alternatively, reduction of risk of nursing home admission could have been associated with better overall health of those who were able to tolerate the continued high dose of tacrine (and to overcome the well documented gastrointestinal side effects). Or these individuals could have had the stronger support systems of family and friends that allowed them to remain on the drug despite any adverse experiences. Nonetheless, the association of reduced nursing home placement with long-term high-dose tacrine use is of considerable interest as a hypothesis for prospective interventions, and demonstrates a useful direction for AD treatment studies.

Not all interventions have been successful in reducing nursing home admissions, however. Lawton (1994a) reports on several well-designed broad scale intervention that failed to result in any significant impact on placement. These included a respite care intervention specifically for AD patients and a large case management intervention (the National Channeling Demonstration) for individuals at risk for nursing home placement-a sample that, presumably, included a large number of AD patients.

Nursing home placement is, unquestionably, a complex outcome. It is comes about through the complex interaction of several characteristics: disability and symptomatology, stress and burden tolerance of the family, and the physical and social environment. This complexity should not eliminate nursing home placement from consideration in AD treatment studies. A useful model for this comes from the area of Parkinson's disease (Parkinson Study Group, 1989). In this trial of deprenyl in Parkinson's disease, a primary outcome was delay in the initiation of use of L-dopa/carbidopa. The decision to initiate this treatment is also complex, and arises from the consideration of levels of symptomatology, individual and family tolerance, and environmental demands. This study should have important implications for the design of AD trials.

Morbidity, Mortality, Disability, Resource Use

None of these factors have been extensively assessed in AD trials. Mortality and disability were assessed in the selegeline/vitamin E trial (Sano et al., 1997), and general impressions of changes in disability are presumed to be a part of the regulatory-oriented studies that include a global rating of overall functioning. Resource use, particularly in general health care, is an especially interesting potential target for intervention in AD.

In comparison to age-matched patients without AD, those with AD patients who are hospitalized for medical reasons have been shown to require twice as much in the way of resources, including extended length of stay (Torian, Davidson, Fulop, et al., 1992). Pfizer, Inc., the marketer of donepezil in the U.S. report in the prescribing information material (Aricept, 1997) that patients with dementias account for close to 2.5 times the treatment costs of non-dementia patients in a large managed care organization.

Quality of Life

Quality of life is a broad and somewhat confusing construct. There is little consistency in conceptualization, dimensionality, or operationalization. General measures have been proposed and have been used in a variety of contexts and conditions. Lawton (1991) has convincingly argued, however, for a more complex, multidimensional, and interactive view of the concept. Although quality of life is widely used in health research (Shumaker, 1993) in general, and in treatment research in particular (Rupp & Kreling, 1997), use of the concept in AD research is very preliminary (Lawton, 1994b). To this point, quality-of-life measures have not been used in AD trials. Albert and colleagues (1996) have suggested an approach to proxy assessment of quality of life that might be amenable to use with a broad range of AD patients, including those who have lost ability for verbal communication.

Family Burden

The measurement of family burden is another area that is well established, with good scales developed specifically for subjective feelings of burden in caregivers of AD patients (Zarit, Todd, & Zarit, 1986). These measures have not, typically, been used in treatment trials, though a new one, the Caregiver Activities Time Survey, has been proposed for consideration (Clipp & Moore, 1995). This instrument was used in a large multisite trial of velnacrine, a cholinesterase inhibitor that was not pursued for further development in the United States. In this trial, caregivers of AD patients randomized to a high dose of this drug report a reduction in time involvement of over 3 hours per day. This time difference, though not statistically significant, represents a considerable advantage to those families.

CONCLUSIONS

A public health view of Alzheimer's disease leads to a broad perspective on issues of effectiveness and on the outcomes of treatment. Extending beyond the management of symptomatology in highly selected patient groups, a new generation of treatment studies is going to be needed. These studies, guided by the pioneering work of M. Powell

Lawton and his colleagues, will include more representative samples of patients and be set in a broader range of health care settings. Outcome measures will be selected to include areas of major public health concern such as function, disability, morbidity, mortality, institutionalization, family burden, and quality of life. In doing this, the field will move toward more general applicability of experimental treatments and more rapid translation of research from the laboratory to the community.

REFERENCES

Albert, S. M., Del Castillo-Castenada, C., Sano, M., Jacobs, D. M., Marder, K., Bell, K., Bylsma, F., Lafleche, G., Brandt, J., Albert, M., & Stern, Y. (1996). Quality of life in patients with Alzheimer's disease as reported by patient proxies. *Journal of the American Geriatrics Society, 44*, 1342–1347.

Alzheimer, A. (1987). About a particular disease of the cerebral cortex [L. Jarvik & H. Greenson, trans.]. *Alzheimer Disease and Associated Disorders, 1*, 5–8. (First published 1907)

American Academy of Neurology. (1994). Practice parameter: Diagnosis and evaluation of dementia. *Neurology, 44*, 2203–2206.

American Psychiatric Association. (1997). Practice guideline for the treatment of patients with Alzheimer's disease and other dementias of late life. *American Journal of Psychiatry, 154*(Suppl), 1–39.

Anand, R., & Enz, A. (1996). Clinical confirmation of preclinical attributes of ENA 713. *Alzheimer Disease and Associated Disorders, 17*, S349.

Anand, R., & Gharabawi, G. (1996). Efficacy and safety results of the early phase studies with Exelon (ENA 713) in Alzheimer's disease: An overview. *Journal of Drug Development and Clinical Practice, 8*, 1–14.

Aricept (donepezil). (1997). [Package insert]. New York: Pfizer.

Clipp, E. C., & Moore, M. J. (1995). Caregiver time use: An outcome measure in clinical trial research on Alzheimer's disease. *Clinical Pharmacology and Therapeutics, 58*, 228–236.

Costa, P. T., Williams, T. F., Somerfield, M., et al. (1996). Recognition and initial assessment of Alzheimer's disease and related dementias. *Clinical Practice Guideline* No. 19, AHCPR Publication No. 97–0702. Rockville, MD: U.S. Department of Health and Human Services, Public Health Service, Agency for Health Care Policy and Research.

DeFriese, G. H. (1990). Measuring the effectiveness of medical interventions: new expectations of health services research. *Health Services Research, 25*, 691–695.

Dickey, B., & Wagenaar, H. (1996). Evaluating health status. In L. I. Sederer & B. Dickey. (Eds.), *Outcomes assessment in clinical practice* (pp. 55–60). Baltimore: Williams and Wilkins.

Drachman, D. A., & Leber, P. (1997). Editorial: Treatment of Alzheimer's Disease: Searching for a breakthrough, settling for less. *New England Journal of Medicine, 336*, 1245–1247.

Ferris, S. H., & Mackell, J. A. (Eds.) (1997). A multicenter evaluation of new treatment efficacy instruments for Alzheimer's disease clinical trials. *Alzheimer Disease and Associated Disorders, 11*(Suppl2).

Finkel, S. I. (Ed.) (1996). Behavioral and psychological signs and symptoms of dementia: Implications for research and treatment. *International Psychogeriatrics, 8*(Suppl 3).

Goldberg, R. J., & Goldberg, J. (1997). Risperidone for dementia-related disturbed behavior in nursing home residents: A clinical experience. *International Psychogeriatrics, 9*, 65–68.

Kalaria, R. N., & Giacobini, E. (1997). Meeting report: The fifth international conference on Alzheimer's disease and related disorders. *Alzheimer Disease and Associated Disorders, 11*, 113–119.

Knapp, M. J., Knopman, D. S., Solomon, P. R., et al. (1994). A 30-week randomized controlled trial of high-dose tacrine in patients with Alzheimer's disease. *Journal of the American Medical Association, 271*, 985–991.

Knopman, D., Schneider, L. S., Davis, K. et al. (1996). Long-term tacrine (Cognex) treatment effects on nursing home placement and mortality. *Neurology, 47*, 166–177.

Lawton, M. P. (1991). A multidimensional view of quality of life. In J. E. Birren, J. E. Lubben, J. C. Rowe, & D. E. Deutchman, (Eds.), *The concept and measurement of quality of life in the frail elderly* (pp. 1–23). New York: Academic Press.

Lawton, M. P. (1994a). Broad spectrum service program effects on caregivers. In E. Light, G. Niederehe, & B. D. Lebowitz (Eds.) *Stress effects on family caregivers of Alzheimer's patients* (pp. 138–155). New York: Springer Publishing Co.

Lawton, M. P. (1994b). Quality of life in Alzheimer disease. *Alzheimer Disease and Associated Disorders, 8*(Suppl 3), 138–150.

Leber, P. (1996). Observations and suggestions on antidementia drug development. *Alzheimer Disease and Associated Disorders, 10*(Suppl 1), 31–35.

Light, E., Niederehe, G., & Lebowitz, B. D. (Eds.) (1994). *Stress effects on family caregivers of Alzheimer's patients*. New York: Springer Publishing Co.

Lohr, K. (1988). Outcome measurement: Concepts and questions. *Inquiry, 25*, 37–50.

Mittelman, M. S., Ferris, S. H., Shulman, E., et al. (1996). A family intervention to delay nursing home placement of patients with Alzheimer's disease: A randomized controlled trial. *Journal of the American Medical Association, 276*, 1725–1731.

Mohs, R. C., Rosen, W. G., & Davis, K. L. (1983). The Alzheimer's Disease Assessment Scale: An instrument for assessing treatment efficacy. *Psychopharmacology Bulletin, 19*, 448–450.

Parkinson Study Group. (1989) Effect of deprenyl on the progression of disability I: early Parkinson's disease. *New England Journal of Medicine, 321*, 1364–1371.

Pollock, B. G., Mulsant, B. H., Sweet, R., Burgio, L., Kirstner, M., Shuster, K., & Rosen, J. (1997). An open pilot study of citalopram for behavioral disturbance of dementia: Plasma levels and real time observations. *American Journal of Geriatric*

Psychiatry, 5, 70–78.

Rogers, S. L., Friedhoff, L. T., and the Donepezil Study Group. (1996). The efficacy and safety of donepezil in patients with Alzheimer's disease: Results of a US multicentre, randomized, double-blind, placebo controlled trial. *Dementia, 7*, 293–303.

Rupp, M .T., & Kreling, D. H. (1997). The impact of pharmaceutical care on patient outcomes: What do we know? *Drug Benefit Trends, 9*, 35–47.

Salzman, C., Vaccaro, B., Lieff, J., & Weirea, A. (1995). Clozapine in older patients with psychosis and behavioral disturbance. *American Journal of Geriatric Psychiatry, 3*, 26–33.

Sano, M., Ernesto, C., Thomas, R. G., Klauber, M. R., et al. (1997). A controlled trial of selegiline, alpha-tocopherol, or both as treatment for Alzheimer's disease. *New England Journal of Medicine, 336*, 1216–1222.

Schneider, L. S., & Olin, J. T. (1996). Clinical global impressions in Alzheimer's clinical trials. *International Psychogeriatrics, 8*, 277–288.

Schneider, L. S., Olin, J. T., Lyness, S. A., & Chui, H. C. (1997). Eligibility of Alzheimer's disease clinic patients for clinical trials. *Journal of the American Geriatrics Society, 45*, 1–6.

Schneider, L. S., Pollock, V. E., & Lyness, S. A. (1990). A meta-analysis of controlled trials of neuroleptic treatment in dementia. *Journal of the American Geriatrics Society, 28*, 553–563.

Scott, J. D. (1993). Hypothesis generating research: The role of medical treatment effectiveness research in hypothesis generation. In N. K. Wenger, (Ed.), *Inclusion of elderly individuals in clinical trials* (pp. 119–125). Kansas City: Marion Merrell Dow.

Shumaker, S. A. (1993). The adequacy of health related quality of life assessment for older populations. In N. K. Wenger, (Ed.), *Inclusion of elderly individuals in clinical trials* (pp. 169–176). Kansas City: Marion Merrell Dow.

Small, G. W., Rabins, P. V., Barry, P. V., et al. (1997). Diagnosis and treatment of Alzheimer's disease: Consensus statement of the American Association for Geriatric Psychiatry, the Alzheimer's Association, and the American Geriatrics Society. *Journal of the American Medical Association, 278*, 1363–1371.

Smith, F., Talwalker, S., Gracon, S., & Srirama, M. (1996). The use of survival techniques in evaluating the effect of long-term tacrine (Cognex) treatment on nursing home placement and mortality in patients with Alzheimer's disease. *Journal of Biopharmaceutical Statistics, 6*, 395–409.

Torian, L., Davidson, E., Fulop, G., Sell, L., & Fillit, H. (1992). The effect of dementia on acute care in a geriatric unit. *International Psychogeriatrics, 4*, 231–239.

Wells, K. B., Sturm, R., Sherbourne, C. D., & Meredith, L. S. (1996). *Caring for depression*. Cambridge, Harvard University Press.

Zarit, S. H., Todd, P. A., & Zarit, J. (1986). Subjective burden of husbands and wives as caregivers: A longitudinal study. *Gerontologist, 26*, 260–266.

Index